Human Frailties

Psychological and Behavioral Aspects of Risk Series

Series Editors: Professor Cary L. Cooper and Professor Ronald J. Burke

Risk management is an ongoing concern for modern organizations in terms of their finance, their people, their assets, their projects and their reputation. The majority of the processes and systems adopted are very financially oriented or fundamentally mechanistic; often better suited to codifying and recording risk, rather than understanding and working with it. Risk is fundamentally a human construct; how we perceive and manage it is dictated by our attitude, behavior and the environment or culture within which we work. Organizations that seek to mitigate, manage, transfer or exploit risk need to understand the psychological factors that dictate the response and behaviors of their employees, their high-flyers, their customers and their stakeholders.

This series, edited by two of the most influential writers and researchers on organizational behavior and human psychology explores the psychological and behavioral aspects of risk; the factors that:

- define our attitudes and response to risk;
- are important in understanding and managing "risk managers"; and
- dictate risky behavior in individuals at all levels.

Titles Currently in the Series Include:

The Fulfilling Workplace
The Organization's Role in Achieving Individual and Organizational Health
Edited by Ronald J. Burke and Cary L. Cooper

Occupational Health and Safety
Edited by Ronald J. Burke, Sharon Clarke and Cary L. Cooper

Corporate Reputation
Managing Opportunities and Threats
Edited by Ronald J. Burke, Graeme Martin and Cary L. Cooper

New Directions in Organizational Psychology and Behavioral Medicine
Edited by Alexander-Stamatios Antoniou and Cary Cooper

Human Frailties

Wrong Choices on the Drive to Success

Edited by

RONALD J. BURKE
York University, Canada

SUZY FOX
Loyola University, USA

CARY L. COOPER
Lancaster University, UK

Routledge
Taylor & Francis Group
LONDON AND NEW YORK

First published 2013 by Gower Publishing

Published 2016 by Routledge
2 Park Square, Milton Park, Abingdon, Oxon OX14 4RN
711 Third Avenue, New York, NY 10017, USA

Routledge is an imprint of the Taylor & Francis Group, an informa business

Gower Applied Business Research
Our programme provides leaders, practitioners, scholars and researchers with thought provoking, cutting edge books that combine conceptual insights, interdisciplinary rigour and practical relevance in key areas of business and management.

British Library Cataloguing in Publication Data
A catalogue record for this book is available from the British Library.

The Library of Congress has cataloged the printed edition as follows:
Burke, Ronald J.
Human frailties : wrong choices on the drive to success / by Ronald J. Burke, Suzy Fox and Cary L. Cooper.
pages cm. -- (Psychological and behavioural aspects of risk)
Includes bibliographical references and index.
ISBN 978-1-4094-4585-2 (hardback) -- ISBN 978-1-4094-4586-9 (ebook) -- ISBN 978-1-4724-0242-4 (epub) 1. Business ethics. 2. Interbehavioral psychology. 3. Emotional intelligence. 4. Fragility (Psychology) I. Title.
HF5387.B847 2013
174'.4--dc23

2013026259

ISBN 13: 978-1-4094-4585-2 (hbk)

Contents

List of Figures

List of Tables

List of Contributors

Neal M. Ashkanasy – University of Queensland Business School, Australia

Carmen Binnewies – University of Muenster, Germany

Ronald J. Burke – York University, Canada

Cary L. Cooper – Lancaster University, UK

Denis Cormier – Concordia University, Canada

Dov Eden – Tel Aviv University, Israel

Suzy Fox – Loyola University Chicago, US

Susanna Galea – Waitemata DHB, New Zealand

Hamid Ghodse (deceased) – London, UK

Verena C. Hahn – University of Muenster, Germany

Itzhak Harpaz – University of Haifa, Israel

Peter J. Jordan – Griffith Business School, Australia

Stacey R. Kessler – Montclair State University, US

Anna Rosa Koch – University of Muenster and University of Mainz, Germany

Janice Langan-Fox – Swinburne University of Technology, Australia

Pascale Lapointe-Antunes – Concordia University, Canada

Michel Magnan – Concordia University, Canada

Lisa M. Penney – University of Houston, US

Cynthia L.S. Pury – Clemson University, US

Philip Riley – Monash University, Australia

Leslie E. Sekerka – Menlo College, US

Raphael Snir – Academic College of Tel Aviv-Yaffo, Israel

Ashlea C. Troth – Griffith Business School, Australia

Mina Westman – Tel Aviv University, Israel

Acknowledgements

The early writing on managerial and executive leadership took the view that all managers and leaders were successful. This belief was soon challenged as more data on managerial and executive performance was accumulated. It has been estimated that about half of those in these positions are falling short. They may be advancing their careers but not making important contributions to organizational success. More attention has now been paid to why highly educated, hard-working managers and professionals fall short, the "dark side of management." Not all managers and professionals are successful, some fail, and some are flawed. This collection is consistent with this growing emphasis. Some managers and professionals make "wrong choices on the road to success," damaging themselves, their families and friends, their organizations, and the wider society.

I thank our outstanding international contributors. Suzy Fox shouldered the bulk of the liaison with our contributors, our publisher and the management of this initiative. We value Martin West and Jonathan Norman at Gower for their continuing support.

My contributions were supported in part by York University.

Ronald J. Burke
Toronto, Canada

To all my former and current PhD students for helping me cope with my human frailties.

Cary L. Cooper
Lancaster, UK

This is a valuable and unique book which reflects a new trend: namely concentrating on the dark side of work. Over half the well written and up-to-date chapters examine the causes and consequences of dark people and dark work situations that reflect the book's subtitle. I very much enjoyed reading many of the chapters in a book that should be of use not only to students and researchers but managers struggling with the forces of darkness in their workplace.

Adrian Furnham, University College London, UK

... a sobering and illuminating collection documenting just how often the desire to succeed can come to override honest ethical behaviour and lead to reckless, destructive and fraudulent behaviour resulting in the courts, prison or death.

Michael Walton, Director, People in Organisations Ltd, UK

PART I

Human Frailties: An Overview

CHAPTER 1

Human Frailties in the Workplace: Their Nature, Consequences and Remedy

RONALD J. BURKE

Hardly a day goes by without stories appearing in the media reporting the consequences of human frailties for individuals, their families and friends, and their organizations.

The current News Corporation events are but one example (Chellel, 2011). In this situation, the reputations and careers of managers, journalists, and police officers have been damaged and in some cases ruined, with the prospect of individuals being convicted of criminal behavior (Watson and Hickman, 2012). Underlying these actions was the pursuit of an edge over other news media, competition leading some individuals to engage in unethical and illegal conduct (e.g., phone hacking, paying bribes, taking bribes for information provided). Organizational cultures that condoned, supported, or turned a blind eye to such activities have been implicated as well. More recently (March 13, 2012), Rebekah Brooks, former News International senior executive, her husband, and four other individuals were arrested and charged with interfering with justice, a possible cover-up of the scandal (*Globe and Mail*, 2012a). They joined reporters, senior news executives, and police officers previously charged, bringing the total now to at least 23. With Andrew Coulson being arrested on May 30, 2012, the list of those arrested and charged continues to grow.

Bribery and phone hacking allegations against some employees of News Corporation in the UK has resulted in 12 current or former employees being charged as of August 2011, the resignation of two high-ranking police officers, the death of one whistleblower, and the loss of billions of dollars' worth of News Corporation value.

This saga is ongoing. A British parliamentary committee called Rupert Murdoch unfit to run his global media empire on May 1, 2012 (Stringer, 2012a). This statement was not made unanimously in the committee, however. In addition, three more senior executives in his media empire were accused of lying to the committee. Rebekah Brooks, a Murdoch protégé and five other employees were formally charged with conspiracy to obstruct justice for their roles in Hackgate in May 2012 (Stringer, 2012b).

Eight people, including Rebekah Brooks and Andy Coulson, were formally charged on July 24, 2012 with intercepting or conspiring to intercept communications. Brooks and

Coulson were charged with paying bribes to public officials for stories and information, along with three others on November 20, 2012 (Cowell and Burns, 2012).

A few days after Dominique Strauss-Kahn was arrested and charged for allegedly sexually assaulting a hotel maid, another senior executive from a Middle Eastern country was similarly charged in New York City. A gathering of house cleaning staff in New York City reported that having guests expose themselves to cleaning staff was a fairly common occurrence. Strauss-Kahn admitted his sexual encounter with a New York hotel maid was a "moral failing" towards his wife, children, and the French citizens (Gauthier-Villars, 2011). He had earlier resigned as head of the IMF and had his hopes of becoming President of France dashed. He also still faces civil suits from the New York City maid as well as from Tristane Banon, a French writer. Banon's mother had claimed an affair with him as well (Hasham, 2012).

Studies of cheating on university campuses have consistently shown that business students engage in higher levels of university cheating than do students studying other disciplines. Students who cheat in universities are also more likely to cheat in their working lives. In addition, many experts believe that efforts to teach "ethical behavior" in business schools generally make little difference.

Many, perhaps the majority of students in high schools, cheat, with high achievers as likely to cheat as others. Cheating is also increasing because it has become easier and more widely tolerated, with neither parents nor learning institutions giving students a clear message of what is allowed and what is not. Unemployed or underemployed teachers and professors are writing papers for students for an on-line service (Seidman, 2012). This service says, however, that this work should not be used to fulfill academic requirements. Who are they kidding?

School systems in the US are coming under increasing pressure to show improvements in student scores on standardized tests. Teachers in a Georgia school system systematically altered and corrected student answers in order to increase the standing of their schools. Test scores of some schools in Ontario, Canada have also recently been eliminated from consideration because of concerns about their validity.

Great Neck, New York, scene of F. Scott Fitzgerald's *The Great Gatsby*, was rocked by the arrest of individuals who took college entrance examinations (the SAT and ACT) for other high school students. These fake test takers, chosen because they did very well on these tests, were paid a few thousand dollars for each sitting (Anderson and Applebaum, 2011). Fake test takers used false IDs, apparently easy to obtain, with one male test taker even sitting the tests for a female student. Test takers were paid as much as US$3,600 to take SAT and ACT tests. Interestingly, one test taker said he took tests for at least 15 clients over three years. He indicated, surprisingly, that he took tests for two girls. Another test taker, Joshua Chefec, is now studying business at Tulane University.

Every year some cyclists in the Tour de France fail drug tests. The football and cricket worlds have been plagued by scandal and match-fixing allegations. Perhaps as many as 680 soccer games have been fixed (Jolly and Borden, 2013). Members of the board of directors of FIFA have been charged with accepting bribes in exchange for their votes for a particular country's bid to host the World Cup. Laroque (2011), who played in the National Hockey League for 13 years and appeared in about 700 games, without naming names, wrote that NHL players took performance enhancing drugs.

Educational institutions such as universities, and business schools in particular, have been engaged in a rankings exercise for the past decade. Higher-ranking universities and business schools attract more donations, "more qualified" faculty, and "better" students. Ranking agencies typically ask universities and business schools to provide the data that is then used to make their rankings. Emory University in Atlanta has admitted inflating their data in order to improve its ranking, with the likelihood that other institutions have done the same. George Odiorne, one of the early proponents of management by objectives, offered an anecdote of a supervisor in an organization who was given a pedometer to indicate how many miles he walked during a given day, the more miles the better. He attached his pedometer to a nearby machine and immediately racked up several miles. So much for beating the system.

This collection places the spotlight on individuals, their behavioral choices, and the consequences that follow. Human frailties encompass flaws such as greed, unethical behaviors, sexually harassing behaviors, work addiction, alcohol and drug addiction, and potentially harmful lifestyle choices such as a lack of exercise, obesity, and smoking. Human frailties end up being an individual's worst enemy. The volume's purpose is to highlight the role played by human frailties in one's life and career and lay out alternative choices and options. When individual human frailties cause pain, the individuals in question generally realize their shortcomings, feel apologetic, and express concern for the pain that their behavior has caused others. They would have, in hindsight, preferred to make different behavior choices. This collection endorses introspection, self-assessment, the identification of central individual values, and goal setting.

There are no easy or quick "fixes" in addressing these self-limiting behaviors but success by some can been achieved. A colleague who smoked for over 30 years decided to stop smoking "cold turkey" about three years ago and has been successful so far. She uses the adage of other approaches to changing harmful habits of taking it "one day at a time."

All managers, all individuals, are flawed but not all flaws are fatal. Some flaws are merely annoying, others career limiting, and still others fatal in the sense of career-ending (Lane, 2012). Mayer, Aquino, Mawritz and Priesemuth (2012) offer the following as examples of leader transgressions outside of work: engages in extremely questionable behavior, thought to be having an extra-marital affair, initiates casual sexual encounters with women, makes frequent trips to gambling cities, visits strip clubs, hires prostitutes, and drinks alcoholic beverages daily after work. For several reasons, human frailties or flaws are more critical now than previously. These reasons include:

- greater scrutiny of individual actions
- greater demands for transparency
- more stakeholders with differing interests
- greater interdependence of business, governments, and the legal system
- greater cynicism about business and government leaders
- more interactions across cultures having different value systems
- more examples of individual and organizational greed, fraud, and corruption

All result in greater attention being paid to ethical and moral issues and individual actions in the workplace.

Consider the following information about men and women in managerial and professional jobs:

- There have been several highly-publicized stories in the media of inappropriate sexual behaviors and relationships in the workplace (more recently – Dominique Strauss-Kahn, Arnold Schwarzenegger, David Petraeus, Silvio Berlusconi – and in the recent past – Bill Clinton, John Edwards, Tiger Woods). In addition, examples of fraud, crime, and corruption appear almost daily (Bernie Madoff, Raj Rajaratnam at the individual level, and Iraq, China, Russia, and India at the country level).
- Sex and fraud sometimes go together (*National Post*, 2012a). The Brazilian lover of a former Volkswagen AG labor leader has been charged in a bribery scandal. She was paid $454,000 in fake contracts from 2002 through 2005. Klaus Volkert, her lover and former labor union leader representative on VWs supervisory board has already been convicted of receiving about $4 million. Union leaders were paid in trips, luxury goods, and prostitutes for favorable votes on VWs policies.
- In spite of the large number of financial scandals in the financial services sector over the past decade, a June 2012 survey of 500 financial services managers and professionals carried out by LabatonSucharow reported that 39 percent of respondents believed that competitors engaged in unethical or illegal activities to be successful, 26 percent had observed wrongdoing in their workplaces, and 16 percent said they would commit the crime of insider trading if they could not be caught (LabatonSucharow, 2012).
- Every year the Tour de France finds that some cyclists cheated by using performance-enhancing drugs. In 2011, the Tour de France boasted that fewer riders took these drugs in 2011 than previously, taking pride in the fact that there were now fewer cheaters. Alberto Contador, three-time winner of the Tour de France, used performance-enhancing drugs when he won in 2010 (Austen, 2012). He will be banned from racing for two years, in a sport plagued by doping scandals.
- The World Anti-Doping Agency (WADA) indicated that their latest research evidence suggested that as many as one in ten athletes who compete internationally may be using banned substances (Leicester, 2012). Indeed, more than 100 athletes were caught doping and sanctioned in the six months leading up to the 2012 London Olympics in a move to eliminate cheats before the games (*National Post*, 2012b). In fact at least one athlete scheduled to compete at the 2012 London Olympics has already been disqualified for taking banned substances. Cheats, however, may get a break since WADA will be cutting back on its programs and drug-testing teams for lack of funds (Waldie, 2012). Athletes are not the only cheats apparently. IOC officials from more than 150 countries are being investigated for selling London Olympic tickets on the black market (Hui, 2012).
- Rumors have swirled around Lance Armstrong, seven time winner of the Tour de France, that he used banned substances (Walsh, 2012). He was charged and cleared of these claims but again faced charges (that now include several other members of his team including managers and doctors) (June 29, 2012), of alleged doping, filed by the US Anti-Doping Agency. Armstrong was found guilty and stripped of his seven Tour de France victories, asked to return the winner's money, banned from competing for life (Vertuno, 2012), and lost several corporate sponsors. Three former Armstrong staff members and consultants received life-time bans from sports on July 10, 2012

and a French Tour de France rider was charged with doping on that same date and suspended from the French cycling team. Armstrong decided in August 2012 that he would no longer fight against doping allegations. As a result he will lose the seven championships that he had previously recorded in the Tour de France. Tour de France organizers now face the daunting task of declaring someone else a winner. Armstrong, after years of denials, sometimes under oath, admitted on the Oprah Winfrey show on January 17, 2013 to using performance-enhancing drugs. This is challenging since so many of the other riders finishing just behind Armstrong have also been found guilty of doping infractions. Hamilton, himself a cyclist and admitted doper, tells how widespread drug use was in cycling over the past decade (Hamilton and Coyle, 2012. Perhaps Charlie Francis, disgraced coach of Ben Johnson, Canadian winner of the Olympic 100 meter dash and disqualified for failing a doping test, known as "Charlie the Chemist," though talking about sprinting, said it best: "It was always a level playing field, it just wasn't at the level you thought it was."

- In football, to address illegal activities of players and officials, FIFA published a new code of conduct on April 26, 2012 for all players and officials (*National Post*, 2012c). It directly ordered them to reject bribery and corruption in the game and to behave ethically and with integrity. As of May 2012, about 50 Italian football players, coaches, and administrators have been charged and arrested in match-fixing scandals.
- Gessen (2011), in reviewing the life of Russian President Vladimir Putin, reported that he plagiarized parts of his PhD thesis, has a multi-million dollar summer home built and paid for by cronies that made billions under Putin, and that Putin himself is likely a billionaire. In her view, Putin is corrupt and ruthless.
- A high-profile European psychologist, Diederik Stapel, has admitting committing scientific fraud by making up data in countless studies saying he had "failed as a scientist" (United Press International). He was suspended from his position at Tilburg University in the Netherlands in September 2011 after three more junior researchers blew the whistle on him. Tilburg University released a preliminary report stating that dozens of papers and perhaps 14 of the 21 theses Stapel supervised contained made up data.
- Semmelweis University has voided the PhD degree of the current president of Hungary, Pal Schnitt, for plagiarism (*Toronto Star*, 2012a). More than 200 pages of his 215-page thesis were direct translations of others work or showed considerable similarity to the work of others.
- Harvard University, in August 2012, indicated that almost half of the undergraduates in a spring Government class were under investigation for cheating (about 125 students).
- A new survey of employers in Canadian retail reported that 33 percent of merchandise unaccounted for – the "shrink rate" – was the result of employee theft, up from 19 percent in 2008 (Shaw, 2012). External theft was now a smaller problem than in 2008. Theft costs the Canadian retail sector about $4 billion a year or about $11 million each shopping day. Employee theft is a more worrisome problem than external theft since employees come to work several days each week.
- Most people are less ethical than they think they are. We have considerable knowledge as to the rationalizations. The "moral hypocrisy" they use to justify their unethical choices and why they are blind to their own and others' unethical choices and behaviors (Kray and Haselhuhn, 2012).

- Yahoo! CEO Scott Thompson, on the job for only four months, resigned after it came to light that his academic credentials were misrepresented (Womack, 2012). Thompson had a degree in accounting not computer science.
- Donald McCabe, professor in the school of business at Rutgers University, has noted that women in business and engineering programs now cheat as much as their male colleagues to remain competitive. Women have historically cheated less than men did, but the level of cheating is highest in both business and engineering programs which have been and still are male-dominated. Both business and engineering are fields with an emphasis on getting the job done regardless of how one does it.
- Everyone lies (Ariely, 2012), and lying may be bad for one's health. Kesterton (2012a) reports the results of a US study in which respondents indicated lying on average 11 times a week. Lies included exaggerating one's accomplishments, making false excuses for being late, avoiding uncomfortable questions. Respondents were divided into two groups with one group asked to stop their lying over a nine-week period. The group that stopped their lying indicated higher levels of well-being and health and better (smoother) interpersonal relationships.
- But lying usually results in an erosion of trust. An increasing number of police officers in Ontario have been found guilty of lying under oath and fabricating evidence (McLean and Bruser, 2012).
- Bruce Dunn, CEO of troubled money-losing Best Buy, resigned during an investigation into his personal conduct, unrelated to the company's financial operations (Bustillo, 2012a). The issue concerns a potential misuse of company assets in an inappropriate relationship with a female co-worker. His resignation was followed in turn by that of Best Buy founder and Chairman, Richard Schulze, for not informing the board of directors of the relationship Dunn was having with a female staff member (Bustillo, 2012b).

Exploring the "Dark Side"

Most of the leadership writing has had a positive bias assuming that leaders are good leaders, and that leadership skills could be taught and good leaders produced as a result, but individuals can have a dark side (Bohart et al., 2013). Hogan and Hogan (2001) estimate that between 50 and 75 percent of leaders are not performing well in terms of improving performance and meeting objectives. More leaders are being terminated and leadership tenure has fallen (Hogan, 1999). This has led to an increase in trying to understand leadership failures. Leaders do not fail because they do not work hard enough, lack the necessary education and experience, lack leadership skills, lack resources to do the job, or were unethical. Walton (2007), based on his consulting, managerial and research experience, suggests that seeing dysfunction and toxicity as normal is more realistic than viewing these as abnormal.

Kellerman (2004) considered two types of bad leadership – ineffective and unethical. Identifying seven types of bad leaders, type refers to a pattern of leader and follower behavior that was maintained over time.

1. incompetent – lacked the will or skill to create effective action or positive change
2. rigid – stiff, unyielding, unable or unwilling to adapt to the new

3. intemperate – lacking in self-control
4. callous – uncaring, unkind, ignoring the needs of others
5. corrupt – lies, cheats, steals, places self-interest first
6. insular – ignores the needs and welfare of those outside the work team
7. evil – does psychological or physical harm to others

Dotlich and Cairo (2003) indicate ways in which leaders can derail their careers by exhibiting flawed behaviors. Leaders fail because of who they are and how they act, particularly when under stress. They identified 11 leaders' behaviors that derailed careers of formerly successful executives. These were arrogance, melodrama – needing to be the center of attention – volatility, excessive caution, habitual distrust, aloofness, mischievousness, eccentricity – being different for the sake of being different – passive resistance, perfectionism, and eagerness to please. McCall and Lombardo (1983) include running roughshod over subordinates, being cold and aloof, focusing on empire building and other kinds of self-aggrandizement, and being overly concerned with getting ahead. Their most common causes of leadership failures and derailment were: an insensitive, abrasive, and bullying style, aloofness or arrogance, betrayal of personal trust, and self-centered ambition.

Hogan and Hogan (1997) created the Hogan Development Survey which measures 11 behavioral tendencies that may cause failure. These are:

1. excitable – moody, easily annoyed, hard to please, and emotionally volatile
2. skeptical – distrustful, cynical, sensitive to criticism, and focused on the negative
3. cautious – unassertive, resistant to change, risk averse, and slow to make decisions
4. reserved – aloof, indifferent to the feelings of others, and uncommunicative
5. leisurely – overtly cooperative but privately irritable, stubborn, and uncooperative
6. bold – overly self-confident, arrogant, with inflated feelings of self-worth
7. mischievous – charming, risk taking, limit testing, and seeking excitement
8. colorful – active, energetic, entertaining, dramatic, and attention seeking
9. imaginative – creative but thinking and acting in unusual and eccentric ways
10. diligent – meticulous, precise, conscientious, hard to please, and perfectionistic
11. dutiful – eager to please and reluctant to act independently or against popular opinion

Najar, Holland and Van Landayt (2004), using the Hogan measure, considered the relationship of leaders' dysfunctional interpersonal tendencies and multi-rater evaluations in a sample of 295 high-potential senior executives from a Fortune 500 company. Raters included immediate supervisors and a composite group of peers and others familiar with the individual's job performance. Criteria included four leadership factors (e.g., business results, people, self) and 11 interpersonal factors (e.g., trusting, resilient, dependable). Four broad hypotheses were considered: characteristics associated with arrogance, cautiousness, excitability, and skepticism and distrust would be associated with lower peer ratings. Their results indicated that dysfunctional behaviors associated with arrogance, cautiousness, volatility, and skepticism negatively affected performance ratings and these effects differed between supervisors and peers.

Wright (2012) considered human frailties among CEOs and members of their top management teams (TMTs). He reported results of a recent survey of Forbes 500 CEOs and Chief Human Resources Officers (CHROs) on: where TMTs could improve their functioning, where CEOs could improve their performance and that of their TMT, and what CHROs do to improve the performance of their CEOs and TMTs. Wright draws a distinction between two "bright-side" characteristics: ego-concerned with the self, and pride-justifiable self-respect, and two "dark-side" characteristics: opportunism – self-interest seeking with guile – and hubris – excessive pride or arrogance. He then outlines signals of CEO movement to the dark side. These include: stops listening to others, surrounded by "yes" people, lays blame for failures on others, takes credit for successes, uses "I" instead of "we," treats others disrespectfully and/or abusively, and believes that the rules do not apply to him/her. Enablers of this movement to the dark side include: past job successes, past promotions, sudden increases in money and fame, increasing positive media exposure, surrounded by praise from others, excessive pay and perks, and increasing status coupled with isolation. Wright then identifies potential "guardrails" for such movement offered by CHROs. These included: providing regular, ongoing, and straight coaching and feedback, telling CEO things that others were afraid to tell them, helping CEOs understand their own wants and why they want these, helping CEOs understand behaviors of TMT members, and serving as a confidential sounding board and confidante. Some work experiences can also help the CEO "get it." These include working on the front lines with employees to better appreciate and understand their circumstances, reducing status barriers with immediate TMT members and other employees, getting involved in charity experiences, and exploring other leadership approaches (e.g., servant leadership).

Chris Mazza, having both an MD and MBA, following a number of scandals, was fired in early 2012 as CEO of ORNGE, a unit of the Ontario government tasked with providing helicopter services in the province to assist accident victims. Donovan (2012) quotes colleagues describing Mazza thus: "He always considered himself the smartest guy in the room," "He was a passionate, tyrannical control freak," "given to obsessive tendencies." He once made a morgue reference – "He's done. Put a toe tag on him" – to indicate that an employee was to be fired. He terminated one employee then hired a private detective to follow him. He required all those fired to sign a confidentiality agreement before they received any severance. He called staff in the middle of the night, often in an abusive tirade. He referred to staff as monkeys. One staff member started taking a painkiller, to which he became addicted, to cope with the abuse; since leaving ORNGE he has recovered. Mazza also spent taxpayer monies to advance a lavish lifestyle including travel, expensive hotels and meals (Donovan and McLean, 2013), greed and materialism being a common human frailty.

Vilkinas (2012) uses the case study of Qantas CEO Alan Joyce and the fortunes of Qantas over the past few years to highlight the influence of a toxic leader on staff relationships and morale as well as economic performance of an organization.

Sutton (2010) includes the story of Scott Rudin who went through 250 personal assistants in a five-year period, an average of an assistant every week or two. Rudin claimed that this number was only 119 but he did not include those that lasted less than two weeks. Hornstein (1997) interviewed over 200 people about "brutal bosses" and how they may have confronted or dealt with them. He identified eight deadly sins typical of brutal bosses: deceit, constraint, coercion, selfishness, inequity, cruelty, disregard, and deification. He then classified brutal bosses as: executioners, dehumanizers, blamers, rationalizers, conquerors, performers, and manipulators. He concluded that brutal bosses don't just survive, they typically thrive since they achieve results that their managers want. Hornstein suggests that victims of brutal bosses talk about their experiences with trusted co-workers. In addition he discourages admitting shortcomings to such bosses since they will use this to badger them even more often. He suggests three possible remedies: changing the victim, changing the brutal boss, and changing the system, concluding that only the last one has value. Futterman (2004) lays out options for victims of brutal bosses including how to maintain healthcare coverage, how to plan and reallocate financial resources, how to apply for disability if the need arises, how to pursue legal remedies, and how to fight attempts of blacklisting.

Former CEO of France Telecom, Didier Lombard, is being investigated with regard to the suicides of more than 30 company employees that followed his restructuring of the company (*National Post*, 2012d). Employee representatives said that harsh practices introduced following privatization included forced moves, impossible-to-achieve performance targets, psychological harassment, and ignoring warnings from company doctors about the mental health of some employees. Lombard, when he retired, said that he was sorry that he did not make efforts to improve staff morale sooner in the privatization process.

There is considerable evidence of the negative consequences of abusive supervision on subordinates (Tepper, 2007, 2000). Interestingly, the consequences of supervisory abuse on supervisors are also negative. Ambrose and Ganegoda (2011) collected data from 314 triads (a focal supervisor, a subordinate of this supervisor, and the focal supervisor's supervisor). Abusive supervision was associated with less favorable job attitudes in both supervisors and subordinates, lower psychological well-being, lower supervisor promotability, and lower levels of workgroup performance. Supervisor abusive behaviors had no benefits to the supervisor either. Porath and Pearson (2013) document the costs of workplace incivility.

Judge and LePine (2007) review the "dark side" of personality. Personality has been found to affect job performance but personality has both "benefits" and "costs," upsides and downsides. They developed a 2 × 2 table with the expected desirable outcomes of "dark" and "bright"-side personality characteristics and the actual effects of both "dark" and "bright"-side personality characteristics as axes. These characteristics include the Big 5 personality traits seen as "bright" side (conscientiousness, emotional stability, extraversion, openness to experience, agreeableness) and four personality characteristics seen as "dark" side (narcissism, impulsivity, trait hostility, Type A behavior). Each of these is seen as having both "bright" and dark" sides, making their use in selection and development complex.

The authors suggest designing selection systems that use narrower traits within a broader personality construct and using personality traits in hiring but adding training that addresses potential or real "dark-side" effects.

Some questions still remain unanswered, however. Each of these dark-side characteristics can be a bright-side characteristic, contributing to success in some circumstances (Judge and LePine, 2007). Do certain dark-side characteristics (e.g., arrogance) matter more later in one's career than earlier? Can a strength become a dark-side characteristic? Are some patterns of dark-side characteristics and strengths acceptable while others are fatal (brilliant but insensitive might derail, while organizational savvy and insensitive might not)? Are there some dark-side characteristics (e.g., cannot be trusted) that transcend any combination of strengths? Do dark-side characteristics operate in the same way at upper and lower organizational levels (success and derailment)? Some dark-side characteristics (emotional instability, arrogance, abrasiveness) may be more critical at higher levels because the jobs are larger and more complex, the stakes higher and the costs of failure greater.

Lilienfeld et al. (2012), in a study of 42 US presidents, examined the effects of psychopathic personality traits and presidential success and failure. They found that Fearless Dominance, the boldness associated with psychopathy, was associated with better-rated presidential performance, leadership, crisis management, persuasiveness, better Congressional relations, the initiation of new projects, and being seen as a world leader. Other psychopathic traits were unrelated to ratings of presidential performance but linked with negative character traits, accepting unethical behavior of staff, and the likelihood of impeachment.

Some themes emerged in the writing on dark-side characteristics and leadership failure. First, failure was associated with inability to develop effective interpersonal relationships (arrogant, stubborn, egocentric). Second, excitable individuals were found to have difficult relationships (impatient, moody, negative, volatile, emotional instability). Third, as Lubit (2002) noted, skepticism and distrust reduced leaders' effectiveness in motivating others (cynical, untrustworthy).

Narcissism

All men are born equal, but quite a few eventually get over it.

– Lord Mancroft, British peer and businessman

Twenge and Campbell (2009) chronicle the increasing levels of narcissism in the US, and in other countries as well. Individuals show higher levels of narcissism in concert with increasing societal values that foster and support it. What is narcissism? Narcissists are obsessed with themselves, feel entitled to things that they haven't earned, feel good about themselves, are supremely confident (overconfident perhaps), and choose to live expensive lifestyles. Narcissists are greedy, self-centered, vain, have superficial relationships, are socially isolated and contributed to the economic recession of 2008, supported the bailouts of failing organizations, and continued to take home large bonuses whether they or their organizations performed well or not. Dubrin (2012) reviews the writing on narcissism in organizations and offers self-assessment instruments so that readers can gauge their own levels of it. Dubrin uses words, at the extreme end, to describe narcissists, such as self-absorbed, self-centered, and self-adoring; narcissists show little concern for others.

Twenge and Campbell (2009) identify four factors that contributed to increasing levels of narcissism: permissive parenting and the self-esteem movement, the media culture of shallow celebrity, inflated self-portrayals by individuals posted on the internet, and the availability of easy credit which allowed narcissists to buy things, look rich, and feel special as a result. Narcissists look out for No. 1. Narcissists are also more likely to be dishonest and engage in sexual affairs (Eliot Spitzer, John Edwards, Tiger Woods, Arnold Schwarzenegger, Mark Sanford, John Kennedy, Silvio Berlusconi, Dominique Strauss-Kahn). Although narcissists have an inflated view of themselves, when objective criteria are considered, narcissists are no different from those scoring lower on these characteristics.

Our MBA program has a one week orientation program to help incoming students navigate their studies. They come to a set of tables, sign in, and are given a name tag. Above these tables hangs a large banner stating "RULING THE WORLD STARTS HERE." A first step on the road to narcissism?

There are some indications that narcissists do not do well as CEOs (Sankowsky, 1995; Conger, 1990; Kets de Vries, 1989; Tourish, 2005). Collins (2001), in his book *Good to Great*, found that CEOs of great companies were generally mild mannered, modest, generous in the praise and support of others, and excellent team players. Chatterjee and Hambrick (2007) found that more narcissistic CEOs of technology companies were associated with more volatile company performance. More narcissistic CEOs undertook more dramatic business strategies, sometimes failing. Yet narcissists are more likely to emerge in executive ranks. But their stay there might be short lived. For example, Enron was staffed by "the smartest guys in the room," but went bankrupt once their frauds were uncovered.

Chatterjee and Hambrick (2011) proposed that narcissism in a CEO will affect his/her response to objective and subjective signs of his/her ability such that the CEO scoring high on narcissism would not pay attention to objective indicators of ability, positive signs would increase risk-taking and negative signs would have little effect on risk-taking. CEOs scoring high on narcissism would be particularly affected by praise. Chatterjee and Hambrick reported data from two studies: risky outlays by CEOs of publicly-owned US companies from 1992 to 2006, and acquisition premiums paid by CEOs of a sample of US acquiring firms from 2001 to 2008. They found that CEOs scoring high on narcissism were less affective, by recent objective performance data, than CEOs lower on narcissism.

Finkelstein (2004) considered the question of why smart executives fail (e.g., Enron, Tyco, WorldCom, Rubbermaid, Schwinn) and found common habits among their executives. These included: seeing themselves and their companies as dominating their environments, identifying completely with their companies so there was no clear boundary between their personal interests and their organization's interests, thinking they have all the answers, ruthlessly getting rid of those not completely behind them, being obsessed with the company's image, constantly seeking attention, and stubbornly clinging to what worked for them in the past. Many of these habits can be subsumed under narcissism. Effective leaders need to give up certain things. These include: the need to be right, to speak first, to decide, to get the credit, and to control others.

Narcissism has been shown to be associated with higher levels of counterproductive work behaviors (Penney and Spector, 2002) and higher levels of work addition (Killinger, 1991; Clark, Lelchook and Taylor, 2010). It is also likely that narcissism among members of the executive suite – feelings of entitlement and of being above the rules – has been associated with recently publicized affairs (David Petreaus, Christopher Kubasek, John Edwards, Bill Clinton, Dominique Strauss-Kahn, Tiger Woods, Harry Stonecipher).

Twenge and Campbell (2009) see narcissism as similar to other destructive behaviors. In the short run, narcissism makes the person feel good, it has short-term benefits but longer-term costs, and similar to other destructive behaviors, narcissism hurts others such as family and friends. Thus, similar to other destructive behaviors, including addictions, narcissism is a "time-delay trap"; narcissism offers desirable outcomes and feelings at the start but negative outcomes over time. Lubit (2004, 2002), providing illustrative case examples, comes to the same conclusions.

Bhattacharya and Marshall (2012), using a sample of top managers indicted for illegal insider trading between 1989 and 2002, found that those managers who were richer (earning higher salaries) were more likely to be indicted for insider trading than were managers who were poorer (earned lower salaries) in matched organizations and industries. They concluded that a rational decision to earn more money because they were poorer was not evident. Instead they suggest that hubris and arrogance, or company cultures supporting such misbehavior, were more likely explanations for engaging in insider trading than a desire for more money.

Roberts (2011), while noting the importance of self-esteem, self-confidence, and a healthy ego in managerial success, noted that too strong an ego can lead to arrogance among narcissistic managers. Roberts argues for a balance, what he terms "egolibrium," between concerns for self and concerns for others – ego-centric versus other-centric positions. Roberts lists nine situations where too much ego can cause problems.

1. controlling versus relinquishing control
2. judgmental versus nonjudgmental reactions
3. doing what you want versus doing the right thing
4. know-it-all versus open to learning
5. holding on versus letting go
6. impatience versus patience
7. closed and defensive versus open and non-defensive
8. resistant versus accepting
9. self-focused versus other-focused

There may be hope for narcissists yet, however. Owens (2012) found that when narcissism was paired with humility, a dark-side trait with a bright-side trait, levels of employee work engagement and performance were higher. Humility may have tempered or blunted the effects of narcissism. Others (e.g., Maccoby, 2004) have noted the paradoxical effects of narcissistic leaders.

Workplace Arrogance

Johnson et al. (2010) considered correlates and consequences of arrogance in the workplace. While likely correlated with narcissism, they are different; arrogance is more social and narrower in scope. Arrogance is also different from hubris and confidence. Sample items in their measure of arrogance included: knowing better than anyone else in any given situation, criticizing others, asserting authority in situations when he/she does not have the required information.

In four studies, some using external views of focal respondents, the following results were reported:

- arrogance was positively related to dominance, anger, superiority, entitlement, and vanity, and negatively related to humility and agreeableness;
- arrogance was positively related to strain and negatively related to engaging in organizational citizenship behaviors;
- self and others' ratings of focal person's arrogance were significantly and positively correlated;

- arrogance was negatively related to task performance and cognitive abilities;
- arrogance was negatively related to self-esteem.

Workplace arrogance therefore costs organizations in terms of negatively impacting the morale of both direct reports and co-workers and adding to a climate of toxicity. Organizations can institute developmental experiences such as coaching and 360-degree feedback that emphasize humility as a counter-weight (Collins, 2001).

Personality Disorders

Furnham (2007) considers personality disorders and career derailment and the positive influence of pathology for career success, particularly in early career.

Pathology refers to personality disorders leading to behaviors dysfunctional to others and to the organization. Pathology is not incompetence, inefficiency, lack of experience, or lack of skill or education Pathologies can be both intra-personal or interpersonal, and the organizational context plays a role in affecting the effects of pathology on outcomes and success. Furnham examines three pathologies – antisocial personalities (psychopaths), narcissists, and histrionic personalities – referred to as the "dark triad of personality" by Paulhus and Williams (2006). Interestingly these three personalities (pathologies) can also be assets in obtaining and maintaining managerial jobs, examples of successful psychopaths.

Psychopathy and the Executive Suite

There has been some recent speculation, but little hard evidence, that psychopaths (see Stout, 2005 for definitions and examples) may end up at the top of organizations (Morse, 2004). DeCovny (2012) wrote that an estimated 10 percent of people in the financial services industry were psychopaths. Babiak and Hare (2006) have estimated that 4 percent of managers and professionals within a one-company sample they studied could be termed psychopaths in contrast with a 1 percent frequency in the general population. Cangemi and Pfohl (2009) describe seven case studies of psychopaths holding leadership roles in a variety of sectors. So psychopaths do exist inside and outside of corporations, but the question of whether psychopathy helps one climb the corporate ladder is still an open one.

Toxic Individuals

Increasing attention has been paid to the prevalence and consequences of abusive supervisors, toxic individuals, and "assholes" in the workplace (Tepper, 2000; Pelletier, 2010; Hornstein, 1997; Lipman-Blumen, 2005; Namie and Namie, 2000; Walton, 2007; Reed, 2004; Kusy and Holloway, 2009; Sutton, 2007, 2010) These individuals have negative impacts on employee satisfaction, job performance, and work unit success (Crowley and Elster, 2009). We know a lot about leadership flaws, how to spot them and how to address them. Padilla, Hogan and Kaiser (2007) propose a "toxic triangle" incorporating characteristics of destructive leaders, susceptible followers, and conducive environments. These three factors make destructive leadership possible, pervasive, and long lasting. To minimize destructive leaders, organizations need to improve leader selection and development processes, develop stronger and empowered followers, and create a workplace that makes people accountable for their behaviors and performance by monitoring behaviors of all employees at every level.

In addition, relationships that exist between supervisors and subordinates, within teams, with customers and clients, and with others outside of the workplace, if toxic, have been shown to have negative effects on individual attitudes, behaviors, and well-being (Eby and Allen, 2012).

Addictions

Addiction refers to a disorder in which an individual becomes preoccupied with a behavior or activity that initially offers positive affect (Mate, 2008). Individuals then lose the ability to stop the behavior or activity, eventually leading to negative experiences and outcomes (Shaffer, 2012a, 2012b). The addiction interferes with the performance of important life roles or diminishes one's enjoyment of them. Individuals may have difficulties in work, social relationships, and leisure, sometimes placing oneself in risky and dangerous situations, experiencing psychological distress, physical injury, legal problems, and financial loss. Individuals can become addicted to substances (cigarettes, alcohol, drugs) or processes (love, sex, eating, work, shopping).

A number of different addictions such as alcohol, drug, sex, pornography, gambling, the internet, and food have been linked with negative outcomes (Hovarth, 1999; Pelchat, 2002; Lesieur and Blume, 1993; Freimuth, 2008). Sussman, Lisha and Griffiths (2011), in a review of the literature, considered 11 potential addictions in terms of prevalence and co-occurrence. They offer speculations on the effects of each of these 11 addictions on a number of outcomes. They found an overall 12-month prevalence of an addiction among US adults varies from 1 percent to 61 percent, settling on a conclusion that 47 percent of the US adult population suffers from maladaptive signs of an addictive disorder over a 12-month period. Griffiths (1996) and Orford (2001) also believe that addictions are widespread. We consider some of these below.

Alcohol Addiction

Real-life super sports agent Leigh Steinberg formed the basis of a character played by Tom Cruise in the movie *Jerry Maguire*. Steinberg today has declared bankruptcy, and saw his sports empire – once the world's largest and most successful – fall on hard times because of his alcoholism (Moore, 2012). Steinberg has had several alcohol-related arrests, and a divorce, winding up both broke and a drunk. He has now embarked on a 12-step recovery program and has been sober for over 700 days.

Bryant (2012) describes his life as a high functioning alcoholic before he accidentally hit a cyclist causing the cyclist's death on August 31, 2009. Bryant states that he was hung-over most mornings but never drunk on the job. He was sober the evening of the accident. Events leading up to the accident, and the accident itself, resulted in Bryant losing a high-paying job, losing his marriage, losing his financial assets as a result of court cases, and losing his reputation. He has since stopped drinking and been sober for three years.

Matthew Barnaby was immediately fired by ESPN as the network's hockey analyst one day after he was charged with drunk driving (*National Post*, 2011). He was arrested after failing a sobriety test and refusing to provide a breathalyzer test.

Two employees of Research in Motion (RIM), both vice-presidents, George Campbell and Paul Wilson, behaving badly while drunk on a flight from Toronto to Beijing caused the flight to be diverted to Vancouver (Bailey, 2011). Both had to be restrained by airline crew. They pled guilty to mischief, were fined $71,757, put on an immediate suspension by RIM, and later were fired.

British Labour MP, Eric Joyce, was accused of assaulting a Tory MP while in a Parliamentary bar (Brennan, 2012). Joyce, while "overly refreshed," shouted at Tory patrons, spilled beer on patrons, punched others, and head-butted Tory Stuart Andrew twice. Police were called and arrested Joyce. Two years earlier, Joyce lost his driver's license for refusing to provide a breathalyzer sample after an automobile accident. Joyce, admitting that he had problems with alcohol and aggression was later fined $6,950. He was suspended from the Labour caucus and announced that he will not seek re-election in 2015.

Alcohol harms individual health, families, lives, and careers. It is also an equal opportunity addiction, with both men and women, boys and girls, falling victim to it. But certain alcoholics – functional alcoholics – can function in some, or several areas, despite their drinking. Some alcoholics can stop their drinking, although this proves to be difficult and the success rate is not very high (Stromberg and Merrill, 2009), but there are some success stories (Moyers, 2007; Stromberg and Merrill, 2007).

Fortunately, there is considerable information available to help organizations manage alcohol problems and issues in the workplace (Tobutt, 2011). Many Canadian workplaces use random drug and alcohol testing for employees working in safety-sensitive jobs. This pits the privacy of workers against the employer's need to provide a safe workplace, an issue that is still contentious (Gray, 2012).

Drug Addiction

> *TTC driver charged in Lawrence Avenue crash: Pot possession among charges laid in collision that killed woman, 43.*
>
> – *Toronto Star*, October 13, 2011, GT4

A TTC (Toronto Transit Commission) bus driver involved in a fatal bus crash has been charged with criminal negligence causing death and the possession of cannabis, according to police.

Eleven employees at a nuclear power station in Ontario were fired with cause for allegedly using drugs on the job (Howlett, 2011). These employees were later reinstated.

Canada's nuclear regulator has suggested new "fitness for duty" rules for its industry. Nuclear companies can use both pre-employment drug testing and testing employees "for cause" (Spears, 2012). This legislation will permit testing for both alcohol and drugs. Canada has laws against drinking and driving, so having laws against drinking and drug use and running a nuclear power plant makes some sense. This legislation constitutes a proactive effort to prohibit the use or possession of alcohol or drugs by employees while on duty. The Toronto Transit Commission referred to above currently tests employees after a serious accident and has developed a policy of random alcohol and drug testing of its employee but has not implemented it yet.

Sussman and Ames (2008) offer guidance on the prevention and cessation of drug use. Brannigan et al. (2004) reported on the quality of highly-regarded substance-treatment programs as well.

Gambling Addiction

About ten years ago I met a man in his forties, working in a blue collar, manufacturing setting, who had earlier been heavily into gambling and apparently did this with a biker gang. He lost money and was in debt to the bikers. They threatened to break his legs if they did not get paid. He indicated to me that, being a body builder, he was prepared to break their legs as well. I am not sure how the gambling debts got sorted out but he tried unsuccessfully to take his own life. Ten years later, he still gambles but relatively infrequently and only with small amounts of money.

The British Columbia Securities Commission alleged that a financial adviser, Lynne Nickford, swindled more than $1 million from her clients in a less-than-two-year period. Nickford used the money to pay her personal expenses including food, clothing and rent, and gambled almost $1 million at casinos in the Vancouver area (*Globe and Mail*, 2012b).

Health experts note a rise in suicide, family breakdown, and illness when people can access gambling (Daubs, 2012; Potenza et al., 2002). Gambling increases when the economy worsens, and poor people are more likely to gamble than are rich people. In gambling, the house always wins. Political parties out of power are always against gambling, but for it when in power. It is estimated that "problem gamblers" represent about 4 percent of the population, and that 30 percent of the revenue from gambling comes from "problem gamblers." Some problem gamblers who lost everything have tried to sue the province for making gambling so freely available and for not stopping them from taking part in it. The province has attempted to stop "problem gamblers" from entering gambling premises but this has not been fully successful.

People spend money at casinos that they might otherwise spend at restaurants, movies, and other entertainment sites. They are also gambling away their mortgage money and accumulating debt to feed their addiction.

I am not sure how well this program is working but Mastercard has created a Next Step Card, a prepaid Mastercard for people fighting addictions (Kesterton, 2012b). The card will not work in casinos, bars, or permit the withdrawal of cash from ATMs.

Sexual Relationships, Hypersexuality, and Sex Addiction

Sexual addiction applies across the life span, including the teenage years (Sussman, 2007). We are beginning to know a lot about sexual relationships, hypersexuality, love addiction, and sexual addiction (Boies, Knudson and Young, 2004; Carnes, 1996, 1991; Hovarth, 1999; Schneider and Irons, 2001; Sussman, 2010; Weiss and Schneider, 2006).

Consider the following examples. Men in various professions (e.g., politics, business, entertainment, television) have exhibited sex addiction (Bill Clinton, Larry Craig, Michael Douglas, Eric Benet, Elliot Spitzer, David Duchovny, Dominique Strauss-Kahn,

Rev. Jesse Jackson, Dr. Martin Luther King). Why would such successful and powerful men behave in ways that will cause them great pain – public humiliation, damaged reputations, embarrassment, shame to family and friends, and in some cases, job loss. Dubbed the "Emperor complex," men in high government and business sector positions in China accumulate mistresses the same way they pursue money and power (MacKinnon, 2012). About 90 percent of the men fired for corruption in China over the past five years have had mistresses. Onstad (2012) writes that the past five French Presidents each had at least one mistress.

Arnold Schwarzenegger (2012) chronicles his life, having being born poor in a small town in Austria, moving to the US, winning several body-building contests, becoming an action movie hero, making lots of money, hanging out with other celebrities, and becoming governor of California. He also includes his life as a serial philanderer, being accused by several women of groping them, admitting to affairs while married, and to fathering a child with the family housekeeper while married to Maria Shriver. The couple has since divorced.

William Armony, who built the United Way into a major charity, went to prison for six years for misusing funds to support a lavish lifestyle and a teenage mistress (McFadden, 2011). He was the CEO of United Way for 22 years. His salary and benefits exceeded $400,000 annually, plus the use of apartments in New York City and Coral Gables, Florida. Armony stated he used these perks to meet corporate donors. Armony and two associates were indicted on 71 counts of fraud, conspiracy, money laundering, and tax evasion. He stole $1 million and gave money to his mistress, took trips with her, and bought her champagne, flowers, and a fax machine to send her love notes.

Bobby Petrino, head football coach at the University of Arkansas, was fired on April 10, 2012, when it was revealed that he had hired Jessica Dorrell without disclosing his relationship with her or the fact that he paid her $20,000 for undisclosed reasons (Voigt, 2012). Though a married father of four, Petrino and Dorrell had exchanged more than 4,300 text messages and about 300 phone calls over the prior seven months. Petrino has since admitted to an affair.

At least a dozen Secret Service agents accompanying US President Barack Obama to Cartagena Colombia for a Summit of the Americas were sent home for misconduct involving prostitutes and drunkenness at the Hotel Caribe (*Toronto Star*, 2012b). At least 20 women were involved in the Colombian incident. Prostitution is legal in particular zones in Cartagena, and the 11 Secret Service agents apparently brought the prostitutes to their rooms. Colombian police were called when one agent had a disagreement with a prostitute over her "fee." Obama's personal security was not breached as these events took place a day before his arrival. The situation was investigated and some of the agents involved resigned and a few others were terminated and had their careers in the Secret Service ended. The Secret Service announced new regulations for its agents: barring taking foreign nationals to their rooms, not visiting "unacceptable" establishments, and no alcohol within 10 hours of going on duty.

The Secret Service was also investigating visits by its agents to strip clubs and the use of prostitutes before Obama's visit to El Salvador in March 2011 (Campbell, 2012). Apparently managers were aware of such activities and turned a blind eye. To believe that the Colombian incident was the first time Secret Service agents "went wild" is naïve.

Why would these men behave so recklessly? Carnes, Murray and Charpentier (2005) and Carnes (2001) suggest several possibilities. First, they lack, partly because of their intense work commitment, opportunities for emotional connection, relaxation, rest, intimacy, and emotional support in their lives so they fill this emotional void in reckless ways. They look for a quick remedy. Second, people in these positions have a need to be continually validated, valued, and admired. These acts make them feel better. Third, they are surrounded by people who are unwilling to tell the truth and thus protect the individual from himself and from making bad choices. Fourth, they may feel invincible. Fifth, they don't think they will get caught, and if they do get caught, they have the resources to minimize the damage.

Anderson (2012) offers as reasons for cheating the following: the addictive power of feeling love, holding a powerful position, and being comfortable with risk taking. He cites a Dutch study of executives that reported 26 percent had cheated on their partners at least once, they could cheat again, and cheating was more common the higher the person's position in the organizational hierarchy. These individuals had access to the key ingredients for cheating: they travelled a lot, given their power they could assume that a potential partner would agree, and they were surrounded by others at work who would say nothing.

Another reason why people cheat is the link between adultery and romantic love. Adultery involves passion, love, and addiction.

Suggestions for the prevention and treatment of love addiction and sexual addiction can be found in Anonymous (1986), Gordon (2007), Peabody (2004), Sussman (2010), and Wolfe (2000). Anonymous describes a 12-step program similar to those advocated for alcoholics, substance abusers, and gambling addicts.

Extra-marital Affairs

> *There comes a time in everyone's life when you're faced with a choice whether you'd like to have sex on your desk at work or remain employed.*
>
> – comedian Jon Stewart, The Daily Show

Most American adults believe that engaging in an extra-marital affair is wrong; about 77 percent in a 1994 survey held this view and this figure has now risen to over 90 percent (Marano, 2012). But the vast majority of respondents also had fantasies about engaging in extra-marital affairs. Eichler (2012) reports that nearly 95 percent of men and women, in a non-representative sample of men and women looking for extra-marital affairs, fantasized about a colleague. Among US couples, 20 to 40 percent of heterosexual married men and between 10 to 25 percent of married heterosexual women will have an affair during their lifetime. During any single year, 1.5 to 4 percent of married individuals had an extra-marital affair. Interestingly, among younger individuals, rates of infidelity among women and men are converging. Women tend to have extra-marital affairs to satisfy emotional needs more so than do men. Surprisingly, affairs result in marital dissatisfaction and problems rather than being caused by marital dissatisfaction and marital problems. The major factor in engaging in extra-marital affairs is situational – opportunity – having access to others, travelling, privacy, socializing together after work, alcohol, and being desirable to others, which is why so many affairs take place at work among work colleagues. Events and experiences that lower one's self control such as exhaustion from travel, excessive work demands, and alcohol increase the likelihood of having an extra-marital affair. Some workplace cultures, the more macho ones, are more conducive to affairs occurring. Miller and Shales (2011) describe the workplace culture in the early days of ESPN as sex, drugs, infidelity, and sexual harassment; likely less prevalent today at this sports network.

Finding out one's partner has had an affair is a devastating experience. Most couples want to stay together after an affair has been revealed. About 70 percent of couples try to rebuild their marriages. Indeed, it is possible to recover from one partner engaging in affairs. Couples can work on rebuilding romance in their relationship. In addition, couples can sign "pacts" to support their good intentions. Pacts may include individuals indicating the circumstances under which they have thoughts of straying, i.e., the high-risk situations. In addition a pact could include reference to the costs of engaging in an affair.

Colleagues who know that other colleagues are having an affair also face a difficult situation. Colleagues may not want to work with these individuals, while those having the affair face their own challenges, and managers in the organization have to deal with all of this. Should organizations censure individuals having an affair? Does having an affair with someone outside the organization limit the effectiveness of an employee?

Sexual Harassment

Dimmock (2012) summarizes a recent RCMP investigative report on the conduct of one of its staff sergeants, Don Ray, head of a polygraph unit in Alberta. Ray held sex and drinking events in his office, sexually harassed female staff, kept a bar fridge full of liquor in his office, exposed himself to a female staff member, asking her first to touch his penis then to have sex with him (she refused both), and had sex with another female staff member in the polygraph office. Ray was docked 10 days' pay and demoted one level, and it was recommended he be transferred. This raises the question of what a person would have to do to lose their job with the RCMP and the Canadian public sector and why the union would, in good conscience, support Ray.

This toxic environment for female Mounties has resulted in a lawsuit being filed against the force (Theodore, 2012). Janet Merlo, a former Mountie, has launched a class action suit against the RCMP targeting the toxic environment within the male-dominated force. More than 100 current and former female members of the force will join. Merlo said it was common for her supervisor to prop up a naked inflatable doll next to his desk and ask her to stand beside it.

Another female former Mountie is also suing the force (Fong, 2012). Cate Galliford says she endured sexual harassment over an 18-year period, leaving the force in 2009 with a diagnosis of PTSD and a dependence on alcohol to cope with her levels of anxiety. The publicity given to sexual harassment of females within the RCMP has taken a toll on its reputation. Less than two-thirds of Canadians, in a recent poll, believed that the RCMP could address and successfully resolve alleged harassment of women officers (*National Post*, 2013).

Selley (2012) presents a litany of wrongdoings by police officers working in British Columbia, most involving sexual harassment and excessive drinking. Unfortunately RCMP and national government policies and regulations make it almost impossible to fire anyone. A male police officer exposing himself to a female staff member, drinking in his office, encouraging other staff members to drink with him in his office, having sex with female staff members in his office, and sexually harassing other staff members is not enough.

A widening sexual misconduct scandal is currently ongoing (July 2012) at Lackland Air Force base in Texas (Forsyth, 2012). Several US Air Force trainers have been found guilty of having unprofessional relationships with female basic trainees. One trainer was sentenced to 20 years in prison for the rape or sexual assault of ten female recruits. A total of 38 women have come forward claiming they were victims of sexual harassment and sexual misconduct and 15 sergeants have been charged or are being investigated in regard to these accusations. In the 1990s, another sex scandal occurred at the Army's Ordinance Center and School in Maryland.

Catalyst (1998) reports that 95 percent of large US employers have developed sexual harassment grievance policies and 70 percent have training programs that address these acts. Thus most employees have come to see sexual harassment as legally wrongful. Sexual harassment claims have fallen in the current economic recession as employees are afraid of losing their jobs if they make such claims. It has become somewhat easier to investigate sexual harassment claims now since e-mail and texting are now more often used in harassing behaviors.

The Sexual Abuse of Children

Priests in the Catholic Church have been accused, and found guilty, of sexually abusing children over at least the past ten years. The issue continues (Kelley, 2012). A high-ranking Catholic priest, Monsignor William Lynn, the most senior US Church official charged with covering up priests' sexual abuse of children, went on trial in Philadelphia on March 26. Lynn is charged with moving priests known to be child abusers to other parishes where they continued molesting children. He is charged with endangering the welfare of children and conspiracy for covering up allegations of priests' sexual abuse. Other co-defendants have already pleaded guilty. Lynn's lawyer said he was powerless to stop the abuse since he was too low in the Church hierarchy. At one point earlier, Lynn went into Church archives and made a list of 35 abusive priests but was ordered by the Church hierarchy to destroy the list. The Cardinal of the Catholic Church in Ireland was under increasing pressure in early 2012 to resign for his role in the cover up of sexual abuse of children by priests.

Louis Freeh, former director of the FBI, investigated the recent child sex abuse scandal at Penn State University, releasing his report on July 12, 2012. Assistant football coach, Jerry Sandusky, now in jail, was convicted on 45 of 48 counts. Senior university officials were aware of these incidents for over a decade, as were the head football coach, another assistant football coach, and several janitors. Several university officials were fired, and may be charged with criminal offenses. The head football coach was fired and has since died. Senior university officials decided not to take action for fear of damaging the university's reputation, and the football program was a huge source of money and prestige. The janitors did not come forward as they feared for their jobs (Mulvihill, Armas and Scolforo, 2012).

Recent information has come to light documenting decades of sexual abuse of young boys within the Boy Scouts of America organization, and the sexual abuse of young boys and girls by DJ and presenter Jimmy Savile while at the BBC. These crimes were horrendous, and illustrate again that the cover up, though not worse than these crimes, ended the careers of several people. Rather than being heroes they ended up letting everybody down. The similarities between the handling of the Penn State child sex abuse scandal, the Boy Scouts of American scandal, Jimmy Savile, and others at the BBC, and the child sexual abuse scandals within the Catholic Church are striking.

Work Addiction

Considerable research attention has been devoted to antecedents and consequences of working long hours, working in intense jobs, and work addiction (Burke, 2010; Bunting, 2004; Hewlett and Luce, 2006; Ng, Sorensen and Feldman, 2007; van der Hulst, 2003; Killinger, 1991; Snir and Harpaz, 2012; Sussman, 2012). Individuals in several countries are now working more hours in more demanding and intense jobs. Some people take great pride in describing themselves as workaholics, and workers in some industries (e.g., financial services) seem to work excessive hours. The evidence generally indicates that working excessively long hours takes a toll on family, relationships, and health. Some executives, however, report high levels of job satisfaction despite excessive work hours because of the rewards and perks of such investments. Interestingly, the intensity of one's job has been shown to have more negative effects on psychological well-being than the number of hours worked.

Research evidence has accumulated over the past decade showing the costs individuals and families endure from workaholism or work addiction (Burke, 2010; Ng, Sorensen and Feldman, 2007; Holland, 2008). Workaholism can be seen as having two dimensions; working compulsively and working excessively (Schaufeli, Taris and Bakker, 2008). Both of these dimensions have been shown to be associated with negative psychological well-being outcomes (Schaufeli, Shimazu and Taris, 2009).

But not all work addicts are equally disadvantaged; those that work long hours and exhibit particular behaviors (perfectionism, unwillingness and inability to delegate), and particular outcomes (higher levels of job stress) were particularly at risk, supporting the notion that it isn't how hard one works but how one works hard that matters.

There are different types of workaholics or work addicts (Burke 2010). Schaufeli and his colleagues (Schaufeli, Taris and Bakker, 2008; van Beek et al., 2012; Schaufeli, Shimazu and Taris, 2009) make a distinction between "good workaholics" and "bad workaholics." The former show a positive association between work addiction and work engagement, while the latter show an association between work addiction and burnout. "Bad workaholics" are pushed, compulsively driven by internal needs, to their work while "good workaholics" are pulled to their work because they love it, see it as fun, and are not stressed by it. Van Beek et al. (2012), in a sample of Chinese healthcare workers, found that levels of two types of work motivations distinguished "good" and "bad" workaholics. Good workaholics showed an association of intrinsic motivations (e.g., work was interesting, enjoyable, satisfying) with work engagement, while bad workaholics showed an association of extrinsic motivations (work to earn a living, to get others' approval) with burnout.

It has also been suggested (Porter, 1996) that work addicts contribute to making the workplace less pleasant. Balducci et al. (2012), in two large samples, found that individuals scoring higher on work addiction also engaged in more aggressive workplace behaviors.

Good work is too often defined by number of hours worked, the notion of face time, being seen to be available by those at higher organizational levels (Wharton and Blair-Loy, 2002; Epstein et al., 1999; Hewlett and Luce, 2006; Kuhn, 2006; Blair-Loy, 2004). A redefinition of what good work means involves changing informal norms and expectations and the formal reward structure of an organization.

An interesting question becomes what would or do people actually do when they work fewer hours. Saffer and Lamiraud (2008) examined what workers in France did when the work week was reduced from 39 to 35 hours in 1998. Workers spent more time reading, listening to music, exercising, being with their children, cleaning, shopping, washing, cooking, and relaxing but not on increased social interaction with organized groups, such as sports clubs, church groups, and parents groups, among others.

Internet Addiction

Susan and I took a two week vacation in Spain in mid-September 2012. We spent 10 days travelling with an early-forties female HR manager working for a large multinational firm headquartered in Munich. We ate breakfast, lunch, and dinners together and spent hours each day walking in Madrid, Granada, and Malaga. She looked at her Blackberry every five minutes or so while eating, flying, taking a bus tour, or walking. After one day I could tell by her facial expressions the tenor of the emails she received. If she smiled, it was from her boyfriend; if she scowled slightly it was from a colleague who had scheduled a meeting upon her return home, and if she used the F-bomb it was from a colleague that had screwed up. She indicated that she kept her Blackberry beside her bed at night since she often thought about work while in bed. She said that she had sent an e-mail to a colleague back in Munich one night at 2:30 am suggesting that an internal candidate seemed like a good fit for a recent job opening. Her behavior describes what Perlow was studying to a T (Perlow, 2012).

Internet addiction has become an increasing concern among adults (Griffiths, 2000a, 2000b) and among boys and girls who spend countless hours playing videogames (Grusser, Thalemann and Griffiths, 2007). In a study of the impact of e-mail communications on employees, Derks and Bakker (2010) found that the costs of e-mail were disproportionately placed on the recipient who has to deal with huge amounts of e-mail and feels pressure to respond to them as soon as possible. In addition, use of smartphones increased opportunity to work from anywhere, thus increasing working hours and the possibility of increasing work–family conflicts. Thus internet addiction and work addiction may co-exist for some.

Mintzberg and Todd (2012) make the case that executives can become more effective by reducing their electronic communications. Silverman (2012) cites findings supportive of Mintzberg and Todd's proposals. Office workers were interrupted about every three minutes (by self or by others). Interruptions included checking one's phone, answering a text, switching to a desktop to read an e-mail, looking at Facebook or Twitter messages, and being interrupted by a colleague coming into one's office. In addition, reading and processing 100 e-mails took more than half a day. And it took an average of 23 minutes to return to the original task. There are clearly more frustrations from technology today than earlier.

As a result, efforts have been undertaken to prevent and/or reduce this addiction (see Young, 1999). Baute (2011) discusses ways that she and others have addressed digital addiction. These include: taking "low tech" breaks such as going for a walk, having a glass of water, and leaving the house to visit friends. Others have asked spouses to change their password. There is also computer software available that blocks one from social media sites.

There is increasing evidence that e-mail is interfering with people's ability to get their work done (Song, Halsey and Burgess, 2012). Bilton (2012) cites a University of California Irvine study showing that employees who do not look at their e-mail on a regular basis at work are less stressed and more productive. Workers asked to stop e-mailing for five days instead focused on single work tasks and showed lower levels of stress assessed by wearing daily heart monitors. He suggests that employees take e-mail vacations over a few days. Silverman (2012) describes the following solutions: instituting a no-device policy at team meetings, blocking out several hours a week without e-mails or meetings, and instituting a no internal e-mail policy while allowing external e-mails.

Inzlicht (2012) describes his internet addiction and how he is going about addressing it. His e-mail behavior at work was actually interfering with him getting his job done. He did the following: disabled devices indicating that an e-mail has arrived, moved his e-mail apps to less visible locations, and checked his e-mail only every four hours. He notes that Volkswagen in Germany has restricted employee e-mail use to business hours only. Some high-end hotels are also now restricting e-mail use.

Perlow (2012) considered the effects of internet use in contributing to working long hours in a sample noted for long work hours, consultants at an international consulting organization. Individuals checked their e-mail when they first got up, before going to bed, dozens of times a day, daily while on vacation, and while doing other things such as having dinner with their family. Individuals were afraid to not check their e-mails for fear of not responding promptly to others, because not doing so would hamper their careers, and because they had a belief that clients wanted immediate information, among other reasons. Perlow summarizes factors causing the consultants to continue being chained to their e-mails as a "cycle of responsiveness." Individuals experience pressure to always be responsive, so they must always be available; others then know that I am always available, I see myself as always being available and liking to keep up with my work, and everyone around me is also connected to their technologies. Perlow began a series of initiatives with work teams within this firm over a five-year period based on the belief that disconnecting from work would result in consultants being more productive, satisfied, and having a more balanced life. Team members were committed collectively to a time when they would not use their e-mails and not conduct work with each other and clients (e.g., on a given night, not after a certain hour – 5:00 pm), referred to as Predictable Time Off (PTO). Comparing PTO and non-PTO consulting teams indicated that the former were more satisfied, worked fewer hours, and were more productive. A key element in this process was encouraging team members to talk openly about their experiences, giving them a voice. Perlow offers guidance to other organizations interested in having its employees be productive while leading more balanced lives.

Fraud, Bribery, and Corruption

Two stories involving bribery and corruption appeared side by side on the same day in the Report on Business (*Globe and Mail*, 2001a, 2001b):

- "China bribe trail cites Ericsson payoff" – Sony Ericsson Mobile Communications AB allegedly paid bribes of US$5.8 million to a Chinese official over a period of years in order to win contracts.
- "Bribery probe stalls Tullow sale in Uganda" – Ugandan lawmakers delayed approval of Tullow Oil PLC's sale of three exploration blocks because of bribery in the awarding of oil concessions.

The Ontario Securities Commission ordered Coventree and three of its top executives to pay $2.5 million in penalties for failing to tell investors about the health of the market for asset-based commercial paper prior to its collapse in 2007 (Greenwood, 2011).

Sex, bribery, and fraud can also go together. Wiretaps of Italian Prime Minister Silvio Berlusconi revealed him ordering women for his parties, perhaps even flying some of them in on state planes, and complaining that his meetings with Chancellor Angela Merkel of Germany, President Nicolas Sarkozy of France, and Pope Benedict XVI were cramping his social life, and that he had sex with eight of eleven women at one of his parties.

Italy has a spoils system based on loyalty that links holding a job with votes, expecting favors with loyalty and jobs – essentially favor trading (Donahue, 2011). One vivid example of this was evident in a government investigation into Gianpaolo Tarantini, a businessman from Bari, accused of bringing prostitutes to Berlusconi. Tarantini said he took women to Berlusconi but did not know they were prostitutes. Tarantini was given a diplomatic visa to join Berlusconi on a trip to China in 2008, during which he tried to find women for Berlusconi.

Two executives at Finmeccanica, a partly state-owned conglomerate, resigned after it was shown that Tarantini obtained prostitutes for Finmeccanica managers in exchange for helping Tarantini obtain contracts. Tarantini was arrested in September 2011 and charged with extorting money from Berlusconi in return for favorable testimony in the prostitution case. Berlusconi paid Tarantini $684,000.

The Ontario Securities Commission, after a lengthy investigation, concluded that Sino-Forest Corp, a Chinese company trading on the Ontario Stock Exchange, committed a large fraud involving inflated assets and receivables (Koven, 2012).

Pook (2008) reports the results of surveys conducted in Bulgaria and Romania in which 88 percent of Bulgarians and 85 percent of Romanians claimed that their public officials were corrupt and took bribes. The cost of corruption in these two countries runs to billions of dollars.

It was somewhat ironic that a Canadian government agency responsible for ethics training of public servants was found by a government ombudsman to have "cooked" contracts for the delivery of these sessions so a former retired employee would get the work (*National Post*, 2012e). This was in violation of the government's policy against sole source contracting.

How can organizations remain corruption free in their dealings with corruption-rife countries such as Russia, India, and China? Bribery is so common in Russia the finance ministry has stated that bribery paid abroad will not be tax deductible (Kesterton, 2012c). Canada's SNC-Lavalin, one of the world's largest construction companies, is engaged in bribery in its dealings with Libya, and Wal-Mart likely engaged in bribery to obtain real estate properties for its stores in Mexico. To avoid corruption, organizations need strong leadership, clear policies, and shareholders willing to take smaller returns as a result of ethical practices. It also helps to have a strong brand and exceptional technology and products. But leadership is key. Enron had a lengthy values statement and we know how little difference this made. It may be difficult but it is possible (Yew, 2012). Ethical leadership matters. Mayer, Aquino, Greenbaum and Kuenzi (2012), in a study of supervisors and work group members from 195 departments, found that leader ethical behavior was associated with more ethical department behavior and fewer relationship conflicts within departments.

Seduction: The Slow Selling of One's Soul

Christensen, Allworth and Dillon (2012) illustrate some "wrong turns on the road to success." Christensen obtained his MBA degree at the Harvard Business School and regularly returned to attend five-year class reunions. At the five-year class reunion almost all graduates came and the vast majority were satisfied with their jobs, careers, and lives. At the ten-year gathering, a few fewer attended, and some expressed dissatisfaction with their jobs and careers, and some grumblings about their marriages. At the 15-year reunion, still fewer came, and there was more dissatisfaction with marriages and family life, some divorces, and more job and career dissatisfaction. At later reunions there were more divorces, more dissatisfaction with home and family life, more job dissatisfaction, and a few graduates were in jail.

Perkins (2006), in his analysis and description of his activities in representing US interests and US firms in contacts with developing countries, highlights steps in the "selling of his soul" in support of activities he had come to see as negative. These included pleasing his boss and being recognized for his sterling efforts at work, being handsomely rewarded in financial terms (being in it for the money and the good life), getting promoted quickly and fast becoming a "star" in his organization, being financially rewarded while also receiving perks and recognition. These become "bribes" for continuing on the path. He lumps these into becoming "rich, famous, and powerful." It is easy to become seduced into doing things one believes are wrong and harmful given the rewards for doing so, in a society where having these rewards are signs of having made it. And it appears that most people are seducible. Greed is infectious (Partnoy, 2009).

Christensen, Allworth and Dillon (2012) also address the slippery ethical slope in living a life of integrity. All of us likely come face to face with a "just this once" situation in which bending the rules would offer an advantage. They use the case of Nick Leeson, trader for Barings Bank, who lost $1.3 billion in investments causing the bank to collapse, cost 1,200 people their jobs, cost him his marriage, and earned him six years in jail. Leeson made some investments that lost a small amount of money. He then made more larger investments to cover up his losses, ended up lying to cover up previous lies, forging documents, misleading auditors, and making misleading statements. "Just this once" thinking can easily lead one down the slippery slope. Christensen, Allworth and Dillon (2012) conclude that being ethical 100 percent of the time is easier than being so 98 percent of the time.

Greed and Materialism

> *Materialism – excessive devotion to the pursuit of material wealth and physical well-being.*
>
> – Cassell's dictionary

When men and women are rewarded for their greed, greed becomes a factor in fraud and corruption (Wang and Murnighan, 2011; Livesey, 2012; Madrach, 2011; O'Shea, 2011; Morgenson and Posner, 2011; Partnoy, 2009). Individuals who "make it" – reflected in their mansions and villas, yachts and private planes, and conspicuous consumption – become the models we are encouraged to emulate. But only a relatively few enjoy these riches while the vast majority barely get by. Capitalism has its flaws but these almost always are the result of human frailties.

Jackson (2004) writes about two US organizations and their leaders that failed the "character" test. One, Sunbeam, was led by Al Dunlap. Dunlap was termed Chainsaw, the Shredder, and Rambo in pinstripes, by the media. He had a reputation for taking a lackluster company and making it profitable by cost cutting and employee downsizing. He undertook these efforts at Sunbeam and company stock price increased. Dunlap, and Sunbeam, had large financial goals and eventually Sunbeam was charged by the SEC with accounting irregularities. Dunlap was fired, and Sunbeam filed for bankruptcy shortly thereafter. Jackson's second example was Enron, led by Kenneth Lay and Andrew Fastow. Enron was also charged with fraud and it eventually filed for bankruptcy. Enron's culture emphasized financial growth and individual initiative leading to an unethical Enron culture having few controls. Interestingly, Enron had a lengthy code of conduct and ethical expectations. Under Fastow, Enron created a "yes man" and "yes woman" culture in which those expressing opposing views were punished. Lay and Fastow were sentenced to lengthy prison terms, though Lay died before beginning to serve his. Enron's auditor, Arthur Andersen, shredded documents and eventually filed for bankruptcy as well.

Aubrey McClendon, CEO of Chesapeake Energy Corp used his firm's money as a personal and family piggy bank (Shiffman, Driver and Grow, 2012). Company money was used to repair his house after it was damaged by hail stones, for him and his family on personal vacations, to fly friends of his wife on their personal vacations, and the purchase of a stake in an NBA basketball team. McClendon also placed friends on the Chesapeake board of directors.

Allen Stanford, found guilty of leading a US$7 billion Ponzi scheme, was sentenced to 110 years in prison on June 14, 2012 (Gilbert and Englesham, 2012). For years, Stanford engaged in a lavish lifestyle involving private jets, luxury yachts, and homes in several countries. Bernie Madoff was sentenced to 150 years in prison for running an even larger Ponzi scheme that also afforded him a lavish lifestyle.

Other North American companies that filed for bankruptcy as a result of fraud and corruption include Keller Peabody, Drexel, Burnham Lambert, Global Crossings, WorldCom, Adelphia, and Livent, among others. Various individuals have also been convicted of fraud including Bernie Madoff, Allen Stanford, Jack Abramoff, Conrad Black, Garth Drabinsky, and Raj Rajaratnam. These individuals and organizations have diminished the reputation of government and business leaders, organizations themselves, and capitalism itself (Henriques, 2010). As a consequence, individuals and organizations that can build and maintain reputational capital will be advantaged.

An association between board of director exit and damaged firm reputation through either financial restatements and lawsuits has also been observed (Arthaud-Day et al., 2006; Cowen and Marcel, 2011; Srinivasan, 2005). In addition, Boivie, Graffin and Pollock (2012) observed that the value of being on the board of a prestigious firm dropped when the firm experienced events that damaged its prestige.

Having a moral character means following the law, developing quality products and services, having financial controls and discipline (Callahan,2006). Such individuals and organizations should only work with forthright and honest people, and drop unscrupulous employees, business partners, and clients. Furthermore, people prefer to work for and enjoy working for organizations that have character and are trustworthy and ethical.

Behaving ethically may have some short-term costs, however. Disclosing the potential adverse effects of drugs, being unwilling to pay bribes to obtain a contract, or just "selling" unnecessary services to customers can be seen as potentially lost opportunities. The risks imposed by these ethical lapses are reflected in the loss of trust, credibility, and reputation. Sears' automotive repair unit suffered these when it was revealed that they sold unnecessary repairs. In the long term, they are a threat to individual and organizational success.

Why Reputation Matters

A good reputation is more valuable than money.

– Publilius Syrus, First Century BC

When information about individual character flaws and organizational toxicity become public, it travels quickly and can tarnish entire industrial sectors (Yu, Sengul and Lester, 2008) Individuals and organizations should realize that they all live in "glass houses." Members of boards of directors have had their reputations tarnished by being associated with firms found guilty of financial fraud (Cowen and Marcel, 2011; Pozner, 2008). Being indirectly associated with organizational fraud indicates a potential failure to fulfill important professional oversight requirements. Compromised directors are often terminated from their present board seats and have difficulty in obtaining future board appointments.

Why Do "Good" People Do "Bad Things"?

The individuals mentioned above were "good people" with few being truly "evil." Almost all incumbents of managerial and professional jobs are "good" not "evil" people. Yet some of these "good people" do bad things. Questions such as "Why do good people do bad things?" and "Why do so many people in power behave so badly?" are increasingly being asked (Zimbardo, 2007).

There are several hypotheses as to why "good people" do "bad things." These include:

- to gain an advantage over others
- a belief that everybody is doing it
- financial and ego-enhancing rewards

- organizational cultures that routinize "bad behavior"
- a focus on the short term
- a belief that the ends justify the means
- a slippery slope – starting small and escalating
- powerful people may view risk differently and engage in reckless behavior as a result
- powerful people may feel entitled
- most people overestimate their ability to behave ethically and are unaware of not acting ethically

Hannah, Avolio and May (2011), in a conceptual review and integration, propose and define the concept of moral capacity and its elements and suggest ways that it can be developed. They identify six moral capacities, in two categories; moral maturation and moral conation. Moral maturation is defined as "the capacity to elaborate and effectively attend to, store, retrieve, process, and make meaning of morally relevant information" (p. 667); moral conation is defined as "the capacity to generate responsibility and motivation to take moral action in the face of adversity and persevere through challenges" (p. 667). The latter includes taking ownership, having moral efficacy, and courage; the former includes having capacities for dealing with complexity and identifying moral issues. They suggest some ways to develop both moral maturation (e.g., social learning, exposure to moral experiences) and moral conation (e.g., encouraging responsibility, highlighting the costs of immoral actions, and providing recognition and rewards for moral actions).

Moore and her colleagues (2012) developed a measure of individual propensity to morally disengage, and in five studies examined its relationship with various unethical organizational behaviors. Individual propensity to morally disengage predicted self-reported unethical behaviors, decisions to commit fraud, self-serving decisions in the workplace, and co-worker and supervisor-reported unethical work behaviors.

Individuals are also more likely to cheat if they believe that cheating will not harm anyone. Some examples would include lying about the number of hours worked in cases of billable hours, and claiming expenses for meals that were provided by fees paid to a sponsoring organization. Individuals who engage in these practices likely feel no guilt. There are costs, however, to their organizations, and perhaps to the reputation of individuals involved.

Low Self-control

I can resist everything except temptation.

– Oscar Wilde

Baumeister and Tierney (2011) conclude that the strongest personal quality that predicts a dissatisfying life, career poor health, and being alone is lack of self-control or low willpower. They see a link between low self-control or low willpower and compulsive spending and borrowing, impulsive violence, underachieving in school, procrastination at work, chronic anxiety, explosive anger, losing friends, being fired, getting divorced, ending up in prison, committing adultery, and making risky loans. People see their lack of control or low willpower as a major failing. Unfortunately there are an endless list of temptations today. People typically experience desires for various things or experiences – fortunately most people are able to resist most of their temptations.

Interest in willpower and character building declined around the 1950s with the self-esteem movement that eventually led to higher incidences of narcissism. An early study showing the power of control and willpower was the famous marshmallow experiment. Children were presented with one marshmallow and told that if they delayed eating it for a while they would receive a second marshmallow. The experimenter then left the room and the children were observed. Some immediately ate the single marshmallow, others looked at it, touched it, then ate it, while still others did not eat it. Willpower was important. A later follow-up of children that participated in this experiment when they were four years of age was then undertaken. It produced some powerful findings. Those that delayed eating the marshmallow at age four, as adults, did better at school and on standardized tests, were more popular with teachers and peers, were less likely to abuse drugs, had healthier body weights, and earned higher salaries, while others experienced higher divorce rates, more domestic violence crimes, and more social problems. Baumeister and Tierney (2011) have suggested that loss of control has become the major social pathology of our times.

The Need for Speed

Gunia et al. (2012), in an experiment involving university students, found that individuals were more likely to do the right thing/make a more ethical choice or decision when they have some time to think about it than when they have to make a snap decision or choice. Immediate decisions were more likely to be selfish. They suggest taking more time to respond or talking with an ethical colleague would reduce the making of small unethical choices. They observed that immediate decisions or self-interested conversations were associated with fewer ethical decisions, whereas individual contemplative decisions or social contemplative decisions resulted in more ethical decisions being made. Slower decision making is likely to be reflected in more ethical decision making. However, it is unlikely that these efforts would reduce large financial frauds. Partnoy (2012) also makes the case for moving slowly.

Can "Dark-Side" Characteristics be Changed?

Hogan, Curphy and Hogan (1994) believe "dark-side" characteristics can be changed but it requires considerably more intensive development than currently found in most leader-training programs. Leader character becomes more important as one rises in an organization, but relatively few individuals seem to want to know themselves better, and the workplace environment limits and hinders an examination and admission of "weakness." In addition, mangers get relatively little honest feedback about their behaviors and the impact of these on others. The power of most managers intimidates others.

Personal awareness of one's dark-side characteristics is critical. Managers are encouraged to get feedback on what they can do to become better leaders, to take a confidante, talk about dark-side characteristics in their management teams, use the services of a coach, use small failures to support awareness, learning, and change.

Costs of Human Frailties

Costs exist at both individual and organizational levels. These include loss of reputation, distress to individuals, their families and friends, career failure, and financial costs. Weimer and Thornton (1997) showed that the negative effects of a culture at Mitsubishi in the US that tolerated sexual harassment persisted for many years after it was acknowledged and changes were pledged. Shapiro and Von Glinow (2007) note the huge financial costs to organizations resulting from "flawed" leadership (e.g., Enron, Martha Stewart Living, Tyco, Arthur Andersen).

News Corp's UK unit has now been sued by almost 70 people since reports of phone hacking at their *News of the World* tabloid were made public (Chellel, 2011). News Corp had already reached financial settlements with some celebrities who said the newspaper hacked their cell phones. News Corp has a US$70 million fund to settle claims but perhaps will need as much as US$150 million.

Mark McGwire, who admitted taking steroids, has now only a slim chance of making it into baseball's Hall of Fame. Voters are holding his cheating against him. Other baseball players likely to be tarnished by cheating include Barry Bonds, Sammy Sosa, and Roger Clemens.

Sometimes the costs of human frailties to perpetrators are small. Teachers that sexually prey on their male and female students face little or no punishment. School boards, teacher watchdogs, and teacher unions have been unable to slow or stop increases in these assaults. The largest school board in one Canadian province, Newfoundland and Labrador, has established a new policy that requires teachers let students who are caught cheating get a second try with no academic penalty (Boesveld, 2011). The teachers association believes that this policy enables students to cheat.

Sometimes the potential costs are large. Ruth Madoff, in a *60 Minutes* interview, said that she and her husband, Bernie, tried to kill themselves after his Ponzi scheme was detected (*Toronto Star*, 2011). Furthermore, Madoff's son, Mark, committed suicide on the second anniversary of his father's admission of guilt.

Not surprisingly, CEOs now have an image problem (Ovsey, 2012). Terms such as greedy, selfish, unethical, dictatorial, lacking character, lacking integrity, and lacking honesty are commonly used to describe CEOs. Ovsey reports that a survey international PR firm Edelman found that CEOs are now rated below politicians on a trust barometer in Canada.

It will take more than PR and spin doctors to turn this image problem around.

Leader Apologies for Transgressions

An increasing number of organizational leaders have made apologies for a variety of personal transgressions, the transgressions of employees, injury and death caused to others by the safety of their products or equipment, or the poor performance of their organization under their stewardship. Transgressions can be integrity-based (sexual harassment, sexual affairs, theft, fraud) or competency-based (lacked knowledge and competence). Kellerman (2006) refers to this as an "apology culture." Apologies are also complex; there is no guarantee they will work. An important question is whether leader apologies have their desired effects.

Byrne, Barling and Dupre (2012) reported the results of two field studies on the effects of leader apologies for transgressions on the well-being of their employees and on the well-being of the leaders themselves. In the first study, respondents assessed either an integrity-based transgression or a competency-based transgression of their leader and its severity, the nature and extent of the leader's apology, and their own emotions (positive and negative) and psychological health. They reported that leader apology moderated the effects of transgression severity and employee well-being. The second study examined these measures from the perspectives of the leaders. Leaders described a time when they offended an employee. Leader apologies moderated the relationship between transgression severity and leader (apologizer) well-being. Thus leader apologies seemed to benefit both the leaders themselves and their employees by lifting the burden/clearing both of the transgression.

Falling from Grace – but How Far?

Although there are some costs that result from human frailties, for some the costs may be small; they may fall from grace but not very far and not for long (Mayer, Aquino, Mawritz and Priesemuth, 2012; Polman, Pettit and Wiesenfeld, 2013). Mayer, Aquino, Mawritz and Priesemuth (2012) examined the effects of scandal on the evaluations and reputations of these individuals. They undertook a field study and two laboratory experiments and reported that (1) high-performing leaders were evaluated more negatively than low-performing leaders for engaging in transgressions outside of work, but (2) high-performing leaders who engaged in transgressions outside of work were evaluated more favorably than low-performing leaders who were ethical outside of work. Thus leaders engaged in transgressions outside of work did not fall very far. Performance trumped transgressions which seems to be case with Bill Clinton, David Letterman, Eliot Spitzer, and Kobe Bryant, among others.

Thus not every individual tarnished by human frailties "falls from grace." Individuals involved in personal and organizational misconduct are stigmatized, but the nature and consequences of this can vary. It is not inevitable that human frailties leading to personal and organizational misconduct lead to career failure. Some studies show negative consequences of personal and organizational misconduct (Cowen and Marcel, 2011; Pozner, 2008); others found little negative effect (see Mayer, Aquino, Mawritz and Priesemuth, 2012). Some directors of failed organizations are now serving on the boards of directors of other companies.

Koyuncu (2012) presents a model to explain why some transgressions are associated with failed careers while others are not. First, perceptions of the transgressions and the corresponding stigma attached to individuals reflects the degree to which the individual and organization can recover, how severe the transgression was, and how visible the transgression was. In addition, the time frame of the transgression, that is, the passage of time, influences the magnitude of the stigma.

Stigmatized individuals are likely to experience negative career consequences. But the magnitude of these negative effects are affected by how accountable the individual was for the transgression, the nature of the evidence surrounding the transgression (clear cut or ambiguous), the stigma management tactics used by the individual, and the relationship between the individual and the organization. The stigma management strategies used by organizations also play a role here.

Our Objectives for this Collection

We focus here on individuals and what both individuals and their employing organizations can do to lessen the incidence and negative consequences of human frailties by developing appropriate attitudes, values, and behaviors consistent with character and integrity. How can individuals avoid becoming a casualty of some risky individual choices and behaviors? What can organizations do to better understand and identify human frailties of employees and address these.

Our purpose is to support the development of healthy individuals and healthy workplaces. Sainforth and his colleagues (2001) write that healthy organizations both are financially successful and have a healthy workforce. Shain and Kramer (2004, p. 643) discuss "what employees bring with them to the workplace in terms of personal resources, health practices, beliefs, attitudes, values and hereditary endowment" (healthy individuals) and "what the workplace does to employees once they are there in terms of organization of work, in both the physical and psychological sense" (a healthy workplace). Organizations can be proactive in addressing human frailties and in creating positive experiences among their employees.

Organizational pathology exists in today's workplace but is typically ignored or hidden. Employees are aware of this but pathology is rarely addressed. Pathology saps morale and hinders work performance. Employees, their families, and customers have to live with the consequences. Pathologies affect both individuals and organizations.

Executive Education Programs

In the last week of his MBA classes, Clayton Christensen (see Christensen, Allworth and Dillon, 2012) and his students discuss the following:

"How can I be sure that ...

- I will be successful and happy in my career?
- My relationships with my spouse, my children, and my extended family and close friends become an enduring source of happiness?
- I live a life of integrity – and stay out of jail?" (Christensen, Allworth and Dillon, 2012, p. 6).

In these sessions they try to apply course content and theories that might predict success in these three areas.

Courage and Character

Rate and Sternberg (2007) see a crisis of courage in organizations, mainly the result of fear among employees. They see large blunders in some organizations being made by managers who are highly educated, skilled, and experienced because of the lack of courage in their workplaces. This raises two central issues: Why do people fail to act with courage? And why and how does one fail to act courageously? They phrase this as "When and why do good people do nothing?"

Doing nothing tends almost always to have negative consequences. But they make a distinction between lacking courage and cowardice. Unfortunately acting courageously can also have negative consequences such as being socially and organizationally ostracized, and experiencing economic and psychological harm.

They define courage as "(a) an intentional act executed after willful deliberation, (b) involving the acknowledgement and endurance of substantial risk to the actor, (c) attempting to bring about a noble good or worthy purpose, (d) persisting perhaps, despite the presence of personal fear" (Rate and Sternberg, 2007, p. 8).

Courage, to them, has several components: intentionality and deliberation, known substantial risk, a noble good, and actions despite personal fear.

They suggest several ways to develop courage in organizations. These include:

- including employees in dealing with work unit and organizational problems
- encouraging employees to question
- emphasizing the heroic, moral and meaningful aspects of work
- creating and supporting a culture in which courageous behavior can be sustained – emphasizing morale, ethics, and voice
- creating programs supporting the free flow of information
- reducing levels of fear in the workplace
- developing a supportive climate for learning
- using stories and examples of courageous behavior
- ultimately creating a workplace in which courage is no longer needed – there is no risk of reprisal, ostracism, loss of one's job, or fear of retribution or public humiliation

Tough (2012), in his research on factors associated with the success of children in their later lives noted that character was a better predictor of future success than was IQ. He listed persistence, curiosity, optimism, conscientiousness and self-control as in part character traits acquired while growing up from parents in families, schools, through role models and mentors.

Your Self Worth Is Not Your Net Worth

Few people, if any, start at the outset of their working life and careers to harm others or behave dishonestly. Even acknowledged criminals such as Bernie Madoff, Jeff Skilling, Nick Leeson, Conrad Black, and Allen Stanford started out living honest lives. But once they made exceptions, "just this one time," it was only a matter of time before they made their next exception, and on and on. Measuring success in monetary terms is likely to lead some women and men astray. Instead they need to consider how they define success and what is most important in their lives. Success is likely not reaching a certain organizational level and making a particular level of salary. Success is having a positive effect on one's family, friends, colleagues at work, the employing organization, and in the wider society (Friedman, 2008; George, 2007).

Rebounding from the Negative Effects of Human Frailties

To err is human, to forgive divine.

– Alexander Pope (1688–1744), English poet

Not all human frailties produce the same negative consequences on individuals, families, and workplaces. Some have limited effects while others have widespread negative effects. Not all human frailties are fatal. In addition, most societies believe in giving individuals who have fallen short a second chance, again depending to some extent on how egregious the effects were. Well known individuals who have shown human frailties and rebuilt their lives and careers include US President Bill Clinton, former New York Governor Eliot Spitzer, Martha Stewart, Tiger Woods, Jeffrey Archer, and Michael Milken. Some of these have served time in jail, others were shamed for their sexual peccadillos. Some of these individuals (Clinton, Milken, Stewart) have even gone on to develop solid reputations following their downfalls.

Common initiatives consistent with rebuilding one's reputation include accepting responsibility for one's actions, offering a sincere and complete apology, being chastened, keeping out of future trouble, being productive, and having some semblance of balance.

How Will You Measure Your Life?

This heading is the title of a recent book by Christensen, Allworth and Dillon (2012). They first debunk the belief that the pursuit of money will bring satisfaction and happiness. The central building block for a meaningful life, to them, is developing a life purpose. Developing a life purpose has three elements.

- a likeness – identifying the person that I want to become
- a commitment – making a deep commitment to realizing one's likeness
- a metric – articulating measures by which one's life will be measured

Living One's Best Life

Try to be better than yourself.

– William Faulkner (1897–1962), US writer and Nobel Laureate

Weinstein (2011) offers five "rules" for living one's best life:

- Do no harm – do not inflict physical or emotional damage on others. Will what I am doing avoid or cause harm?
- Make things better for yourself and others. Will this make things better for myself and others?
- Respect others – honor the values, preferences and rights of others. Is this respectful?
- Be fair – treat all fairly and equally. Is it fair?
- Be loving. Is this loving?

Living an Authentic and Meaningful Life

Be yourself, everyone else is taken.

– Oscar Wilde

Sharma (2011) suggests that leadership skills begin with self-leadership. He offers the following guidelines to minimize the risks of human frailties:

1. live an authentic life – live by your own values and pursue original goals
2. embrace your fears – get out of your comfort zone
3. live with kindness – be kinder and more generous than expected
4. make small daily progress – small wins
5. do your best to lead your best life – use your talents
6. choose your influences well – spend time with people that uplift you
7. find the greatest joy in the simplest places
8. understand life's true purpose – to live well
9. stand for something bigger – the journey is everything and make it enjoyable

We Get By with a Little Help from Our Friends

McDonald and Westphal (2011) studied factors associated with CEOs' willingness to offer social support to other CEOs who were experiencing important personal problems (marital difficulties, problems in relationships with a child, health problems of a loved one). They found that CEOs who identified with the corporate elite were more likely to offer social support to other CEOs, and that CEOs receiving social support from other CEOs were more likely to engage in effective managerial behaviors (resulting in fewer effects from their personal problems and greater reduction in the effects of personal problems on important managerial behaviors (e.g., mentoring subordinates, interactions with colleagues).

When CEOs suffer personal problems, support from fellow CEOs was found to be more helpful than support from family or friends. CEO personal problems caused CEOs to pull back from important interpersonal behaviors with their direct reports and other subordinate managers.

Westphal et al. (2012) found that when CEOs said good things about other CEOs, it had the effect of countering negative assessments of the CEOs' performance. In addition, CEOs saying positive things about other CEOs tended in return to receive positive comments from those previously praised. Their study considered impressions of CEOs and their performance following a poor financial performance event. There are obviously other "failures" or transgressions which are unlikely to be affected by the good things other CEOs say about a focal CEO.

Interventions

Interventions have been developed that focus on individuals (Nash and Stevenson, 2004). These include training and development initiatives, managerial coaching, employee counseling and therapy, and employee assistance programs. These efforts have considered ethics in the workplace, the development of psychological capital, the development of courage and employee voice, addressing toxic behavior, enhancing positive and lifestyle behaviors.

Interventions have also been undertaken at the organizational level. Targets of some of these efforts have addressed harassment in the workplace, corporate wellness programs, ethical issues such as conflict of interest, employee behaviors, and individual and corporate reputations, and workplace sources of stress (Seldman and Seldman, 2008; Loehr and Schwartz, 2003).

Employees have a part to play in preventing workplace violence. Employees need to be convinced in making personal security a commonplace habit. This includes keeping car doors locked while driving and when one gets out of the car, checking your car before entering it to make sure it is empty, walking in busy, well-lit areas and being alert for muggers, entering a busy store if you feel unsafe, carrying your purse, briefcase, and computer close to your body, letting others know when you are working late and keeping close to a phone, reporting unauthorized unknown individuals to security, and taking any threats or harassment seriously and reporting them to your manager.

It is also possible, through coaching, training, and development, to address leadership that falls short (Boyatzis and McKee, 2005; Burke and Cooper 2012; George, 2003).

Manzoni (2013) makes the case for why a higher level of integrity is critical today (higher expectations, less tolerance for unethical behavior) and the high costs of unethical behaviors (e.g., UBS, Société Générale, Enron, Parmalat, WorldCom). Organizational culture makes the difference. He distills four lessons for executives. First, the rules, regulations, and rewards for ethical behavior need to be clear and in place. Second, all employees need to be "educated" to deal with human frailties in information processing and decision making leading to unethical behavior, with repeated refreshers offered as well. Third, executives must constantly reinforce the message that performance requires living within their rules. Fourth, employees are encouraged to voice any concerns about pending actions or decisions which they think may violate their rules.

We have assembled current thinking and research evidence, relevant to enhancing the satisfaction individuals achieve from all their life roles – the whole person. Instead of money, individuals should emphasize relationships, love, fun, and memories – the richness of one's time spent. It is clear that for most of us, failing in one aspect of one's life diminishes overall satisfaction and performance. And while difficult, it is possible for most of us to do a better job of maximizing our satisfaction and performance if we have a better sense of what is important to us and how we are doing at present (Friedman, 2008). This volume starts the reader on this journey.

Contents of the Collection

Ronald Burke, in Part I, this introductory chapter, reviews what is known about human frailties and transgressions by managers and professionals (bad behavior) in and outside of their organizations. Power has an inevitable downside. These frailties include alcohol and drug addiction, gambling addiction, work addiction, sex addiction and pornography, bribery, fraud and corruption, discrimination and harassment, and bullying, among others. Real life examples are provided. Human frailties have negative effects on individuals, their families, their organizations, and if relevant, their victims. Human frailties and transgressions are more important today because of greater scrutiny, cynicism about leaders, and a call for greater transparency – the world is watching and bad news travels fast. All individuals are flawed but not all flaws or transgressions are fatal; some flaws are merely annoying. Frailties and transgressions are associated with levels of individual and organizational narcissism, hubris, self-interest and guile, and personality disorders. Reasons why "good people do bad things" are offered (e.g., low self-control, fatigue). The role of apologies following transgressions is explored along with crisis management initiatives. Individuals need to examine at an early stage of their working lives how they will measure their lives.

Part II examines antecedents and consequences of human frailties for individuals, families, workplaces, and society at large. Susanna Galea and the late Hamid Ghodse examine substance abuse and addiction in the workplace. Levels of drug abuse have remained basically unchanged over the past few decades. Individuals with substance abuse problems (alcoholism, drug use) almost always hold jobs. Galea and Ghodse provide statistics showing the prevalence of substance abuse globally. Illicit drug use is also associated with particular health problems. In addition, there has also been an increase in the use of prescription drugs by young people. The authors show how substance abuse affects work performance, industrial injuries, and alertness. They also illustrate the huge financial costs associated with substance abuse. These costs affect individuals, families, employers, and society at large. They go further by indicating the signs and symptoms of commonly abused substances. Both occupation and workplace culture enable substance abuse but they can also discourage it. Job demands and job stress is a common antecedent of substance abuse. The authors conclude with suggestions for addressing substance abuse problems. These include: workplace policies, workplace drug testing, employee assistance programs, and employee wellness programs.

Ronald Burke then writes about greed, money, and materialism. Hardly a day goes by without stories of fraud, bribery, theft, cheating, and corruption appearing in the media. Underlying almost all these reports is greed, the desire for or pursuit of money. Money is a versatile currency satisfying a variety of needs. Examples of greed associated with money and lavish lifestyles are offered from several countries; greed and materialism know no boundaries. Companies, reflected in the behaviors of their executives, can also be greedy, cutting corners or engaging in fraud in order to boost their profits, in a win-at-all-costs world, and increase levels of executive pay. Obscene levels of pay have produced a backlash against executive compensation. Interestingly money is only weakly associated with levels of individual happiness. In fact the pursuit of money, for many, hasn't brought about the satisfactions that were expected. Time affluence in fact is more strongly associated with happiness than is material affluence. Antecedents of greed and materialism are identified. Suggestions of ways of using money to increase happiness are offered. Finally, individual, organizational, and societal changes likely to reduce greed and materialism are proposed.

In a related chapter, Michel Magnan, Denis Cormier and Pascale Lapointe-Antunes, using a number of Canadian case examples, examine the role of managerial hubris in financial reporting fraud. They make the case that over-confidence, an elevated opinion of themselves, led executives to commit, or be oblivious to, fraud. Senior managers do in fact commit the largest frauds. Favorable media coverage and the receipt of awards are indicators of managerial over-confidence, fraud being committed to enrich managers. Financial reporting fraud is generally undertaken to overvalue a company. Managers' personalities and attitudes play a central role here. Overconfident managers are more likely to ignore employee input, centralize and make unilateral decisions. The authors examined 15 fraudulent financial manipulation cases between 1995 and 2005 in Canada in publicly-traded firms. Frauds involved accounting violations, asset misappropriation, and incomplete or fraudulent disclosures.

Suzy Fox examines narcissism, a personality trait, in the workplace. She considers both adaptive and maladaptive aspects of narcissism – the bright side and dark side – as it adds to or detracts from performance and leadership. The first looks at narcissism as a personality disorder then as a sub-clinical, multi-dimensional personality trait, taking a nuanced view of it. She considers various types of narcissists: healthy, group, helpful, compensated, oblivious, hypervigilant, ruthless, helpless and amorous. She then moves to narcissism in the workplace. Organizations are rife with narcissists, and most writers view it negatively. Studies have found links between narcissism and counterproductive work behaviors, toxic politics and culture. Some writers see it being positively associated with creativity, leadership emergence, and career progress. Thus whether narcissism has positive or negative outcomes depends on the context. Fox then looks at narcissism and leadership more explicitly, narcissism again having both positive and negative effects. She argues for a consideration of sub-traits associated with narcissisms to better understand their potential effects. Narcissists might profit from executive coaching and cognitive behavioral therapy to help them better understand their motivations, behaviors and their consequences.

Although emotional intelligence has been promoted as an important construct increasing our understanding of behavior in the workplace and in minimizing individual shortcomings or human frailties, Peter Jordan, Ashlea Troth and Neal Ashkanasy wonder if in fact this is the case. They examine individual emotional abilities comprising the emotional intelligence construct, considering ways in which each of these abilities reduces or prevents acts of human frailty. They conclude that the suggested association of emotional intelligence with fewer individual shortcomings can be challenged. In fact they argue that high levels of emotional abilities may in fact increase human frailty.

Raphael Snir and Itzhak Harpaz then present the concept of Heavy Work Investment (HWI) and its two dimensions, time and effort. They describe possible negative outcomes of the heavy investment of time and effort to work. Since HWI is multifaceted, various subtypes are possible. The authors also address the challenges that HWI poses for individuals, families, workplaces, and society alike. They post and address interesting questions such as which dimension of work investment should be valued more – time or effort; should employers care about HWI and its outcomes; if outcomes of HWI are mixed, how should they be weighed; should employers strive towards a one-size-fits-all notion of work–life balance or should balance be individually-suited; should employers prefer heavy work investors over typical full-time employees of other subtypes of heavy work investors; should organizations address mismatches between actual and preferred work investment of their employees, and how should global organizations deal with cross-cultural differences in HWI?

Philip Riley and Janice Langan-Fox look at an aspect of abusive supervision, bullying in the workplace. It is a sad irony that some of the "helping professions" are more heavily burdened by workplace bullying than the general population. Thus for those having chosen a profession that seeks to help others, often as a "professional calling," the impact of workplace bullying on their ability to aid others is reduced. The authors review the literature on the impact of bullying experiences among two specific groups in the "helping" professions, namely Australian school principals and health professionals. They include data from the first wave of a longitudinal study of bullying in these two groups. The experience of workplace bullying takes a toll on both psychological health and effectiveness. The usefulness of a variety of workplace interventions is also addressed.

In the final chapter in Part II, Lisa Penney and Stacey Kessler focus on what motivates employees to engage in counterproductive work behavior (CWB). CWB involves behaviors that can potentially harm an organization and the people connected to it. CWB has costs to organizations. CWB is commonly seen as employee responses to negative work experiences and resulting negative emotions. CWB can also result from work stressors. Individual differences also play a role in CWB, with employees higher on negative affect more likely to engage in them. Narcissism and Machiavellianism were also found to predict CWB. A recent view sees CWB as instrumental-goal directed. Instrumental goals included revenge and retaliation. An additional instrumental goal of CWB is the management of workplace emotions, often termed coping. CWB can also represent cognitive as opposed to emotional processes. Penney and Kessler conclude with solutions that employees and workplaces can undertake to reduce CWB. Individuals can better learn how to cope with boredom and job stressors. Organizations can help here as well. In addition, organizations can select employees less likely to engage in CWB, reduce job demands, lessen workplace restraints that interfere with job performance, minimize interpersonal workplace conflicts, and deal with feelings of injustice.

Part III considers ways of addressing human frailties in the workplace. First, Anna Koch, Verena Hahn and Carmen Binnewies examine research on recovery from work stress and its effects on employee well-being and performance. Recovery is likely to both reduce CWB and foster energy. Distressed and depleted employees are less able to manage human frailties. Recovery involves unwinding and replenishing resources. Recovery has been fostered through the use of vacations, activities during leisure time such as reading a book, engaging in social and physical activities, and participating in volunteer initiatives. Psychological detachment from work in the evenings and on weekends has also shown positive recovery effects. Finally, short work breaks can also allow employees to restore their energies.

Dov Eden and Mina Westman then summarize early research findings from respite research as well as more recent work. Spawned from methodological considerations, early respite research considered a variety of off-the-job respites including forced leave due to computer shutdowns, holidays, vacations, semester breaks, reserve military duty, and business trips. Research has grown over time and considered a greater variety of respites. Researchers have studied the effects of short respites such as evenings and weekends at home and much longer respites such as year-long sabbatical leave. Research methodologies have also become more sophisticated. Important factors determining the success of respites include how, where, and with whom off-the-job respite time is spent. Respites are increasingly relevant to managing long work hours, work addiction, the work–family interface, managing one's energy, participating in leisure activities and voluntary organizations, and adding to life satisfaction and happiness.

The final two chapters in this part look at individual character. Cynthia Pury, noting that writing and research on courage is a relatively new phenomenon, reviews historical and current courage writing and research. She positions the lack of courage as a human frailty, often tied to fear. Interestingly, more courageous people may experience less fear. Different types of courageous behaviors have been identified (e.g., physical versus moral courage), but it is often difficult to classify some courageous acts. Courage typically involves the voluntary taking of risks in the pursuit of valuable goals. Frailties of courage include cowardice, rashness, indecision, indifference, ineffectiveness, and "bad" courage. Pury examines each of these frailties of courage in some detail. She concludes with some preliminary examples of courage interventions.

Finally, Leslie Sekerka considers ways of establishing ethical strength in organizations, using a positive health and well-being model. For employees to retain their ethical health, they need to exercise their ethical/moral muscles. Compliance-driven policies too often fall short. Societies are continually facing a series of unethical actions by individuals and their organizations. Sekerka first examines why we so often exhibit ethical lapses. She then offers suggestions to address this problem advocating the importance of developing moral courage in the workplace primarily as a result of training. Using the balanced experiential inquiry process. She describes this approach in some detail.

References

Ambrose, M.J. and Ganegoda, D.B. (2011) Why treat people like this? Supervisor consequences of abusive supervision. Paper presented at the Annual Meeting of the Academy of Management, San Antonio, TX, August.

Anderson, C. (2012) Why people cheat: As the Petraeus affair seems to suggest, its partly the addictive power of love, partly the lure of power, partly the desire to take risks. *Globe and Mail*, November 16, L4.

Anderson, J. and Applebaum, P. (2011) College-exam scandal tarnishes affluent Great Gatsby suburb. *Globe and Mail*, December 3, A20.

Anonymous (1986) *Sex and Love Addicts Anonymous*. Boston, MA: The Augustine Fellowship, Sex and Love Addicts Anonymous, Fellowship-Wide Services.

Ariely, D. (2012) *The (Honest) Truth about Dishonesty: How We Lie to Everyone – Especially Ourselves*. New York: HarperCollins.

Arthaud-Day, M.L., Certo, S.T., Dalton, C.M. and Dalton, D.R. (2006) A changing of the guard: Executive and director turnover following corporate financial restatements. *Academy of Management Journal*, 49, 1119–36.

Austen, I. (2012) Contador guilty of doping court rules: 2010 Tour de France winner to be stripped of title. *Globe and Mail*, February 7, B7.

Babiak, P. and Hare, R. (2006) *Snakes in Suits*. New York: Regan Books.

Bailey, T. (2011) Rowdy RIM pair plead guilty after Beijing flight disrupted. *Globe and Mail*, December 2, A12.

Balducci, C., Cecchin, M., Fraccaroli, F. and Schaufeli, W.B. (2012) Exploring the relationship between workaholism and workplace aggressive behavior: The role of job-related emotion. *Personality and Individual Differences*, 53, 629–34.

Baumeister, R. and Tierney, J. (2011) *Willpower*. New York: Penguin Press.

Baute, N. (2011) Curbing the cravings of my digital addiction. *Toronto Star*, December 6, E6.

Bhattacharya, U. and Marshall, C.D. (2012) Do they do it for the money? *Journal of Corporate Finance*, 18, 147.

Bilton, N. (2012) Taking e-mail vacations reduce stress, study finds. *Globe and Mail*, May 5, B17.

Blair-Loy, M. (2004) Work devotion and work time. In C.F. Epstein and A. Kalleberg (eds) *Fighting for Time: Shifting Boundaries of Work and Social Life*. New York: Russell Sage, pp. 282–316.

Boesveld, S. (2011) Policy says it's OK to cheat, teachers warn: Dishonest students to get second chance with no penalty. *National Post*, October 25, A7.

Bohart, A.C., Held, B.S., Mendelowitz, E. and Schneider, K.J. (2013) *Humanity's Dark Side: Evil, Destructive Experience, and Psychotherapy*. Washington, DC: American Psychological Association.

Boies, S.C., Knudson, G. and Young, J. (2004) The internet, sex, and youths: Implications for sexual development. *Sexual Addiction and Compulsivity*, 11, 343–63.

Boivie, S., Graffin, S.D. and Pollock, T.G. (2012) Time for me to fly: Predicting director exits at large firms. *Academy of Management Journal*, 55, 1334–59.

Boyatzis, R. and McKee, A. (2005) *Resonant Leadership: Renewing Your Self and Connecting with Others Through Mindfulness, Hope and Compassion*. Boston, MA: Harvard Business School Press.

Brannigan, R., Schackman, B.R., Falco, M. and Millman, R.B. (2004) The quality of highly regarded adolescent substance abuse treatment programs: Results of an in-depth national survey. *Archives of Pediatrics and Adolescent Medicine*, 158, 904–9.

Brennan, R.J. (2012) UK MPs butt heads – literally. *Toronto Star*, February 24, A21.

Bryant, M. (2012) *28 Seconds: A True Story of Addiction, Tragedy, and Hope*. Toronto Viking.

Bunting, M. (2004) *Willing Slaves: How the Overwork Culture Is Ruling Our Lives*. New York: HarperCollins.

Burke, R.J. (2010) Work hours, work intensity and work addiction: Weighing the costs. In R.J. Burke and C.L. Cooper (eds) *Risky Business: Psychological, Physical and Financial Costs of High Risk Behaviors in Organizations*. Farnham: Gower, pp. 67–106.

Burke, R.J. and C.L. Cooper (2012) *The Fulfilling Workplace: The Organization's Role in Achieving Individual and Organizational Health*. Farnham: Gower.

Bustillo, M. (2012a) BestBuy CEO quits amid conduct probe: Dunn's resignation over "personal" behavior adds to concerns of electronics retailer. *Globe and Mail*, April 11, B14.

—— (2012b) BestBuy chairman to resign after probe of former CEO. *Globe and Mail*, May 15, B13.

Byrne, A., Barlng, J. and Dupre, K. (2012) Leaders' apologies: Understanding and mitigating negative outcomes for leaders and subordinates. Paper presented at the Annual Meeting of the Academy of Management, Boston, MA, August.

Callahan, D. (2006) *Moral Center: How We Can Reclaim Our Country from Die-Hard Extremists, Rogue Corporations, Hollywood Hacks, and Pretend Patriots*. Boston, MA: Houghton-Mifflin Harcourt.

Campbell, A.A. (2012) Secret service prostitution probe widens to include trip to El Salvador. *Globe and Mail*, April 27, A9.

Cangemi, J.P. and Pfohl, W. (2009) Sociopaths in high places. *Organization Development Journal*, 27, 85–96.

Carnes, P.J. (1991) *Don't Call It Love: Recovery from Sexual Addiction*. New York: Bantam.

—— (1996) Addiction or compulsion: Politics or illness? *Sexual Addiction and Compulsivity*, 3, 30–34.

—— (2001) *Out of the Shadows: Understanding Sexual Addiction*. Center City, MN: Hazelden.

Carnes, P.J., Murray, R.E. and Charpentier, L. (2005) Bargains with chaos: Sex addicts and addiction interaction disorder. *Sexual Addictive Behaviors*, 12, 79–120.

Catalyst (1998) *Advancing Women in Business: The Catalyst Guide*. San Francisco, CA: Jossey-Bass.

Chatterjee, A. and Hambrick, D.C. (2007) It's all about me: Narcissistic CEOs and their effects on company strategy and performance. *Administrative Science Quarterly*, 52, 351–86.

—— (2011) Executive personality, capability cues, and risk taking: How narcissistic CEOs react to their successes and stumbles. *Administrative Science Quarterly*, 56, 202–37.

Chellel, K. (2011) Lawsuits against News Corp escalate. *National Post*, October 5, FP12.

Christensen, C.M., Allworth, J. and Dillon, K. (2012) *How Will You Measure Your Life?* New York: Harper Business.

Clark, M.A., Lelchook, A.M. and Taylor, M.L. (2010) Beyond the big five: How narcissism, perfectionism, and dispositional affect relate to workaholism. *Personality and Individual Differences*, 48, 786–91.

Collins, J. (2001) *Good to Great: Why Some Companies Make the Leap, ... and Others Don't*. New York: HarperCollins.

Conger, J. (1990) The dark side of leadership. *Organizational Dynamics*, 19, 44–55.

Cowell, A. and Burns, J.F. (2012) Former Murdoch aides to be charged with bribery. *Globe and Mail*, November 21, A14.

Cowen, A.P. and Marcel, J.J. (2011) Damaged goods: Board decisions to dismiss reputationally compromised directors. *Academy of Management Journal*, 54, 509–27.

Crowley, K. and Elster, E. (2009) *Working with You Is Killing Me*. New York: Business Plus.

Daubs, K. (2012) Casino fuels addiction fears: Hikes in suicides, illness tied to gambling access say health experts. *Globe and Mail*, March 15, GT5.

DeCovny, S. (2012) The financial psychopath next door. *CFA Magazine*, 23, 22–3.

Derks, D. and Bakker, A.B. (2010) The impact of e-mail communication on organizational life. *Cyberpsychology: Journal of Psychosocial Research on Cyberspace*, 4, 41–83.

Dimmock, G. (2012) Internal RCMP investigation uncovers disturbing behavior. *Ottawa Citizen*, May 22, 2.

Donahue, R. (2011) How Berlusconi endures. *International Herald Tribune*, September 22, 2.

Donovan, K. (2012) "He's done: Put a toe tag on him": What ex-ORNGE boss Chris Mazza said when an employee's time was up. *Toronto Star*, February 8, A1, A6.

Donovan, K., and MacLean, J. (2013) ORNGE: "First-class Chris" billed us 75 cents for parking, $1.50 for cookies, $8 for fizzy water, and $14 for nuts. *Toronto Star*, January 18, A12.

Dotlich, D.L. and Cairo, P.C. (2003) *Why CEOs Fail*. San Francisco, CA: Jossey-Bass.

Dubrin, A. (2012) *Narcissism in the Workplace: Research Opinion and Practice*. Cheltenham: Edward Elgar.

Eby, L.T. and Allen, T.D. (2012) *Personal Relationships: The Effect on Employee Attitudes, Behavior, and Well-being*. London: Routledge.

Eichler, L. (2012) Keeping the bedroom out of the boardroom: Being unfaithful to one's partner doesn't necessarily mean losing the trust of employees, shareholders or constituents. *Globe and Mail*, November 17, B18.

Epstein, C.F., Sevon, C., Oglensky, B. and Saute, R. (1999) *The Part-Time Paradox: Time Norms, Professional Lives, Family, and Gender*. New York: Routledge.

Finkelstein, S. (2004) *Why Smart Executives Fail and What We Can Learn from Their Mistakes*. New York: Portfolio.

Fong, P. (2012) Mountie sues force over sexual harassment. *Toronto Star*, May 11, A4.

Forsyth, J. (2012) Senator calls for probe in US Air Force sex scandal: Sergeant guilty. *National Post*, August 3, A11.

Freimuth, M. (2008) *Addicted? Recognizing Destructive Behavior Before It's Too Late*. Lanham, MD: Rowman and Littlefield.

Friedman, S.D. (2008) *Total Leadership: Be a Better Leader, Have a Richer Life*. Boston, MA: Harvard Business School Press.

Furnham, A. (2007) Personality disorders and derailment at work: The paradoxical positive influence of pathology in the workplace. In J. Langan-Fox, C.L. Cooper and R.J. Klimoski (eds) *Research Companion to the Dysfunctional Workplace: Management Challenges and Symptoms*. Chichester: Edward Elgar, pp. 22–39.

Futterman, S. (2004) *When You Work for a Bully: Assessing Your Options and Taking Action*. Montvale, NJ: Croce Publishing.

Gauthier-Villars, D. (2011) Strauss-Kahn: Admits to "moral failing." *Wall Street Journal*, September 19, 3.

George, W. (2003) *Authentic Leadership: Rediscovering the Secrets to Creating Lasting Value*. San Francisco, CA: Jossey-Bass.

—— (2007) *True North*. San Francisco, CA: Berrett-Koehler.

Gessen, M. (2011) *The Man without a Face: The Unlikely Rise of Vladimir Putin*. New York: Riverhead.

Gilbert, D. and Englesham, J. (2012) Ponzi schemer Stanford sentenced to 110 years. *Globe and Mail*, June 15, B5.

Globe and Mail (2001a) China bribe trail cites Ericsson payoff. October 12, B12.

—— (2001b) Bribery probe stalls Tullow sale in Uganda. October 12, B12.

—— (2012a) UK police arrest Brooks in hacking probe. March 14, B9.

—— (2012b) BCSC alleges advisor gambled client funds. August 1, B8.

Gordon, R.M. (2007) *I Love You Madly! Workbook Insight Enhancement about Healthy and Disturbed Relations*. Allentown, PA: IAPT Press.

Gray, J. (2012) Supreme court to rule on random alcohol testing. *Globe and Mail*, May 9, B10.

Greenwood, J. (2011) Coventree to pay $2.25 M in penalties: Fallout from ABCP mess. *National Post*, November 10, FP2.

Griffiths, M.D. (1996) Behavioral addictions: An issue for everybody? *Journal of Workplace Learning*, 8, 19–25.

—— (2000a) Internet addiction: Time to be taken seriously? *Addiction Research*, 8, 413–18.

—— (2000b) Does internet and computer "addiction" exist? Some case study evidence. *CyberPsychology and Behavior*, 3, 211–18.

Grusser, S.M., Thalemann, R. and Griffiths, M.D. (2007) Excessive computer game playing: Evidence for addiction and aggression? *CyberPsychology and Behavior*, 10, 290–92.

Gunia, B.C., Wang, L., Huang, L.J., Wang, H. and Murnighan, J.K. (2012) Contemplation and conversation: Subtle influences on moral decision making. *Academy of Management Journal*, 55, 13–33.

Hamilton, T. and Coyle, D. (2012) *The Secret Race*. New York: Random House.

Hannah, S.T., Avolio, B.J. and May, D.R. (2011) Moral maturation and moral conation: A capacity approach to explaining moral thought and action. *Academy of Management Review*, 36, 663–85.

Hasham, A. (2012) Mrs. DSK in spotlight for right reasons. *Toronto Star*, January 24, A13.

Henriques, D.B. (2010) *The Wizard of Lies: Bernie Madoff and the Death of Trust*. New York: St. Martin's Griffin.

Hewlett, S.A. and Luce, C.B. (2006) Extreme jobs: The dangerous allure of the 70-hour work week. *Harvard Business Review*, December, 49–59.

Hogan, R. (1999) Trouble at the top: Causes and consequences of managerial incompetence. *Consulting Psychology Journal*, 46, 1061–7.

Hogan, R. and Hogan, J. (1997) *Hogan Development Survey Manual*. Tulsa, OK: Hogan Assessment Systems.

—— (2001) Assessing leadership: A view of the dark side. *International Journal of Evaluation and Assessment*, 9, 40–51.

Hogan, R., Curphy, G.J. and Hogan, J. (1994) What do we know about leadership? *American Psychologist*, 49, 493–501.

Holland, D.W. (2008) Work addiction: Costs and solutions for individuals, relationships and organizations. *Journal of Workplace Behavioral Health*, 22, 1–15.

Hornstein, H. (1997) *Brutal Bosses and Their Prey: How to Identify and Overcome Abuse in the Workplace*. New York: Penguin.

Hovarth, A.T. (1999) *Sex, Drugs, Gambling, and Chocolate: A Workbook for Overcoming Addictions*. San Luis Obispo, CA: Impact.

Howlett, K. (2011) Nuclear plant workers fired for drug use: Ontario Power Generation insists safety not compromised as employees had no role in operation of Pickering station. *Globe and Mail*, November 29, A8.

Hui, S. (2012) IOC probing claims of black market ticket sales. *Globe and Mail*, June 18, S4.

Inzlicht, M. (2012) Confessions of an e-mail addict. *Globe and Mail*, April 14, F9.

Jackson, K.T. (2004) *Building Reputational Capital: Strategies for Integrity and Fair Play That Improve the Bottom Line*. Oxford: Oxford University Press.

Johnson, R.E., Silverman, S.B., Shyamunder, A., Swee, H-Y., Rodopman, O.B., Cho, E. and Bauer, J. (2010) Acting superior but actually inferior?: Correlates and consequences of workplace arrogance. *Human Performance*, 23, 403–27.

Jolly, D. and Borden, S. (2013) Fixing suspected in 680 games: Investigation. *Globe and Mail*, February 5, S2.

Judge, T.A. and LePine, J.A. (2007) The bright and dark sides of personality: Implications for personnel selection in individual and team contexts. In J. Langan-Fox, C.L. Cooper and R.J. Klimoski (eds) *Research Companion to the Dysfunctional Workplace: Management Challenges and Symptoms*. Chichester: Edward Elgar, pp. 332–55.

Kellerman, B. (2004) *Bad Leadership*. Boston, MA: Harvard Business School Press.

—— (2006) When should a leader apologize and when not? *Harvard Business Review*, 84, 72–81.

Kelley, D. (2012) Trial begins for priest accused in sex coverup. *National Post*, March 27, A16.

Kesterton, M. (2012a) Honesty is healthy. *Globe and Mail*, August 22, L7.

—— (2012b) Master cards for addicts. *Globe and Mail*, September 6, L7.

—— (2012c) Bribes not tax deductible. *Globe and Mail*, September 6, L7.

Kets de Vries, M.R.F. (1989) Leaders who self-destruct: The causes and cures. *Organizational Dynamics*, 17, 5–17.

Killinger, B. (1991) *Workaholics: The Respectable Addicts*. New York: Simon and Schuster.

Koven, P. (2012) SINO faked facts, OSC: Company fabricated contracts to hype deals regulator says. *National Post*, May 23, FP1, FP2.

Koyuncu, B. (2012) Oops, I am stigmatized! A model of stigma frame and individual career outcomes. Paper presented at the Annual Meeting of the Academy of Management, Boston, MA, August.

Kray, L.J. and Haselhuhn, M.P. (2012) Male pragmatism in negotiators ethical reasoning. *Journal of Experimental Social Psychology*, 48, 1124–31.

Kuhn, T. (2006) A "demented work ethic" and a "lifestyle firm": Discourse, identity, and workplace time commitments. *Organization Studies*, 27, 1339–58.

Kusy, M. and Holloway, E. (2009) *Toxic Workplaces! Managing Toxic Personalities and Their Systems of Power*. New York: John Wiley.

LabatonSucharow (2012) *Wall Street, Fleet Street, and Main Street: Corporate Integrity at a Crossroads*. New York: LabatonSucharow.

Lane, W. (2012) *Losing It: Behaviors and Mindsets That Ruin Careers*. London: *Financial Times*.

Laroque, G. (2011) *The Story of the NHL's Unlikeliest Tough Guy*. Toronto: Viking Press.

Leicester, J. (2012) WADA suggests one in ten athletes cheating. *Globe and Mail*, February 8, S5.

Lesieur, H.R. and Blume, S.B. (1993) Pathological gambling, eating disorders and the psychoactive substance abuse disorders. *Journal of Addictive Behavior*, 12, 79–120.

Lilienfeld, S.O., Waldman, I.D., Landfield, K., Watts, A.L., Rubenzer, S. and Faschingbauer, T.R. (2012) Fearless dominance and the US Presidency: Implications of psychopathic personality traits for successful and unsuccessful political leadership. *Journal of Personality and Social Psychology*, 103, 489–595.

Lipman-Blumen, J. (2005) *The Allure of Toxic Leaders: Why We Follow Destructive Bosses and Corrupt Politicians – And How We Can Survive Them*. New York: Oxford University Press.

Livesey, B. (2012) *Thieves of Bay Street: How Banks, Brokerages, and the Wealthy Steal Billions from Canadians*. Toronto: Random House Canada.

Loehr, J. and Schwartz, T. (2003) *The Power of Full Engagement: Managing Energy, Not Time Is the Key to High Performance and Personal Renewal*. New York: Free Press.

Lubit, R.H. (2002) The long-term organizational impact of destructively narcissistic managers. *Academy of Management Executive*, 16, 127–38.

—— (2004) *Coping with Toxic Managers, Subordinates … and Other Difficult People: Using Emotional Intelligence to Survive and Prosper*. Upper Saddle River, NJ: Prentice Hall.

Maccoby, M. (2004) Narcissistic leaders: the incredible pros, the inevitable cons. *Harvard Business Review*, 82, 92–101.

MacKinnon, M. (2012) Business, political elite flaunt success with mistresses: Powerful men in China said to accumulate women the same way they desire money and power. *Globe and Mail*, October 19, A23.

Madrach, J. (2011) *Age of Greed: The Triumph of Finance and the Decline of America, 1970 to the Present*. New York: Knopf.

Manzoni, J.F. (2013) Nurturing a high integrity culture. *Rotman Management*, Winter, 22–7.

Marano, M.E. (2012) From promise to promiscuity. *Psychology Today*, August, 60–69.

Mate, G. (2008) *In the Realm of Hungry Ghosts: Encounters with Addiction*. Toronto: Vintage Canada.

Mayer, D.M., Aquino, K., Greenbaum, R.L. and Kuenzi, M. (2012) Who displays ethical leadership, and why does it matter: an examination of antecedents and consequences of ethical leadership. *Academy of Management Journal*, 55, 151–71.

Mayer, D.M., Aquino, K., Mawritz, M.B. and Priesemuth, M. (2012) Fallen from grace … but not that far: The impact of transgressions and performance on perceptions of leaders' moral character. Unpublished manuscript, University of Michigan, Ross School of Business.

McCall, M. and Lombardo, M. (1983) *Off the Track: Why and How Successful Executives Get Derailed*. Technical Report No. 21. Greensboro, NC: Center for Creative Leadership.

McDonald, M. and Westphal, J.D. (2011) My brother's keeper: CEO identification, with the corporate elite, social support among CEOs and leader effectiveness. *Academy of Management Journal*, 54, 661–93.

McFadden, R. (2011) Former United Way leader jailed for defrauding charity. *Globe and Mail*, November 17, S7.

McLean, J. and Bruser, D. (2012) Crown reports officers "inaccurate" testimony: Attorney General alerted under new policy after judge suggests Toronto policeman was deceitful under oath. *Toronto Star*, November 16, A1, A33.

Miller, J.A. and Shales, T. (2011) *Those Guys Have All the Fun: Inside the World of ESPN*. New York: Little, Brown and Company.

Mintzberg, H. and Todd, P. (2012) The offline executive. *Strategy and Business*, Winter, 11–14.

Moore, C., Detert, J.R., Trevino, L.K., Baker, V.L. and Mayer, D.M. (2012). Why employees do bad things: Moral disengagement and unethical organizational behaviors. *Personnel Psychology*, 65, 1–48.

Moore, D.L. (2012) Former super-agent seeking long term deal: Bankrupt Steinberg reveals battle with bottle: "I got to the blackout point … I was unreliable." *Toronto Star*, February 22, S3.

Morgenson, G. and Posner, J. (2011) *Reckless Endangerment: How Outsized Ambition, Greed, and Corruption Led to Economic Armageddon*. New York: New York Times Books.

Morse, G. (2004) Executive psychopaths. *Harvard Business Review*, October, 71–3.
Moyers, W.C. (2007) *Broken*. New York: Penguin.
Mulvihill, G., Armas, G.C. and Scolforo, M. (2012) Report says Paterno buried abuse claims: Former FBI director says alleged cover-up was done to avoid bad publicity for Penn State football program. *Globe and Mail*, July 13, A12.
Najar, M.J., Holland, B.D. and Van Landyt, C.R. (2004) Individual differences in leadership development. Paper presented at the SIOP Conference, Chicago, IL, April.
Namie, G. and Namie, T. (2000) *The Bully at Work: What You Can Do to Stop the Hurt and Reclaim the Dignity on the Job*. Naperville, IL: Sourcebooks.
Nash, L. and Stevenson, H. (2004) *Just Enough: Tools for Creating Success in Your Work and Life*. New York: John Wiley.
National Post (2011) Barnaby fired by ESPN after arrest for drunk driving. December 6, S8.
—— (2012a) VW scandal grows, as labor leader's lover charged for her role in breach of trust. March 17, FP10.
—— (2012b) Doping police sanction more than 100 athletes leading up to Olympics. July 25, S6.
—— (2012c) FIFA's new code aims to curb corruption. April 27. S7.
—— (2012d) Ex-France Telecom CEO investigated in suicides. July 5, FP4.
—— (2012e) Ethics contracts "cooked": Ombudsman. July 6, A6.
—— (2013) Canadians confidence in RCMP has dropped "significantly": In a new poll. January 2, A6.
Ng, T.W.H., Sorensen, K.L. and Feldman, D.C. (2007) Dimensions, antecedents, and consequences of workaholism: A conceptual integration and extension. *Journal of Organizational Behavior*, 28, 111–36.
Onstad, K. (2012) The Petraeus affair: Maybe it's time we quit feigning outrage over infidelity. *Globe and Mail*, November 16, L4.
Orford, J. (2001) *Excessive Appetites: A Psychological View of the Addictions*, 2nd edn. Chichester: John Wiley.
O'Shea, J. (2011) *The Deal from Hell: How Moguls and Wall Street Plundered Great American Newspapers*. New York: Public Affairs.
Ovsey, D. (2012) Will anyone repair the C-suite brand? *National Post*, March 13, FP7.
Owens, B.P. (2012) Synergistic and paradoxical leader trait couplings: The synergy of humility and competence and the paradox of humility and narcissism. Paper presented at the Annual Meeting of the Academy of Management, Boston, MA, August.
Padilla, A., Hogan, R. and Kaiser, R.B. (2007) The toxic triangle: Destructive leaders, susceptible followers, and conducive environments. *Leadership Quarterly*, 18, 176–94.
Partnoy, F. (2009) *Infectious Greed: How Deceit and Risk Corrupted the Markets*. New York: Public Affairs.
—— (2012) *Wait: The Art and Science of Delay*. New York: Public Affairs.
Paulhus, D.L. and Williams, K.M. (2006) The dark triad of personality: Narcissism, Machiavellianism, and psychopathy. *Journal of Research in Personality*, 36, 556–63.
Peabody, S. (2004) *Addiction to Love: Overcoming Obsession and Dependency*. Berkeley, CA: Ten Speed Press.
Pelchat, M.L. (2002) Of human bondage: Food craving, obsession, compulsion, and addiction. *Physiological Behavior*, 76, 347–53.
Pelletier, K.L. (2010) Leader toxicity: An empirical investigation of toxic behavior and rhetoric. *Leadership*, 6, 373–89.
Penney, L.M. and Spector, P.E. (2002) Narcissism and counterproductive work behavior: Do bigger egos mean bigger problems? *International Journal of Selection and Assessment*, 10, 126–34.
Perkins, J. (2006) *Confessions of an Economic Hit Man*. New York: Plume.

Perlow, L.A. (2012) *Sleeping with Your Smartphone: How to Break the 24/7 Habit and Change the Way You Work*. Boston, MA: Harvard Business Review Press.

Polman, E., Pettit, N.C. and Wiesenfeld, B.M. (2013) Effects of wrongdoer status on moral licensing. *Journal of Experimental Social Psychology*, 49, 619–23.

Pook, L.A. (2008) Impact of corruption on the development of information and communications infrastructures in Bulgaria and Romania. *Journal of East-West Business*, 14, 101–13.

Porath, C. and Pearson, C. (2013) The price of incivility. *Harvard Business Review*. January–February, 46–53.

Porter, G. (1996) Organizational impact of workaholism: Suggestions for researching the negative outcomes of excessive work. *Journal of Occupational Health Psychology*, 1, 70–84.

Potenza, M.N., Fiellin, D.A., Heninger, G.R., Rounsaville, B.J. and Mazure, M.C. (2002) Gambling: An addictive behavior with health and primary care implications. *Journal of General Internal Medicine*, 17, 721–32.

Pozner, H.E. (2008) Stigma and settling up: An integrated approach to the consequences of organizational misconduct for organizational elites. *Journal of Business Ethics*, 80, 141–50.

Rate, C.R. and Sternberg, R.J. (2007) When good people do nothing: A failure of courage. In J. Langan-Fox, C.L. Cooper and R.J. Klimoski (eds) *Research Companion to the Dysfunctional Workplace: Management Challenges and Symptoms*. Cheltenham: Edward Elgar, pp. 3–21.

Reed, G.E. (2004) Toxic leadership. *Military Review*, 84, 67–71.

Roberts, R. (2011) *The Well-balanced Leader*. New York: McGraw-Hill.

Saffer, H. and Lamiraud, K. (2008) *The Effect of Hours of Work on Social Interaction*. Cambridge, MA: National Bureau of Economic Research.

Sainforth, F., Kapsh, B., Broske, B.L. and Smith, M.J. (2001) Applying quality improvement principles to achieve healthy work organizations. *Journal of Quality Improvement*, 27, 465–83.

Sankowsky, D. (1995) The charismatic leaders as narcissist: Understanding the abuse of power. *Organizational Dynamics*, 23, 57–71.

Schaufeli, W.B., Shimazu, A. and Taris, T.W. (2009) Being driven to work excessively hard: The evaluation of a two-factor measure of workaholism in the Netherlands and Japan. *Cross Cultural Management*, 43, 320–48.

Schaufeli, W.B., Taris, T.W. and Bakker, A.B. (2008) It takes two to tango: Workaholism is working excessively and working compulsively. In. R.J. Burke and C.L. Cooper (eds) *The Long Work Hours Culture: Causes, Consequences and Choices*. Bingley: Emerald, pp. 203–26.

Schneider, J.P. and Irons, R.R. (2001) Assessment and treatment of addictive sexual disorders: Relevance for chemical dependency relapse. *Substance Use and Misuse*, 36, 1795–820.

Schwarzenegger, A. (2012) *Total Recall: My Unbelievably True Life Story*. New York: Simon and Schuster.

Seidman, K. (2012) Professors paid to write student papers: Online services. *National Post*, September 13, A6.

Seldman, M. and Seldman, J. (2008) *Executive Stamina: How to Optimize Time, Energy and Productivity to Achieve Peak Performance*. New York: John Wiley.

Selley, C. (2012) Bad boys, bad boys: Watchagonna do? *National Post*, May 30, A15.

Shaffer, H.J. (2012a) *APA Addiction Syndrome Handbook*. Vol. 1, *Foundations, Influences, and Expressions of Addiction*. Washington, DC: American Psychological Association.

—— (2012b) *APA Addiction Syndrome Handbook*. Vol. 2, *Recovery, Prevention, and Other Issues*. Washington, DC: American Psychological Association.

Shain, M. and Kramer, D.M. (2004) Health promotion in the workplace: Framing the concept; reviewing the evidence. *Occupational and Environmental Medicine*, 61, 613–18.

Shapiro, D. and Von Glinow, M.A. (2007) Why bad leaders stay in good places. In J. Langan-Fox, C.L. Cooper and R.J. Klimoski (eds) *Research Companion to the Dysfunctional Workplace: Management Challenges and Symptoms*. Cheltenham: Edward Elgar, pp. 90–109.

Sharma, R. (2011) *The Secret Letters of the Monk Who Sold His Ferrari*. Toronto: Collins.

Shaw, H. (2012) Workers steal 33% of missing goods, up from 19%. *National Post*, October 31, FP1, FP5.

Shiffman, J., Driver, A. and Grow, B. (2012) A lavish and leveraged life. *National Post*, June 8, FP3.

Silverman, R.E. (2012) Why you won't finish reading this article at work. *Globe and Mail*, December 15, B20.

Snir, R. and Harpaz, I. (2012) Beyond workaholism: Towards a general model of heavy work investment. *Human Resource Management Review*, 22, 232–43.

Song, M., Halsey, V. and Burgess, T. (2012) *The Hamster Revolution: How to Manage Your E-mail Before It Manages You*. San Francisco, CA: Berrett-Koehler.

Spears, J. (2012) Nuclear plant staff face drug, alcohol tests: Proposed new rules a "proactive" way to improve safety commission says. *Toronto Star*, April 18, A12.

Srinivasan, S. (2005) Consequences of financial reporting failure for outside directors: Evidence from accounting restatements and audit committee members. *Journal of Accounting Research*, 41, 291–334.

Stout, M. (2005) *The Sociopath Next Door*. New York: Broadway Books.

Stringer, D. (2012a) Murdoch called unfit to lead company. *Globe and Mail*, May 2, B13.

—— (2012b) Murdoch's protégé charged over role in phone hacking. *Toronto Star*, May 16, A19.

Stromberg, G. and Merrill, J. (2007) *The Harder They Fall: Celebrities Tell Their True-Life Stories of Addiction and Recovery*. Minneapolis, MN: Hazelden Publishing.

—— (2009) *Second Chances: Top Executives Share Their Stories of Addiction and Recovery*. New York: McGraw-Hill.

Sussman, S. (2007) Sexual addiction among teens: A review. *Sexual Addiction and Compulsivity*, 14, 257–78.

—— (2010) Love addiction: Definition, etiology, treatment. *Sexual Addiction and Compulsivity*, 17, 33–45.

—— (2012) Workaholism: A review. *Journal of Addiction: Research and Therapy*, 16, 1–10.

Sussman, S. and Ames, S.L. (2008) *Drug Abuse: Concepts, Prevention and Cessation*. New York: Cambridge University Press.

Sussman, S., Lisha, N. and Griffiths, M. (2011) Prevalence of the addictions: A problem of the majority or the minority? *Evaluation and the Health Professions*, 34, 3–56.

Sutton, R.I. (2007) *The No Asshole Rule: Building a Civilized Workplace and Surviving One That Isn't*. New York: Business Plus.

—— (2010) *Good Boss, Bad Boss: How to Be the Best ... and Learn from the Worst*. New York: Business Plus.

Tepper, B.J. (2000) Consequences of abusive supervision. *Academy of Management Journal*, 43, 178–90.

—— (2007) Abusive supervision in work organizations: Review, synthesis, and research agenda. *Journal of Management*, 33, 261–89.

Theodore, T. (2012) Former Mountie suing RCMP. *Toronto Star*, March 28, A3.

Tobutt, C. (2011) *Alcohol at Work: Managing Alcohol Problems and Issues in the Workplace*. Farnham: Gower.

Toronto Star (2011) Madoff's wife revealed they attempted suicide: Couple took overdose of sleeping medication on Christmas eve, 2008. October 27, A4.

—— (2012a) President's PhD void over plagiarism. March 30, A21.

—— (2012b) US agents sent home for "misconduct": Prostitution scandal rocks Obama visit. April 15, A8.

Tough, P. (2012) *How Children Succeed: Grit, Curiosity and the Hidden Power of Character*. New York: Houghton Mifflin Harcourt.

Tourish, D. (2005) Charismatic leadership and corporate cultism at Enron: The elimination of dissent, the promotion of conformity and organizational collapse. *Leadership*, 1, 12–26.

Twenge, J.M. and Campbell, W.K. (2009) *The Narcissism Epidemic: Living in the Age of Entitlement*. New York: Free Press.

van Beek, I., Hu, Q., Schaufeli, W.B., Taris, T.W. and Schreurs, B.H.J. (2012) For fun, love, or money: What drives workaholics, engaged, and burned-out employees at work? *Applied Psychology: An International Review*, 61, 30–55.

van der Hulst, M. (2003) Long work hours and health. *Scandinavian Journal of Work, Environment and Health*, 2, 171–88.

Vertuno, J. (2012) Agency charges Armstrong with alleged doping. USADA cites blood sample "manipulation." *National Post*, June 14, S5.

Vilkinas, T. (2012) Toxicity in leadership: A case study of Qantas to explore the impacts of leadership. Paper presented at the Annual Meeting of the Academy of Management, Boston, MA, August.

Voigt, K. (2012) The coach, the mistress and 4,300 messages: Deception costs Petrino $3.5 million football job. *Toronto Star*, April 13, S1, S2.

Waldie, P. (2012) Financial constraints cripple WADA's effectiveness director general says. *Globe and Mail*, June 7, S1, S5.

Walsh, D. (2012) *Seven Deadly Sins: My Pursuit of Lance Armstrong*. New York: Simon and Schuster.

Walton, M. (2007) Leadership toxicity: an inevitable affliction of organizations? *Organizations and People*, 14, 19–27.

Wang, L. and Murnighan, J.K. (2011) On greed. *Academy of Management Annals*, 5, 279–316.

Watson, T. and Hickman, M. (2012) *Dial M for Murdoch: News Corporation and the Corruption of Britain*. London: Allen Lane.

Weimer, D. and Thornton, E. (1997) Slow healing at Mitsubishi: It's clearing up sexual harassment charges but ill will lingers. *Business Week*, September 22, 74–6.

Weinstein, B. (2011) *Ethical Intelligence*. New York: New World Library.

Weiss, R. and Schneider, J.P. (2006) *Untangling the Web: Sex, Porn, and Fantasy Obsession in the Internet Age*. New York: Alyson Books.

Westphal, J.D., Park, S.H., McDonald, M.L. and Hayward, M.L.A. (2012) Helping other CEOs avoid bad press: social exchange and impression management support among CEOs in communications with journalists. *Administrative Science Quarterly*, 57, 217–68.

Wharton, A. and Blair-Loy, M. (2002) The "overtime culture" in a global corporation: A cross-national study of finance professionals' interest in working part-time. *Work and Occupations*, 29, 32–63.

Wolfe, J.L. (2000) Assessment and treatment of compulsive sex/love behavior. *Journal of Rational-Emotive and Cognitive-Behavior Therapy*, 18, 235–46.

Womack, B. (2012) CEOs fake degree sparks Yahoo shift. *National Post*, May 14, FP1.

Wright, P.M. (2012) Stars on the executive leadership team: Human frailties in action. Paper presented at the Annual Meeting of the Academy of Management, Boston, MA, August.

Yew, M.A.-T. (2012) Corporations can resist bribery urge: But experts say it takes strong leadership, clear policy and understanding shareholders. *Toronto Star*, May 3, B5.

Young, K.S. (1999) The evaluation and treatment of internet addiction. In L. Vandecreek and T. Jackson (eds) *Innovations in Clinical Practice: A Source Book*. Sarasota, FL: Professional Resource Press, pp. 17–31.

Yu, T.Y, Sengul, M. and Lester, R.H. (2008) Misery loves company: The spread of negative impacts resulting from an organizational crisis. *Academy of Management Review*, 33, 452–72.

Zimbardo, P. (2007) *The Lucifer Effect: Understanding How Good People Turn Evil.* New York: Random House.

PART II

Human Frailties: Antecedents and Consequences

CHAPTER 2

Substance Abuse and Addiction in the Workplace

SUSANNA GALEA AND HAMID GHODSE

Introduction

The global challenge of substance abuse and addictions within all societies calls for concerted and collaborative efforts to promote societies free of drugs. In June 1998 the Special Session of the United Nations General Assembly acknowledged the importance of promoting social systems free of drugs – with the workplace being recognized as one of the most significant social systems, outside the family, within which most individuals interact and function (United Nations, 1998).

Substance abuse and addiction problems have been a cause for concern over the last few decades. The chronic relapsing nature of substance abuse and addictions contributed significantly to maintaining the global prevalence at almost a stable level over that time (UNODC, 2012). Ongoing efforts to address such problems acknowledge the chronic nature through promoting recovery and well-being, and attempting to effectively re-integrate individuals with substance abuse and addiction problems within societies and social systems. Integrating individuals within environments such as the workplace creates an opportunity to shift human suffering related to substance abuse and addiction from a realm of powerlessness to one of functionality and gradual empowerment. The recovery approach builds upon personal and societal attitudes and approaches, making efforts to effectively integrate individuals within more empathetic social systems, with the aim of achieving a greater good for all.

Around the world large, a number of individuals with alcohol-related problems (around 70 percent) and individuals with drug-related problems (around 60 percent) are estimated to hold some form of employment (International Labour Organization, 1998) indicating that a significant proportion of the workforce is likely to be afflicted with substance abuse and addiction problems and related complications such as hepatitis, relational problems and other psychosocial problems. Recognizing the workforce as a convenient environment for detection of substance abuse and addiction and provision of help promotes an effective, integrated recovery approach to addressing the global challenge of addiction.

The Nature and Extent of the Problem

The use of mind altering substances by humans for both medical and non-medical purposes is no new phenomenon. The legitimate use of substances for various purposes has been well recognized among various societies since the existence of humankind. For instance, the chewing of Erythroxylon coca leaves containing cocaine, by South American indigenous people, was recognized by such people as a means of survival – chewing the coca leaves gave them the strength and energy needed for hunting in cold conditions (Petersen, 1977; Gay et al., 1975). Currently individuals use coffee or chocolate as socially acceptable substances enhancing physical alertness.

In more recent years, the use of mind-altering substances has gradually diverged away from legitimate use to a pattern of use associated with biological, psychological and social adverse consequences. Improvement in scientific rigour, transport and communication methods have resulted in more potent mind-altering substances found within reach of households and local communities. Greed for acquisition of power promotes the production, distribution, marketing and ease of access of mind-altering substances without much concern for associated harm.

Recent data (UNODC, 2010) indicates that globally 230 million people, i.e., 5 percent of the world's adult population – are estimated to have used an illicit substance at least once within that year. Problem drug users are estimated at 27 million, i.e., 0.6 percent of the world adult population, and around 12 percent of the population of drug users. These figures and data from previous UNODC reports indicate that the extent of global adult illicit drug use has remained relatively stable in the past five years. The two most commonly used substances are cannabis (prevalence between 2.6 and 5 percent) and amphetamine-type stimulants (excluding ecstasy) (prevalence between 0.3 and 1.2 percent). Treatment demand in Asia and Europe is predominantly related to opioid abuse. Opioids also contribute significantly to the demand for treatment in Africa, North America and Oceania. In Africa treatment demand is predominantly due to cannabis abuse. Treatment demand related to cocaine use is mainly in the Americas; and that related to amphetamine-type stimulants is mainly in Asia.

Complications related to illicit drug abuse contributed significantly to the global burden of disease – with prevalence rates of hepatitis C as high as 46.7 percent among injecting drug users. Mortality is also concerning. In 2010, between 99,000 and 253,000 deaths (0.5–1.3 percent of all-cause mortality) were attributed to illicit drug use (UNODC, 2012).

The abuse of prescription drugs has been recognized as an issue of concern in more recent years especially among the younger generation. Most commonly abused substances include those prescribed for pain relief, such as oxycodone, and tranquilizers such as benzodiazepines. Factors contributing to the increasing global problem of the abuse of prescribed substances are trends of increased prescribing of substances with potential abuse liability leading to increased ease of access to prescription drugs, poor awareness of the potential risks related to handling of mind-altering substances, and misconceptions about the safety of prescription drugs, all contribute to the increasing global problem with the abuse of prescribed substances. Epidemiological data from America shows that among adolescents, prescription and over-the-counter medications account for most drug abuse, when excluding cannabis. In 2010, 2.7 per cent of the US population (around 7 million people) were using psychotherapeutic drugs non-medically (National Institute on Drug Abuse, 2011).

The global use of alcohol also contributes significantly to the burden of disease and mortality rates. Alcohol is associated with a large number of diseases, injuries and social problems, with 4 percent of all deaths worldwide attributable to alcohol abuse. Almost half of all men and one third of all women worldwide have consumed alcohol in the past year. In 2005, an estimated 6.13 litres of pure alcohol was consumed by every person aged 15 years or older (World Health Organization, 2007, 2011).

Such epidemiological data indicates that despite worldwide trends and variations, substance abuse and addiction problems remain a significant challenge to all societies. The extent of the problem within the community is likely to be mirrored within the workplace given that the majority of individuals with drug and/or alcohol problems hold some form of employment. This makes the workplace a convenient environment to recognize and address these issues.

Recognizing the Impact: Substance Abuse and Addiction in the Workplace

The use of substances by the workforce, whether within or outside working hours, affects the work and workplace environment in many ways. Early detection and responsive employee assistance can effectively reduce the negative impact that the abuse of substances can have on the workplace.

Performance, alertness and concentration at work can be affected by various states of substance abuse or addiction – e.g., during states of intoxication, withdrawal, or even drug taking states. For instance, the excessive abuse of alcohol by individuals outside working hours can have an impact on one's alertness on the job even the following day, depending on the drinking pattern of that individual. The workplace can also be affected indirectly through the potential covert nature of substance abuse. Generally employees with substance abuse or addiction problems will attempt to hide their problem from their employers, probably due to shame and fear of possible negative consequences related to disclosure. Such behaviour contributes to lack of trust and transparency within the workplace. Disproportionate and perhaps relatively unpredictable managerial time attributed to managing such problems within the workplace can also significantly impact on the work environment, delaying productivity and diverting attention away from organizational vision (Ghodse, 2005).

Recognizing and qualifying the impact of substance abuse and addiction on the workplace is no easy task. The different effects of substances, the varying states of abuse and addiction, and the different demands and expectations within the workplace environment contribute to the difficulty in recognizing and measuring the impact. The implementation of policies provides good ground to standardize the management of such problems and permits better quantification of impact and outcomes.

The impact of substance abuse and addiction can be divided into three main headings – impact related to the employee, impact related to the workplace environment and impact on finances. Table 2.1 below provides an outline of potential impact factors (Ghodse, 2005).

Table 2.1 Impact of substance abuse and addiction in the workplace

Employee	Workplace Environment	Costs
• Performance • Productivity • Absenteeism • Behaviours • Appearance and attitude • Safety hazards • Preoccupation with drug seeking interfering with attention and concentration	• Management time • De-motivating environments • Trust • Transparency • Health and safety workplace issues • Employment relations with other employees	• Disproportionate burden • Illegal activities in the workplace – e.g., selling drugs to other employees • Cost related to treatment and rehabilitation • Costs from reduced productivity and absenteeism • Costs due to substance-related injuries or illnesses • Costs due to disability claims • Increased employee turnover (change of job; premature death or injuries)

The impact on performance and reduced productivity was reported in a number of studies. Earnings were equated with individual productivity (MacDonald and Shields, 2001; Rannia, 2003) and studies showed a sharp reduction in wage premium as alcohol consumption increased from moderate drinking to higher levels of drinking. However, moderate drinkers had higher wage premium when compared to non-drinkers.

The early recognition of workforce substance abuse and addiction is an important factor in the effective management of such situations. Performance issues such as carelessness or increased number of errors, difficulty concentrating, inconsistent work quality, erratic work patterns, inconsistent work pace, signs of fatigue, withdrawal from social networks, and an inability to meet deadlines are indicative of possible substance abuse. In an American report, 47 percent of all industrial injuries and 40 percent of all industrial fatalities could be linked to alcohol abuse and addiction (Bernstein and Mahoney, 1989). Other factors, such as absenteeism, late arrival at or early departure from work, unexplained absences, excessive time spent on the phone, and small property theft (such as theft of mobile phones, wallets, etc.) could also be indicative. Attitudes and behaviour such as irritability, deterioration in appearance and hygiene, defensiveness, blaming others for concerns, frequent financial problems, and inconsistency in event reporting with probable fabrication are all indicative of potential substance use (National Council on Alcoholism and Drug Dependence, n.d.). Such behaviours and attitudes *may* be indicative of substance abuse and addiction problems but are not necessarily so.

Absenteeism was also shown to be higher among alcohol abusers due to alcohol-related illnesses as well as due to increased accidents among alcohol abusers (Rannia, 2003). The rate and level of absenteeism was shown to be determined more by the pattern of alcohol consumption rather than by the actual amount of alcohol consumed. The frequency of heavy episodic drinking over the previous month was positively correlated with number of days absent from work in the subsequent 12-month period. Volume of alcohol consumption did not show the same correlation (Bacharach, Bamberger and Biron, 2010). Similarly, the incidence and severity of comorbid physical and mental health problems due to excessive drinking over time was positively correlated with the level of employee sickness absenteeism (Gmel and Rehm, 2003; Jones, Casswell and Zhang, 1995).

Specific substances can be responsible for characteristic signs and symptoms (see Table 2.2). Awareness and recognition in the workplace of such presentations can give an indication on the substance involved and facilitate more effective management of the situation (Ghodse, 2010; World Health Organization, 1994).

Table 2.2 Characteristic signs and symptoms of commonly abused substances

Substance	Effects of intoxication	Effects of withdrawal
Opioids (e.g. heroin; morphine; oxycodone)	Drowsiness and slowness Slurred speech Inability to feel pain Impaired attention Impaired performance Decreased responsiveness Needle marks (complicate use) Pin-point pupils	Runny nose Watery eyes Yawning Diarrhoea Dilated pupils Abdominal cramps Muscle aches
Alcohol	Impaired attention Disinhibition Irritability Unstable mood Impaired performance Slurred speech Unsteady on feet Smell of alcohol	Sweating Nausea/vomiting Tremors Risk of seizures
Cannabis	Disinhibition Euphoria Agitation Suspicious Impaired attention Slowness Oddness (due to hallucinations, depersonalization, etc.)	Irritability Suspicious
Sedatives or hypnotics (e.g. benzodiazepines)	Impaired attention Irritability Slowness Drowsiness Lack of coordination Euphoria	Irritability Suspicious Risk of seizures
Stimulants (e.g. cocaine; amphetamine)	Euphoria Marked agitation Argumentative Abusive Suspicious Inability to complete tasks Easily distracted Unstable mood Weight loss (long-term use)	Dysphoria Lethargy Hunger Agitation

The characteristic symptoms and signs outlined in Table 2.2 are by no means comprehensive and all do not necessarily need to be present. They are only indicative of potential substance abuse and addiction. It is important to note that the presentations outlined can result from other conditions with a specialist assessment being required for appropriate diagnosis.

Table 2.3 Financial burden on employees

Impact of substance abuse and addiction	Cost translation to employer
Absenteeism	Decreased productivity Lost time Reduced profits
Impaired workplace performance	Decreased productivity Decreased profits Poorer quality Impaired organizational reputation Reduced competitive organizational strength
Health issues	Sickness benefits Costs of employer's share of medical insurance
Injuries and accidents	Insurance costs Legal costs
Inappropriate behaviour	Management time Disciplinary process costs Costs related to employee morale
Job losses	Recruitment costs Training costs Performance management costs Loss of organizational knowledge
Theft and other crime	Reduced profits Property destruction Violence-related costs Security costs
Negative relations and morale	Decreased productivity Decreased performance Decreased profits Poorer quality Impaired organizational reputation

Source: Adapted from Alcohol Advisory Council of New Zealand, New Zealand Drug Foundation and Accident Compensation Cooperation New Zealand, 2008.

The financial burden of substance abuse and addiction on employers and on the wider society is significant. Within the United States, reductions in productivity due to substance abuse and addiction were estimated to cost the American economy around $80.9 billion, with $66.7 billion attributed to alcohol problems and $14.2 billion to other drug problems (National Institute on Drug Abuse and National Institute on Alcohol Abuse and Alcoholism, 1992). Within New Zealand, social costs due to decreased productivity from alcohol problems were estimated at $1.8 billion, i.e. 2.5 percent of the GDP. Loss of productivity was calculated from reduced quantity of work as well as reduction due to premature deaths. Life years lost due to alcohol problems contributed to an estimated 17,000 less people in the working-age workforce (Easton, 1997). Table 2.3 indicates how substance abuse and addiction translate into a financial burden for employees (Alcohol Advisory Council of New Zealand, New Zealand Drug Foundation and Accident Compensation Cooperation New Zealand, 2008; Mattman, 2001; International Labour Office, 1996).

Workplace Culture

The workplace culture may enable or discourage substance abuse and addiction and substance-related work problems. Norms, values and expectations within the workplace play an important role in shaping the way employees behave on a day to day basis. Organizational cohesiveness and collaboration can be manifested in several ways and can directly or indirectly promote or discourage substance abuse. For example, some organizations support team building days by ending with free drinks all around, indirectly promoting a drinking culture. Other organizations may support ending the day with socializing but drinks to be purchased by the employee, giving the message that drinking is not an organizational expectation.

Some occupations and workplaces are high-risk enablers of substance abuse and addiction. Studies identified jobs within the drinking trade, caterers, armed forces, merchant navy, fishermen, medical doctors and journalists as high-risk occupations (Royal College of Psychiatrists, 1986). Professional and managerial status jobs are also associated with higher alcohol consumption (Rikards et al., 2004). Other jobs which involve working unsociable hours such as postmen, are also considered as high risk (Galea and Ghodse, 2005). Occupations shown to have lowest rates of illicit drug use include: administrative workers, teachers, child care or social services jobs, and police and detective work (National Council on Alcoholism and Drug Dependence, n.d.).

A number of factors contribute to high-risk enabling occupations. Ease of access to substances, such as jobs in the entertainment industry, are associated with increased rates of substance abuse. Occupations which lack inadequate support and supervision, stressful and highly demanding jobs, and busy or mobile occupations which do not allow time for bonding and cohesiveness among employees are associated with higher levels of alcohol use. Occupations with less sociable hours and high earnings making it financially feasible to spend money on substances are also considered as high-risk enabling occupations. Other factors not directly related to the particular occupation include: workers employed in three or more jobs in the previous five years being twice as likely to be illicit drug users, and unmarried (divorced, separated or never married) workers having twice the rate of illicit substance and heavy alcohol use (Galea and Ghodse, 2005; National Council on Alcoholism and Drug Dependence, n.d.; Hoffman, Brittingham and Larison, 1996).

Tackling the Problem

Conduct, performance or attendance issues at work, whether related to substance abuse and addictions or whether due to other conditions, tend to be followed by managerial procedures. Managers need to be aware of the possibility of substance abuse and addiction causing or contributing to the performance to be addressed, and follow clear processes that can effectively tackle the problem. Early recognition and reduction of employee substance abuse and addiction problems will reduce the employer's financial burden related to such problems.

WORKPLACE POLICIES

Most organizations have policies in place for tackling substance abuse problems in the workplace. In more recent years workplace policies for tackling substance abuse have increasingly emphasised improving the health, safety and productivity of all employees through provision of assistance, treatment, rehabilitation and follow-up for those employees with substance abuse and addiction problems. Purposes and objectives of policies are to promote the safety and well-being of all employees, to facilitate early identification and management of substance abuse and addiction problems, to promote a standardized non-judgemental approach to dealing with staff with addiction problems, and to embrace addiction problems as a norm within societies and cultures, including the workplace culture. Standardizing an approach to tackling such problems also safeguards organizations from claims of unfair or unjust treatment and makes clear the organizational stance.

Some organizations have a legal obligation to address workplace or occupational substance abuse and addiction. These are generally industries where personal or public safety and/or security are at risk. For instance, the British Airways Drug and Alcohol Policy includes expectations of drug and alcohol testing of staff suspected of substance abuse and addiction problems; a random test can be done within the first six months of employment, and random tests can be required of employees after treatment and rehabilitation. These measures are balanced by positive encouragement for employees to come forward to be offered support to deal with the problems (Gakhal, 2005).

WORKPLACE DRUG TESTING

Workplace drug testing is aimed at early detection and at promoting the health and safety of the workforce and of the wider public. It is an approach that has been adopted by many organizations in the US, UK and other countries – but continues to raise ethical dilemmas around the need to balance early detection and prevention of deterioration, tackling productivity concerns, and promoting the health, safety and well-being of all the workforce, whilst respecting the privacy and freedom of individual workers.

Workplace drug testing by organizations can be implemented pre-employment and during the course of employment. Drug testing during the course of employment is implemented by most organizations when there is a high index of suspicion of substance abuse problems. However, other organizations may also adopt random testing with employees who consent or regular testing at predictable times again with employee consent.

The provision of informed consent by employees for workplace drug testing is an important part of the process. Implementing a policy to promote the safety and well-being of all employees and to ensure competency in performing specific jobs is dependent upon an effective collaborative approach between the employer and employee – highlighting the relevance of obtaining informed consent and maintaining confidentiality and ensuring integrity of testing approaches.

EMPLOYEE ASSISTANCE PROGRAMMES

Employee assistance programmes are cost-effective worksite-based programmes designed to assist organizations in addressing performance and productivity issues, and to assist employees in addressing personal concerns that may impact on job performance. Substance abuse and addiction is one of the concerns dealt with within employee assistance programmes. Organizations supporting such programmes tend to deal with fewer grievances, improve workplace morale and motivation, promote workplace co-operation, are successful in recruiting and retaining workforce, are perceived as a caring employer, decrease absenteeism and improve performance and productivity, and improve the overall safety within the workplace.

Employee assistance programmes to address substance abuse and addiction problems are an effective advantageous approach given that the programmes function both at an organizational and at an individual level. The programmes are instrumental in provision of adequate support to the employee, reducing stigma towards substance abuse within the workplace and facilitating appropriate, non-judgemental attitudes and processes adopted by the employer. Such programmes are generally staffed by professionals who are capable of providing information, support, counselling, short-term solutions and referrals to other healthcare providers as necessary. Employee assistance programmes can provide confidential substance abuse and addiction screening and testing, as well as support during the recovery period post-treatment.

WORKPLACE HEALTH AND WELLNESS PROGRAMMES

These programmes are aimed at the prevention of ill health through promoting healthy lifestyles. Healthy eating campaigns, walking competitions, promotion of use of bicycles to and from work, and other health promotion initiatives are effective in promoting wellness and giving a message that substance abuse and addiction is an unhealthy lifestyle to engage in.

Conclusion

This chapter discusses how a wrong turn into a lifestyle of substance abuse and addiction can lead one onto a road away from success. Substance abuse and addiction problems present a global challenge to all societies. The chronic nature of such conditions is mirrored within the workplace and can have a significantly negative impact on the workplace environment, the employees, and the financial burden of the organization. Employee morale can easily be eroded and the organization's reputation can easily be at stake, due to factors such as reduced productivity and poor quality of assets delivered.

The workplace culture has the potential to enable or discourage substance abuse and addiction. Employers need to be mindful of the values and norms held by its employees and move towards promoting drug and alcohol free environments. Early and timely detection of substance abuse within the workforce is facilitated by the implementation of drug and alcohol workplace policies. The effectiveness of such policies is dependent upon the application of programmes providing support whilst protecting individual privacy. Organizational attention to such measures will see employees slowly moving back on to the road to success.

References

Alcohol Advisory Council of New Zealand, New Zealand Drug Foundation and Accident Compensation Cooperation New Zealand (2008) *Alcohol and Other Drugs in the Workplace: Employer Guide*.

Bacharach, S.B., Bamberger, P. and Biron, M. (2010) Alcohol consumption and workplace absenteeism: The moderating effect of social support. *Journal of Applied Psychology*, 95, 334–48.

Bernstein, M. and Mahoney, J.J. (1989) Management perspectives on Alcoholism: The employer's stake in alcoholism treatment. *Occupational Medicine*, 4, 223–32.

Easton, B. (1997) *The Social Costs of Tobacco Use and Alcohol Misuse*. Wellington: Department of Public Health.

Gakhal, R. (2005) British Airways: drug and alcohol policy. In H. Ghodse (ed.) *Addiction at Work: Tackling Drug Use and Misuse in the Workplace*. Aldershot: Gower, pp. 249–51.

Galea, S. and Ghodse, H. (2005) Drugs misuse and the work culture. In H. Ghodse (ed.) *Addiction at Work: Tackling Drug Use and Misuse in the Workplace*. Aldershot: Gower, 33–40.

Gay, G.R., Inaba, D.S., Sheppard, C.W. and Newmeyer, J.A. (1975) Cocaine: history, epidemiology, human pharmacology, and treatment. a perspective on a new debut for an old girl. *Clinical Toxicology*, 8(2), 149–78.

Ghodse, H. (2005) Drugs and alcohol in the workplace. In H. Ghodse (ed.) *Addiction at Work: Tackling Drug Use and Misuse in the Workplace*. Aldershot: Gower, 3–9.

—— (2010) *Ghodse's Drugs and Addictive Behaviour: A Guide to Treatment*, 4th edn. Cambridge: Cambridge University Press.

Gmel, G. and Rehm, J. (2003) Harmful alcohol use. *Alcohol Research and Health*, 27, 52–62.

Hoffman, J.P., Brittingham, A. and Larison, C. (1996) *Drug Use among US Workers: Prevalence and Trends by Occupation and Industry Categories*. Rockville, MD: Substance Abuse and Mental Health Services Administration.

International Labour Office (1996) ILO policies and activities concerning vocational rehabilitation, Section II – Workplace Alcohol and Drug Prevention, Part 1 – Problems and Issues. Committee on Employment and Social Policy, Geneva. Available at: http://www.ilo.org/public/english/standards/relm/gb/docs/gb273/esp-3.htm [accessed November 24, 2012].

International Labour Organization (1998) *Mobilising Small Business to Prevent Substance Abuse*. Report of the International Labour Organization Workshop, Geneva, May 12–16, 1997.

Jones, S., Casswell, S. and Zhang, J. (1995) The economic costs of alcohol-related absenteeism and reduced productivity among the working population of New Zealand. *Addiction*, 90, 1455–61.

MacDonald, Z. and Shields, M. (2001) The impact of alcohol consumption on occupational attainment in England. *Economica*, 68, 427–53.

Mattman, S. (2001) Preventing violence in the workplace. Workplace Violence Research Institute. Available at: http://noworkviolence.com/articles/preventing_violence.htm [accessed November 24, 2012].

National Council on Alcoholism and Drug Dependence (n.d.) Drugs and the workplace. Available at: www.ncadd.org/index.php/learn-about-drugs/workplace/242-drugs-and-the-workplace [accessed November 4, 2012].

National Institute on Drug Abuse (2011) *Prescription Drug Abuse: A Research Update from the National Institute of Drug Abuse*. Washington, DC: US Department of Health and Human Services.

National Institute on Drug Abuse and National Institute on Alcohol Abuse and Alcoholism (1992) *The Economic Cost of Alcohol and Drug Abuse*. Washington, DC: US Department of Health and Human Services.

Petersen, R.C. (1977) History of cocaine. In R.C. Petersen and R.C. Stillman (eds) *Cocaine: 1977*, National Institute of Drug Abuse Research Monograph Series. Rockville, MD: Department of Health, Education and Welfare, Public Health Service, pp. 26–43.

Rannia, L. (2003) *Alcohol Misuse: How Much Does It Cost?* London: Strategy Unit Cabinet Office.

Rikards, L., Fox, K., Roberts, C., Fletcher, L. and Goddard, E. (2004) *Living in Britain: Results from the 2002 General Household Survey, No. 31*. London: Office of National Statistics.

Royal College of Psychiatrists (1986) *Alcohol: Our Favourite Drug. New Report on Alcohol and Alcohol-related Problems*. Royal College of Psychiatrists Special Committee on Alcoholism. London: Tavistock.

United Nations (1998) *Special Session of the General Assembly, Guiding Principles of Drug Demand Reduction*. IV E.15 (June). New York: United Nations, pp. 8–10.

UNODC (2010) *World Drug Report 2010*. E.10.XI.13. New York: United Nations.

—— (2012) *World Drug Report 2012*. E.12.XI.1. New York: United Nations.

World Health Organization (1994) *International Classification of Mental and Behavioural Disorders* (ICD-10). Geneva: World Health Organization.

—— (2007) *Alcohol and Injury in Emergency Departments: Summary of the Report from the WHO Collaborative Study on Alcohol and Injuries*. Geneva: World Health Organization.

—— (2011). *Global Status Report on Alcohol and Health*. Geneva: World Health Organization.

CHAPTER **3**

Materialism and its Discontents[1]

RONALD J. BURKE

Introduction

This chapter examines what we know about materialism, money, and greed. While these concepts are different from each other they are inter-related. This chapter builds on and updates my chapters in earlier studies (Burke, 2009, 2011). I believe that greed underlies almost all acts of crime and corruption in organizations, and that crime and corruption seem to be flourishing today in organizations because "that's where the money is."

> *Greed – "avarice, insatiable desire or covetousness"*
>
> *Materialism – "excessive devotion to the pursuit of material wealth and physical well-being"*
>
> – Cassell's Concise Dictionary (1997)

Greed is the selfish desire for or pursuit of money, wealth, food, or other possessions (Wang and Murnighan, 2011). It is generally considered a vice and is one of the seven deadly sins in Catholicism. Greed has been a factor in human behavior since the beginning of time. A simple desire to increase one's wealth is generally acceptable in all societies and is not considered to be greed. Making money by itself isn't undesirable. Greed is the extreme form of this desire. Greed is likely to lead to materialism; materialism is greedy behavior. But one needs to consider the motives for making this money and how the money was made. One can also distinguish economic winners versus economic cheaters. One can use money to buy a yacht but not a congressman. Some people believe that greed is good and has positive effects. Greed drives capitalism and competition. But greed was also behind several recent unethical and immoral actions by both individuals and organizations and was associated with extreme examples of executive and organizational excesses. McQuaig (2001) contends that greed and materialism have become central organizing principles in today's capitalistic societies, with Atwood (2008) seeing the pursuit of money and being in debt having a long history.

1 Preparation of this manuscript was supported in part by York University.

Consider the following:

- The greed of the US banking system has cost taxpayers a heavy price. Banks in the US lent billions of dollars to individuals who would have great difficulty in paying it back, sometimes misrepresenting the conditions involved in order to continue to sell their products and services. Managers and individual professionals achieved higher performance and received bonuses based on these suspect transactions. This created the sub-prime mortgage crisis which devastated the US economy and had lesser effects in several other countries. When individuals defaulted on their loans, the housing market collapsed, the risk of an economic recession increased, and the central banking system (the US government) decided to bail out these institutions to avoid further economic meltdown. Some leading bankers recently admitted they "made mistakes."

Some recent examples of greed:

- Kweku Adoboli was charged with committing a $2.3 billion fraud at UBS, a large Swiss bank (September 17, 2011). He was charged with fraud and false accounting. Amazingly, UBS risk staff failed to spot these losses. It was not clear whether Adoboli personally benefited from his transactions though he appeared to have an expensive set of habits (Harris and Martin, 2011).
- The UBS rogue trading scandal, now estimated at US$2.3 billion, resulted in the resignation of Oswald Grubel, UBS CEO. Other UBS senior managers had their reputations tarnished in this scandal (e.g., Carsten Kengeter). Adoboli was sentenced to seven years in jail for his actions on November 20, 2012 (Shirbon, 2012).
- A UK property tycoon, Achilleas Kallakis, and two others, was found guilty of defrauding banks of millions of dollars (*Globe and Mail*, 2013). Kallakis had a fleet of chauffeur-driven Bentleys, a private jet, a private helicopter, a luxury yacht moored in Monaco, and expensive art works.
- Société Générale, responding to Jérôme Kerviel's fraud (US$7.2 billion), imposed tough internal control measures but Société Générale, over three years later, is still seen as a riskier bank than its competitors. Société Générale fired some of Kerviel's supervisors, and several of Société Générale's managers had their careers tarnished.
- Olympus Corp. has admitted it covered up investment losses for decades (Dvorak and Wakabayashi, 2001). Several other Japanese companies (e.g., Yamaichi Securities, Livedoor Co.) fudged their books as well.
- A senior Iranian banker who resigned following a massive embezzlement scandal has fled Iran and is living in Toronto in a $3 million home (Freeze and Hu, 2011). The amount of money involved was estimated to exceed $2 billion.
- Hosni Mubarak's closest aide, Hussein Salem, and his son and daughter, were sentenced in October 2011 in absentia to seven years in jail and a combined fine of more than US$4 billion for money laundering and profiteering (*Globe and Mail*, 2011, October 18, A16).
- James Ibari returned to Nigeria from the UK where he worked as a cashier to become governor of the Delta state in 1989 (Raynar, 2012). In the next eight years he defrauded his country of $250 million, amassing a personal fortune of $80 million. He bought four houses in the UK, a $5 million property in Johannesburg, a house in Houston, Texas, a fleet of luxury cars, and when arrested was trying to buy a $24 million private jet.

- Jacob Zuma, President of South Africa, reportedly spent over $23 million of taxpayer monies renovating one of his four houses (Mumumdza, 2012). And Wen Jaibao, China's Premier, and his family reportedly amassed a US$2.7 billion fortune over the past 20 years in outside banks (*Globe and Mail*, 2012a).
- More recently (Chowdhry, 2013) the Supreme Court of Pakistan ordered the arrest of Prime Minister Pervez Ashraf and 15 others on corruption charges.
- Quebec police arrested construction magnate, Antonio Accurso, and 13 others in an anti-corruption sweep. They were charged with bribery and fraud in obtaining lucrative construction contracts (LeBlanc and Peritz, 2012). Accurso had a $100,000 clothing budget, a sprawling mansion outside Montreal, and a 119-foot luxury yacht called *Touch*, moored in the Caribbean, which had four king-size beds, a six-person hot tub, mahogany walls and furniture, gold faucets, and marble counters, and in which he entertained politicians, union leaders, and other businessmen. His company received favorable treatment in return for cash and/or services.
- The US administration is seeking to seize $71 million in allegedly corrupt assets from the son of the leader of Equatorial Guinea (*Globe and Mail*, 2011a). The US has accused Teodoro Nguema Obiong Mangua, the son of President Teodoro Nguema Obian Mbasago, of fraudulently obtaining more than $100 million. The African dictator's son spent money on luxuries including a private jet, Malibu and Beverly Hills mansions, Michael Jackson memorabilia, 24 sports cars, shopping sprees for designer clothes, and speed boats (Allen, 2011). The dictator, his son, and close associates were engaged in corruption, bribery, and money laundering. Seventy percent of his country's population lives below the poverty level and tens of thousands have no access to electricity or clean water.
- Former Irish Prime Minister, Bertie Ahern received $277,000 in secret payments while in office which he lied about under oath, and two of his former cabinet colleagues were charged with corruption (Pogatchnik, 2012).
- The French government is investigating at least three African leaders accused of embezzling money from their home countries (Chrisafis, 2012). The Bongo family from Gabon, relatives of the late leader of Gabon, Omar Bongo, own 39 properties in France, mostly in Paris and on the French Riviera, 70 French bank accounts, and at least seven luxury cars. Sassou Nguesso, leader of the Republic of Congo, spent more than US$855,000 on clothes over a 12 month period. His family owns 24 properties in France, 112 bank accounts, and various sports cars. The Bongo family from Gabon, the Nguesso family from the Congo, and the Obgtang family from Equatorial Guinea, own assets of at least US$295 million, penthouses, villas, bank accounts, and luxury vehicles.
- Former Haitian dictator, Jean-Claude "Baby Doc" Duvalier, will face charges pertaining to corruption during his 15 year rule (Delva, 2012). Duvalier is accused of embezzling between $300 and $800 million. Duvalier had spent the past several years living in luxury in Paris.
- Zine El Abidine Ben Ali, former Tunisian dictator (1982–2011), is now living in Saudi Arabia. His personal fortune is thought to be $5 billion.
- A total of $861 million was diverted from Kabul's largest bank in a massive fraud scheme (Farmer, 2012).
- Why should country turmoil or a massacre and war crimes against a country's citizens put a damper on greed and materialism? The Arab Spring has shone a light on the excesses of

the wives of dictator husbands. These women emerge as partners in crime (Ward, 2012). Asma Assad (Syria) continues to shop for expensive art, jewelry, home furnishings, and $1,600 crystal-encrusted shoes by Christian Louboutin. Suzanne Mubarak (Egypt), Leila Trabelsi (Tunisia), and Sofia Farkash (Libya) amassed huge fortunes (Mirsky, 2012).

- William Wise, now on the lam, is accused of running a $129 million Ponzi scheme (Findlay, 2012). His assets included a Challenger jet, two 2009 Cadillac Escalades, three Mercedes and two yachts in St. Vincent. Wise spent money on foreign escorts, meals costing several thousands of dollars, international travel, a $500,000 wine collection, and a $12,000 weekly allowance for his wife. He paid $20,000 for two meals in Atlanta, and took 50 people to St. Vincent for a New Year's Eve party in 2008. He also owned more than 170 Swarovski crystal figurines and several expensive paintings.
- Greg Mortenson, US author and Nobel Prize nominee, has been found guilty of "financial transgressions" in running his charity (a code word for fraud). Mortenson used his charity money to support a personal lifestyle of excess which included family vacations and millions on charter flights and gifts for employees and family members (*Globe and Mail*, 2012b). He was ordered to pay $1 million back to his charity. Mortenson was also alleged to have "made up" parts of the books he wrote in support of his charity and his efforts while maintaining they were true.
- Robert Waxman, former Philip Services Corp executive was sentenced to eight years in jail and ordered to pay a $18 million restitution for diverting more than $17 million from his now bankrupt company to his own use (*Globe and Mail*, 2011b). He spent the money on jewelry, horses, watches, art, and wine. A fine of US$15.5 million was also imposed on Waxman.
- Jean Chalette and Serge Beaugre were found guilty in March 2010 of more than 100 charges of fraud and producing false documents (*Globe and Mail*, 2011c). Both worked for and with Vincent Lacroix, who had already been sentenced to 13 years in prison. Money was diverted to Lacroix for his personal use. This became one of the largest frauds in Canadian history.
- Leblanc (2011) identified nine federal employees of the Canadian Revenue Agency (CRA) socializing with businessmen involved in tax evasion leading to a lengthy RCMP investigation. These auditors received free trips, home renovations, and a bank account in the Bahamas containing over $800,000. In addition, copies of CRA tax documents were found in the hands of one of the businessmen and his accountants. Five of the auditors were fired and one has resigned. Leblanc noted that this investigation began in Montreal and has now spread to other cities in Quebec.
- London police are investigating a Russian banker, George Uromov, who is charged with defrauding Otrithe Financial Corp of US$183 million (*Globe and Mail*, 2011d).
- John Corzine, CEO of the now bankrupt MF Global, testified before a US congressional committee that he does not know where the missing US$1.2 billion went (Wagner and Gordon, 2011). His two chief executives (COO, Bradley Abelow, CFO, Henri Steinberg) said they do not know where the money went either.
- Chesapeake Energy CEO, Aubrey McClendon, with board approval, took $1.1 billion in personal loans on an ownership stake in gas wells the company had given him, constituting a conflict of interest (Daily and Driver, 2012). McClendon said he was "deeply sorry" for the mess his personal financial dealings had created. Chesapeake's stocks fell sharply. McClendon also ran a $200 million hedge fund that traded in the same products that Chesapeake produced.

- Former Credit Suisse trader David Higgs and his subordinate, Salmaan Siddiqui, pled guilty to criminal conspiracy and fraud charges (Bray, 2012). Other Credit Suisse employees were also charged. By manipulating the value of bonds in the trading book, these individuals were able to obtain large year-end bonuses in 2007. One individual's bonus was $1.76 million in 2007 and his incentive share award was $5.2 million.
- Eleven people, which included two doctors and a former union president, were charged on October 27, 2011 with participating in a massive fraud in which hundreds of Long Island Rail Road workers submitted false pension claims involving disability (Rashbaum, 2011). A network of doctors and union employees helped workers to file claims that they were disabled. Doctors ran "disability mills," being paid in cash ($800 to $1,500) for each fake assessment. One "disabled" employee regularly played tennis and golf.
- William Armony, who built the United Way into a major charity, went to prison for six years for misusing funds to support a lavish lifestyle and a teenage mistress (McFadden, 2011). He was the CEO of United Way for 22 years. His salary and benefits exceeded $400,000 annually, plus the use of apartments in New York City and Coral Gables Florida. Armony stated he used these perks to meet corporate donors. Armony and two associates were indicted on 71 counts of fraud, conspiracy, money laundering, and tax evasion. He stole $1 million and gave money to his mistress, for trips with her, and for champagne, flowers, and a fax machine to send her love notes.
- Tavi Erez, previously charged with running a Ponzi scheme, has been charged with ten counts of fraud through fake publishing contracts in which he promised returns of between 20 and 36 percent (Rush, 2011). Individuals lost between $275,000 to $1 million and $2 million. In an earlier alleged fraud case, charges were dropped because it would cost too much to pursue; Erez defrauded more than 70 investors of $27 million in a large Ponzi scheme.
- Two billionaire brothers in Hong Kong, Thomas Kwok and Raymond Kwok, were arrested on March 29 in connection with bribery charges (Hui and Ng, 2012). Their firm is one of the world's largest real estate developers. Rafael Hui, formerly the number two official in Hong Kong, was also arrested on possible bribery and misconduct in public office.
- Financial controller, Timothy Bodkin, stole $12 million from his employer over a five-to-six-year period. He spent $3.4 million to buy a house for a girlfriend living in California and then bought a Lotus for her driveway, he bought another girlfriend an Audi and a less expensive home in Ontario, and for yet another girlfriend he bought a $54,000 engagement ring. He bought himself a house for $433,482, then spent over $660,000 in renovations and upgrades. He also bought himself and his friends Harley-Davidson motorcycles (Edwards, 2012).
- The Securities and Exchange Commission (SEC) is now investigating SAC Capital Advisors, a US hedge fund. While not yet formally charged (though charges may be forthcoming), CEO Steve Cohen lives in a 3,000 square-meter house, with its own ice skating rink and Zamboni ice cleaner, and an art collection containing many of the grand masters (Slater, 2012).
- Barclay (2012) cites "made up" or unreliable Chinese data, and increased corruption, as contributing to the decline of China's economic performance. He writes that the 70 wealthiest government officials in China have amassed assets of US$90 billion, and almost 3,000 Chinese bureaucrats have been arrested for corruption since 2007. Corruption is common in the construction industry resulting in poorly constructed buildings leading to hundreds of citizen deaths.

- A Canadian doctor living in Texas, Jacques Roy, and five other associates have been charged (February 29, 2012) with the largest healthcare fraud in US history totaling about $375 million (Brennan, 2012). Roy and his associates billed the US government for fraudulent patients, unnecessary medical services that were not provided, and for unnecessary medical equipment. The government seized Roy's bank accounts, several cars, and two sailboats. At his home, police found a fake passport, fake driver's licenses, and a book titled *Hide Your A$$ets and Disappear: A Step-by-Step Guide*, as well as bank statements from the Cayman Islands.
- Oshawa Hospital fired its CEO after forensic accountants found money and charity management problems (*Toronto Star*, 2011). Jim Sizemore made side arrangements that benefited him without informing the hospital's board of directors. There were unfortunately few financial controls. Sizemore hired his own company as the charity's fundraising arm, took a $7,000 charity auction gift without paying for it, and could not explain international trips he and others had taken. His company was paid at least $307,000 since 2005 for fund raising initiatives.
- In the ten years since the invasion of Afghanistan, foreign donors have given more than US$57 billion in aid. Unfortunately, the Afghan government is one of the most corrupt governments in the world. Armstrong (2011), using data from the UN Office on Drugs and Crime, lists the following.

  - US$2.5 billion – amount paid in bribes in a year
  - US$2.8 billion estimated revenues from Afghanistan's opium trade
  - 59 – percentage of Afghans who consider the daily experience of corruption a bigger threat than insecurity (54 percent) and unemployment (53 percent)
  - 52 – percentage saying they had to pay at least one bribe to a public official in the past year
  - 56 – percentage saying that the request was stated explicitly
  - 25 – percentage who had to pay police
  - 75 – percentage saying they paid in cash
  - 50 – percentage of large bribes (US$1,000 or more) paid to law enforcement officials such as police and judges
  - 63 – percentage who say reporting corruption is a waste of time
  - 54 – percentage who believe NGOs and international organizations are in Afghanistan to get rich
  - 40 – percentage of senior politicians believed to be receiving bribes
  - The UN fired three officials in charge of the US Afghanistan police trust in early June 2012, a $1.4 billion fund, for mismanagement and possible misconduct (Nussenbaum, 2012).

The Scary World of Off-shore Finance

I am not sure why I was on their mailing list but I received two announcements for a conference titled the Offshore Alert Conference to be held in Miami, Florida. It featured 60 speakers. Here is a sample of some session titles.

- Tax avoidance and evaders: An update
- Enticing the top echelon: How the IRS, SEC and CFTC attract high-level whistle-blowers
- Ponzi tsunami: Lessons learned (so far) from the proliferation of Ponzi litigation
- China and OFCs: The dark side
- Russia exposed: The Serge Magnitsky affair
- The role of OFCs in global corruption
- Global shell game: Who's worse – onshore or offshore?
- Exploiting tax loopholes: How US companies like Google shift profits offshore
- A film screening of "We're not broke" about corporate tax scandals in the US

After reading the brochure I was not sure whether I should be even more fearful of the financial sector or comforted by this content.

Offshore Tax Havens

Using data from the World Bank, International Monetary Fund, United Nations, and central banks, James Henry, writing for the UK-based Justice Network, estimated that the rich held $32 trillion in offshore tax havens (*Toronto Star*, 2012a). This represented a loss of $280 million in tax revenues. Focusing on 139 developing countries, Henry found that the richest people in these countries since the 1970s held between $7.3 and $9.3 trillion in "unrecorded offshore wealth."

One consequence for countries noted to be tax havens (e.g., Switzerland, Cayman Islands) is a poor reputation (McLean, 2012). Both the haves and have-nots see these countries as repositories for "dirty money." Tens of billions of dollars from Libya are still housed in Swiss accounts. Switzerland has been attempting to return "dirty money" to several countries (e.g., Tunisia, Libya, Egypt, Peru, Nigeria, the Philippines, and the Democratic Republic of Congo) over the past decade.

Greedy Companies

The US Savings and Loan debacle, Enron, the US sub-prime mortgage fiasco, Bernie Madoff, JPMorgan, and Libor – companies, as well as individuals, can be greedy (Bakan, 2004; McQuaig, 2001; Cohan, 2011; Partnoy, 2009; Tett, 2009; Toffler and Reingold, 2003; O'Shea, 2011; Morgenson and Posner, 2011; Eichenwald, 2005; Madrach, 2011; Martin, 2011; Berenson, 2003; Allaire and Firsirotu, 2012, 2009).

Tens of thousands of women in France reported being given faulty cheap breast implants (Chrisafis, 2011). Poly Implant Prosthesis, a world leader in silicone implant products, was saving about US$1.5 billion a year using industrial silicone instead of medical grade fillers in their breast implants.

Merck and Co., the second largest US drug maker agreed to pay US$950 million, with a company unit pleading guilty to a criminal charge in connection with its sale of the painkiller Vioxx (Feeley and Voreacos, 2011). The drug was misbranded and sold for unapproved uses. Vioxx was Merck's third largest selling drug, generating annual sales of US$2.5 billion. Vioxx was found to be associated with increased risk of heart attacks.

Merck also agreed to pay US$4.85 billion to settle thousands of patient lawsuits about their injuries and US$1.9 billion for legal costs.

Johnson and Johnson became the model of how to respond to the crisis it faced when it was discovered that someone had tampered with their Tylenol product. Johnson and Johnson today seems like just another greedy company. It was recently reported that Johnson and Johnson sold joint replacement products that were found to not meet US safety standards in other countries throughout the world that had lower safety standards. While not illegal, this action raised some eyebrows in terms of ethical standards.

Furthermore, drug companies spend hundreds of millions of dollars annually to develop new drugs that have few benefits to patients but through intense marketing efforts, again costing hundreds of millions of dollars, support their use (Light and Lexchin, 2012).

ING Bank NV agreed to pay US$619 million to settle charges that it violated US sanctions against Iran, Cuba, and other countries (Freifeld, 2012). Other banks (e.g., Credit Suisse, Lloyd's, Barclays) had earlier paid to settle similar charges. ING told clients how to disguise transactions, and falsified and concealed transactions.

Samsung was found guilty in August 2012 of infringing on Apple's patents and fined $1 billion (Elias, 2012). A few days later, Samsung received negative publicity for mistreating workers in China and illegally using child labor (Lee, 2012).

In 2005, a former executive at Wal-Mart in Mexico sent an e-mail to a senior Wal-Mart lawyer in the US indicating that bribery was undertaken in Mexico by Wal-Mart to obtain permits to build stores (Barstow, 2012). The former executive provided names, dates, and amount of bribes paid. An internal investigation of these claims found evidence of widespread bribery involving US$24 million. Wal-Mart executives in the US knew about the bribes and undertook steps to hide them. Wal-Mart executives in the US then apparently stopped the investigation. One might also now ask whether Wal-Mart acted similarly in other countries in which they recently entered and are growing (e.g., China). Wal-Mart lost US$10 billion on Monday, April 23 following the announcement of a bribery investigation into its Mexican operations (*Globe and Mail*, 2012c). If true, these bribery practices would violate the US Foreign Corrupt Practices Act and create lengthy problems for Wal-Mart. A short time later, Wal-Mart lawyers included Brazil, China, India and South Africa, in addition to Mexico, in their investigation of potential bribery by Wal-Mart (Viswanatha, 2012).

Bribes are paid to obtain contracts in much of the world and seem to be increasingly common (Reguly, 2012). Bribes used to constitute 5 percent of a contract's value but are now 20 percent. In recent months, SNC-Lavalin, Wal-Mart, and Finmeccanica were being investigated for paying bribes to gain a competitive advantage. Bribery also hurts the countries who solicit them. Reguly cites a study of 98 Brazilian companies undertaken by Campos, Estrin and Proto in 2010 showing that corruption was the biggest barrier to entry into new markets, reduced legitimate competition, and allowed lower quality projects to "win."

Avon Products Inc. is in talks with the US Justice Department and the Securities and Exchange Commission to settle an investigation into the possible bribery of foreign officials in China and elsewhere (Palazzolo and Glazer, 2012).

Biomet Inc., a US-based maker of medical devices, agreed to pay US$22.9 million to settle US accusations it bribed foreign doctors in China, Brazil, and Argentina to obtain business. Payments were recorded as commissions, royalties, and scientific incentives (*National Post*, 2012a).

The pharmaceutical industry seems to represent a number of greedy organizations. Research studies sponsored by the pharmaceutical industry, when published in peer-reviewed journals, were four times more likely to be favorable to a sponsor's drug, device, or treatment than were non-industry sponsored studies, in a review of 30 studies reported in the *British Medical Journal*. Another review of 205 drug studies reported that in industry-funded studies, 66 percent were favorable to the study drug with only 46 percent favorable in studies that were not industry funded.

Hochman and McCormick (2011) analyzed all randomized medication trials published in the six highest rated general medicine journals between June 2008 and September 2010, and concluded that most intended to mislead readers.

A common practice in medical research is for respected scholars to add their names in support of particular drugs and particular studies (always for pay and/or perks), a practice that is decried but still persists (Wilson and Singer, 2009). A common practice is "ghostwriting" in which respected scholars add their names to reports or articles that they had not written (again for pay and perks). It has been proposed that these scholars should have "legal liability" should problems emerge later.

GlaxoSmithKline PLC pled guilty to misdemeanor criminal charges on July 2, 2012, and was fined US3 billion to settle what the US government called the largest healthcare fraud in history (Ingram, 2012). GlaxoSmithKline undertook several illegal activities including marketing drugs to children that were only approved for adults, failing to provide safety data to the government, using misleading journal articles, and giving doctors meals and spa treatments.

But fraud and bribery exists in all industrial sectors. The CEO of SNC-Lavalin resigned on March 26 when the company found that $56 million was charged to contracts that did not exist to pay agents it cannot name (Yew, 2012). SNC is one of Canada's most recognized companies. SNC-Lavalin made hundreds of millions of dollars in Libya when the Gaddafi regime was in power; one could not get work without knowing the Gaddafis. The departing CEO, who worked in the company for 12 years, will receive several million dollars in severance compensation and pension (Silicoff, 2012).

The RCMP made a second visit to obtain documents from SNC. These documents related to investigations of SNC's activities in Canada, Bangladesh, India, Mexico, and Libya, along with the missing $556 million referred to above (Waldie, Peretz and Smith, 2012). This was the second raid at SNC in six months. Most of the countries involved (excluding Canada) have high levels of corruption so it is probably not surprising that companies get involved in unsavory business practices.

Not surprisingly, not only did SNC offer bribes to others to obtain contracts, apparently company executives solicited bribes from others (Reguly, 2012). A Tunisian businessman claimed he lost out on a contract because he refused to pay a bribe of $100,000. Furthermore, Ben Aissa took care of his family members as well. His sister was hired to design a massive Libyan prison and a company run by his mother sold computers to SNC's Tunisian subsidiary (McArthur et al., 2012). Riadh Ben Aissa, a Tunisian working for SNC and their point man in dealings in the Middle East was terminated in February 2012 for a possible role in fraud and bribery, and was arrested in Switzerland on April 27, 2012 for possible corruption, fraud, and money laundering. Ben Aissa had close ties with the Gaddafi family in Libya (Chung, 2012).

A $1.5 billion class action lawsuit was filed against SNC-Lavalin on May 9 alleging it violated securities laws by misrepresenting that it had controls and procedures that endured accurate disclosure and financial reporting (*Toronto Star*, 2012b). An earlier class action lawsuit filed by other investors was for $250 million. SNC's shares dropped by more than 20 percent at the end of February, a $1.5 billion drop in market value. Ben Aissa, currently in jail, was charged by Swiss authorities with fraud, money laundering, and corruption in November 2012 (McArthur, 2012). Pierre Duhaime, former President of SNC, has also been charged with fraud (Woods, 2012). With the addition of Duhaime it is hard to see this as the work of a single rogue executive. Indeed, with pressure from shareholders for immediate financial results, demands on organizations to show short-term profits rather than long-term sustainability have increased.

Companies have also been accused of greed in their treatment of foreign workers making their products abroad. In the past decade, Disney, Nike, Gap, and Apple have all come under scrutiny and criticism. Apple has recently asked an outside firm to examine working conditions in Foxconn, one of its overseas factories, in response to public outcry. The findings suggested that employees were required to work excessive hours (over 60 per week) and were underpaid. Apple has agreed to work with Foxconn (Gupta and Chan, 2012) to improve pay and working conditions. Foxconn has also agreed to lower the required work hours to 50 and to improve levels of pay as a result.

Apple is now the world's most valuable company. However, it also avoids paying billions in US taxes by using subsidiaries in low-tax countries such as Ireland, the Netherlands, and the British Virgin Islands, among others (*Toronto Star*, 2012c). This is not illegal but part of a world-wide strategy to cut its taxes by billions each year.

US Federal safety regulators have imposed a US$162.4 million fine against American Airlines for alleged safety violations over a several-year period (Koenig, 2012). American Airlines is currently under bankruptcy protection.

Jamie Dimon, CEO of JPMorgan, who for years has argued against greater regulation of the financial services sector and called CEOs of banks that failed "reckless," acknowledged a recent $2 billion trading error as "stupid" and "egregious" (Robertson, 2012); this figure has now grown to $9 billion. What is different in this case is that three senior executives resigned on May 11 in the wake of this example of excessive risk taking with more departures likely to follow. If any JPMorgan employee is found guilty of violating their rules and regulations it is possible that these employees could be asked to pay back some of their salaries. The FBI has begun an investigation into the losses at JPMorgan. Dimon, meanwhile, has referred to the loss as "a bump in the road," and although at the company's annual shareholder meeting, Dimon came under criticism, he was still able to retain both his CE and Board Chairman positions (Henry, 2012). Two class action lawsuits have been filed by shareholders against JPMorgan and Jamie Dimon for providing misleading information to clients about its control of risk. This incident is likely to strengthen calls for greater regulation of the financial sector. Moreover, US citizens' support for capitalism has dropped from 80 percent a decade ago to 60 percent today.

Barclays Bank, in the UK, was fined $453 million by British and US regulators for falsifying interest and borrowing rates between 2005 and 2009. The chairman of the bank's board of directors, Marcus Agius, CEO Bob Diamond, and COO Jerry del Missier, have all resigned as a result (*Toronto Star*, 2012d). Barclays was warned at least four months before it was fined that its culture was too aggressive (e.g., use of rate rigging, tax avoidance schemes). Under Diamond, Barclays became known as a hard-driving bank that paid large salaries and bonuses (Slater, 2012a). Diamond will still walk away with millions of dollars in pay. Other banks are also now being investigated. Paul Tucker, deputy governor of the Bank of England, in testimony before a UK parliamentary committee referred to Barclays as a "cesspit."

Both UBS and Barclays agreed to pay fines for their role in rigging Libor rates, with other banks likely to do the same (Heilprin, 2012). As fallout of the Libor scandal, UBS fired 18 of the 40 or so people involved in rigging Libor rates from 2006 to 2009, while others had voluntarily left the bank (Slater and Bart, 2013). Although some were paid huge salaries during this period, their careers have been blemished. In a more dramatic ending, Wegelin and Co., a 250-year-old Swiss bank closed following a guilty plea to helping US citizens avoid paying taxes through secret accounts. (Raymond, 2013).

The city of London has worked hard to become a major financial center in international banking over the past decade. It said it would apply a "light touch regulation" scheme in its' effort to entice more banks and banking investments. Recent events in the London banking community have done considerable damage to its reputation (e.g., Barclays, HSBC, Standard Chartered). Seven more banks were subpoenaed in New York and Connecticut on August 15 with regards to the manipulation of the Libor (McLaughlin, 2012). Banking regulations have thus become a joke and banking regulators a laughing stock. Is it now time for "hard touch regulations"?

Calls for stricter regulations increased following the 2008 economic meltdown. However, this sector has vigorously fought against tighter regulation, Dimon's being one of the louder voices. Regulations to date have had little effect, though. Thus traders seem to take huge risks that will make them a lot of money if they succeed, while they will be "bailed out" if they fail. Dimon offered a non-apology for mistakes and losses, and on the evening before Dimon was to testify before the US Senate he said that traders in their London office didn't understand the risks they were taking and were not properly monitored (Kopecki and Mattingly, 2012). Who was minding the store?

More recently, a US Federal Judge ordered JPMorgan to explain why it should not turn over e-mails in an investigation of potential energy market manipulations (Schoenberg, 2012). JPMorgan also agreed to pay a $100 million fine for improperly boosting credit card holder minimum payment fees (Stempel, 2012).

HSBC, one of the largest banks in the world, admitted to the US Senate that it had done a poor job in controlling the laundering of drug money over the previous decade (Slater, 2012b). HSBC had a branch in the tax haven Cayman Islands having 50,000 accounts, $2.1 billion in assets, and no staff. HSBC also removed information about countries that were not allowed to bring money into the US. US regulators were also found to be lax. David Bagley, head of the bank's compliance group, apologized and resigned, and HSBC's CEO called their operation in Mexico "shameful." HSBC will have to pay a fine, reported to be in excess of $2 billion (Colchester and Munoz, 2012).

Standard Chartered PLC was accused of violating US money-laundering laws in its dealings with Iranian banks (Finch, 2012). US regulations made such transactions illegal. Standard Chartered handled US$250 billion in dealings with Iranian banks over a seven year period and earned hundreds of millions of dollars in fees. Standard Chartered attempted to hide these transactions.

> *Modern international bankers form a class of thieves the likes of which the world has never seen before.*
>
> – Robert Scheer, *The Nation*

This spate of banking scandals seems to support the following conclusions.

- Massive bailouts provided to banks at citizen expense were accompanied by bank executives taking home large bonuses.
- Outright fraud occurred in several cases.
- Many of the banking losses resulted from excessive bank recklessness.
- Banking executives came across as greedy and arrogant.
- Incompetence of senior banking executives seems to have pushed Greece and Spain into near bankruptcy.
- Banking executives say they are sorry, they apologize, and claim to have learned their lessons, and government bureaucrats say that regulations will be tightened-until the next scandal occurs.
- In 2008, the phrase was "too big to fail"; in 2012, the phrase seems to be "too complex to understand."
- In 2012, HSBC was fined US$1.9 billion for lax monitoring of money laundering. Critics wondered why this bank did not face criminal charges. Some suspected that if HSBC fell it would seriously damage worldwide financial markets. HSBC was "too big to jail."
- We can now add this to "too big to regulate," "too big to run," and "too big to behave."

Given this sample of bad behavior, it seems safe to conclude, as Edwards (2010) and Sinclair (2011) do, that business won't save the world. If business can't even fix itself, why should we believe it can fix the world?

Corruption Knows No Country Boundaries or Political System

Corruption exists in countries that were formerly Communist (e.g., Russia, North Korea) and formerly socialist (China, Cuba). Kane (2012) reported that Cuba recently convicted 12 individuals for corruption.

Sadly Things Do Not Seem To Be Getting Any Better

In spite of the number of financial scandals over the past decade, there is little evidence of change. A recent survey (June 2012) of 500 financial service managers and professionals in the US and the UK undertaken by law firm Labaton Sucharow reported the following (Labaton Sucharow, 2012):

- 39 percent reported that their competitors were likely to have engaged in unethical or illegal activity in order to be successful;
- 24 percent believed that financial services managers and professions may need to engage in unethical or illegal activity to be successful;

- 26 percent indicated that they had seen or had firsthand knowledge of wrong doing in their firms;
- 16 percent said they would commit a crime – insider trading – if they could get away with it;
- 30 percent reported that their compensation and bonus plans created pressure to compromise ethical standards or break the law;
- 22 percent reported other pressures that lead to unethical or illegal activity;
- 22 percent of females and 12 percent of males indicated that they would face retaliation if they reported wrongdoing in their firms – if they became whistleblowers;
- 39 percent felt current SEC legislation deterred wrong doing.

The report expressed surprise in the extent of potential unethical or illegal activity in this sector given recent events, i.e., the lack of ethical integrity in the financial service industry. In addition, 20 percent of respondents were uncertain and/or skeptical about how their firm would handle allegations of wrongdoing (Henry 2012).

At the Trough

A seemingly endless list of men and women abusing their office –elected officials, government bureaucrats, and private sector executives – seems to have developed. Consider the following:

- Yamani (2011) reports that Prince Sultan's fortune was estimated to be $270 million at his death, which he distributed to his sons. The ratio of "Royals" to commoners in Saudi Arabia is 1 to 1,000, compared to 1 in 5,000,000 in the UK. So managing privileges, money, and jobs is a challenge for the royal family. Royal perks include life-time jobs in senior positions in the civil service, and allowing princes to award contracts and receive commissions on top of their salaries.
- Talaga (2012) identifies a number of individuals who seemed to be "at the trough" at ORNGE, a unit of the Ministry of Health in Ontario. These included the CEO Chris Mazza, his girlfriend Kelly Long, other senior executives, the members of the board of directors, the daughter of the board chairman, Anne Brunet, and several lawyers and consultants.

In contrast, François Hollande, newly elected president of France, introduced some new rules for his cabinet: taking the train instead of flying for trips of three hours or less, refusing gifts and holidays that are valued over $190, and declaring financial conflicts of interest (*National Post*, 2012b).

Are Karl Marx and Chairman Mao Rolling Over in Their Graves?

Russia now has 96 billionaires. These individuals control $373 billion, representing 20 percent of Russian's GDP. Sixty-nine percent of these billionaires live in Moscow. Eighty percent of this Russian billionaire wealth, however, comes from non-productive industries such as real estate and oil, raising questions about the future of the Russian economy.

Vladimir Putin declared an income of $113,000 in 2011 and listed three old domestic cars and a car hitch passed down by his father (*National Post*, 2012d). He also owns 11 watches valued at $687,000 retail, has access to, $1 billion in aircraft – one with a $75,000 toilet – four yachts – one with a spa pool, waterfall and wine cellar – and two dozen official residences. Yet over 20 million people in Russia live in poverty.

A Chinese research group reported that China had 1.02 million millionaires in 2011 up 6.3 percent from 2010. The report also indicated that there may be an additional 2 million millionaires that are still "unknown" (*National Post*, 2012c).

The Salaries of CEOs: The Armageddon of Greed

Poor men wanna be rich, rich men wanna be king.
And a king ain't satisfied till he rules everything.

– Bruce Springsteen

Although the world-wide economic recession has had major effects on employment, job prospects, and wages, CEOs still are raking it in. Canadian comparisons of the top 100 CEOs' salaries compared with the average Canadian's salary increased from 85 times as much in 1995, to 104 times as much in 1998, to 174 times as much in 2008. During this period, the average Canadian lost 6 percent when inflation was factored in while CEOs' salaries outpaced inflation by 70 percent.

The Canadian experience is not unique. Stephen Hester, CEO of the UK bank, Royal Bank of Scotland, admitted that even his parents believed that he was paid too much. It is not surprising then that governments in several countries (France, UK, US) want either to limit CEO pay and pay increases, or increase taxes on those earning very high salaries.

Ford gave CEO Alan Mulaly US$58.3 million in stock as a reward for turning around its fortunes (Naughton, 2012). Bob Dudley, CEO of BP PLC topped his pay in 2011 over 2010 receiving US$ 6.8 million in 2011 and US$1.74 million in 2010. Dudley took over as CEO of BP after the Gulf of Mexico oil spill (*Globe and Mail*, 2012d). Forbes listed a record 1,226 billionaires from 58 countries in 2011 compared to 1,210 in 2010. Bill Gates, Paul Allen, and Warren Buffett made more money in one year than the 30 poorest countries, a quarter of the world's population combined.

Interestingly, corporate boards of directors having more highly-paid CEOs as members awarded higher levels of salary and salary increases to their organization's CEOs. Furthermore, corporate directors with financial expertise tended to exert considerable influence in board deliberations but not necessarily in the interest of shareholders (Guner, Malmendier and Tate, 2008). Hastings (2011) bashes bankers, stating they had learned nothing from the financial meltdown of 2008. Instead they are fighting changes to make them accountable. Banks are still paying exorbitant salaries to executives, and no one has gone to jail.

Paying excessive salaries can sometimes lead to an organization's collapse (Smith and Jones, 2012). Dewey and LeBoeuf filed for bankruptcy protection on May 28, 2012, having paid extravagant salaries to lure partners from other firms, even guaranteeing a number of millions to lawyers over several years. They also used huge salaries to keep lawyers from joining other firms. This practice left little money for lower ranked partners and staff. The salaries of some partners might, however, be clawed-back by creditors.

The Wages of Sin May Be More Wages

Former News International CEO, Rebekah Brooks, resigned early in 2011 as a result of the phone hacking scandal, forcing the *News of the World* to fold. She was also arrested by police with regard to the hacking but has not yet been charged. It was reported that Rupert Murdoch paid her $2.7 million, gave her the use of an office, and the use of a limousine and driver for two years (Sabbagh, 2011). Brooks also received a US$ 11 million "payoff" in October, 2012, following her departure. Clive Goodman, former *News of the World* editor, who was jailed for his involvement in "Hackgate," also received a "hefty" severance payment after he launched an unfair dismissal claim. George Entwhistle, Director General of the BBC, left the BBC because of the child abuse scandal after serving less than three months and received a severance package of $720,000 (Chu, 2012).

Jerry del Missier, a Canadian working for Barclays, resigned as a result of the Libor rate-rigging scandal. He left Barclays with a payout of US$14.2 million (Slater and Vellacott, 2012). Shareholders and politicians were outraged, stating it was a reward for failure.

A small consulting niche has emerged to assist white collar criminals in making the transition from life on the outside to life in prison. Former criminals provide coaching assistance on the dos and don'ts of prison life. Nick Leeson, since released after serving four years in a Singapore prison for his rogue trading of $1.3 billion that caused the collapse of Barings Bank, is on the lecture circuit, telling what he learned from this incident (wished he had someone to talk to when the losses were small) and why it could happen (not enough financial controls, overly complex financial instruments that many people did not understand). Leeson charges $12,000 to $20,000 per speech.

There has also been an upsurge in individuals and firms providing services in forensic accounting, the detection of fraud, and the undertaking of efforts to recover stolen monies. Cinar is one company trying to find company money, after the termination of its co-CEOs (Ronald Weinberg and Micheline Charest, since deceased, husband and wife), claiming they sent $11 million to Barrington Bank International in the Bahamas and US$1.7 million to a bank in the Turks and Caicos, both tax havens beyond the reach of Canadian laws (Livesay, 2011).

Ryan (2009) chronicles the activities of Martin Kenney, a Canadian living in the Caribbean, whose firm pursues fraud artists. Kenney moved to the Caribbean because that is where much of the fraudulently-obtained money ends up.

While most people are not averse to individuals earning high salaries, it is the way in which these salaries are made and how they are displayed that give cause of concern. Steve Jobs made a lot of money as did Bernie Madoff. Job's income was honestly earned while Madoff's was theft. Jobs pursued a modest lifestyle while Madoff pursued a lavish lifestyle.

Another group reaping financial benefits from greed, alleged crime, and corruption is lawyers and advisers (Gray, 2013). In a four year trail involving Nortel Networks' bankruptcy, pensioners and former disabled employees had their benefits cut while Nortel paid $630 million in fees to lawyers, accountants, bankers, and advisers.

The Wages of Sin May Be Jail Time

Bernie Madoff was sentenced to 150 years in jail. More recently, Allen Stanford was convicted on March 1, 2012 of running a US$7 billion Ponzi scheme and is possibly facing a 20-year prison term. Canadian Garth Drabinsky is currently in jail for his role in the Livent fraud. Jeff Skilling and Dennis Kozlowski were also found guilty of fraud and are serving jail time.

Prosecutors in the US plan to charge and arrest individual traders in the UK involved in manipulating global benchmark interest rates (Libor – the London Interbank Offered Rate); there was also the possibility some banks would be fined (*Toronto Star*, 2012e).

The Wages of Failure May Be More Wages

The fired CEOs of Home Depot, Merrill Lynch, Pfizer, and Citigroup walked away with severance of $40 million to $200 million. All of them had failed. The top 1 percent of income earners also include the incompetent executives who led Enron, Nortel, BP, and those who contributed to the Wall Street meltdown in 2008.

BC Hydro executives pocketed hundreds of thousands in bonuses based on profits that the provincial auditor said never existed (*National Post*, 2011a). Performance bonuses were based on the utility turning a profit, but evidence showed that BC Hydro actually lost money. Through accounting chicanery, however, hundreds of millions of dollars in expenses were deferred. Yet in 2009–10, five executives took home over $500,000 in bonuses tied to financial performance though the utility lost $249 million that year.

Not to be outdone, Toronto Hydro executives earned incentive bonuses totaling $2.9 million over the past five years, despite the company's failure to meet reliability standards set by the Ontario Energy Board (Spears, 2012). Meeting these standards should be considered part of their jobs instead of an arena for bonuses.

Milstead (2012) examined the pay awarded to executives of Canada's five major banks and concluded that average performance received outstanding pay. Banks justified these pay levels in terms of retention, motivation, aligning executive pay with shareholders goals and expectations, and discouraging excessive risk-taking by executives. We have heard this all before.

Companies such as these use human resource consulting firms that specialize in compensation (e.g., Mercer). Talk about a conflict of interest. Would you employ a compensation consulting firm that proposed lowering pay, smaller bonuses, and tighter criteria for the receipt of bonuses?

The Wages of Sin May Involve Returning the Money

Raj Rajaratnam was ordered to pay a US$92.8 million civil penalty in addition to serving a jail sentence (Bray, 2011). He also had to pay $53.8 million in criminal forfeiture. But don't feel sorry for Raj, apparently his net worth is several times greater than these financial penalties.

In addition, executives at several financial services institutions, who historically have received large bonuses, may have to give some back. Lloyd's Banking Group PLC plans to take back parts of bonuses paid to present and past executives, with more than $1.57 million potentially being clawed back (*Globe and Mail*, 2012e). The Royal Bank of Scotland (RBS) reduced the bonuses of CEO Stephen Hester by half the amount he received in 2010. The bonus was still over $1.5 million, and was received in addition to his salary of $11.5 million. Meanwhile, RBS announced plans to cut more than 4,000 jobs and to close large parts of its investment banking business. The Bank's stock price fell 48 percent in 2011.

Finally, Sir Fred Goodwin is now merely Fred Goodwin (Winnett and Mason, 2012). Goodwin, the former Royal Bank of Scotland CEO, lost his knighthood for his role in the Bank of Scotland's collapse, which resulted in a $71 billion UK government bailout. Dubbed "Fred the shred" for his cost cutting methods at RBS, he has been criticized for his role in the near collapse of RBS.

The Wages of Sin May Be Death or Disappearance

In a two-week period, two US executives either tried to commit suicide or attempted to fake a suicide and then disappear. In the first case, Russell Wasendorf, CEO of Peregrine, tried to commit suicide by attaching a hose to his exhaust pipe, though he was unsuccessful, ending up in a coma in a hospital in Iowa. Wasendorf was accused of misappropriating more than $100 million (Lessing and Ustinova, 2012). Wasendorf had a $100,000 personal wine collection that he stored at a restaurant he owned called MyVerona, a jet worth between $7 to $10 million, a condominium in downtown Chicago, and a home in Cedar Falls, Iowa worth over $1 million. The second case, Aubrey Lee Price, a US bank director, wrote a rambling confession to financial regulators then suggested he was going to commit suicide (Brumback, 2012). In his case, $17 million was missing. Price acknowledged fraud and bought a one-way ferry ticket from Florida along with some weights. Price also owned property in Venezuela and a boat large enough to reach there.

Fraud without Guilt

The Ontario Securities Commission (OSC) has changed the rules making it possible for those charged with fraudulent activities to pay a fine without acknowledging guilt or wrongdoing (Gray, 2011). This saves money in preventing lengthy and costly trials. The US SEC has been doing this for some time, recovering hundreds of millions of dollars in the process. Organizations paying these fines do not admit wrongdoing. Some North American and UK examples include the following.

Goldman Sachs	$550 million
Barclays	$450 million
State Street	$300 million
Citigroup	$285 million
JPMorgan	$210 million
Bank of America	$150 million
Charles Schwab	$118 million
RBC	$30.4 million
TD Ameritrade	$10 million

The OSC only offers this option to first-time offenders and to those who cooperate. Organizations using this option avoid acknowledging guilt, thus preventing future lawsuits against them by shareholders and investors. This process also addresses the volume of securities investigation and their backlog. Unfortunately the public often sees this option as both confusing and hypocritical. There is still a public stigma attached to organizations involved

Citigroup paid a fine of $590 million in late August 2012 to settle legal claims by shareholders that it mislead them about financial problems before the financial crisis. The bank denied the allegations but said it settled to avoid a lengthy and costly court case (*Toronto Star*, 2012f).

The Wages of Sin May Be Difficulty in Finding Another Job

Chris Mazza, fired CEO of ORNGE discussed above, may also find it difficult to find another job. Recent allegations (Donovan, 2012a) indicated that the daughter of ORNGE's chairman of the board and Mazza's girlfriend (Carrie Anne Brunet and Kelly Long) did very little work on a $6.7 million project for a client, the money going to ORNGE. This client had earlier bought helicopters from ORNGE, raising the specter of this being a kickback given the small amount of work done on the project. Both Brunet and Long were supported by Mazza and ORNGE to undertake an executive MBA at a cost to ORNGE of almost $200,000.

Have All Societies Become Cheating Societies?

Individuals cheat so they can have an advantage. These ill-gotten advantages may in the short run make the individual feel superior and in the long-run lead to greater success that ultimately will increase fame and fortune (Callahan, 2006, 2004). In the past few years, for example, scandals have arisen involving the use of banned substances in many major sports (e.g., cycling, baseball). Baseball players take banned substances so they can land jobs in the major leagues, perform better, and play longer all of which means they can make more money. So many baseball players have now admitted taking steroids in the 1990s that it was dubbed the "steroid era" in baseball. Unfortunately some players taking steroids (Barry Bonds, Sammy Sosa, Mark McGuire, Roger Clemons) set baseball records (career home runs, single season home runs) and all four mentioned were likely to be elected to the baseball Hall of Fame before news of their "cheating" was revealed. Alex Rodriguez, on track to becoming the lifetime career home run hitter, admitted in early 2009 to taking steroids. When asked if he cheated, Rodriguez ducked the question saying it was for others to decide. Marion Jones admitted to the illegal use of banned substances after winning five medals at the Sydney Olympics, medals she parlayed into financial success on the speaker circuit. Winners of the Tour de France can parlay their victory into lucrative product endorsements. Teenaged boys take steroids so they can better compete with their peers in athletics and garner university scholarships. Two Pakistani cricketers were found guilty (November 1, 2001) of fixing a cricket match and of accepting money as part of a betting scandal (Condie, 2011). Both were sentenced to jail time. A third Pakistani cricketer had already pled guilty to these charges and received a jail sentence.

Cheating thus appears to be widespread as individuals strive for any advantage they can turn to short- or long-term benefits, in some cases financial. Cheating may be seen as critical to success in a winner-takes-all society (Frank and Cook, 1995). In a survey of 2,500 traders undertaken in 2007, more than half indicated that they would take advantage of an illegal tip if they were certain they would not get caught.

Unfortunately, there seems to be a movement to not punish cheating. The largest school board in one Canadian Province, Newfoundland and Labrador, has established a policy that requires teachers to let students caught cheating get a second try with no academic penalty (Boesveld, 2011). The teachers' association believes this policy enables students to cheat.

Win at All Costs: The Ends Justify the Means

The following three stories appeared in Toronto newspapers on the same day – February 28, 2012.

Donovan (2012b) wrote about the head of aviation at ORNGE, Rich Potter, an Ontario government unit tasked with providing helicopter and air ambulance services to injured citizens, pretending to have an MBA degree to attract potential investors. ORNGE CEO Chris Mazza suggested he do so. Potter was terminated on March 7, 2012.

Lyall (2012), reporting findings of the Levesen inquiry in the UK, stated that large sums of money went to police officers as well as "corrupted individuals" in the military and the government.

Two of Canada's major political parties fired staff members for engaging in "dirty tricks" during the country's most recent national election (Woods and MacCharles, 2012). The Conservatives fired a person for initiating "robo-calls" to individuals likely to vote for another party telling them that their polling station had been moved and sending them to another address which had no polling station. The Liberal party fired a staff member for posting leaks about the personal life, a messy divorce, of a Conservative candidate who at the time of the election served in the Conservative cabinet.

Economics, Business Education, and Greed

It is likely that the majority of those in the 1 percent earned their money in business, and likely studied economics and business in some form and at some time. Recent research has shown that studying economics and business is associated with more positive views on greed and more greedy behavior (Buckholz, 2012). Wang, Malhotra and Murnighan (2012), in three interrelated studies, reported that (1) economics majors and students taking more economics courses engaged in more greedy behavior in a laboratory task, (2) economics education was associated with more positive attitudes towards greed and toward one's own greedy behavior, and (3) that short statements about the benefits of self-interest – the hallmark of economics education – increased the acceptability of greed, even among non-economics students.

The assumptions and language of economics and business strategy have been examined by some (e.g., Ferraro, Pfeffer and Sutton, 2005; Ghoshal, 2005; Pfeffer, 2005; Bazerman and Malhotra, 2006; Rocha and Ghoshal, 2006). In this writing, the line between self-interest and greed is a blurry one; when does self-interest become greed? Balot (2001, p.1) defines greed as "an excessive desire to get more ... a primarily materialistic type of desire." However, what is excessive to one person may not be excessive to another. Economics and business strategy writing encourages self-interest, encourages rationality instead of emotions and empathy, and encourages competition between people since all others are equally self-interested. Wang, Malhotra and Murnighan (2012) address this by defining self-interest as individual behavior that increases one's personal well-being while greed is excessive self-interest that harms others.

Other research has shown that business students cheat more while in university than do students majoring in other areas of study (McCabe, Dukerich and Dutton, 1993a, 1993b). Davis (1997) found, in a longitudinal study of business students, that business students begin their programs at lower stages of moral development than do non-business students, and graduate with little change in their stage of development while non-business students increase their levels of moral development.

Gandal et al. (2005), in a review of five studies, reported that economics students attribute more importance to self-enhancement values and less importance to universalism values than do students in other fields of study. This pattern appears in their first year of study and persists throughout their education.

Social Class, Greed, and Unethical Behavior

A recent study (Piff et al., 2012) showed that richer people, individuals in the upper class, engaged in more unethical behaviors than did poorer people, individuals in the lower class. Behaviors included breaking the law while driving, taking valued goods from others, cheating to increase chances of winning a prize, believing that "greed is good," and endorsing unethical behaviors at work. This was attributed to more positive attitudes towards greed among wealthier people. In addition wealthier people have more freedom, resources, and independence from others that might contribute to more selfish behaviors. One might think that poorer people who have less would be more prone to unethical behaviors but this was not the case here. Other research has shown that poorer people give a larger amount of their money to charity than do wealthier people (Piff et al., 2010). Furthermore, it has been suggested that the greed of wealthy individuals contributed to the current economic crisis (Galperin, Bennett and Aquino, 2011).

The Younger Generation Is Even More Materialistic

If you think this picture painted thus far is depressing, the current Millennial generation seems to be even more greedy and materialistic. Twenge, Freeman and Campbell (2012) compared the traits of young people in high school and entering college today with those of baby boomers and Gen Xers at the same age from 1966 to 2009. Their data showed increases in the value of money, image, and fame rather than inherent principles such as self-acceptance, affiliation, and community. Being well-off financially was ranked eighth in 1971 but has been ranked first since 1989. Twenge and her colleagues refer to the Millennials as "Generation Me" rather than "Generation We." Young people today put their own needs first and focus on feeling good about themselves (Twenge et al., 2010: Twenge and Campbell, 2009; Twenge, 2006). Interest in the environment, political participation, trust in government, and concern for others has waned as well.

Money and Materialism as Factors in Relationships and Relationship Distress

Berger and Newman (2012), in an edited collection, examined the role played by money in individual psychological distress and relationship difficulties from a psychoanalytic perspective. Money was rarely talked about by patients or analysts, being still a taboo subject, but the economic downturn of 2008 increased money concerns among both patients and therapists.

Carroll et al. (2011), in a study of couples, found that high materialism (placing a high value on money and the accumulation of possessions) in both partners was associated with less responsiveness to the other partner, less emotional maturity, poor communication, and higher levels of conflict. Love of money, in one or both partners, was associated with less relationship satisfaction and less relationship stability. Individuals scoring high on materialism spent more money than they had, thus creating debt and financial stress.

Materialism has also been found to affect a country's birth rate. At a macro level, people living in Singapore are more materialist, and less satisfied with their lives than people living in the US and have a lower desire for children as a result (Li et al., 2011). Children cost money!

Another "Dark Side" of Materialism

While some individuals are actually rich, others pretend that they are. The latter do so by buying counterfeit goods on the black market carrying famous brand names such as Louis Vuitton, Nike, Chanel, Gucci, Versace, Armani, Rolex and Prada (Phillips, 2005). The buying of fake goods harms legitimate businesses (Nunes and Mulani, 2008). Moreover, almost all of these fake goods are made in developing countries in order to keep the costs low so those pretending they are rich can afford them. This results in not only low wages for workers in these countries, but sometimes unsafe workplaces. The recent fire in a garment factory in Bangladesh in which over 100 workers burned to death as the factory had no fire escapes and doors were locked is just one example. Hundreds of workers have died in Bangladesh over the past decade (Onstad, 2012). Swatuk (2012) tells about passing a garment factory in Dhaka stating that it had ISO14001 approval. The building soon collapsed killing several hundred workers, many children. He asked how the building obtained ISO14001 approval initially. He was told the owners paid for the banner. This is still another example of the "dark side" of wanting more.

The 1 Percent

Taibbi (2012) noted that the Bank of America has not paid taxes for the past two years, claiming a pre-tax loss of US$5.4 billion in 2010. It still paid hundreds of millions in 2010 in executive bonuses and compensation, however.

The *National Post* (2011b) reported that the average annual compensation paid to directors of publicly traded companies in Canada rose by over a third over a two year period (between 2008 and 2010) to $112,651. Directors said they spend an average of 128 hours a year on board business. Flavelle (2011) framed it as a 400 percent increase in the pay board directors saw in the past decade while company revenues increased by only 33 percent.

Interestingly, while the pay of board directors has increased, their contribution to organizational performance and the presence of company financial fraud has not been stellar. Several scandals in the past decade illustrate what happens when boards and their directors themselves behave badly. Widely publicized examples include: Enron, Worldcom, Nortel Networks, Hewlett-Packard, Adelphia, Research in Motion, Parmalat, Satyan, Tyco, and Olympus. Modest changes in the role and behavior of individuals serving on corporate boards of directors have occurred recently. Directors today are less passive and more likely to give voice to discussions of company objectives, processes, and performance. Directors now operate more independently of management.

In Canada, the top 100 CEOs were paid an average of $8.4 million in 2010, a 27 percent increase over 2009 (Flavelle, 2012). Meanwhile, the average Canadian earned $44,366 in 2010, an 11 percent increase over 2009. The top 100 earned 189 times the average Canadian's salary in 2010. Rexrode and Cardon (2012) note, also, that the typical American worker would have to work 244 years to earn what the typical CEO earns in one year.

Besides huge salaries, executives also have access to a wide range of expensive perks. It is difficult out find out what these are in the private sector but becoming easier in the public sector. Howlett and Mills (2012) and Ogilvie and Stone (2012) report some of the perks received by senior executives in Ontario's major hospitals, though hospitals in Ontario rushed to reduce executive perks in response to having to post these contracts on line. These included: memberships in private clubs, free parking privileges, car allowances, an allowance for plastic surgery and for a weight loss program for a female executive, six weeks of paid vacations, generous severance packages paying more than $1 million, luxury car leases, and annual $100,000 pension top ups. Some also received $50,000 bonuses for their job performance. Hospitals indicated that they had to offer these in order to be competitive.

The 99 percent aren't going to take it anymore. Wall Street protests grew in number and the occupy movement has spread to over 1,000 cities worldwide, protesting against corporate greed. One percent of the US population controls 40 percent of the wealth. Meanwhile youth unemployment grows worldwide. The current economic recession has brought about a dramatic increase in the levels of youth unemployment (International Labour Office, 2012). Youth unemployment in Spain and Greece is over 40 percent and almost 30 percent in Ireland, Italy, and Portugal. Being unemployed in one's youth also has a large negative effect of one's lifetime earnings.

Capitalism, nearly imploded in 2008, until banks and the financial sector received a massive financial bailout by and at the expense of taxpayers. Yet banks and investment houses continued to give out extravagant bonuses following the bailout. The public has also become skeptical about the investment advising business and the stress placed on increasing shareholder value by organizations (Edesess, 2007; Stout, 2012; Johnson, 2007; Hartmann, 2007; Korten, 2011).

Anna Hazare's Indian anti-corruption movement, which he started by going on a hunger strike, appears to be alive and well several months later (Glekin, 2011). His grass roots movement caused the Indian government to jail some people and to create an independent anti-corruption ombudsman. Hazare believes, as do the majority of Indians, that payoffs, patronage, and theft are commonplace in their country. Unlike the Occupy Wall Street movement, Hazare has very specific objectives: fire those caught in wrongdoing, change laws previously bought by special interests, and make government records public.

Kay (2012) cogently argues that income inequality is a major threat to capitalism. A consumer-oriented mass market economy cannot function with people at the two income extremes. Poor people do not buy very much, and the very rich spend only a small fraction of their income on goods. Yet few people see inequality as a threat to capitalism. In fact most Americans underestimate the gap between the 1 percent and the 99 percent. This seems to be changing, though as more Americans are becoming concerned about the size of the income gap between the rich and poor, and an increasing number of Americans want America to be a more equal country (Hartmann, 2007).

An increasing trend towards allowing shareholders to vote on CEO pay levels has arisen, though this vote is not binding, only informative. Some countries have made such voting mandatory. While negative voting has been increasing only slowly, it catches the attention of corporate boards of directors and seems to be having some effect (Cauchi and Guevarra, 2012). Indeed, protests made by shareholders against excessive levels of executive pay resulted in three CEOs resigning in early 2012 (Andrew Moss of Aviva, and the CEOs of both AstraZeneca and Trinity Mirror). In addition CEO pay levels at other organizations (e.g., Barclays, Citigroup, Credit Suisse) were voted down.

Even some insiders are rebelling. Shareholders vetoed a board of directors plan to give retiring CEO Ian Greenberg a $25 million thank you for building his company, Astral (Ladurantaye, 2012). In addition, Apple CEO, Tim Cook, gave up $75 million in stock dividends, though he still earned $375 million in 2011.

Adam Smith Made a Mistake: For Several, Selfishness Knows No Bounds

Adam Smith, in his *The Wealth of Nations*, proposed that the motivational force for progress and growth was "selfishness" – the desire to make more money benefited everyone because this extra money produced more jobs and sales. He believed that, in general, honest people able to freely pursue their own interests would fare better than they would if someone dictated what they should do. Individuals pursuing their own interests would reduce inefficiencies and allocate resources where they would most benefit the larger society. Some interpreted his work to suggest that greed was good and that unlimited greed was even better (see Lanchester, 2012; Coates, 2012). But Smith also thought that such "selfishness" was self-regulating, or at least had some limits. Smith's second book, *The Theory of Moral Sentiments*, is less well-known, but in it he stated that individuals would also be interested in the well-being of others.

Money and Meanness

Being poor is like being a child. Being rich is like being an adult: you get to do whatever you want. Everyone is nice when they have to be; rich people are nice when they feel like it.

– Fran Leibowitz, American author

Over the past decade, emerging research findings have suggested a link between money and meanness, referred to as a money-empathy gap (see Miller, 2012, for a review). Miller reports research results showing that rich people are "meaner" and more likely to behave in less humane ways. She cites the work of Piff and his colleagues (Piff et al., 2012), indicating that people in higher social classes (having more money) are more likely to condone and engage in unethical behavior. Other research has indicated that rich people put their own interests before the interests of others, are more likely to dehumanize people, are more selfish and less compassionate (Piff et al., 2010). Vohs, Mead and Goode (2006, 2008) have found that merely thinking about money made people less interested in others. It seems that having money affects one's view of the world and the people in it. Other people are seen as allies or obstacles to one's own aspirations. Rich people tend to attribute an individual's success to abilities and efforts of the individual and individual failures to limitations or weaknesses of an individual; poorer people tend to attribute individual successes and failures more to outside uncontrollable events and unequal circumstances.

Interestingly Judge, Livingston and Hurst (2012) found that individuals rated as more disagreeable were also earning higher incomes.

Money: A Versatile Currency

Money doesn't mind if we say it's evil, it goes from strength to strength. It's a fiction, an addiction, and tacit conspiracy.

– Martin Amis, British novelist

Why would anyone need or want money? There are a lot of needs that money meets (Kets de Vries, 2007). At the most basic level, money is necessary for survival in that it provides food, water, clothing, and shelter. Money provides for one's family and their well-being. In addition, money allows one to participate in activities that provide pleasure such as eating in restaurants, going to movies and concerts, buying books for personal enjoyment and learning, going on vacations for rest, relaxation, new experiences, learning, and adventure. Money can serve as a reward for investing in education, for outstanding performance, and as a benchmark that permits comparisons with others. Money can be used to help others by giving to those in need. Money can serve as a vehicle for bolstering one's self-esteem; to the degree that an individual is conspicuous about his or her money, others will look up to this person as a person of some status and worth, and in turn the person can value themselves. Kets de Vries (2007) suggests three motives for money:

1. Fuck you money – I am now not beholden to anybody, I am invincible;
2. In your face money – flaunting wealth, oneupmanship;
3. Keeping score money – looking at the Forbes richest people list to see if I am on it.

What Do We Know About Money?

Money never made a man happy yet, nor will it. The more a man has, the more he wants. Instead of filling a vacuum, it makes one.

– Benjamin Franklin, American statesman 1706–90

Research findings support the following conclusions:

- There is a positive relationship between income and subjective well-being assessed by various indicators (Diener, 1984) but in North America they correlate only about .15 (Diener et al., 1993).
- Materialism is negatively correlated with life satisfaction, subjective well-being, and general affect (Belk, 1985; Richins and Dawson, 1992; Solberg, Diener and Robinson, 2004).
- Pursuing the American Dream of financial success (extrinsic goals, having instead of being, seeking the approval and respect of others) distracts people from achieving life satisfaction (Nickerson et al., 2002).
- Some individuals adapt better than others to higher incomes. Motives for money (Srivastava, Locke and Bartol, 2001), the meaning of money (Barber and Bretz, 2000), and love of money (Tang, 2007) have been shown to influence the money and well-being relationship. Tang proposed and found, for example, that income leads to lower quality of life for people obsessed with money but had no relationship with quality of life for all others.
- More materialistic people are less happy (Solberg, Diener and Robinson, 2004).
- Motives for money matter (Srivastava, Locke and Bartol, 2001). If people value money to achieve power, show off, overcome self-doubts, or to look better when compared to others (negative motives for money), money will be associated with lower levels of well-being. For these people, the more money they have the more money they want (Kets de Vries, 2007).
- Money has less importance as individuals rise in the organizational hierarchy. Higher incomes are associated with a lower marginal utility of money.
- As nations get richer, increases in wealth are associated with smaller increases in well-being.
- Within countries, increased income is associated with higher levels of well-being mainly among the poor. Increased incomes are not associated with increased well-being among those above the poverty level (Diener and Oishi, 2000; Csikszentmihalyi, 1999).
- Importance of money was associated with lower levels of life satisfaction among college students from 41 countries (Diener and Oishi, 2000).
- Achieving high incomes is associated with higher levels of work stress and work–family conflict. Spending more time at work may lead to higher incomes but reduce time available for other meaningful and satisfying activities (e.g., leisure, family, socializing, self-development). Realizing the American Dream of financial success may have a dark side (Nickerson et al., 2003).
- Money has become more important to individuals in North America, and likely in many other countries, over the past 50 years. More students say they go to university to earn more money, pay has become more a more important, job characteristic,

lack of money has become the biggest source of dissatisfaction among university students, and organizations increasingly use money to attract, retain and motivate employees.

- Pay dissatisfaction is associated with counter-productive work behaviors (turnover, theft).
- Tang (2007) has developed and shown correlates of a "love of money" scale. This scale measures wanting to be rich (affective), seeing money as important and a sign of success (cognitive), and spending money carefully (behavioral). Tang reported the following findings. Love of money is negatively related to pay satisfaction. Men have a higher love of money than do women. Love of money is positively related to unethical behaviors in the workplace.
- With increasing economic growth and prosperity, more people are pursuing the "good life" through consumption. But this pursuit may have a "dark side." There is a negative correlation between materialism and subjective well-being, self-esteem, self-actualization, and meaning in life, and a positive correlation with impulsive buying and neuroticism. Money can come to possess the person instead of the person possessing the money. It takes more than money to feel rich, to be satisfied with one's life.
- Materialists put possessions and their acquisition at the center of their lives (centrality), see possessions as important for their satisfaction (happiness), and judge their own and others' success in terms of the quality and quality of their possessions (success). Materialists see themselves as the sum of their possessions.
- People who strongly desire wealth and money are less happy than those who do not. Thus, avoiding poverty, living in a rich country and emphasizing goals other than wealth are associated with higher levels of happiness.

Materialism

Net worth is not the same as self-worth.

– Rick Warren

Sirgy (1998) proposed a theory of materialism and overall life satisfaction. Life satisfaction is partly determined by one's satisfaction with one's standard of living. Satisfaction with one's standard of living is determined by one's actual standard of living compared to a set goal. Materialists place high value on material possessions, wealth and income. Materialists experience a greater dissatisfaction with their standard of living than do non-materialists, which in turn, lowers their satisfaction with life. Materialists experience greater dissatisfaction with their standard of living because their standard of living goals are unrealistically high. These goals are influenced by perceptions of wealth, income, and material possessions of others having more (upward social comparisons). Materialists also compare their own standard of living with others based on income and work effort and conclude that others have more income and work no harder than they do. Theses comparisons lead to feelings of unfairness, envy, and anger. Materialists may also spend more money than they earn, with debt ensuing as a result. There has been a steady increase in materialism displayed in magazine advertising over the past 80 years (Belk and Pollay, 1985).

I shop, therefore I am.
Spend it like Beckham.

– Satyajit Das

Richins and Dawson (1992) defined materialism as

> *a value that guides people's choices and conduct in a variety of situations including, but not limited to, consumption arenas. With respect to consumption, materialism will influence the type and quantity of goods purchased. Beyond consumption, materialism will influence the allocation of a variety of resources, including time. A materialist, for instance, might choose to work longer hours and earn more money instead of using that time for leisure activities. (p. 307)*

Richins and Dawson (1992) developed a measure of materialism having three components: acquisition centrality, acquisition as the pursuit of happiness, and possessions-defined success. High scores desired a higher level of income, placed greater emphasis on financial security and less on interpersonal relationships, preferred to spend more on themselves and less on others, engaged in fewer voluntary, simplicity behaviors, and were less satisfied with their lives.

Kasser (2002) reviewed the scientific evidence relating materialism and happiness. The pursuit of wealth not only does not lead to happiness, it actually makes many people unhappy, even when they are successful in achieving wealth. Kasser believes that materialism does not directly cause unhappiness but instead that both reinforce each other. Unhappy people are often the most materialistic. He argues that insecurity leads to materialism and that the pursuit of materialistic goals not only does not increase happiness but also diminishes close relationships, health, and the happiness of others in their close relationships.

Kasser makes an important distinction between extrinsic and intrinsic aspirations. Extrinsic aspirations include wealth, fame, and image; intrinsic aspirations include meaningful relationships, personal growth, and community contributions. Research has shown that having strong relative aspirations for extrinsic outcomes was associated with poorer mental health outcomes (Kasser, 2004). Having a stronger preference for intrinsic outcomes was associated with positive mental health. Self-reported attainment of intrinsic aspirations was associated with well-being; attainment of extrinsic aspirations was not.

Individuals high on materialism value possessions that are related to appearance and status than ones more instrumental in nature. Individuals low on materialism value possessions that have a symbolic interpersonal nature. High materialists are bound to be less satisfied with family and friends and have less fun and enjoyment as a consequence (Ryan et al., 1996). Belk (1985, 1984) views it as valuing material possessions and being envious of others who have a material object that you do not. These definitions downplay the spiritual dimensions of human existence (Richins and Dawson, 1992), the non-material (values such as character, friendship, and romantic love). Focusing on the material may even reduce the pleasure one might get from making money by diminishing the link between the material and the spiritual or non-material (Lane, 2000; Myers, 2000, 2003; Needleman, 1991, 1998).

Deckop, Jurkiewicz and Giacalone (2010) investigated the relationship of materialistic values and work-related personal well-being in a longitudinal study involving 274 employed men and women. They found that materialistic values were negatively associated with a number of indicators of quality of working life including affective organizational commitment, intrinsic and extrinsic reward satisfaction, job satisfaction, career satisfaction, and job burnout. In another workplace study involving 308 managers and professionals in the US, Giacalone, Jurkiewicz and Deckop (2008) found that materialistic values were associated with lower standards of ethics and lower social responsibility at work.

While materialism generally has negative connotations, not all aspects of materialism are bad. The desire for goods may cause employees to work harder or longer, increasing their incomes and standard of living, a strong motive to succeed and be self-sufficient. High levels of consumption by individuals can increase the profitability of organizations, leading them to invest more heavily in new technology and research and development, which in turn leads to higher levels of productivity and new products and ultimately to higher living standards.

Money by itself is not harmful; in fact it is beneficial in satisfying a variety of needs and values. Money is harmful if it is used to fill needs it cannot fill. Money cannot buy happiness, love, or character. Money cannot reduce self-doubt because a lack of money is not the cause of self-doubt or low self-esteem (Kets de Vries, 2007; Locke, McClearey and Knight, 1996).

Financial success was the core of the American Dream; people came to believe that money leads to happiness and success (Diener and Biswas-Diener, 2002). But some suggested a dark side to this dream; pursuing wealth comes to be seen as empty or shallow and limiting relationships with family, friends, community, and one's self-actualization (Fromm, 1976). Fromm made the distinction between "having" – a consumption orientation – and "being" – an experiential orientation to life. Money is an external incentive for behavior that is contingently given; this limits self-actualization, resulting in greater distress. Deci and Ryan (1991) reported also that personal strivings for power (desire to control, impress, or manipulate others) were associated with more negative affect and greater distress.

Can Money Buy Happiness?

All I want is the chance to prove that money can't make me happy.

– Spike Milligan

Money can't buy happiness but it allows you to choose your own misery.

– Unknown

The US movie actor W.C. Fields once said, "I've been rich and I've been poor and rich is better." And although rich people tend to be happier than poor people, the effects are small.

Steve Jobs knew what matters. In his recently published memoir, Steve Jobs stated that he was never consumed by his wealth (Isaacson, 2011). He had high quality products in his home and kept a few expensive cars, but his home was modestly furnished (Irish, 2011).

I watched people at Apple who made a lot of money and felt they had to live differently.

Some of them bought a Rolls Royce and various houses, each with a house manager and them someone to manage the house managers. Their wives got plastic surgery and turned into those bizarre people. This was not how I wanted to live. It's crazy, I made a promise to myself that I was not going to let money ruin my life. (Steve Jobs, quoted in Isaacson, 2011)

There is only a very small correlation, generally around .15 to .20, between income and satisfaction. Several hypotheses have been offered to explain this low relationship. These include the following: adaptation – we get used to the income very quickly; comparison – there is always someone richer than you are; alternatives – as one gets more money, other things (leisure, family) seem more valuable. There are other important sources of happiness than money – family, friends, leisure, and health. When one has money, one can worry about things other than money. There is, however, a strong relationship between income and happiness among those with lower incomes. For this group, money buys the things they need or want. For the middle class, the "expenditure cascade" by which people of this class try to emulate the very rich has actually impoverished their lives. For example, moving to the suburbs to get a bigger house may add to commuting congestion and longer commuting time. This also creates more pollution and elevated levels of stress. Furthermore, people compare the past with the present: the past was good; people expect the present to be even better, but it isn't. Their reality does not match what was promised. Higher levels of income did not buy them happiness. Some have argued (e.g., Murray, 2012) that increasing levels of financial improvements have been associated with a reduction in the social fabric.

Instead, people get satisfaction from relationships with family and friends, the love they give and receive, the meaning they get from work, service, hobbies, and religion. Happiness depends heavily on individual character – some people will always smile while others will always complain – and national culture – Swedes and Danes are happier than Americans who in turn are happier than the French, Germans, and Italians.

In summary, happiness is associated with focusing on goals individuals define for themselves rather than extrinsic goals such as money, image, and fame.

Becoming and Staying Happy

Money is human happiness in the abstract. He, then, who is no longer capable of enjoying human happiness in the concrete, devotes his heart entirely to money.

– Arthur Schopenhauer, German philosopher (1788–1860)

An interesting question becomes what makes people happy and can they maintain high levels of happiness. To add to our understanding of this, Sheldon and Lyubomirsky (2012) first surveyed 481 people about their happiness, then asked them six weeks later to identify a recent positive change in their lives that made them happy, and again asked them about their level of happiness six weeks later. For most individuals levels of happiness remained the same supporting their view that most people have a happiness set point from which they rarely deviate. Those reporting higher levels of happiness were still able to appreciate what they had experienced (the positive event) and have encountered new positive experiences. They concluded that becoming happy and remaining happy is achieved by wanting what you have and seeking new experiences (additional life-changing/enhancing experiences), and remaining appreciative of what one has and not wanting more too soon.

Motives for Money Matter

Both what you want and why you want it are important predictors of well-being (Carver and Baird, 1998; Kasser et al., 2004). Srivastava, Locke and Bartol (2001) considered whether people's reasons for making money affected their psychological well-being. First, they developed a scale to measure people's motives for making money, identifying ten such motives: security, family support, market worth, pride, leisure, freedom, satisfying impulses, charity, social comparisons, and overcoming self-doubt. In two other studies of employed professionals, managers and employed entrepreneurs, after controlling for gender and actual income, people who placed a higher importance on money, when compared to other goals such as a satisfying family life or doing work one enjoys, were more likely to report lower subjective well-being. Only individuals who valued money but had negative motives for making it (e.g., social comparison, overcoming self-doubt) reported lower well-being, however. This was not the case for those wanting to make money for positive reasons (e.g., supporting one's family). The association of materialistic values and reduced well-being have also been documented in two studies of business students (Kasser and Ahuvia, 2002; Vansteenkiste et al., 2006).

Time or Money?

Consider the famous Charles Dickens story, *A Christmas Carol.* Ebenezer Scrooge only becomes happy when he stops thinking about and counting his money following a visit by the Ghost of Christmas Past. He then enjoys a Christmas gathering with Bob Cratchit and his family – a social activity.

Your money or your life? It has been said that rich people have money and wealthy people have time. One can replace lost money but one cannot replace lost time. Time is finite. Time is money: time and money are the two major resources individuals have at their disposal. Mogliner (2010) reports findings on the effects of merely thinking about time or money. People continue to believe that money and happiness are related even though the evidence shows they are not. As incomes rose in North America, increases in working hours also occurred though levels of satisfaction or happiness remained the same. Interestingly, in Europe, as incomes rose working hours decreased while levels of satisfaction and happiness increased (Layard, 2005). Generally work in not seen as leading to happiness whereas spending time with others is. The pursuit of money results in a forfeit of time, interpersonal relationships, and health (Kets de Vries, 2007).

Time and money are probably the two most important resources people have. Most people desire happiness in life, and both money and time can contribute to happiness or subjective well-being. Yet money has been generally shown to have a weak relationship to happiness or subjective well-being.

There has been considerable research devoted to understanding the association of money and happiness but relatively little attention paid to the time and happiness association. Mogliner (2010) considered this relationship in three laboratory and field experiments. In her first study, respondents were primed to think about time, money, or neither. Respondents primed to think about time increased their time spent socializing and engaging in intimate social relationships (more happy activities), and spent less time working and commuting (less happy activities). Respondents primed to think about money indicated spending more time working and less time engaging in social and personal relationship activities. In her second experiment, a replication of the first but using a low income sample to see whether level of income would affect the results, yielded similar results to the first study. Her third study took place in a coffee shop. She examined how long individuals spent working or socializing after being primed to think about time or money. Individuals primed to think about money worked longer and individuals primed to think about time spent more time socializing.

Regardless of how much money people had, thinking about money caused them to work more. Thus thinking about money had stronger effects on work commitment and work hours than the amount of money people actually had. Yet work is an activity that most people say does not make them happy. Thinking about time in terms of money (e.g., the phase "time is money," has been shown to increase time pressure and stress (DeVoe and Pfeffer, 2011).

Kasser and Sheldon (2009) proposed that time affluence was likely to be a more important contributor to happiness or well-being than material affluence. Time, like money, is a limited resource. Time can be saved, spent, or wasted. Some people seem to have lots of time while others are always short of time. And people in some countries have more time (i.e., they work less) than people in other countries.

Why should time affluence increase happiness or well-being? First, it takes time to undertake and participate in activities and events that are satisfying (Lyubomirsky, Sheldon and Schkade, 2005). Second, time is needed for activities that lead to personal growth, the development of meaningful relationships, and contributing to one's community and the wider world (Kasser, 2002). Third, time pressures and the shortage of time can reduce the experience of flow (Csikszentmihalyi, 1999) and mindfulness (Brown and Ryan, 2003), both of which have been shown to increase happiness.

Kasser and Sheldon (2009) reviewed the results of three studies that support a relationship of time affluence and happiness. Kasser and Brown (2003) found that work hours was negatively correlated with life satisfaction in a sample of adults while income had no relationship with happiness. Van Boven and Gilovich (2003) reported that people were happier with things or activities they did than with things they had bought, the former taking time to pursue. Finally, Diener, Diener and Diener (1995) concluded that the happiest countries were those with relatively low work hours.

Kasser and Sheldon (2009) developed measures of material affluence and time affluence, then considered the relationship of these with indicators of job and family satisfaction in a series of studies. In their first study, time affluence predicted both job and family satisfaction after controlling for material affluence (income). In a second study, they reported that short-term changes in well-being were related to changes in time affluence (about a month lag), controlling for changes in material affluence. In their two further studies, both mindfulness and need satisfaction (operationalized as autonomy, competence, and relatedness) partially mediated the relationship of time affluence and well-being.

DeVoe and House (2011), in a series of laboratory experiments, found that asking people to think about money or calculate their recent hourly wages indicated lower levels of happiness with different experiences. They concluded that thinking about time in terms of money lessened their ability to derive happiness from pleasurable experiences. They viewed impatience that resulted from putting a price on time reduced people's ability to derive happiness from pleasurable experiences.

Thinking about money creates a specific mindset in individuals (DeVoe and Pfeffer, 2009). An economic mindset maximizes the economic value of one's time. Thinking about time in terms of money increases people's willingness to give up leisure to earn more money (DeVoe and Pfeffer, 2007a) or volunteer their time (DeVoe and Pfeffer, 2007b; Pfeffer and DeVoe, 2009).

If We're So Rich Why Aren't We Happy?

While the standard of living of citizens in many countries has risen over the past few decades, women's and men's levels of satisfaction and happiness have fallen during this same period (Herbst, 2011). Others have reported similar results (e.g., Stevenson and Wolpers, 2008; Sousa-Poza and Sousa-Poza, 2003; Blanchflower and Oswald, 2004). Declines have been reported in self-confidence and various indicators of mental and physical well-being along with increases in regrets about the past. These declines in satisfaction and happiness have been attributed to drops in social and civic engagement (Putnam, 2000), interpersonal trust, and financial security.

A Broader Index of Well-being

For the past 50 years or more, policy makers have used the GDP as an indicator of the well-being of their citizens in their countries. This seems to be changing somewhat. An increasing number of countries are also using other measures to gauge the well-being of their citizens, many reflecting the "happiness" of their citizens. France, the UK, and Canada, among others, now use a "happiness" index involving several components. Recent evidence indicates that in Canada, for example, though the GDP has risen steadily over the past 20 years, the index of happiness has increased much less slowly. Furthermore, GDP measures economic output not the "costs" of achieving these gains (work–life imbalance, work and family stress, the time crunch) or the way this additional wealth is distributed.

Indeed, not everything can be measured in dollars and cents (Munoz de Bustillo, Fernandez-Macias and Esteve, 2011). Hence, for example, Munoz de Bustillo, Fernandez-Macias and Esteve (2011) designed and tested in several European countries a model of job quality using five different dimensions.

Similarly, the Canadian Index of Well-being contains eight dimensions; living standards, community vitality, democratic engagement, education, health, environment, leisure and culture, and how people spend their time. This Index is a broader/wider measure of progress. But obviously one still needs to consider the GDP. In Canada, the GDP increased 31 percent from 1994 to 2008, while the Index of Well-being rose just 11 percent. In two areas, time crunch and income inequality, evaluations got worse during this time period. Canadians are now spending more time working and less time with their families and friends, more are working non-standard hours, and more women are working at two jobs – one outside the home and a second being responsible for home and family functioning. Most of the gains in wealth went to the richest Canadians.

Brean (2012), reporting results of an international study of happiness, included a Canadian study that examined income and life satisfaction in various cities. It found that people living in Canada's richest cities (Toronto, Calgary, Ottawa) were less happy than people living in the smaller and less rich cities (Quebec City, St. John's, Charlottetown). The international study indicated that major predictors of happiness were family and friends, good health, material sufficiency, freedom, and the pleasures of living in a justifiably trusting community and country.

Practical Implications

This chapter, focusing as it does on materialism, money, and greed, emphasizes "bad apples," the behavior of individuals or groups of individuals that participate in acts of crime, corruption, and fraud. Greed leads to crooked police officers, crooked politicians, crooked world leaders, and the endless list of corporate scandals that daily appear in our media. Greed is responsible for the dramatic increases in salaries of CEOs, the payment of huge salaries to CEOs of failing companies, the under-reporting of company losses, the over-reporting of company profits, and the wide-spread cheating in a winner-takes-all culture. Greed wrongly connects material wealth with happiness.

Greed has been part of the human condition for thousands of years. It would be naive for anyone to think that greed can be stopped; the best one can hope for is that we can reduce the level of greed and the dysfunctional aspects of greed. If greed is to be reduced, it must be addressed at multiple levels: individual, organizational, and societal. It is important to also state that the purpose of this chapter was not to bash the US, developed countries, or capitalism. Capitalism has improved the life circumstances of countless millions of people around the world. Unbridled capitalism, however, has sometimes produced negative consequences.

Individual Change

Be yourself, everyone else is taken.

– Oscar Wilde

Individuals are less likely to be greedy if they live a more authentic and meaningful life, claims Sharma (2011), who goes on to make the following suggestions. People should strive to be authentic. A key question then becomes "Who am I and how do I want to live?" Answering this involves understanding yourself, your skills, your talents, your goals, your dreams, and becoming comfortable with who you are. You should live with kindness and generosity. It is also important to challenge your fears. Every week do at least one thing that frightens you. When you do this you gain power. Move out of your comfort zone. Individuals need to invest in relationships; these are the greatest source of happiness. Individuals should spend time with people that uplift them. Strive to be positive and optimistic; inspire yourself. Work on your mind, body, emotions and spirituality. Individuals can find joy in the simplest activities and the simplest places. Individuals need to understand life's true purpose – to live well. Finally, seeing one's job as a craft or calling, and not as work, adds to positive feelings and attitudes. Reynolds (2011), in his reasons why people fail, includes money obsession. He writes that building your life around the accumulation of money will lead to misery rather than happiness; he argues, instead, that one should build one's life around relationships, community, and serving others.

Brett Wilson (2012), a very successful Canadian entrepreneur and philanthropist, made a lot of money in his early career but sacrificed his health, his marriage, and his relationships with his children. He recently wrote about what he learned on his journey and how success should really be measured. He described himself as having earlier been in "personal bankruptcy." The key questions became what would he want his children, or his friends and colleagues, to write on his epitaph.

Willis and Garn (2011) advocate that individuals develop lives of prosperity – prosperity being a function of money, happiness, and sustainability. Money is obviously important in creating a prosperous life, but it is the "want" of money that can create difficulties. People need enough money to support their goals, values, and principles. Happiness includes holding positive feelings about oneself and one's world, living one's life consistent with one's beliefs and values, commitment to family and friendships, and being healthy and well. Sustainability includes feelings of loving what you are doing, the belief that you can sustain this passion and interest, acting ethically and morally, and making the world a better place. Willis and Garn offer self-assessments and exercises to help readers become prosperous.

Furthermore, individuals and their families can begin to take steps to reduce the levels of their materialism. At the heart of these efforts is a commitment to live more simply; that is, a making a c choice to focus on what is essential to a good life while ignoring tendencies to acquire possessions that add little but cost a lot (Kasser and Kanner, 2003; Needleman, 1991). We must all move beyond selfishness (Mintzberg, Simons and Basu, 2002). Terms such as "downshifting" and "simplicity" have been used to describe these lifestyles. Following Izzo (2005), making time for friends, family, recreation, and spirituality appear to be worthwhile expenditures of one's efforts and energy. Intimacy not materialism enriches one's life. Since time is finite, individuals also need to manage their time expenditures wisely (De Graaf, 2003; Honore, 2004; Needleman, 1998). Ensuring time for physical and social activities is a must. Although technology has been billed as a time saver, it often has the opposite effect. Individuals need to ensure that their latest gadgets nourish rather than deplete their lives.

Saying "no" to the demands of children is necessary as well. Materialism develops very early in children in the developed world. Two-year-olds begin to ask for products by name and eight-year-old girls and boys can identify 200 branded products. The average American teenager watches over three hours of television every day and watches an estimated 40,000 commercials in a year (Schor, 2004). It makes sense to limit the television-watching of children.

Finally, there are two ways to be rich; one is to work and achieve more money, the other is to want less (Kets de Vries, 2007: Roberts, 2011).

Organizational Change

Organizations need also to move beyond selfishness (Mintzberg, Simons and Basu, 2002). Organizations can downplay their use of financial rewards; financial rewards should still be used to reinforce excellence but in a lower profile way. In addition, designing work spaces to minimize status or level distinctions would help. Perks should be aligned to performance deliverables and space assigned to those that need it rather than those at higher levels in the organization.

Mintzberg (2009) makes the radical case for scrapping executive bonuses entirely. He argues that executive bonuses, particularly in the form of stock and option grants, are a form of legal corruption that has hampered large organizations. Too many CEOs have become gamblers with other people's money, they get rewarded when it looks as if their organizations are doing well when they really aren't, they get paid even when their organizations are doing poorly, they get paid for signing merger agreements, and they get paid for staying with the company (those retention bonuses). These factors encourage CEOs to take great risks. They can't lose.

Mintzberg identifies several flaws in the notion of giving bonuses. These include: a company's health is reflected by financial measures alone, financial measures reflect the true strength of a company, and the CEO and his team are mainly responsible for company performance. Too many executives use bonuses for their own personal benefits: feeding their egos, meeting narcissistic needs, and satisfying greed. The CEO of a US$14 trillion economy (Barack Obama) receives US$400,000 a year. Why should the CEO of a much smaller organization be paid millions?

Organizations need to make it harder to commit fraud. A 2011 global survey of about 4,000 senior executives undertaken by PwC showed pervasive workplace fraud (Johns, 2011). About 35 percent said their company had experienced at least one case of fraud in the past year, with 40 percent being committed by an employee. Companies lose about 5 percent of their revenue to fraud, totaling more than US$2.9 trillion. Small businesses are more vulnerable than medium or large firms. Three types of fraud were commonly found: theft or misappropriation of assets, corruption or conflicts of interests, and fraudulent reporting.

An interesting question is who commits fraud. The following were noted: those with a desperate need for money, those feeling resentment against an employer, and those motivated by just plain greed. Those committing fraud were usually "good people" caught in a "bad situation."

Suggestions for guarding against fraud included:

1. identifying weak spots, the most vulnerable areas of the company
2. distributing control to several people
3. conducting regular checks
4. acting quickly and strongly when fraud is suspected
5. supporting whistleblowers and use of an internal crime hotline

Business schools are also in the vanguard of change. "Years ago, the choice of which inspirational figure to stick behind a lectern, in front of your new MBA class was a simple one. It had to be a high-flying financier in the Gordon Gecko mould or naught" (Symonds, 2011).

Times have changed. While some MBAs still seek careers in financial services, the background and dreams of MBA students are much more varied. Greed is no longer good. And a recent survey of business schools conducted by the Aspen Institute found that MBA programs and business schools more generally were now focusing on ethics. Roose (2012) reports that a 2011 survey of 6,700 young professionals conducted by consulting firm Universum found Google, Apple, and Facebook were the most coveted workplaces with the highest ranking bank, JPMorgan Chase, being only 41st.

Conclusion: Societal Change

McKnight and Block (2012) make a compelling case documenting the limits of consumption which has produced lives of scarcity for some and lives of over-consumption for others. Lives of over-consumption have created costs to individuals, neighborhoods, and societies. They suggest that individuals can choose instead to work towards creating a culture characterized by lives of abundance and cooperation.

The Occupy movement, which began in the US and has since spread to dozens of other countries, has highlighted the gap between the 1 percent and the 99 percent (van Gelder, 2011; Collins, 2012). This movement has increased the proportion of North American citizens who now believe that the gap between the rich and the poor has not only widened but is unsustainable. Bruce Springsteen's seventeenth album, "Wrecking Ball," released March 6, 2012, took direct aim at the 1 percent.

The Occupy Movement has increased calls to revise the tax system, a call that President Obama heard and supported in his 2012 State of the Union address. Warren Buffett was the first billionaire to suggest increasing taxes on the rich, and his secretary was in the gallery at Obama's address. Furthermore, in a note to a Republican congressman, Buffett wrote: "I hope you succeed in getting the ultra-rich, who as a group are paying less of their income to the federal government than their receptionists, to share in the sacrifice many millions of Americans soon will be asked to do."

It will definitely be an uphill struggle to reduce levels of materialism and greed. Why such a pessimistic view? Because it seems that in 2012 everything is for sale (Sandel, 2012; Hochschild, 2012; Kuttner, 1997). Sandel claims that we have moved from a market economy to a market society. Those with money can use riches to make their lives "easier." You can now pay someone to do just about anything (see Hochschild, 2012), but one needs money to purchase these services. The provider of these services needs money as well, in order to survive. Sandel believes that putting a price on everything has increased the gap between the haves and the have nots. This marketization also corrupts and degrades moral values.

It is important that countries raise the standard of living of their citizens. China, among other, countries has raised its standard of living over the past 50 years. But as China raises its standard of living, there has been an increase in the pursuit of luxury goods and the trappings of excessive materialism (Wheeler, 2012). This change may be inevitable. When people become rich, they desire the trappings associated with being rich.

The current economic recession is having the effect on individuals at all economic levels to think about their financial situation and cut back their spending. Houses are being built smaller, McMansions no longer being in vogue; some restaurants have lowered their prices and cut the sizes of their portions, air travel is down, as is consumer spending.

It is too soon, however, to conclude that these trends will continue. There are signs that conspicuous consumption and excess are still very much the order of the day.

American Express transaction analysis from 2009 through 2011 showed that members of Generation Y, women and men born since 1983, have boosted their spending on luxury goods, travel, and fine dining (Infantry, 2012). A generation told that they deserve it and they should have it are now spending.

Some believe that once the recession is over it will be business as usual. Consumers in China still appear to be materialistic as their economy remains relatively buoyant. Others argue that these changes, particularly as they influence the young, may continue into the future. Only time will tell. The material reviewed in this chapter, however, indicates that greed, fraud, corruption, and materialism is alive and well, and spreading to other parts of the developing world. Krishna (2012) comes to a similar conclusion. He believes that accounting fraud and the sizes of financial frauds will increase in the future.

I would concur. Countless examples of greed and materialism leading to theft, fraud, crime, and corruption are being reported daily. One day after Bob Diamond appeared at the House of Commons hearing convened to understand the failings at Barclays, Spain opened a criminal investigation of Bankia that included its former Chairman, Rodrigo Rato and 32 other board members, charging them with fraud and misappropriation of funds, and falsifying 2011 annual results (Bjork, 2012). It seems that an increasing number of organizations worldwide are greedy and will do anything to make a dollar. With their pay tied to stock prices, they will do anything to raise stock prices including lying, cheating, and stealing. The perpetrators of these crimes, particularly at the managerial and executive levels, are rarely punished; hardly anyone ever goes to jail. Fines to the organization are merely the cost of doing business. Penalties for bad behavior are small compared to the rewards. Most walk away from their organizations taking with them hefty salaries and pensions. Instead the public pays a price in terms of lost pensions, as in the Canadian Nortel case, and having to pay higher interest rates for loans and mortgages, as in the Barclays Bank example. Many pay a price in being shamed, Bob Diamond, the departing CEO of Barclays, was accused of being incompetent at the House of Commons inquiry, but shame seems to have little, or only a short-term effect, once these individuals leave their jobs. Diamond received about US$200 million in the seven years he was with Barclays; his life will go on pretty much the same.

References

Allaire, Y. and Firsirotu, M. (2009) *Black Markets – and Business Blues*. Montreal: Institute for Governance of Private and Public Organizations.

—— (2012) *A Capitalism of Owners*. Montreal: Institute for Governance of Private and Public Organizations.

Allen, N. (2011) Dictators son blows $100 m on lavish living. *National Post*, October 27, A2.

Armstrong, J. (2011) The campaign for civility: Ten years after the fall of the Taliban, Afghanistan still can't deliver services. *National Post*, October 17, A12.

Atwood, M. (2008) *Payback: Debt and the Shadow Side of Wealth*. Toronto: House of Anansi Press.

Bakan, J. (2004) *The Corporation: The Pathological Pursuit of Profit and Power*. New York: Free Press.

Balot, R.K. (2001) *Greed and Injustice in Classic Athens*. Princeton, NJ: Princeton University Press.

Barber, A.E. and Bretz, R.D. (2000) Compensation, attraction and retention. In S.L. Rynes and B. Gerhart (eds) *Compensation in Organizations: Current Research and Practice*. San Francisco, CA: Jossey-Bass, pp. 32–60.

Barclay, S. (2012) Warning signs flashing for china: Slowing manufacturing, rising corruption, a string of concerning statistics, and shaky wealth creation packages spark concern. *Globe and Mail*, September 3, B7.

Barstow, D. (2012) Bribery hushed up by Wal-Mart: Report uncovers company executives nixed investigations into corrupt dealings with politicians and bureaucrats in Mexico. *Globe and Mail*, April 23, B5.

Bazerman, M.H. and Malhotra, D. (2006) Economics wins, psychology loses, and society pays. In D. deCremer, J.K. Murnighan and M. Zeelenberg (eds) *Social Psychology and Economics*. Mahwah, NJ: Lawrence Erlbaum, pp. 263–80.

Belk, R.W. (1984) Three scales to measure constructs related to materialism: reliability, validity, and relationships to measures of happiness. In T.C. Kinnear (ed.) *Advances in Consumer Research*, vol. 11. Provo, UT: Association for Consumer Research, pp. 291–7.

—— (1985) Materialism: Trait aspects of living in a materialistic world. *Journal of Consumer Research*, 12, 265–80.

Belk, R.W. and Pollay, R. (1985) Images of ourselves: The good life in twentieth century advertising. *Journal of Consumer Research*, 11, 887–97.

Berenson, A. (2003) The numbers: *How the Drive for Quarterly Earnings Corrupted Wall Street and Corporate America*. New York: Random House.

Berger, B. and Newman, S. (2012) *Money Talks in Therapy, Society and Life*. New York: Routledge.

Bjork, C. (2012) Spain opens criminal probe into Bankia: Ex-chairman, 32 board members to be investigated. *National Post*, July 5, FP10.

Blanchflower, D. and Oswald, A. (2004) Well-being over time in Britain and the USA. *Journal of Public Economics*, 99, 1359–86.

Boesveld, S. (2011) Policy says it's OK to cheat, teachers warn: Dishonest students to get second chance with no penalty. *National Post*, October 25, A7.

Bray C. (2011) Rajaratnam fined $92.8 million in SEC case. *Globe and Mail*, November 9, B11.

(2012) Guilty pleas in "stunning" mortgage fraud. *Globe and Mail*, February 2, B10.

Brean, J. (2012) Money isn't everything, report says. *National Post*, April 3, A6.

Brennan, R.J. (2012) Canadian charged in massive fraud case: Officials allege $375M in illegal health claims. *Toronto Star*, March 1, A1.

Brown, K.W. and Ryan, R.M. (2003) The benefits of being present: Mindfulness and its role in well-being. *Journal of Personality and Social Psychology*, 84, 822–48.

Brumback, K. (2012) US banker confesses, disappears: $17 million missing. *National Post*, July 12, A10.

Buckholz, R. (2012) *Reforming Capitalism: The Scientific World-view and Business*. London: Routledge.

Burke, R.J (2009) Greed. In R.J. Burke and C.L. Cooper (eds) *Research Companion to Corruption in Organizations*. Cheltenham: Edward Elgar, pp. 33–59.

—— (2011) Show me the money. In R.J. Burke, E.C. Tomlinson and C.L. Cooper (eds) *Crime and Corruption in Organizations*. Farnham: Gower, pp. 69–96.

Callahan, D. (2004) *The Cheating Culture: Why More Americans Are Doing Wrong to Get Ahead*. Orlando, FL: Harcourt.

—— (2006) *Moral Center: How We Can Reclaim Our Country from Die-Hard Extremists, Rogue Corporations, Hollywood Hacks, and Pretend Patriots*. Boston, MA: Houghton-Mifflin Harcourt.

Carroll, J.S., Dean, L.R., Call, L.L. and Busby, D.M. (2011) Materialism and marriage: Couple profiles of congruent and incongruent spouses. *Journal of Couple and Relationship Therapy*, 10, 287–308.

Carver, C.S. and Baird, E. (1998) The American dream revisited: Is it what you want or why you want it that matters? *Psychological Science*, 9, 289–92.

Cassell (1997) *Cassell Concise Dictionary*. London: Cassell.

Cauchi, M. and Guevarra, V. (2012) Aviva CEO resigns after pay revolt. *Globe and Mail*, May 9, B14.

Chowdhry, A. (2013) Pakistan rocked by corruption charges. *Globe and Mail*, January 16, A3.

Chrisafis, A. (2011) Plastic surgery scandal rocks France. *Globe and Mail*, December 15, A22.

—— (2012) France impounds African autocrats' "illegally-gotten gains." *The Guardian*, August 6.

Chu, H. (2012) BBC scrambles to contain crisis: Two senior editors "step aside" as outrage grows over payout to departing director general. *Toronto Star*, November 13, A12.

Chung, A. (2012) Ex-SNC exec held in Swiss probe: Arrest of former VP with ties to Gadhafi clan deepens crisis at Canadian engineering giant. *Toronto Star*, April 30, A1, A4.

Coates, J. (2012) *The Hour between Dog and Wolf: Risk-Taking, Gut Feelings and the Biology of Boom and Bust*. Toronto: Random House.

Cohan, W. (2011) *Money and Power: How Goldman Sachs Came to Rule the World*. New York: Doubleday.

Colchester, M. and Munoz, S.S. (2012) HSBC takes $2-billion hit for flaws. *Globe and Mail*, July 31, B7.

Collins, C. (2012) *99 to 1: How Wealth Inequality Is Wrecking the World and What We Can Do about It*. San Francisco, CA: Berrett-Koehler.

Condie, S. (2011) Two guilty in cricket fixing trial: Cricket's worst scandal for more than a decade. *Toronto Star*, 2, S2.

Csikszentmihalyi, M. (1999) If we are so rich, why aren't we happy? *American Psychologist*, 54, 821–7.

Daily, M. and Driver, A. (2012) "Deeply sorry" Chesapeake CEO, calls reports "misinformation." *Globe and Mail*, May 3, B8.

Davis, L. (1997) Moral judgment development of graduate management students in two cultures: Minnesota and Singapore. Unpublished manuscript, University of Minnesota.

Deci, E. and Ryan, R.M. (1991) A motivational approach to self integration in personality. In R. Dienstbier (ed.) *Nebraska Symposium on Motivation*, vol. 38. Lincoln, NB: University of Nebraska Press, pp. 237–88.

Deckop, J.R., Jurkiewicz, C.L. and Giacalone, R.A. (2010) The effects of materialism on work-related personal well-being. *Human Relations*, 63, 1007–30.

De Graaf, J. (2003) *Take Back Your Time: Fighting Overwork and Time Poverty in America*. San Francisco, CA: Berrett-Koehler.

Delva, J.G. (2012) Duvalier faces trial on charges of corruption. *Toronto Star*, January 31, A17.

DeVoe, S.E. and House, J. (2011) Time, money and happiness: How does putting a price on time affect our ability to smell the roses? *Journal of Experimental Social Psychology*, 48, 466–74.

DeVoe, S.E. and Pfeffer, J. (2007a) When time is money: The effect of hourly payment on the evaluation of time. *Organizational Behavior and Human Decision Processes*, 104, 1–13.

—— (2007b) Hourly payment and volunteering: The effect of organizational practices on decisions about time use. *Academy of Management Journal*, 50, 783–98.

—— (2009) When is happiness about how much you earn? The effect of hourly payment on the money-happiness connection. *Personality and Social Psychology Bulletin*, 35, 1602–18.

—— (2011) Time is tight: How higher economic value of time increases feelings of time pressure. *Journal of Applied Psychology*, 96, 668–76.

Diener, E. (1984) Subjective well-being. *Psychological Bulletin*, 95, 542–75.

Diener, E. and Biswas-Diener, R. (2002) Will money increase subjective well-being? *Social Indicators Research*, 57, 119–69.

Diener, E., Diener, M. and Diener, C. (1995) Factors predicting the subjective well-being of nations. *Journal of Personality and Social Psychology*, 69, 851–64.

Diener, E. and Oishi, S. (2000) Money and happiness: Income and subjective well-being across nations. In E. Diener and E.M. Suh (eds) *Culture and Subjective Well-being*. Cambridge, MA: MIT Press, pp. 185–218.

Diener, E., Sandvik, E., Seidlitz, L. and Diener, M. (1993) The relationship between income and subjective well-being: Relative or absolute? *Social Indicators Research*, 28, 195–223.

Diener, E. and Seligman, M.E.P. (2004) Beyond money: Towards an economy of well-being. *Psychology in the Public Interest*, 5, 1–31.

Donovan, K. (2012a) Girlfriend, daughter of ORNGE brass headed $6.7M project: Filled 2 small binders with clippings, Google research. *Toronto Star*, April 25, A1,A8.

—— (2012b) ORNGE official faked having MBA: Aviation chief says he embellished his credentials in a bid to solicit investors. *Toronto Star*, February 28, A1, A8.

Dvorak, P. and Wakabayashi, D. (2011) Olympus's answers raise many questions: Admission that the Japanese company covered up losses causes speculation about its viability. *Globe and Mail*, November 9, B10.

Edesess, M. (2007) *The Big Investment Lie: What Your Financial Advisor Doesn't Want You to Know*. San Francisco, CA: Berrett-Koehler.

Edwards, M. (2010) *Small Change: Why Business Won't Save the World*. San Francisco, CA: Berrett-Koehler.

Edwards, P. (2012) Accountant jailed for bilking employer of $12 M. *Toronto Star*, May 18, GT1, GT7.

Eichenwald, K. (2005) *Conspiracy of Fools: A True Story*. New York: Broadway Books.

Elias, P. (2012) Samsung hit with $1B patent verdict. *Toronto Star*, August 25, B1, B2.

Farmer, B. (2012) $861M diverted by Kabul bank, audit finds: Ponzi scheme. *National Post*, November 28, A18.

Feeley, J. and Voreacos, D. (2011) Merck to pay US$950 million to end US Vioxx probe. *National Post*, FP4.

Ferguson, W. (2012) *419*. Toronto: Viking Press.

Ferraro, F., Pfeffer, J. and Sutton, R.I. (2005) Economics language and assumptions: How theories can become self-fulfilling. *Academy of Management Review*, 30, 8–24.

Finch, G. (2012) Standard Chartwell may be hit with US 5.5B in costs: Iran dealings may lead to fine, lost market value, revenues. *National Post*, August 8, FP2.

Findlay, S. (2012) Ex-OHL owner on lam in $129M Ponzi scheme. *Toronto Star*, March 12, A1.

Flavelle, D. (2011) 400 is the percentage jump board directors have seen in their pay in the past decade as company revenues have averaged a 33% hike. *Toronto Star*, December 14, B1, B4.

—— (2012) The top 10% of Canadians earned ten times as much as the bottom 10%: Canada eases above the global average in inequality. *Toronto Star*, December 6, B1, B2.

Frank, R.H. and Cook, P.J. (1995) *The Winner-Take-All Society*. New York: The Free Press.

Freeze, C. and Hu, T.T. (2011) Banker in Iran scandal said to be in Toronto: Biggest fraud in Iranian history hurting the political fortunes of President Mahmoud Ahmadinejad. *Globe and Mail*, October 1, A3.

Freifeld, K. (2012) ING to pay US619M over Cuba, Iran: US sanctions. *National Post*, June 13, FP7.

Fromm, E. (1976) *To Have or to Be?* New York: Harper and Row.

Galperin, B.L., Bennett, R.J. and Aquino, K. (2011) Status differentiation and the protean self: A social-cognitive model of unethical behavior in organizations. *Journal of Business Ethics*, 98, 407–24.

Gandal, N., Roccas, S., Sagiv, L. and Wrzesniewski, A. (2005) Personal value priorities of economists. *Human Relations*, 58, 1227–52.

Ghoshal, S. (2005) Bad management theories are destroying good management practices. *Academy of Management Learning and Education*, 4, 75–91.

Giacalone, R.A., Jurkiewicz, C.L. and Deckop, J.R. (2008) On ethics and social responsibility: The impact of materialism, postmaterialism and hope. *Human Relations*, 61, 483–514.

Glekin, J. (2011) Anti-graft movement here to stay. *Globe and Mail*, October 31, B7.

Globe and Mail (2011a) US seeks $71m in corrupt gains. October 26, A24.

—— (2011b) White collar crime: Former Philips executive sentenced. October 26, B13.

—— (2011c) Norbourg pair get eight year terms for fraud: Judge says the stiff sentences are needed to send a strong messages in scam that fleeced more than 9,000 investors of US$115 million. October 1, B8.

—— (2011d) UK probes Russian in bank fraud. December 17, B12.

—— (2012a) Wen Jaibao family denies NYT report of hidden riches. October 29, A12.

—— (2012b) Probe censures "Three cups" author: Greg Mortenson is ordered to pay $1 million to his own charity after a finding of "financial transgression." April 6, A17.

—— (2012c) Wal-Mart value plunges $10-billion amid bribe claim. April 24, B7.

—— (2012d) BP chief tripled pay in 2011. March 7, B8.

—— (2012e) Lloyd's to claw back executive bonuses. February 21, B6.

—— (2013) UK property tycoon found guilty of bank fraud. January 17, B10.

Gray, J. (2011) How OSC's new tack will change the game. *Globe and Mail*, October 26, B17.

—— (2013) Nortel nightmare a $630-million dream for advisers. *Globe and Mail*, January 16, B1, B8.

Guner, A.B., Malmendier, U. and Tate, G. (2008) Financial expertise of directors. *Journal of Financial Economics*, 88, 323–54.

Gupta, P. and Chan, E. (2012) Apple, Foxconn vow to improve worker conditions in China. *Globe and Mail*, March 30, B3.

Harris, P. and Martin, A. (2011) Champagne, girls and an obsession for making money. *Daily Mail*, September 16, 5.

Hartmann, T. (2007) *Screwed: The Undeclared War on the Middle Class*. San Francisco, CA: Berrett-Koehler.

Hastings, M. (2011) Looters in suits. *Daily Mail*, September 17, 16, 17.

Heilprin, J. (2012) UBS becomes second bank to settle its Libor case. *Toronto Star*, December 20, B6.

Henry, D. (2012) FBI probes US$2B loss at JPMorgan: Dimon gets through AGM unscathed. *National Post*, May 6, FP1, FP5.

Herbst, C.M. (2011) Paradoxical decline? Another look at the relative reduction in female happiness. *Journal of Economic Psychology*, 32, 773–88.

Hochman, M. and McCormick, D. (2011) Endpoint selection and relative (versus absolute) risk reporting in publications in medical studies. *Journal of General Internal Medicine*, 26, 1246–52.

Hochschild, A.R. (2012) *The Outsourced Self: Intimate Life in Market Times*. New York: Metropolitan Books.

Honore, C. (2004) *In Praise of Slow*. Toronto: Alfred Knopf.

Howlett, K. and Mills, C. (2012) Hospitals scrapping executive perks: Range of benefits on the chopping block as transparency requirements call for contracts with top earners to be posted on line. *Globe and Mail*, January 4, A4.

Hui, P. and Ng, J. (2012) Hong Kong tycoons arrested in corruption probe. *Globe and Mail*, March 30, B9.

Infantry, A. (2012) Generation buy splurges on luxury: Young Canadians shell out for designer denim, high-end travel and dining despite rising debt. *Toronto Star*, June 19, B5.

Ingram, D. (2012) Glaxo to pay US 3B fine after guilty plea in drug case: Government calls it the largest health care fraud in history. *National Post*, July 3, FP2.

International Labour Office (2012) *Global Employment Trends for Youth 2012*. Geneva: International Labour Office.

Irish, P. (2011) Apple magic not ruled by money. *Toronto Star*, October 25, E2.

Isaacson, W. (2011) *Steve Jobs*. New York: Simon and Schuster.

Izzo, J. (2005) *The Five Secrets You Must Discover before You Die*. Lions Bay, BC: Fairwinds Press.

Johns, M. (2011) Don't fall victim to an inside job: More than half the fraud a company experiences is committed by an employee, a global survey of senior exec's finds. *Globe and Mail*, December 15, B10.

Johnson, D.C. (2007) *Free Lunch: How the Wealthiest Americans Enrich Themselves at Government Expense (and Stick You with the Bill)*. New York: Portfolio.

Judge, T.A., Livingston, B.A. and Hurst, C. (2012) Do nice guys – and girls – really finish last? The joint effects of sex and agreeableness on income. *Journal of Personality and Social Psychology*, 102, 390–407.

Kane, L. (2012) Cuba convicts 12 of corruption. *Toronto Star*, August 22, B2.

Kasser, T. (2002) *The High Price of Materialism*. Cambridge, MA: MIT Press.

—— (2004) The good life or the goods life? Positive psychology and personal well-being in the culture of consumption. In P.A. Linley and S. Joseph (eds) *Positive Psychology in Practice*. New York: Wiley, pp. 55–67.

Kasser, T. and Ahuvia, A.C. (2002) Materialistic values and well-being in business students. *European Journal of Social Psychology*, 32, 137–46.

Kasser, T. and Brown, K.W. (2003) On time, happiness, and ecological footprints. In J. de Graaf (ed.) *Take Back Your Time: Fighting Overwork and Time Poverty in America*. San Francisco, CA: Berrett-Koehler, pp. 107–12.

Kasser, T. and Kanner, A.D. (2003) *Psychology and Consumer Culture: The Struggle for a Good Life in a Materialistic World*. Washington, DC: APA Books.

Kasser, T. and Sheldon, K.M. (2009) Material and time affluence as predictors of subjective well-being. *Journal of Business Ethics*, 84, 243–55.

Kasser, T., Sheldon, K.M., Ryan, R.M. and Deci, E.L. (2004) The independent effects of goal contents and motives on well-being: It's both what you do and why you do it. *Personality and Social Psychology Bulletin*, 30, 475–86.

Kay, J. (2012) Obama is right: Inequality is a threat to capitalism. *National Post*, January 26, A14.

Kets de Vries, M. (2007) Money, money, money. *Organizational Dynamics*, 36, 231–43.

Koenig, D. (2012) American Airlines may face $162M in safety fines. *Toronto Star*, August 8, B2.

Kopecki, D. and Mattingly, P. (2012) JPMorgan traders didn't understand risks: Dimon US $2 Billion loss. *National Post*, June 13, FP2.

Korten, D.C. (2011) *Agenda for a New Economy: From Phantom Wealth to Real Wealth*. San Francisco, CA: Berrett-Koehler.

Krishna, V. (2012) Fraud isn't likely to disappear: Accounting securities fraud to keep evolving. *National Post*, March 28, FP7.

Kuttner, R. (1997) *Everything for Sale: The Virtues and Limits of Markets*. New York: Alfred Knopf.

Labaton Sucharow (2012) *Wall Street, Fleet Street and Main Street: Corporate Integrity at a Crossroads*. New York: Labaton Sucharow.

Ladurantaye, S. (2012) Astral bows to shareholders on CEOs rich send off. *Globe and Mail*, May 23, B1, B12.

Lanchester, J. (2012) *Capital*. Toronto: McClelland and Stewart.

Lane, R.E. (2000) *The Loss of Happiness in Market Democracies*. New Haven, CT: Yale University Press.

Layard, R. (2005) *Happiness: Lessons from a New Science*. London: Penguin.

LeBlanc, D. (2011) RCMP widens Canada revenue investigation. *Globe and Mail*, November 4, A1.

LeBlanc, D. and Peritz, I. (2012) Accurso arrested in anti-corruption sweep: Construction magnate, 13 others charged in probe of provincial construction industry. *Globe and Mail*, April 18, A4.

Lee, Y. (2012) Samsung in hot seat over alleged abuse of workers. *Toronto Star*, September 6, B3.

Lessing, M. and Ustinova, A. (2012) Fall of Peregrine's founder foretold. *Globe and Mail*, July13, B6.

Li, N.R., Patel, L., Balliet, D., Tov, W. and Scollon, C.N. (2011) The incompatibility of materialism and the desire for children: Psychological insights into the fertility discrepancy among modern countries. *Social Indicators Research*, 101, 391–404.

Light, D.W. and Lexchin, J.R. (2012) Pharmaceutical research and development: What do we get for all that money. *British Medical Journal*, August 7, 345.

Livesay, B. (2011) The defender. *Report on Business*, October, 56–62, 64, 66.

Locke, E., McCleary, K. and Knight, D. (1996) Self esteem and work. In C. Cooper and I. Robertson (eds) *International Review of Industrial and Organizational Psychology*. New York: Wiley, pp. 1–32.

Lyall, S. (2012) "Culture of illegal payments" at Murdoch's Sun. *National Post*, February 28, A11.

Lyubomirsky, S., Sheldon, K.M. and Schkade, D. (2005) Pursuing happiness: The architecture of sustainable change. *Review of General Psychology*, 9, 111–31.

Madrach, J. (2011) *Age of Geed: The Triumph of Finance and the Decline of America, 1970 to the Present*. New York: Knopf.

Martin, R.L. (2011) *Fixing the Game: Bubbles, Crashes and What Capitalism Can Learn from the NFL*. Boston, MA: Harvard Business School Press.

McArthur, G. (2012) Former SNC executive charged: Swiss authorities accuse Riadh Ben Aissa of fraud, money laundering and corruption. *Globe and Mail*, November 26, B1.

McArthur, G., Smith, G., Reguly, E. and Waldie, P. (2012) SNC-Lavalin executive's sister was hired to design Libyan prison. *Globe and Mail*, April 25, A12.

McCabe, D.L., Dukerich, J.M. and Dutton, J.E. (1993a) Values and moral dilemmas: A cross-cultural comparison. *Business Ethics Quarterly*, 3, 117–30.

—— (1993b) Context, values and moral dilemmas: Comparing the choices of business and law school students. *Journal of Business Ethics*, 10, 951–60.

McFadden, R. (2011) Former United Way leader jailed for defrauding charity. *Globe and Mail*, November 17, S7.

McKnight, J. and Block, P. (2012) *The Abundant Community: Awakening the Power of Families and Neighborhoods*. San Francisco, CA: Berrett-Koehler.

McLaughlin, D. (2012) US expands bank probe over LIBOR: Subpoenas sent. *National Post*, August 16, FP6.

McLean, C. (2012) Swiss fight reputation as dirty money haven. *Globe and Mail*, August 7, B7.

McQuaig, L. (2001) *All You Can Eat: Greed, Lust and the New Capitalism*. Toronto: Penguin.

Miller, L. (2012) The money-empathy gap. *New York*, July 9, 18–23, 78–9.

Milstead, D. (2012) Average performance, outstanding pay: At Canada's biggest banks mediocre results barely dent executives' compensation. *Globe and Mail*, April 3, B13.

Mintzberg, H. (2009) No more executive bonuses! *Wall Street Journal*, November 30, 2009.

Mintzberg, H., Simons, R. and Basu, K. (2002) Beyond selfishness. *MIT Sloan Management Review*, Fall, 67–74.

Mirsky, J. (2012) As Syria burns, the Assads 1. Share songs and Youtube clips, 2. Shop for $1600 shoes and bullet-proof clothes. 3. track down latest Harry Potter movie. *National Post*, March 15, A1, A11.

Mogliner, C. (2010) The pursuit of happiness: Time, money and social connections. *Psychological Science*, 21, 1348–54.

Morgenson, G. and Posner, J. (2011) *Reckless Endangerment: How Outsized Ambition, Greed, and Corruption Led to Economic Armageddon*. New York: New York Times Books.

Mumumdza, R. (2012) South Africa's Zuma spends $23M of public money on home reno. *Toronto Star*, October 13, A3.

Munoz de Bustillo, R., Fernandez-Macias, E. and Esteve, F. (2011) *Measuring More Than Money: The Social Economics of Job Quality*. Cheltenham: Edward Elgar.

Murray, C. (2012) *Coming Apart: The State of White America, 1960–2010*. New York: Crowne Forum.

Myers, D.G. (2000) *The American Paradox: Spiritual Hunger in an Age of Plenty*. New Haven, CT: Yale University Press.

—— (2003) The social psychology of sustainability. *World Futures: The Journal of General Evolution*, 59, 201–11.

National Post (2011a) BC Hydro executives' bonuses based on non-existent profits. November 1, A6.

—— (2011b) Compensation for company directors soars by more than a third in two years: $880 an hour. December 8, FP5.

—— (2012a) Biomet to pay nearly US$23-million to settle bribery accusations. March 27, FP5.

—— (2012b) French president introduces code of ethics for cabinet ministers. May 18, A11.

—— (2012c) Millions of millionaires in China, and more are horseback riding. August 2, FP5.

—— (2012d) Not too shabby for "a galley slave." August 29, A3.

Naughton, K. (2012) Ford awards CEO US $58.3 M in stock. *National Post*, March 7, FP5.

Needleman, J. (1991) *Money and the Meaning of Life*. New York: Doubleday/Currency.

—— (1998) *Time and the Soul: Where Has All the Meaningful Time Gone – and Can We Get It Back?* San Francisco, CA: Berrett-Koehler.

Nickerson, C., Schwartz, N., Diener, E. and Kahneman, D. (2003) Zeroing in on the dark side of the American Dream: A closer look at the negative consequences of the goal of financial success. *Psychological Science*, 14, 531–6.

Nunes, P.F. and Mulani, N.P. (2008) Can knock-offs knock out your business? *Harvard Business Review*, October, 41–50.

Nussenbaum, D. (2012) UN removes police trust fund managers. *Globe and Mail*, June 11, A16.

Ogilvie, R. and Stone, L. (2012) Hospital executives' perks revealed: Newly disclosed contracts give CEOs generous bonuses. *Toronto Star*, January 4, GT1, GT5.

Onstad, K. (2012) The price of always wanting: The latest fatal garment factory fire in Dhaka reminds us that those cheap clothes we love to buy at the big chains have a dark side. *Globe and Mail*, November 30, L3.

O'Shea, J. (2011) *The Deal from Hell: How Moguls and Wall Street Plundered Great American Newspapers*. New York: Public Affairs.

Palazzolo, J. and Glazer, E. (2012) Avon begins settlement talks in US bribery probe. *Globe and Mail*, August 2, B6.

Partnoy, F. (2009) *FIASCO: Blood in the Water on Wall Street*. New York: Norton.

Pfeffer, J. (2005) Why do bad management theories persist? A comment on Ghoshal. *Academy of Management Learning and Education*, 4, 96–100.

Pfeffer, J. and DeVoe, S.E. (2009) Economic evaluation: The effects of money and economics on attitudes about volunteering. *Journal of Economic Psychology*, 30, 500–508.

Phillips, T. (2005) *Knockoff: The Deadly Trade in Counterfeit Goods*. London: Kogan Page.

Piff, P.K., Kraus, M.W., Cote, S., Cheng, B.H. and Keltner, D. (2010) Having less, giving more: The influence of social class on prosocial behavior. *Journal of Personality and Social Psychology*, 99, 771–84.

Piff, P.K., Stancato, D.M., Cote, S., Mendoza-Denton, R. and Keltner, D. (2012) Higher social class predicts increased unethical behavior. Proceedings of the National Academy of Sciences, 109, 4086–91.

Pogatchnik, S. (2012) Irish ex-PM received $277,000, says 15 year, $260 million probe. *Toronto Star*, March 23, A19.

Putnam, R.D. (2000) *Bowling Alone: The Collapse and Revival of American Community*. New York: Simon and Schuster.

Rashbaum, M. (2011) US railroad workers charged in pension scam: Report alleges a network of phony doctors' assessments, massive payments and supposedly disabled employees playing golf. *Globe and Mail*, October 28, A18.

Raymond, N. (2013) Swiss bank closes after guilty plea on aiding US tax evaders. *National Post*, January 4, FP10.

Raynar, G. (2012) Ex-cashier bilked Nigerian state of $80M. *National Post*, April 18, A14.

Reguly, E. (2012) New allegations arise in SNC-Lavalin probe: Tunisian businessman claims he lost an infrastructure contract for refusing to pay a bribe of $100,000. *Globe and Mail*, April 23, A3.

Reynolds, S. (2011) *Why People Fail*. San Francisco, CA: Jossey-Bass.

Rexrode, C. and Cardon, B. (2012) Typical CEO in US made $9.6 million last year; the average worker, $39,300. *Globe and Mail*, May 26, B3.

Richins, M.L. and Dawson, S. (1992) A consumer value orientation for materialism and its measurement: Scale development and validation. *Journal of Consumer Research*, 19, 303–16.

Roberts, J.A. (2011) *Shiny Objects: Why We Spend Money We Don't Have in Search of Happiness We Can't Buy*. New York: HarperOne.

Robertson, G. (2012) JPMorgan laments $2-billion blunder. *Globe and Mail*, May 11, B1.

Rocha H.O. and Ghoshal, S. (2006) Beyond self-interest revisited. *Journal of Management Studies*, 43, 585–619.

Roose, K. (2012) Wall Street losing luster among campus recruits: Reputation sullied. *National Post*, March 28, FP16.

Rush, C. (2011) Accused in alleged Ponzi scheme facing new fraud charges: Man surrenders after 120 people claim to have lost $9M. *Toronto Star*, October 27, GT4.

Ryan, N. (2009) Never mind the death threats. *Report on Business*, November, 54–8.

Ryan, R.M., Sheldon, K.M., Kasser, T. and Deci, E.I. (1996) All goals are not created equal: An organismic perspective on the nature of goals and their regulation. In P.M. Gollwitzer and I.A. Bargh (eds) *The Psychology of Action*. New York: Guilford Press, pp. 7–26.

Sabbagh, D. (2011) James Murdoch readies for session with British MPs: News Corp. boss is preparing to concede the company should have taken more action on allegations of phone hacking earlier. *Globe and Mail*, November 7, A16.

Sandel, M. (2012) *What Money Can't Buy: The Moral Limits of Markets*. New York: Farrar Strauss and Giroux.

Schor, J.B. (2004) *Born to Buy: The Commercialized Child and the New Consumer Culture*. New York: Simon and Schuster.

Sharma, R. (2011) *Daily Inspiration*. Ahmedabad: JAICO Publishing.

Sheldon, K. and Lyubomirsky, S. (2012) The challenge of staying happier: Testing the Hedonic Adaptation Prevention (HAP) model. *Personality and Social Psychology Bulletin*, 38, 670–80.

Shirbon, E. (2012) Ex-UBS trader draws seven-year jail term. *Globe and Mail*, November 21, B7.

Silicoff, S. (2012) Payout to former SNC chief will total millions. *Globe and Mail*, March 28, B1.

Sinclair, H. (2011) *Confessions of a Microfinance Heretic: How Microlending Lost Its Way and Betrayed the Poor*. San Francisco, CA: Berrett-Koehler.

Sirgy, M.J. (1998) Materialism and quality of life. *Social Indicators Research*, 43, 227–60.

Slater, D. (2012) SEC zeroes in on a hedge-fund giant. *Globe and Mail*, November 29, B1, B12.

Slater, S. (2012a) UK regulators warned Barclays over aggressive culture: Financial Services Authority told bank as early as February it was pushing the boundaries. *Globe and Mail*, July 6, B6.

—— (2012b) HSBC failed to control drug-money laundering, Senate finds. *Globe and Mail*, July 18, B1, B4.

Slater, S. and Bart, K. (2013) Swiss bank UBS moves past Libor scandal. *National Post*, January 10, FP7.

Slater, S. and Vellacott, C. (2012) Outrage over Barclays payout: Former CEO receives millions in compensation: Shareholders and politicians say it was "reward for failure." *Globe and Mail*, July 27, B8.

Smith, J. and Jones, A. (2012) Legal giant seeks bankruptcy shield: Dewey and LeBoeuf's financial troubles tied to extravagant pay packages, used to lure and keep legal talent, observers say. *Globe and Mail*, May 30, B10.

Solberg, E., Diener, E. and Robinson, M. (2004) Why materialists are less satisfied. In T. Kasser and A. Kanner (eds) *Psychology and the Consumer Culture*. Washington, DC: American Psychological Association, pp. 29–48.

Sousa-Poza, A. and Sousa-Poza, A.A. (2003) Gender differences in job satisfaction in Great Britain, 1991–2000: Permanent or transitory? *Applied Economics Letters*, 10, 691–4.

Spears, J. (2012) Hydro executives get fat bonuses as utility misses benchmarks. *Toronto Star*, January 27, A1, A10.

Srivastava, A., Locke, E.A. and Bartol, K.M. (2001) Money and subjective well-being: It's not the money, it's the motives. *Journal of Personality and Social Psychology*, 80, 959–71.

Stempel, J. (2012) JPMorgan to pay $100-million in credit card suit. *Globe and Mail*, July 25, B6.

Stevenson, B. and Wolpers, J. (2008) Happiness inequality in the United States. *Journal of Legal Studies*, 37, S33–S79.

Stout, L. (2012) *The Shareholder Value Myth: How Putting Shareholders First Harms Investors, Corporations, and the Public*. San Francisco, CA: Berrett Koehler.

Swatuk, L. (2012) Cheap's costly toll. *Globe and Mail*, December 1, F8.

Symonds, M. (2011) New words of welcome for the MBA class of 2012. *Forbes*, October.

Taibbi, M. (2012) Too crooked to fail: The crimes of the Bank of America. *Rolling Stone*, March 14, 17–23.

Talaga, T. (2012) Ethics chief queried ORNGE "lobbying." *Toronto Star*, April 25, A8.

Tang, T. (2007) Income and quality of life: Does the love of money make a difference? *Journal of Business Ethics*, 72, 375–93.

Tett, J. (2009) *Fool's Gold: The Inside Story of J.P. Morgan and How Wall Street Greed Corrupted Its Bold Dream and Caused a Financial Catastrophe*. New York: Free Press.

Toffler, B.L. and Reingold, J. (2003) *Final Accounting: Ambition, Greed and the Fall of Arthur Andersen*. New York: Broadway Books.

Toronto Star (2011) Charity fires boss, calls in cops: Oshawa Hospital Foundation's former CEO hired own company to run fundraisers. October 27, A1, A22.

—— (2012a) Rich hold $32 trillion in offshore tax havens: Money in accounts represents $280M in lost tax revenues. July 23, A3.

—— (2012b) $1.5-billion class action suit launched against SNC-Lavalin. May 10, B3.

—— (2012c) Apple avoids billions in US taxes: Its subsidiaries are set up in low-tax countries. April 30, B8.

—— (2012d) Exodus continues at troubled Barclays. July 4, B3.

—— (2012e) Prosecutors close to making Libor arrests: Individual traders to be charged in UK's rate-rigging scandal. July 23, A2.

—— (2012f) Citigroup settles with shareholders. August 30, B7.

Twenge, J.M. (2006) *Generation Me: Why Today's Young Americans Are More Confident, Assertive, Entitled – and More Miserable Than Ever Before*. New York: Free Press.

Twenge, J.M. and Campbell, W.K. (2009) *The Narcissism Epidemic: Living in the Age of Entitlement*. New York: Free Press.

Twenge, J.M., Campbell, S.M., Hoffman, B.J. and Lance, C.E. (2010) Generational differences in work values: Leisure and extrinsic values increasing, social and intrinsic values decreasing. *Journal of Management*, 36, 1117–42.

Twenge, J.M., Freeman, E.C. and Campbell, W.K. (2012) Generational differences in young adults' life goals, concern for others, and civic orientation, 1966–2003. *Journal of Personality and Social Psychology*, 102, 1045–62.

Van Boven, L. and Gilovich, T. (2003) To do or to have? That is the question. *Journal of Personality and Social Psychology*, 85, 1193–202.

van Gelder, S. (2011) *This Changes Everything: Occupy Wall Street and the 99% Movement*. San Francisco, CA: Berrett-Koehler.

Vansteenkiste, M., Duriez, B., Simons, H.J. and Soenens, B. (2006) Materialistic values and well-being among business students: Further evidence of their detrimental effect. *Journal of Applied Social Psychology*, 36, 2892–908.

Viswanatha, A. (2012) Wal-Mart bribery review expands to Brazil, China. *National Post*, June 13, FP7.

Vohs, K.D., Mead, N.L. and Goode, M.R. (2006) The psychological consequences of money. *Science*, 314, 1154–6.

—— (2008) Merely activating the concept of money changes personal and interpersonal behavior. *Psychological Science*, 19, 49–54.

Wagner, D. and Gordon, M. (2011) Corzine defends role as MFGlobal chief: Former CEO apologizes and says he doesn't know where clients' $1.2 billion has gone since the brokerage firm's collapse. *Globe and Mail*, December 9, B8.

Waldie, P., Peritz, I. and Smith, G. (2012) RCMP make second search of SNC-Lavalin: Raid at engineering giant's Montreal head office part of ongoing probe into allegations of corruption and bribery. *Globe and Mail*, April 11, A4.

Wang, L., Malhotra, D. and Murnighan, J.K. (2012) Economics, education and greed. *Academy of Management Learning and Education*, 10, 643–60.

Wang, L. and Murnighan, J.K. (2011) On greed. *Annals of the Academy of Management*, 5, 279–316.

Ward, O. (2102) Dictators' wives show off Arab bling: Syria, Libya, Tunisia and Egypt may be in turmoil, but these first ladies are used to living in style. *Toronto Star*, March 16, A12, A13.

Wheeler, C. (2012) For luxury goods, China fast becoming the People's Republic of Gucci. *Globe and Mail*, June 20, B9.

Willis, E. and Garn, R. (2011) *Prosper: Create the Life You Really Want*. San Francisco, CA: Berrett-Koehler.

Wilson, B. (2012) Rethinking your legacy: What epitaph would my children write? *National Post*, September 10, FP4.

Wilson, D. and Singer, T. (2009) Ghost writing rife in medical journals. *New York Times*, September 10, 34.

Winnett, R. and Mason, R. (2012) A knight no longer. *National Post*, February 1, A2.

Woods, A. (2012) Ex-SNC boss faces fraud charges. *Toronto Star*, November 29, A6.

Woods, A. and MacCharles, T. (2012) Meet the Conservatives' call guy. *Toronto Star*, February 28, A1.

Yamani, M. (2011) Saudi Arabia's old regime grows older. *Globe and Mail*, October 25, B7.

Yew, M.A-T. (2012) Where did $56 million go? *Toronto Star*, March 27, A1, A8.

CHAPTER 4

Like Moths Attracted to Flames: Managerial Hubris and Financial Reporting Fraud

MICHEL MAGNAN, DENIS CORMIER AND PASCALE LAPOINTE-ANTUNES

Introduction

1993: Canadian Entrepreneur of the Year

1994: Outstanding Achievement Award winner for Women in Television and Film

1997: Honorary doctorate from a Canadian university

1997: 19th among the 50 most powerful women in the world's entertainment industry

1999: Appointed director of BCE Inc., one of Canada's largest and most widely-owned companies

The above refer to critical steps in the meteoric rise of Micheline Charest, former co-CEO and controlling shareholder of CINAR Corporation (CINAR). CINAR, a media and entertainment company co-founded by Ms. Charest and her husband and co-CEO, Ron Weinberg, was once the darling of the investment community. At its peak, the firm reached stock market capitalization of $1.9 billion. However, at the pinnacle of Ms. Charest's fame and power, the company began to unravel, becoming embroiled in allegations of copyright, tax, financial reporting and cash management cover-ups, and frauds in the tens if not hundreds of millions of dollars.[1] The events at CINAR led to a legal and regulatory saga that, in 2009, is still going on. Through that process, the Charest-Weinberg couple

1 On March 15, 2002, without admitting any guilt, Ms. Charest and Mr. Weinberg each agreed to pay an unprecedented $1,000,000 fine to the Quebec Securities Commission and to abstain from exercising the voting rights related to the shares they owned in CINAR for five years. Other litigations with taxation authorities and their former firm were settled out of court.

lost their positions, the control of their company, their reputation, and, most likely, a significant share of their fortune.[2]

Inspired by the CINAR story, this chapter addresses two related questions. First, why does such a celebrated business figure as Micheline Charest risk her reputation to engage in and pursue fraudulent and/or dubious activities? Second, do directors, auditors, and regulators help prevent and/or detect financial reporting fraud when they are dealing with successful and highly reputable individuals such as Micheline Charest? Focusing on a sample of fraud cases pursued by securities regulators during the 1995–2005 period, our chapter addresses both questions in the following ways.

We argue that overconfidence or an elevated opinion of themselves, ignite and accelerate the propensity of senior executives to commit or be oblivious to fraud. The focus on top management is warranted by the fact that they tend to commit the largest frauds that are most likely to affect the reliability of financial statements (Peltier-Rivest, 2007). However, such overconfidence should be held in check by various internal and external monitors: audit committees, boards of directors, auditors, analysts, and media. Hence, our analysis encompasses both signals of managerial overconfidence as well as observable measures of monitoring effectiveness. Signals of managerial overconfidence are captured by favorable media attention (Hayward, Rindova and Pollock, 2004). Prior research shows that hubris can be fed and magnified when there is too much self-reflection of success and achievements.

We document the market, management, governance, and industry contexts that underlie corporate frauds. The evidence that we provide in the chapter is consistent with managerial overconfidence, fed by a fawning or favourable press, being a key determinant of financial frauds. Like moths attracted to the flames that ultimately kill them, managers under the spotlight will gain in self-assurance and a feeling of invincibility, thus leading them to take more risks in their fraudulent activities.

The rest of the chapter proceeds as follows. The next section provides a brief overview of prior research on the determinants of financial reporting fraud. The third section develops our conceptual arguments underlying the role of overconfidence in fraud. The fourth section describes our sample and the methodology used in our analysis. Our analysis and findings are then discussed. The last section provides a discussion and a conclusion.

Fraudulent Financial Reporting

TOP MANAGEMENT AND FINANCIAL REPORTING FRAUD: PRIOR RESEARCH OVERVIEW

The issue of top management fraud encompasses a vast literature covering many years. The scope of prior research reflects the diversity of what constitutes top management fraud, i.e., willfully undertaking actions to mislead others: embezzlement, insider trading, self-dealings, lying about facts, failing to disclose significant events, corruption, cover-ups, etc. Zahra, Priem and Rasheed (2005) provide an exhaustive overview of prior research on the antecedents and consequences of top management

2 Ms. Charest died on April 14, 2004.

fraud. According to them, most studies on financial reporting adopt a governance perspective, with findings generally supporting the view that fraud is committed to enrich managers. However, studies on financial reporting frauds typically focus on proximate indicators, or red flags, rather than attempting to establish underlying causes or antecedents.

Why a firm's top management decides to engage in unethical or fraudulent financial reporting remains, to a large extent, a puzzle. While it is relatively easy to identify environmental, organizational or individual attributes that seem to be associated with the incidence of financial reporting that violates generally accepted accounting principles (GAAP), one can also find such attributes in many other organizational contexts that do not exhibit GAAP violations. Moreover, beyond external or objectives characteristics, it is difficult to infer the interior motives, personalities or combinations of organizational context and personal weakness that drive successful individuals to take the slippery slope of unethical behavior. An additional puzzle is why top managers often willingly expand the scope and the scale of their financial reporting manipulations. Several models have been put forward to provide a structured understanding of these questions.

FRAUDULENT FINANCIAL REPORTING: A MARKET AND INCENTIVE PERSPECTIVE

Jensen (2005) argues that top managers of firms whose shares are overvalued have an incentive to engage in aggressive financial reporting. In his view, a firm's stock market overvaluation, i.e., the difference between a firm's stock market value and its underlying intrinsic value, essentially reflects investors' inflated expectations with respect to future earnings. Because these expectations are unlikely to be achieved, management may be tempted to engage in accounting manipulations to raise the level of reported earnings that match the investors' implied target. While some initial manipulations may be within GAAP, decline in the underlying business or the continuation of a stock market bubble may bring managers to violate GAAP to stay afloat. Since they have more to lose if the firm's share price deflates, managers with extensive stock or option holdings are more likely to feel pressure to manipulate earnings.

Jensen's model has the appeal of putting financial reporting fraud into a broader stock market context in which there is a dynamic interplay between managers and investors. However, Jensen's perspective on the drivers behind financial reporting fraud does not integrate many individual, intra-organizational or social factors that relate to fraudulent behavior. As such, the fraud pattern that emerges from Jensen's argument is consistent with an agency theory view that managers are solely, and rationally, driven by financial incentives, even in terms of their own ethics. In other words, at any point in time, many firms may be in a situation where their shares are overvalued, thus potentially inducing management to engage in financial misreporting.

Jensen's intuition is corroborated by at least one empirical study. Efendi, Srivastava and Swanson (2007) find that instances of financial statement misrepresentation are indeed associated with corporate overvaluations and extensive stock option holdings for managers. With much unrealized stock option holding gains at stake and aggressive market expectations, managers are greatly tempted to resort to manipulations to achieve earnings targets.

However, not all managers fall into that trap, only a minority. Why? To answer this question, it is necessary to use slightly different lenses and perhaps integrate other drivers of human behavior. We now review three studies showing that an individual's attitudes, social referents, and firm size emerge as key drivers of the intention to engage in fraudulent or unethical financial reporting.

FRAUDULENT FINANCIAL REPORTING: A BEHAVIORAL PERSPECTIVE

Through a survey of current Chief Financial Officers (CFOs), Gillett and Uddin (2005) investigate the factors linked with CFO intentions to engage in fraudulent financial reporting, relying on the theory of reasoned action. The final model that emerges reveals that negative belief evaluations may contribute to a reduction in the occurrence of fraudulent financial reporting. A manager's referent groups strongly influence his/her subjective norms and can also attenuate intentions to engage in fraudulent financial reporting. Nevertheless, CFOs in large firms exhibit greater intentions to engage in fraudulent financial reporting. The need for achievement, a positive view of fraudulent actions, and managers' compensation structure do not seem to influence CFO attitudes.

Carpenter and Reimers (2005) use the theory of planned behavior to examine managers' decision to engage or not in fraudulent financial reporting. The planned behavior theory assumes control over behavior. Hence, the key to explain an individual's behavior is intentions, which are driven by attitudes toward the behavior, subjective norms, and perceived control over the behavior. Results from a survey and from an experiment provide strong support for the theory, with attitude having the most influence in predicting behavioral intent.

Cohen et al. (2010) provide evidence that is consistent with the fraud triangle being enriched by integrating the theory of planned behavior. According to Cohen et al. (2010), the theory of planned behavior provides insights into the importance of managers' personality traits as fraud risk factors. By looking at ex-post rationalizations for discovered fraud cases, as published and discussed in media reports, they infer the role of managers' personality and attitudes in the commitment of fraud. In their view, managers' attitudes toward fraud as well as their ethical values are an important factor to consider when assessing the potential for a fraud to be committed. Overall, they consider that the theory of planned action maps reasonably well into the fraud triangle model and allows for an enhancement in its explanatory power.

Managerial Overconfidence or Hubris: The Missing Link?

RECONCILING RESEARCH AND INSTITUTIONS

The COSO framework, as well as audit standards that are derived from it, maps fraudulent financial reporting in a way that is broadly consistent with Jensen's (2005) argument. Fraudulent financial reporting is perceived to be more likely when top management has incentives and/or feels pressure by analysts and market participants to engage in fraudulent financial reporting. Such financial incentives underlie Jensen's perspective.

The opportunity for top management to commit fraud is increased if there is weak governance or internal controls, a view that has empirical support. The rationalization, which may appear to be a behavioral antecedent, is actually ex-post and unlikely to provide the upfront impetus to commit fraud.

Behavioral models such as Carpenter and Reimers (2005) or Gillett and Uddin (2005), which picture fraud in a more intricate way, do not seem to have made much of an impact on institutions. A potential reason for their limited practical impact is the difficulty, in the context of an audit or through regulatory interventions, to measure employees' and managers' attitudes as well as their intentions. The intent to engage in fraudulent financial reporting does not necessarily imply the commitment of such fraud: there seems to be a missing element, or step, between intent and actual action in the behavioral models.

MANAGERIAL OVERCONFIDENCE

Managerial overconfidence, sometimes labeled hubris when it reaches an extreme form, is defined as exaggerated pride or self-confidence often resulting in retribution (Merriam-Webster Online Dictionary; Hayward and Hambrick, 1997). Hubris derives from Greek mythology in which it was deemed to be man's fatal flaw. "Those excessively confident, presumptuous, blindly ambitious or otherwise lacking humility were relentlessly struck down by the gods" (Grimal, 1986, as reported in Hayward and Hambrick, 1997, p. 106). In practice, managerial hubris has been identified as a potential explanation of three widespread business phenomena or events: (1) the overbidding taking place in many large takeover fights (e.g., Hayward and Hambrick, 1997), (2) the decision to engage in a takeover despite widespread evidence that most acquisitions fail to create value (e.g., Brown and Sarma, 2007), and (3) the tendency for entrepreneurs to launch new ventures in the shadow of high venture failure rates (e.g., Hayward, Shepherd and Griffin, 2006).

MANAGERIAL OVERCONFIDENCE AND FRAUD

One of the advantages of using managerial hubris to explore the underlying causes of fraud is that it manifests itself in directly observable actions or decisions. Hiller and Hambrick (2005) note that hubris contributes to enhance an executive's core self-evaluation, i.e., how executives evaluate themselves and their relationship with the environment. In their view, executives with very high or hyper core self-evaluation are free of anxiety and have little concern about negative outcomes because they feel that they will ultimately prevail. In other words, "the upper reaches of core self-evaluation may be thought of as a scientifically validated hubris factor" (Hiller and Hambrick, 2005, p. 306).

MANAGERIAL HUBRIS AND GOVERNANCE

CEO hubris is not completely unrestricted in most firms. There is evidence that vigilant boards, or strong governance or monitoring, can influence corporate outcomes, even those that directly relate to the CEO such as executive compensation (e.g., Core,

Holthausen and Larcker, 1999). Hayward and Hambrick (1997) argue, and provide evidence demonstrating, that vigilant boards can moderate CEO hubris and attenuate its impact on takeover premiums.

The interface between hubris and governance is less straightforward with respect to fraudulent reporting or asset misappropriation. In contrast to executive compensation or takeovers, which must be formally approved by the board, managerial frauds are not typically a topic of board discussion beforehand. Furthermore, formal governance attributes such as directors' independence have been shown to be ineffectual if not associated with competence, expertise, and/or intense activity (e.g., Chen and Zhou, 2007). Finally, politically or socially astute CEOs with hyper core self-evaluation may "engage in centralized and unilateral decision-making but will still allow others in the organization to have the impression that they have a voice or input to the decision" (Hiller and Hambrick, 2005, p. 311). Appearances of good governance or intense external monitoring will help reinforce a CEO's own self-image and conviction that he is beyond reproach, even as frauds are under way. If governance and monitoring mechanisms that appear strong are actually ineffectual, this may reinforce rather than constrain managerial overconfidence, ultimately leading to hubris.

Methodology

The chapter focuses on the population of fraudulent financial misreporting cases that occurred between 1995 and 2005 in Canada among publicly traded firms. The selection criterion was for a firm to have been pursued and/or sanctioned by securities authorities during that period for GAAP violations or asset misappropriations which were not properly disclosed. Hence, other cases of securities fraud such as insider trading or embezzlement are not covered (unless they relate to GAAP violations or asset misappropriations). Fifteen such firms were identified from the web site of the Ontario Securities Commission (OSC) as having had cease-trading orders accompanied by financial statement refilings or errors. We adopt a clinical study approach, which allows us to delve into the rich stories underlying each instance of misreporting.

The information used for the analysis is obtained solely from public sources: proxy statements, audited financial statements, annual reports, management discussion and analysis, OSC briefs or reports, press releases and media articles, and briefs for court proceedings.

Findings and Analysis

OVERVIEW

Table 4.1a provides an overview of the study's cases as well as some summary information regarding the legal and economic outcomes from the fraud or impropriety. The improprieties fall into three broad categories: (1) GAAP violations (accounting), (2) asset misappropriations (assets), and (3) incomplete or fraudulent disclosure (disclosure). However, the specifics of each case are quite varied. Atlas

Cold Storage's 2002 earnings were found to be overstated by $37.4 million due to overstatements of accounts receivable, prepaid expenses, capital assets, and goodwill; and understatements of accounts payable and accruals. More than $100 million in assets evaporated at Philip Services in its metals recycling business due to improper trading. The discovery of a major gold deposit by Bre-X was eventually exposed as a hoax. Finally, CINAR was accused to have falsely represented the citizenship of its artistic creators to obtain special tax credits from the Canadian government. Over $120 million in the firm's liquid assets were found to have been transferred to the Caribbean without the board's approval, with more than $40 million still missing to this day.

Very few cases were settled in court. One particularity of the Canadian legal system concerning white collar crime is the slowness of the procedures. While the Conrad Black-Hollinger case was tried in the United States because it related to a US-based subsidiary of Hollinger, the OSC civil proceedings against Conrad Black and other senior executives of Hollinger are still pending and were recently postponed (such proceedings were started more than four years ago). Similarly, while the frauds allegedly took place between 1993 and 1998 in the Livent case, criminal court proceedings only started in the summer of 2008, with a verdict being pronounced in 2009. The monetary fines or penalties that were eventually imposed on parties involved in fraudulent reporting are also relatively minor compared with the magnitudes of the amounts involved. Only the initiation of civil class action suits allows investors to be partially compensated for their losses (although the perpetrators of the frauds themselves are rarely affected). The $120 million settlement in the YBM Magnex case was paid from the firm's assets ($35 million) and by a group of former auditors, directors, investment bankers, and attorneys ($85 million).

The economic sanctions are of greater consequence. In almost all cases, when comparing the firm's share price peak prior to the announcement of the fraudulent incident to the value as of July 2008, it appears that investors lost almost everything. Eleven out of 15 firms ultimately went bankrupt and were either liquidated or restructured, with pre-fraud investors' ownership being extensively diluted if not eliminated altogether. In the two takeover cases, Atlas and CINAR, Atlas shareholders were able to recoup about 50 percent of CINAR investors who received less than 10 percent of the firm's former peak value. In all firms except Laidlaw and Mount Real, the principals involved in the fraudulent activities also lost significant amounts of money, if not all their firm-specific wealth, as they were significant shareholders. Table 4.1b allows for a comparative analysis of the sample firms' peak stock market valuation, and sales and earnings, as initially reported, in the period preceding or concurrent to the fraudulent activities.

Table 4.1a Overview of cases and outcomes

Case	Nature of Business	Type of Impropriety Sanctioned by Securities Regulators*	Ultimate Regulatory Sanctions (as of June 30, 2008)	Economic Sanction (Stock Market Value Decline from Peak until 31/07/2008)	Ultimate Outcome
Atlas Cold Storage	Freezer operations	Accounting	CFC and controller fined and barred. Charges against CEC dropped for lack of evidence. $40 million settlement of class action suit approved by Ontario Superior Court of Justice in June 2008.	$300,000,000	Takeover
Bre-X	Mining exploration	Disclosure Assets	CEO died during proceedings. $10,000,000 settlement. Chief geologist cleared of all charges.	$6,000,000,000	Bankruptcy and liquidation
CINAR	Film and TV production	Tax evasion Disclosure Assets	Co-CEOs fined and barred. Out-of-court settlements for tax and misappropriation cases.	$1,900,000,000	Takeover
Fareport	Taxi and ground transportation	Accounting Assets	Both president and COO resigned. Insider cease trading order.	$150,000,000	Restructuring and change of control
Getty Copper	Mining exploration	Assets	Chair and CEO resigned. Royal Canadian Mounted Police investigation. Lawsuits still pending.	$400,000,000	
Hollinger	Newspapers	Disclosure Assets	Owner-CEO and executives convicted in criminal US proceedings. OSC proceedings still pending.	$1,000,000,000	Bankruptcy
Knowledge House	Internet-based learning and education	Insider stock trading and stock price manipulation	Chair of audit committee fined $50,000 for lack of monitoring.	$93,000,000	Bankruptcy
Laidlaw	Ground transportation and waste management	Accounting	Out-of-court settlement with claimants.	$7,000,000,000	Bankruptcy and restructuring

Case	Nature of Business	Type of Impropriety Sanctioned by Securities Regulators*	Ultimate Regulatory Sanctions (as of June 30, 2008)	Economic Sanction (Stock Market Value Decline from Peak until 31/07/2008)	Ultimate Outcome
Livent	Live theater production	Accounting Assets	Ongoing criminal trial against controlling shareholders.	$300,000,000	Bankruptcy and liquidation
Mount Real	Accounting services and magazine subscription management	Accounting Assets Illegal sale of securities	Criminal and civil lawsuits still pending.	$150,000,000	Bankruptcy and liquidation
Philip Services	Waste management and recycling	Accounting Assets	Senior management fined $500,000 and barred. Criminal proceedings against another executive still pending.	$3,700,000,000	Bankruptcy and restructuring
Semi-Tech	Sewing machines and electronics	Accounting Assets	Former CEO sentenced to six years in prison by Hong Kong court on one count of false accounting, other charges dropped. Guilty verdict overturned on appeal.	$1,300,000,000	Bankruptcy and liquidation
St. Genevieve	Mining exploration	Assets	Admission of guilt. Owner-CEO removed.	$120,000,000	Bankruptcy and restructuring
Tee-Comm Electronics	Direct-to-home entertainment products and services	Disclosure	Class action lawsuits still outstanding.	$500,000,000	Bankruptcy and liquidation
YBM Magnex	Industrial magnets	Accounting Assets	$120 million settlement. Five former directors, brokerage firms for IPO sanctioned and fined $1.2 million. 5-year ban for directors.	$1,000,000,000	Bankruptcy and liquidation

*Legend – Type of Impropriety Sanctioned by Regulators.

Accounting: GAAP violations.

Assets: Improper use of assets and asset misappropriation.

Disclosure: Non-disclosure of material facts.

Table 4.1b Overvaluation

Case	Date	Approximate Stock Market Capitalization at Peak	Reported GAAP Sales Immediately before Fraud Discovery or Concurrent to It	Reported GAAP Earnings (Loss) Immediately before Fraud Discovery or Concurrent to It
Atlas Cold Storage	2002	$600,000,000	$295,733,000	$19,045,000
Bre-X	1996	$6,000,000,000	Negligible	Negligible
CINAR	1998	$1,900,000,000	$150,978,000	$21,832,000
Fareport	2004	$150,000,000	Not available	($1,656,000)
Getty Copper	2002	$400,000,000	Negligible	($251,000)
Hollinger	1999	$1,000,000,000	$3,860,000,000	*($259,000,000)
Knowledge House	2000	$93,000,000	$39,182,000	($6,911,000)
Laidlaw	1998	$7,000,000,000	$2,056,000,000	*$245,000,000
Livent	1997	$300,000,000	$331,732,000	$11,053,000
Mount Real	2002	$100,000,000	$38,257,000	$9,722,000
Philip Services	1997	$3,700,000,000	$1,125,510,000	$52,742,000
Semi-Tech	1997	$1,300,000,000	$1,799,400,000	($110,100,000)
St. Genevieve	1997	$120,000,000	Negligible	Loss
Tee-Comm	1996	$500,000,000	Not available	Not available
YBM Magnex	1997	$1,000,000,000	$90,326,000	$17,072,000

*Excluding certain dilution gains and gains on disposal of long term assets.

RED FLAGS AS RED HERRINGS?

Table 4.2 provides an analysis of the cases through the lens of the "red flag" template that is often used in auditing and internal control procedures. Since the analysis relies on public documents, many red flags cannot be identified. Nevertheless, we can observe that the red flag template does seem to capture antecedents of Canadian cases of fraudulent reporting reasonably well. In that sense, a priori, the relationship between red flags and fraudulent reporting does appear to be consistent with prior evidence.

But the red flags can also be perceived to be red herrings and, as such, not very useful for auditors and regulators. First, red flags considered to represent opportunities for fraudulent financial reporting can be observed in large swaths of Canada's business landscape. However, most other firms do not seem to exhibit any fraudulent activities. Therefore, relying on these red flags can translate into an inefficient use of audit and regulatory resources as there are so many firms that can potentially be chased on that basis.

For example, around 50 percent of Canada's large publicly traded firms have a significant blockholder, often a family or an individual who also occupies senior executive position(s) (Craighead, Magnan and Thorne, 2004). Complex corporate structures also are a staple of Canadian business. More than 20 percent of firms on the Toronto Stock Exchange Index have a dual class share structure (Khalil, Magnan and Cohen, 2008). During the 2000–2008 period, income trusts or limited partnerships represented up to 15 percent of Canada's total

Table 4.2 "Red flags" summary analysis

Case	Opportunity				Incentives/Pressures/Motivation			Rationalization[8]
	Owner-CEO Control[1]	Complex Corporate Structure[2]	Active M&A Strategy[3]	Unique or Uncommon Business Model[4]	Unrealistic Earnings Expectations[5]	Incentives[6]	Lifestyle[7]	
Atlas Cold Storage	X	X	X	X	X	Bonuses Share issue		
Bre-X	X		X	X	X	Bonuses Share issues and sales	X	
CINAR	X		X	X	X	Bonuses Share issue	X	X
Fareport	X		X	X	X	Personal gains		
Getty Copper	X			X	X	Personal gain to CEO		X
Hollinger	X	X	X		X	Bonuses Special fees	X	X
Knowledge House	X		X	X	X	Bonuses Share sales		
Laidlaw		X	X		X	Bonuses		
Livent	X		X	X	X	Bonuses Share issue	X	X
Mount Real	X	X	X	X	X	Share and debt issues		X
Philip Services	X	X	X	X	X	Share issue		
Semi-Tech	X	X	X	X	X			X
St. Genevieve	X	X	X	X	X	Propping up of related party firm Share issue		X
Tee-Comm	X		X	X	X	Bonuses Share issue		
YBM Magnex	X	X	X	X	X	Share issue		X

1 CEO and/or CEO family own at least 5 percent of shares.

2 Numerous subsidiaries, affiliates; foreign affiliates.

3 Recent acquisitions.

4 Complex or unclear business model.

5 Stock market price unjustified by earnings.

6 Earnings-based bonus plan, share or debt issue, primary and/or secondary.

7 Media mention about CEO's lifestyle.

8 Evidence of public declaration to justify fraudulent behavior (CINAR, St. Genevieve, Hollinger), known history of fraudulent background or connections (Mount Real, Semi-Tech, YBM Magnex), evidence of owner-manager not distinguishing between personal and business (CINAR, Hollinger, Livent).

stock market capitalization (Cormier, Lapointe-Antunes and Magnan, 2011).[3] Pyramidal arrangements are quite common, encompassing many of Canada's leading corporate empires such as Weston-Loblaw, Power Corporation, Quebecor or Sobeys. The past decade witnessed a surge in M&A activity in all industrial sectors (Andre, Khalil and Magnan, 2007). Finally, Canada is home to the world's largest junior mining exchange alongside London (UK), a sector that is typically short of cash and always striving to raise new capital.

A similar observation can be made regarding red flags considered to represent motivations for fraudulent financial reporting. Unrealistic earnings expectations are rampant in bull markets such as the ones experienced between 1995 and 2000, and between 2002 and 2005. Similarly, personal incentives in terms of bonuses, share issues or share sales are prevalent in most firms. In retrospect, the red flag template works but, in the broader context in which auditors and regulators want to prevent or detect fraudulent financial reporting, red flags essentially morph into red herrings that may lead to numerous and unfruitful wild investigation chases. While red flags can be deemed to be proximate causes of fraudulent activities, the causality relationship is actually more complex than what the template may suggest.

GOVERNANCE AND MARKET MONITORING: A PRELUDE TO HUBRIS?

It appears that governance mechanisms and external monitoring did not prevent fraud in sample firms. First, 12 out of 15 firms had a majority of independent directors on their board in the period immediately preceding the discovery of the fraudulent activities. All boards also had an audit committee comprising independent directors (as required by the Toronto Stock Exchange). Second, at least seven out of 15 firms had "star" directors who brought considerable credibility or clout to the board. CINAR's board included one of Canada's leading retail executives who was also an accountant by trade. It also included an experienced merchant banker. A former Canadian ambassador to the United States was on Hollinger's board. Knowledge House had one of the region's leading attorneys on its board as well as a former aide to the country's prime minister. YBM Magnex had a former premier of the Province of Ontario on its board. But Livent's board was perhaps the most star-studded with four of North America's most experienced and well-connected private equity investors and merchant bankers sitting on it. Finally, 12 out of 15 firms also had Big 4 auditors, the only exceptions being Fareport, Getty Copper, and YBM Magnex.

From a market monitoring perspective, most of the sample firms were screened by some of Canada's leading financial intermediaries (see Table 4.3). For example, it appears that nine out of the 15 firms retained prestige investment bankers during the period immediately preceding or coinciding with the discovery of fraudulent activities. Atlas retained TD Capital for a share issue. Bre-X and its affiliates Bresea issued shares through TD Securities, Scotia McLeod, and Midland Walwyn Capital. CINAR issued shares through CIBC Wood Gundy and Salomon Canada. Hollinger issued notes through the investment banking subsidiaries of all of Canada's largest banks. Livent issued shares through CIBC Wood Gundy and First Marathon. Philip Services' last share issue is especially noteworthy as it was subscribed by

3 These corporate structures often involve a dual governance oversight system (a board of trustees plus a board of directors), have intricate legal arrangements (trust deeds) instead of corporate charters and often mix unincorporated entities with corporations (Cormier, Lapointe-Antunes and Magnan 2011).

Table 4.3 Governance and market monitoring

Case	Governance				Market Monitoring		
	Majority of Independent Directors	Existence of Audit Committee	Presence of Star Directors[1]	Prestige Auditor[2]	Prestige Investment Banker[3]	TSX Index[4]	Analyst Coverage[5]
Atlas Cold Storage	X	X		X	X		X
Bre-X		X		X	X	X	X
CINAR	X	X	X	X	X	X	X
Fareport	X	X					
Getty Copper	X	X					
Hollinger		X	X	X	X		X
Knowledge House	X	X	X	X			X
Laidlaw	X	X	X	X	X	X	X
Livent	X	X	X	X	X		X
Mount Real	X	X		X			
Philip Services	X	X		X	X	X	X
Semi-Tech		X		X		X	X
St. Genevieve	X	X	X	X	X		X
Tee-Comm		X		X		X	X
YBM Magnex	X	X	X		X	X	X

1 Presence of a director who sits on more than one board of a publicly traded firm.
2 Auditor is one of the large world-wide accounting firms (Big 4, 5, 6 or 8).
3 Equity or debt issue managed or co-managed by a subsidiary of one of Canada's banks or New York-based old-line investment bank.
4 Firm was part of the Toronto Stock Exchange composite Index at some point.
5 Evidence of analyst following from analysts' reports or recommendations.

a who's who of Canada's investment banking community: Salomon, Merrill Lynch, CIBC Wood Gundy, TD, RBC Dominion, First Marathon, and Midland Walwyn.

At least six of the sample firms were also at some point a component of the Toronto Stock Exchange Index, a status that is typically preceded by an investigation by the Exchange authorities and which is accompanied by increased scrutiny by market participants. Finally, while the data is sketchier in that regard, it does appear that 12 out of 15 firms were subjected to active analyst coverage during the period, albeit not always positive.

Hence, from both governance and market monitoring perspectives, sample firms were subjected to what would appear to be appropriate oversight and scrutiny by well-informed and independent "principals" or "monitors" such as directors, auditors, investment bankers, analysts, and stock market authorities, with the above-mentioned red flags being visible to all these agents at most times. Such a finding contrasts with Hayward and Hambrick (1997) who provide evidence that vigilant boards may be less influenced by managerial hubris, thus attenuating takeover premiums.

That governance and market monitoring failed so dramatically in these instances raises two questions. First, were some players being co-opted by financial incentives, i.e., additional fees in the case of auditors, investment bankers, and even directors? This is a possibility but independence, in fact, is difficult to test for many of these parties. Second, adopting a counter-intuitive approach, was the appearance of good governance and active market monitoring used by fraud perpetrators as a cover for their fraudulent activities? By creating an aura around top management and actions, governance actors and market monitors prevented further inquiry and comforted fraud perpetrators' sense of control over the course of events. Hence, fraudulent activities could keep going on despite governance and monitoring that was in appearance quite good. In some sense, visible governance and market monitoring mechanisms may have facilitated fraudulent activities, not hindered them. Hayward, Rindova and Pollock (2004) actually allude to this potential outcome.

Table 4.4 Managerial hubris

Case	Top-Rated CEO or Senior Executive[1]	Media Coverage Corporate Success[2]
Atlas Cold Storage		X
Bre-X	X	X
CINAR	X	X
Fareport		X
Getty Copper		
Hollinger	X	X
Knowledge House	X	X
Laidlaw	X	X
Livent	X	X
Mount Real		X
Philip Services	X	X
Semi-Tech		X
St. Genevieve		
Tee-Comm		X
YBM Magnex		X

1 The CEO and/or other members of the top management team have received prizes, awards or accolades in the period preceding or coinciding with the fraudulent activities.
2 Favorable or flattering media coverage.

MANAGERIAL HUBRIS

Table 4.4 provides a summary of how the case firms and/or their senior executives were assessed by the media before their downfall. The use of media mentions and public awards to measure managerial hubris is consistent with arguments put forward by Hayward, Rindova and Pollock (2004). It is striking that all sample firms received coverage that can have enhanced executives' self-confidence or arrogance and comforted them in their ability to engage in fraudulent activities without being caught, i.e., fed their hubris.

We now briefly review some of the most noteworthy quotes or mentions that illustrate the table.

Bre-X

- 1997: David Walsh, CEO, is named Developer of the Year and John Felderhof, Chief Geologist, Prospector of the Year by the Prospectors and Developers Association of Canada

CINAR

- 1998: Micheline Charest is named Canadian Woman in Communications of the Year
- 1998: Cinar is recognized by an analyst as "extremely well-managed" and "second to none in terms of delivering shareholder value" (Analyst's report)
- 1999: Micheline Charest ranks as the nineteenth most influential woman in the entertainment world by *The Hollywood Reporter*
- 1999: Micheline Charest is in the top three of the 100 most successful women-owned businesses according to *Canadian Business* (largest Canadian independent business magazine)

Fareport Capital

- 1998: The company is pointed out as an example of successful taxi strategy in the *Report to Review the Toronto Taxi Industry* by the Toronto Task Force to Review the Taxi Industry: "The principles in the Fareport strategy are all supported in the proposed recommendations"

Hollinger

- CEO-owner Conrad M. Black is reviewed in two-well known biographies
- P.C. Newman. *The Establishment Man: A Portrait of Power*. Toronto: McClelland and Stewart, 1982
- Richard Siklos. *Shades of Black*. Toronto: McClelland and Stewart, 1995
- 1990: Conrad M. Black made an officer of the Order of Canada

- 1992: Conrad M. Black appointed to the Queen's Privy Council in Canada
- 1993: Conrad M. Black writes his own biography (*Conrad Black: A Life in Progress*, 1993)
- 1998: Largest newspaper group in Canada and third largest in the world
- 2001: Conrad M. Black takes a seat as Peer of the United Kingdom, Lord Black of Crossharbour

Knowledge House

- 2000: Named New Business of the Year at the Metro Halifax Business Awards
- 2000: Ranks first in year-over-year sales and employee growth among Top 101 companies in Atlantic Canada
- 2000: Chosen as the Canadian training agency for Intel of Canada's Teach to the Future program
- 2001: Dan Potter, CEO, is appointed as chairman of Nova Scotia Business

Laidlaw

- 1998: The Alumni Achievement Award (Ryerson University) is awarded to James Bullock, CEO
- James Bullock serves as Governor and Chair of the Board of Governors of Ryerson University for six years

Livent

- 1994–1995: "Show Boat" is the highest grossing production on Broadway, setting the all-time record for the largest box office advance for a revival/re-creation, and repeatedly breaking the record for the highest weekly Broadway box office gross in history
- 1994–1995: "Show Boat" is most honored show on Broadway, winning five Tony Awards
- 1994–1995: "Show Boat" is the winner of five New York Drama Desk Awards
- Other awards and acclaims for Phantom of the Opera, Kiss of the Spiderwoman, etc.

Mount Real

- 2003: Honeybee Technology, an affiliate, places twelfth on Deloitte and Touche Canadian Technology Fast 50 Winners according to Canadian Corporate News
- 2002–2003: Lino Matteo, CEO, and Joseph Petticchino, COO, are highlighted in the advertising campaign of a major Canadian university after Mount Real agrees to finance a scholarship

Philip Services

- 1994: Named Canada's fastest growing company by *Canadian Business*, Canada's most widely read business monthly magazine

- 1994: CEO-founder and COO-founder are named Entrepreneurs of the Year by the jury of the Ernst and Young Entrepreneur of the Year Awards. Award given by Canada's Governor-General (*Business Wire*, November 2, 1994)
- 1995 and 1996: Places top 10 on *Profit Magazine*'s Top 100 most profitable companies list

Semi-Tech

- June 1997: Fourth on the list of the world's 200 fastest growing companies compiled by Deloitte and Touche Consulting Group
- Fall 1997: Named Canada's tenth largest employer
- Fall 1997: Member of Team Canada delegation to China, headed by country's prime minister

St. Genevieve

- "I could have predicted this would happen because [Gauthier] is the best promoter of this generation," said MacDonald Mines president Frank Smeenk regarding a major discovery in Cuba and the announcement of major international financing (as reported by Peter Kennedy, *Financial Post*, February 1, 1996, p. 25)

Tee-Comm

- 1995–1996: Popular stock for investor wanting to get on the satellite TV trend according to Silicon Investor web site

YBM Magnex

- March 1996: Listed on the TSX and in the TSE 300 index. Receives glowing buy recommendations from Nesbitt Burns and First Marathon

These quotes and citations show that at some point prior to the discovery of fraudulent activities, almost all sample firms or their top executives were the objects of glowing media, society or stock market reports. In our view, the prevalence of such favourable coverage may have either enhanced the willingness of perpetrators of fraudulent activities to pursue their actions or removed successful CEOs from carefully monitoring their executive team. A comment by one of Canada's richest investors, Hal Jackman, former Lieutenant-Governor of Ontario and controlling shareholder of a financial empire, further illustrates the potential removal from business reality that hubris can create. Talking about Conrad Black, a former friend, who was moving up on the British social circuit, he labeled him "a parvenu drifting away from reality. I can't understand his priorities. He does too much entertaining and not enough business" (Tom Bower, Conrad the Barbarian, *Sunday Times*, October 22, 2006).

Overall, using the conceptual and empirical frameworks developed by Hiller and Hambrick (2005), it does appear that senior executives or CEOs involved in the fraud cases reported in this study may have built up hubris, as reflected in a fawning press or analyst coverage. Such hubris may help us understand how frauds were committed and grew as strategic decision-making appeared more intuitive and centralized than formalized and decentralized.

TOWARD A NEW FRAUD FRAMEWORK

Our analysis suggests that prior models of fraud involvement such as the red flag approach or the reasoned action model are incomplete as they do not capture the rich institutional, governance and mental backgrounds that facilitate, if not accelerate, the perpetration of financial reporting fraud and impropriety. Figure 4.1 summarizes the emergent model of fraud involvement that we propose as a result of our analysis of the above case firms.

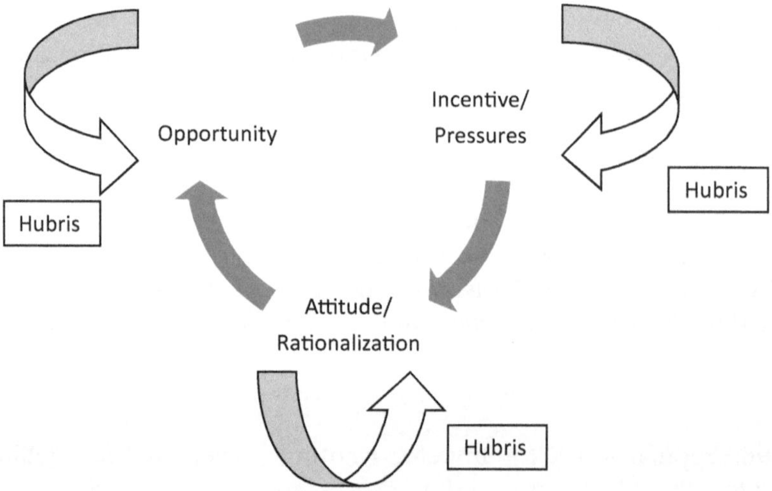

Figure 4.1 Emergent model of fraud involvement with hubris

In our view, for fraud or impropriety to be committed, governance and market monitoring conditions need to be present as they provide additional cover that may retard discovery. Moreover, as executives engage in the slippery slope of deception that accompanies fraud, impropriety or deception, their hubris can be fed or enhanced by positive or fawning external exposure as well as by precedent obscure or forgotten events that comfort them into their likelihood of success in avoiding detection. Our observation is consistent with Schrand and Zechman (2007) who note that executive over-confidence can often be seen as a prelude to fraud.

The study provides auditors and regulators with a rich template to identify or analyze cases of financial reporting fraud and severely undermines the view being put forward by many institutional investors that "check-list" governance is an effective monitoring tool. Managerial hubris, while captured in this chapter by media quotes or mentions, is likely to be transparent when asking executives about their plans, realizations, future strategies, coups, etc. Inconsistencies between executives' statements and observable facts or realities, outlandish claims, and a lack of concern for operational details can be signals that managerial hubris has set in, creating further risk for auditors and regulators.

Conclusion

This chapter analyzes cases of fraudulent financial reporting or disclosure that took place between 1995 and 2005 in Canada. A few key findings emerge. First, similar to prior evidence, many red flags can be identified for all cases. However, such red flags may be identified in scores of other Canadian firms that are without any hint of impropriety. Second, we conclude that, in almost all cases, sample firms had adequate cover for fraud or impropriety as a result of good governance in appearance and extensive stock market scrutiny through the use of prestige investment bankers or analyst coverage. Third, we discover that almost all sample firms and/or their CEOs were the objects of positive media or analyst coverage in the period preceding or concurrent to the fraudulent activities. In our view, such coverage translated into a higher sense of self-confidence or invulnerability among the executives, i.e., managerial hubris. Managerial hubris either led guilty executives further down the path of deception and fraud or, alternatively, pulled their supervising executives away from efficient and effective monitoring.

The study provides an extension as well as a powerful contrast to prior US-based evidence. The picture of fraudulent financial reporting and disclosure that emerges is not linear, and is unlikely to be solely driven by red flags which, in any case, would describe a large fraction of corporate Canada. More attention needs to be given to signals and indications that create an appearance of good governance but are in reality deception once looked at through the prism of managerial hubris.

The study also brings the pursuit of fraud by managers outside the realm of managerial rationalism that has characterized much prior research on the phenomenon. So far, the economic (e.g., agency theory) or behavioral (e.g., planned behavior) theories that have been used to investigate managerial fraudulent intent and/or actions essentially assume rationality. Inferring that irrationality, as reflected in hubris, may explain corporate frauds is consistent with findings on other managerial actions such as takeover fights.

The study's key limitation is the small sample size (15 firms), which does represent the population of firms sanctioned by the OSC with a cease-trade order for improper or fraudulent financial reporting or disclosure. However, the small sample does allow for a deeper investigation of the context surrounding each fraud case. In addition, while we provide no formal statistical inferences, our analysis suggests that prior research may be misleading in its identification of rational or corporate attributes as fraud determinants, thus omitting the human element that hubris represents from their canvas. Finally, while our tentative model is more explanatory than predictive, it opens up a new research area as it brings a new concept into accounting research.

References

Andre, P., Khalil, S. and Magnan, M. (2007) Termination fees in mergers and acquisitions: Protecting investors or managers? *Journal of Business Finance and Accounting*, 34(3–4), 541–66.

Brown, R. and Sarma, N. (2007) CEO overconfidence, CEO dominance and corporate acquisitions. *Journal of Economics and Business*, 59, 358–79.

Carpenter, T. and Reimers, J. (2005) Unethical and fraudulent financial reporting: Applying the theory of planned behavior. *Journal of Business Ethics*, 60, 115–29.

Chen, K. and Zhou, J. (2007) Audit committee, board characteristics and auditor switch decisions by Andersen's clients. *Contemporary Accounting Research*, 24(4), 1085–117.

Cohen, J., Ding, Y., Lesage, C. and Stolowy, H. (2010) Corporate fraud and managers' behavior: Evidence from the press. *Journal of Business Ethics*, 95, 271–315.

Committee of Sponsoring Organizations (COSO) (1999) *Fraudulent Financial Reporting: 1987–1997 – An Analysis of US Public Companies*. New York: Committee of Sponsoring Organizations of the Treadway Commission.

Core, J., Holthausen, R. and Larcker, D. (1999) Corporate governance, Chief Executive Officer compensation and firm performance. *Journal of Financial Economics*, 51, 371–406.

Cormier, D., Lapointe-Antunes, P. and Magnan, M. (2011) Revisiting the relevance and reliability of non-GAAP reporting: The case of income trusts. *Contemporary Accounting Research*, 28(5), 1585–1609.

Craighead, J., Magnan, M. and Thorne, L. (2004) The impact of mandated disclosure on performance-based CEO compensation. *Contemporary Accounting Research*, 21(2), 1–30.

Efendi, J., Srivastava, A. and Swanson, E. (2007) Why do corporate managers misstate financial statements? The role of option compensation and other factors. *Journal of Financial Economics*, 85(3), 667–708.

Gillett, P. and Uddin, N. (2005) CFO intentions of fraudulent financial reporting. *Auditing: A Journal of Practice and Theory*, 24(1), 55–75.

Grimal, P. (1986) *The Dictionary of Classical Mythology*. New York: Blackwell.

Hayward, M. and Hambrick, D. (1997) Explaining the premiums paid for large acquisitions: Evidence of CEO hubris. *Administrative Science Quarterly*, 42, 103–27.

Hayward, M., Rindova, V. and Pollock, T. (2004) Believing one's press: The causes and consequences of CEO celebrity. *Strategic Management Journal*, 25, 637–53.

Hayward, M., Shepherd, D. and Griffin, D. (2006) A hubris theory of entrepreneurship. *Management Science*, 52(2), 160–72.

Hiller, N. and Hambrick, D. (2005) Conceptualizing executive hubris: The role of (hyper) core self-evaluation in strategic decision-making. *Strategic Management Journal*, 26, 297–319.

Jensen, M. (2005) Agency costs of overvalued equity. *Financial Management*, 34(1), 5–19.

Khalil, S., Magnan, M. and Cohen, J. (2008) Dual-class shares and audit pricing: Evidence from the Canadian markets. *Auditing: A Journal for Theory and Practice*, 27(2), 199–216.

Peltier-Rivest, D. (2007) *Detecting Occupational Fraud in Canada: A Study of Its Victims and Perpetrators*. Austin, TX: Association of Certified Fraud Examiners.

Schrand, C. and Zechman, S. (2007) *Executive Overconfidence and the Slippery Slope to Fraud*. Working Paper. University of Pennsylvania.

Zahra, S., Priem, R. and Rasheed, A. (2005) The antecedents and consequences of top management fraud. *Journal of Management*, 31(6), 803–26.

CHAPTER

5 The Narcissistic Leader: The One We Love to Hate or Hate to Love?

SUZY FOX

Introduction

Narcissism is an increasingly popular subject of both scholarly and popular media inquiry. Once the domain of psychotherapists, narcissism is currently viewed as either a pathological disorder or a personality trait. It is the latter form of narcissism, a sub-clinical, stable personality disposition, that predominates in a growing body of organizational and managerial scholarship. With rare exceptions, the literature has a marked tendency to assign to narcissists weighted, indeed reified judgments, and to associate narcissistic characteristics with dysfunctional or even toxic organizational behavior (e.g., counterproductive work behavior (CWB), workplace bullying, and abusive supervision).

This chapter will consider not only maladaptive but also adaptive aspects of narcissism, as they contribute to or detract from behaviors and outcomes associated with performance and leadership. The crux of the argument is that just as there are positive and negative ramifications of leadership behavior, there are positive and negative ramifications of narcissism. To be meaningful, our investigations of both must look beyond the typical, linear definitions and recognize the complex intermingling of good and evil, health and poison in our workplace reality.

Narcissism as Personality Disorder (NPD)

The traditional clinical view of narcissism as a basically unidimensional pathology is defined in the *Diagnostic and Statistical Manual of Mental Disorders* (DSM-IV: APA, 2000) as a disorder in which an individual suffers from a "pervasive pattern of grandiosity (in fantasy or behavior), lack of empathy, and hypersensitivity to the evaluation of others" (p. 689). Symptoms include exaggerated self-importance, fragile self-esteem, strong concern with recognition, admiration, success, power, brilliance, and admiration; a sense of entitlement to special favorable treatment; and relationships characterized by arrogance, envy, exploitativeness, and a lack of empathy. Grandiose self-assessment lies at the core of narcissism, whether or not this self-assessment is accurate.

While the DSM implies mental illness or dysfunction is inherent in narcissism, cognitive behavioral therapist and scholar Arthur Freeman (Freeman and Fox, 2012) argues the pathological or psychiatric nature of narcissism derives from the suffering experienced by the narcissist when this grandiose self-assessment is not continuously supported or validated from the social environment. Considerations of eliminating the NPD as a psychiatric pathology from the upcoming revision of the manual (DSM-V, scheduled for release in 2013) were met with quite an uproar from the clinical community, and the NPD appears likely to be retained as a personality disorder. This controversy reflects an underlying ambiguity as to whether narcissism should be viewed less as a disorder than as a personality trait (that is, a sub-clinical set of individual dispositional characteristics within the realm of "normalcy").

In contrast to the DSM-IV's yes/no clinical diagnosis, the dispositional approach is to view narcissism as a complex, a multi-faceted personality type. As an alternative way of distinguishing between narcissism as a disorder verses disposition, some psychologists consider the difference to be a matter of severity, with the more extreme, incapacitating occurrence considered as a psychiatric or "clinical" disorder; and narcissism in clinically normal individuals considered as a "sub-clinical" personality trait. Most discourse on narcissism in leadership and organizational behavior approaches narcissism as a personality type or trait. However, it would be inaccurate to view the clinical/pathological and sub-clinical/personality approaches as separate or competing silos; some of the leading researchers of narcissism and organization studies or leadership come from psychotherapeutic or psychoanalytic disciplinary backgrounds (e.g., Michael Maccoby and Manfred Kets de Vries).

A final distinction between the psychoanalytic and personality approaches might point to a greater complexity and contradictory nature of pathological narcissism. According to Kets de Vries and Miller (1985), the narcissist's apparent self-sufficiency and independence from emotional bonds with others may actually stem, not from a low need for affiliation, but rather from the belief that she cannot rely on love or loyalty from others; it is to cope with resulting feelings of emptiness, deprivation, and insecurity that the narcissist develops the exaggerated aura of self-sufficiency and independence from socio-emotional relationships, moving toward the extreme of interpersonal exploitativeness. Similarly, descriptions of narcissism as a personality trait focus on the grandiose self-assessment; a pathological view of narcissism emphasizes the fragile vulnerability of this self-concept, and the chronic need to obtain external affirmation (Morf and Rhodewalt, 2001).

A Sub-clinical Approach to Narcissism as a Multi-dimensional Personality Trait

The current chapter is developed around the notion of narcissism as a complex, multi-dimensional personality trait, as it is this conceptualization rather than the more extreme manifestation as a pathological disorder that is relevant to organizational phenomenon in general and leadership in particular. Recent clinical and organizational psychology scholarship categorizes this trait into dimensions (or locates characteristics along continua) such as adaptive–maladaptive, functional–dysfunctional, or covert–overt (e.g., Federn, 1952; Hill and Yousey, 1999; Rose, 2002), depending on severity, context, and outcomes of resulting behaviors and interactions.

The more nuanced the view of narcissism, the more important life context becomes in judging its ramifications. Campbell (2001) questions the prevailing clinical view of narcissism as inherently dysfunctional. From a personality-social perspective, he wonders how negative it can be when narcissistic individuals are depicted as happier, having less social anxiety, depression, shame, and guilt, are closer to their ideal selves, think of themselves as smarter and better-looking, are more extraverted, energetic, and competitive, and more likely to seek new challenges than non-narcissists. This positive relation between narcissism and subjective well-being may be due to the likelihood of narcissists adopting self-concordant personal goals, and feeling that they are successful at fulfilling these goals (Rose and Campbell, 2004). If it is not the actuality of goal achievement, but rather the perception that enhances subjective well-being, this would be consistent with narcissists' high self-evaluations of their abilities and performance. Campbell advocates a balanced view, of course including inter- and intrapersonal downsides of narcissism (anger, aggression, fragility, health risks, self-deception, inability to achieve intimacy, etc.).

Emmons (1984) likewise remarks on the paradox that narcissism correlates positively with self-esteem, extraversion, dominance, and independence. He points to earlier psychologists (such as Cattell and Fromm) who noted that narcissism has positive aspects as well, and suggests a possible curvilinear relationship between adjustment and narcissism.

Another view of narcissism is contributed by cognitive behavioral theorist Arthur Freeman (2009), based on extensive clinical practice. He differentiates nine styles of narcissism, which may be functional or dysfunctional in different life contexts. These distinct but overlapping styles, which he labels healthy, real, group, helpful, compensated, oblivious, hypervigilant, ruthless, and amorous narcissism, are distinguished based on their relationships to positive self-esteem, the accuracy of the individuals' social perception and schemas, and sensitivity to their own and others' emotions. To these individual factors I add the critical organizational and cultural contexts. Freeman's descriptions may provide nuanced insight into organizational behaviors we may associate with narcissism, such as citizenship, counterproductive work behavior, and leadership.

"HEALTHY" NARCISSISM

These individuals have attributes that they consider to be special or superior to their peers. Their desire to maintain this sense of superiority may motivate them to greater effort and achievement. They do not, however, flaunt their "gifts." The co-worker who is highly competitive and focused on self–other comparisons, but does not necessarily have to bring public attention to the comparison others' inferiority, may contribute greatly to workgroup or organizational goals through enhanced personal performance and citizenship behaviors, without the downside of incivility or bullying. This form of narcissism, however, may become a problem when the narcissist places his personal agenda above the interests of the group, particularly in a cultural context in which collectivistic or communal norms are violated.

"REAL" NARCISSISM

This style most closely corresponds to mainstream conceptualizations of narcissism. These individuals view themselves overall as superior to others, and are likely to point this out to others, often frequently and loudly. This view encompasses both the grandiose self-assessment and the constant drive for validation from others. Objective facts and the judgments of others may or may not support the narcissist's high self-judgments. The leader who, implicitly or explicitly, demands agreement, flattery, and supportive data from subordinates fits this mold.

"GROUP" NARCISSISM

These individuals' special status is conferred and maintained by membership in a group. Without the group the status is lost and is not transferable. For example, the members of a particular gang, ethnicity, or work organization may see themselves as special, and believe that members of "lesser" groups are also "lesser" people. Depending on the context of the work organization (or greater cultural context), group narcissism may enhance productivity and social cohesiveness of the group, resulting in greater goal achievement, morale, and rewards. It can, however, become dysfunctional (or deadly) when it so exacerbates inter-group rivalry that conflict and interference with superordinate organizational or societal goals ensue. Throughout the ages, leaders have honed the "us versus them" mentality of group members to assure compliance and dissolve potential resistance.

"HELPFUL" NARCISSISM

These individuals offer their wisdom or assistance to others they believe are in need of their superior advice or skill. They may be unaware that their "helpfulness" at guiding and correcting others may not be sought or appreciated. They may correct peers, colleagues, or strangers, or jump in to complete tasks for which others are responsible. They may go to great lengths to create the impression that their efforts are prosocial or good citizenship behavior, or may themselves believe they are contributing extra efforts that benefit everyone involved. They may even see themselves as intervening heroically to rescue the organization, and be unaware or uncaring regarding whose toes (or reputations) get stepped on along the way. One key component of "organizational citizenship behavior" is helping co-workers with their work tasks or problems (Fox et al., 2012). Particularly when the individual feels compelled to help an underperforming co-worker, and attributes that underperformance to poor job attitudes (e.g., commitment), lack of effort (e.g., social loafing), or other controllable deficits, the narcissist may treat the underperforming co-worker with less than perfect grace, and in fact may respond with heightened stress, anger, and bullying behavior toward the very person being helped. On the other hand, particularly in work processes designed to be highly interdependent and team-based, this type of "helpfulness" may be necessary, in the face of underperforming team members, to get the job done.

"COMPENSATED" NARCISSISM

These individuals feel so badly about themselves that they create a super-person to make up for their perceived lacks and failures, often inflating their image by exaggerating their own accomplishments or denigrating others. This depiction is probably most akin to the classic psychoanalytic view of narcissism. It also resonates with current scholarly, human resource practitioner, and public concern with workplace bullying and abusive supervision.

"OBLIVIOUS" NARCISSISM

These individuals are unaware of their effect on others. They may be excluded from groups or social settings and have no idea as to why they are excluded. Leaders and employees alike may be rewarded for achieving revenue, sales, or other quantitative goals, without regard for how these outcomes are achieved. This is a key factor in bully cultures, in which leaders may directly reward, or at a minimum be unconcerned about bullying tactics that accompany goal attainment. At a higher level, the leaders themselves may be replicating behaviors they have always found to be, at least in the short-term, successful, and while they may be dissatisfied with their relationships with peers and subordinates, they may not understand the effects of their behavior on others. We may distinguish between two types of bullies: those who overtly and proudly behave toward their subordinates with dominance, aggression, and tyranny (which we will describe as based on "ruthless" narcissism); and those who believe they are excellent, strong leaders, but are clueless that others may find their leadership abusive. Executive coaches may find the "oblivious narcissist" most responsive to efforts to reshape her leadership behavior and build a healthier workplace culture. The strategy of the coach is to make the leader aware of how her behaviors are experienced by members of the organization, what psychological, strategic, and financial costs and risks may ensue as a result, and how these narcissistic behaviors are undercutting her own goal attainment and professional recognition (Fox and Freeman, 2011).

"HYPERVIGILANT" NARCISSISM

These individuals are constantly scanning for any tiny insult, denigration, or possibility of being uncovered as less exceptional or accomplished as they see themselves. They respond to negative feedback as a severe threat, and are likely to view the evaluator as incompetent or hostile. This narcissist is, in a sense, pre-disposed to see hostility in critical feedback (perhaps coupled with a hostile attribution bias that infers intentional harm from other people's behavior or communications: Matthews and Norris, 2002). This narcissist is particularly susceptible to narcissistic injury when criticized, which occurs when his view of self is challenged or threatened, and may respond to this perceived loss or threat with anger, frustration, or aggression. A hypervigilant narcissistic leader is likely to surround himself with gatekeepers and "yes-persons," resulting in a culture of groupthink and one-way communication.

"RUTHLESS" NARCISSISM

These individuals gain satisfaction and enjoyment from the discomfort of others. Whereas some forms of narcissism may be viewed as by-products of a particular (e.g., competitive) environment, and in fact go unrecognized by the individual (as in oblivious narcissism), in this case the narcissist actually enjoys being the source of this discomfort by teasing, insulting, embarrassing, pointing out the flaws of others, or making jokes at others' expense. This is classic workplace bullying or supervisory tyranny.

"HELPLESS" NARCISSISM

These individuals are at war with everyone around them, and operate in a strategic defense mode. They may appear helpless and even incompetent, depressed, or withdrawn. This self-handicapping behavior may enable them to avoid having to meet the same criteria that others meet, or having the expectations for their work and productivity reduced.

"AMOROUS" NARCISSISM

These individuals gain gratification from the ongoing erotic and seductive conquests that "prove" their worth, value, and desirability. This is so common in living and historical leaders, the only surprise is how surprised we are every time new revelations hit the headlines that pull yet another Kennedy or Clinton down from the pedestal.

Most survey studies of narcissism in leadership and organizational behavior use some form of the Narcissistic Personality Inventory (Raskin and Hall, 1979). Several factor structures of this measure have been suggested, resulting in subscales of the measurement but also reflected in dimensional views of trait narcissism. An early effort (Raskin and Terry, 1988) supported a seven-factor solution: authority, exhibitionism, superiority, vanity, exploitativeness, entitlement, and self-sufficiency. Dimensions of the trait have differentially been associated with positive/adaptive/functional or negative/maladaptive/dysfunctional outcomes. For example, Ackerman et al. (2011) propose a three-factor model consisting of Leadership/Authority (tending toward adaptive outcomes), Grandiose Exhibitionism (maladaptive), and Entitlement/Exploitativeness (maladaptive).

The contradictory tendencies of these dimensions raise questions about how we may interpret associations between global NPI scores and organizational outcomes and behaviors (Ackerman et al., 2011). Some NPI items are toxic (e.g., willingness to exploit others), while others relate to potentially useful or even outright desirable characteristics such as confidence, leadership ability, and social potency. The conflation of positive and negative characteristics aggregated within a narcissism measure hardly gives us confidence in the meaningfulness of associations with aggregates of behavioral items, which in themselves may conflate positive and negative behaviors, depending on the circumstances (see Fox et al., 2011; Spector and Fox, 2010, for discussions of ambiguous positivity and negativity associated with organizational citizenship and counterproductive work behavior).

Michael Maccoby (2007) offers a dramatically different and largely positive view of narcissism. He rejects the view held by mental health professionals, researchers, and lay persons alike, equating narcissism with bad-mannered, self-absorbed, or self-centered behavior. On the contrary, he asserts that the single most defining quality of narcissists is their desire to change the world – according to their precise view of how things should be. This is actually more than a desire – it is a "sense of mission and crusade" (p. 3). Narcissists reject the status quo, refusing to listen to the voice of authority. Rather than an illness, narcissism is a personality type, which may be productive or unproductive, healthy or toxic, generous or selfish. Productivity of narcissists depends on their ability to carry out their vision of change. Abraham Lincoln and Steve Jobs epitomize productive narcissism.

Workplace Narcissism

Organizations are rife with interpersonal and political manifestations of narcissism. Most discussions of narcissism in the workplace have assumed its negative or maladaptive qualities. Studies have linked narcissism with self-aggrandizing social presentation, abusive supervision, toxic leadership, and counterproductive work behavior (Judge, LePine and Rich, 2006; Penney and Spector, 2002; Rosenthal and Pittinsky, 2006).

Writers who argue that there are positive aspects of narcissism in the workplace are in the minority (e.g., Hill and Yousey, 1999; Lubit, 2002). The extent to which narcissism contributes to successful or healthy outcomes depends in large part on situational factors, occupational demands, and the organization's culture and rewards structure. Many narcissistic characteristics parallel highly researched antecedents of academic, creative, or professional success (Fox and Freeman, 2011; Hill and Yousey, 1999; Kernberg, 1975), such as a confident and self-enhancing social presentation, authoritativeness, persuasiveness, non-conventional creativity, self-efficacy, preferences for challenging goals and diagnosticity (key indicators of McClelland's need for achievement, specifically linked by Wallace and Baumeister [2002], to motivation of narcissists), and internal loci of control. We find narcissists in leadership roles in corporations, governments, academic institutions, healthcare facilities, and the arts.

On the negative side, studies have demonstrated links between narcissism and counterproductive work behavior (O'Boyle et al., 2012; Penney and Spector, 2002). Samier and Atkins (2010) associate university administrators' destructive narcissism ("illegitimate sense of entitlement, inappropriate need for admiration and attention, lack of empathy, and projection of negative traits onto others," p. 581) with toxic university politics and culture. Wu and Lebreton (2011) add narcissism to Machievellianism and psychopathy as components of the "Dark Triad," characterized by entitlement, self-enhancement, antagonisms, and social malevolence. They link counterproductive work behavior with the narcissist's focus on dominating others, adversarial stance, hostile attributions and perceptions of hostile intent in others, their own hostility, and obstructionism.

A few scholars have countered that narcissistic characteristics can be beneficial in the workplace. The advantages of adaptive narcissism, primarily in areas related to creativity, career ascension, and leadership emergence, are highly contextual, of course. Whether narcissism is adaptive or maladaptive depends on factors such as the occupation, organizational culture, and rewards structure (Fox and Freeman, 2011), as well as macro-level cultural factors such as national preferences regarding individualism/collectivism, power distance, and task/relationship orientation.

"Adaptive" narcissists would likely have an advantage when jobs reward confident social presentation, persuasiveness, authoritativeness, and non-conventional creativity. Narcissists may excel at job tasks that have high diagnosticity of superior performance, but perform indifferently when they perceive little opportunity for self-enhancement (e.g., the collective organization of tasks in teamwork) (Hill and Yousey, 1999; Wallace and Baumeister, 2002). The implication is that narcissism may be adaptive in high-pressure, high-profile, individualized professions but not in jobs that reward harmony, cooperation, and teamwork.

A major arena in which narcissistic personality characteristics may be of advantage is leadership. Regardless of actual performance effectiveness, narcissists tend to rise to positions of leadership in organizations (Rosenthal and Pittinsky, 2006). Conversely, narcissism may be associated with the most toxic, abusive, and unethical aspects of leadership. In the remainder of this chapter we turn to narcissism and leadership, with particular focus on the phenomenon of charisma.

Narcissism and Leadership

This section weaves the complexities of adaptive and maladaptive narcissism into notions of constructive and destructive leadership, with an emphasis on charismatic and transformational leadership. The Janus-like nature of narcissism can explain much about our ambivalence toward charisma. The literature on charismatic leadership (Bass, 1990; Bryman, 1992) is replete with the same descriptive characteristics we have been associating with narcissism: extreme self-confidence, energy, drive for power and prestige, magnetic enthusiasm, vision, and political skill. This becomes even more complex when we distinguish between leadership emergence and effectiveness: the very personality attributes that contribute to an individual's rise to power may also contribute to her downfall.

NARCISSISM AND LEADERSHIP EMERGENCE

Narcissists rise to positions of leadership in many organizations (Rosenthal and Pittinsky, 2006). On the motivational side, narcissism may be what drives people to strive for positions of power (Chatterjee and Hambrick, 2007). Research has linked narcissism with attributes and behaviors that are associated with promotions and the acquisition of organizational power. Experimental evidence has been found in laboratory studies of leadership emergence in leaderless groups (Brunell et al., 2008). This may be attributed to implicit theories, that is, people's schemas associating leaders with extraversion, social skill, interpersonal dominance, decisiveness, and psychological masculinity (Brunell et al., 2008; Lord, De Vader and Alliger, 1986).

It has been suggested that narcissists employ self-promotion, impression management, and skillful organizational politics to attain quicker promotion (O'Boyle et al., 2012). A rapid rise within organizational hierarchies or acquisition of positions of leadership may be attributed to even more unambiguously negative qualities: ruthlessness, Machievellianism, manipulative impression management, ingratiation, stealing credit for successes, scapegoating others for failures, and sabotaging the work or reputations of competitors.

A POSITIVE VIEW OF NARCISSISM AND LEADERSHIP EFFECTIVENESS

Once having achieved positions of leadership, narcissists may exhibit either effective or ineffective, and on another level, healthy or toxic leadership behaviors. Depending on the occupation, organizational culture, and rewards structure, narcissism may be advantageous when the tasks and context call for self-confidence, energy, drive for power and prestige, magnetic enthusiasm, charisma and vision, ability to make tough decisions, resource acquisition, and organizational politics.

Kets de Vries and Miller (1985) trace interest in narcissistic leadership to Freud, who declared that the leader need love no one but himself, and characterized the leader as absolutely narcissistic, self-confident, masterful, and independent. They cite two prominent object relations theorists, Kernberg (1975) and Kohut (1971) who drew upon classic psychoanalytic theory to elaborate links between narcissistic characteristics (e.g., intense need for prestige and power; absolute certainty and self-confidence) with top leadership roles.

DuBrin (2012) summarizes a number of arguments associating narcissism with positive aspects of visionary, charismatic, and inspirational leadership. Maccoby (2000) pinpoints two essential qualities that are associated with both narcissists and great leaders: the ability to formulate bold visions and the ability to attract followers. He further suggests that, like it or not, we may be dependent on the type of leadership narcissists are able to provide: "More and more large corporations are getting into bed with narcissists. They are finding that there is no substitute for narcissistic leaders in an age of innovation" (p. 9).

Maccoby (2007) believes that narcissistic leaders are driven by their desire to change the world. The difference between productive and unproductive leaders is that the productive narcissistic leaders are able to convince others to buy into their vision for change. "They communicate a sense of meaning that inspires others to follow them, whereas the unproductive types retreat into their own world and blame others for their isolation" (p. 10). For Maccoby then, the critical factor determining the productivity of the leader's narcissism is the extent to which the narcissist fits the strategic contingencies in which she leads – or perhaps the extent to which she has the "strategic intelligence" to match her leadership behaviors to the requirements of her environment.

Chatterjee and Hambrick (2007) provide empirical evidence supporting Maccoby's notions of productive narcissism and strategic fit. They used unobtrusive measures of CEOs' narcissism, such as prominence of photos and first-person singular pronouns in annual reports and interviews, and found significant links between these measures and strategic dynamism, risk-taking, grandiosity, acquisitions, and other bold, visible, and extreme actions. However, they found that on average, the firms of narcissistic CEOs performed neither better nor worse than other firms, although they did exhibit more extreme fluctuations in performance. Like Maccoby, they speculate that the outcome of narcissistic leadership depends on the strategic contingencies in which they operate, such as engendering better performance in highly dynamic industries than in stable settings.

THE DOWNSIDE OF NARCISSISM AND LEADERSHIP EFFECTIVENESS

An important caveat is that assessments of the narcissists' leadership effectiveness may well depend on who is doing the assessing. The narcissist's self-evaluations of abilities and competence are typically inflated relative to others' evaluations, and are likely less accurate (John and Robins, 1994; Judge, LePine and Rich, 2006).

Even when the narcissist acquires a position of power, leadership may fail, to the extent the narcissist evinces a focus on self-enhancement, low empathy for concerns of subordinates and constituents, devaluation/envy of others' contributions, a suspicious, hypersensitive, argumentative stance toward others, difficulties with teamwork, bullying and abusive supervision style, excitement-seeking, and high risk-taking. The narcissistic leader may create a culture of fear, toxicity, groupthink, and stifling of dissent, and may model and reward ineffective/toxic management at lower managerial levels.

Studies of abusive organizational leadership, often under the rubric of workplace bullying, explicitly or implicitly describe the toxic leader or bully as the prototypical narcissist. DuBrin (2012) summarizes aspects of the narcissistic personality that research has linked to destructive leadership: arrogance; inferiority feelings; profound need for recognition, superiority, power wealth, and admiration; intense competitiveness, anger, hypersensitivity and paranoia; poor listening and communication skills; lack of empathy; amorality, irrationality, inflexibility, and inconsistency.

The narcissistic leader need not be the actual bully in a bully organizational culture. Serving as a role model for aggressive or bullying behavior, the narcissistic leader may implicitly or explicitly reward a bullying management style at lower managerial levels, and "rule over" a fear-based culture that discourages candor – leading to groupthink and lack of critical assessment and upward communication of negative information (Morrison and Milliken, 2000).

Einarsen and colleagues define "destructive leadership" as "the systematic and repeated behaviour by a leader, supervisor or manager that violates the legitimate interest of the organisation by undermining and/or sabotaging the organisation's goals, tasks, resources, and effectiveness and/or the motivation, well-being or job satisfaction of subordinates" (Einarsen, Aasland and Skogstad, 2007, p. 208). Their observation that the same actor may engage in both constructive and destructive leadership behaviors is consistent with our notion of underlying adaptive and maladaptive aspects of the same narcissistic individual.

So we have a rather mixed bag of perspectives on whether narcissism makes for good or poor leadership. Some distinguish between productive and unproductive, others between good and evil. A potentially useful theoretical lens through which to view links between narcissism and leadership is McClelland's motivational needs theory. Here we look at how narcissism interacts with achievement, affiliation, power, and self-control (inhibition of activity) needs as bases of leadership and other workplace behavior. As described by Bass (1990), it may be generalized that leaders tend to be high in need for power and low in need for affiliation. Leaders with an "imperial motive pattern" will be high in need for power, low in need for affiliation, and high in inhibition of activity, that is a self-control that may lead to ruthless, efficient organizing and loyalty to the organization, while leaders with a "conquistador motive pattern" will be high in need for power, low in need for affiliation, and low in inhibition of activity, resulting in active rejection of institutional constraints, establishment of personal authority through sheer force, and a belief that some individuals have a natural right to rule.

Both patterns of leadership motives share aspects of narcissism, perhaps best exemplified by Freeman's "real" narcissism. The high need for power is consistent with the leadership/authority dimension of the NPI. The low need for affiliation is consistent with Freeman's oblivious, helpful, and ruthless narcissism as well as with several characteristics typically associated with narcissism: self-sufficiency, lack of intimacy in interpersonal relationships, lack of empathy, etc. The key differentiating factor between the imperial and conquistador motives is inhibition of activity, or self-control. The implication is that the leader with the imperial pattern may offer a more socialized approach to leadership that includes concern for the welfare of the group and its members, while the conquistador encompasses the more toxic or dysfunctional narcissistic attributes, such as entitlement, arrogance, hypervigilance, exploitativeness, and ruthlessness.

Narcissism and Charisma

Kets de Vries and Miller (1985) note that leaders are able to "reawaken primitive emotions in their followers" (p. 585). Charismatic leaders manipulate symbols that seem to elevate themselves above their followers as superhuman or extraordinary persons (Weber, cited in Kets de Vries and Miller, 1985). The charismatic leader appears in time of crisis to offer salvation through his extraordinary persona. Maccoby (2007) describes historical narcissist leaders in a similar fashion – FDR, Napoleon, Mao, Gandhi – who "emerged during periods of great upheaval, creating new order often out of chaos, with both positive and negative outcomes" (p. 10).

Maccoby (2007) again differentiates between productive and unproductive charisma. Not to be confused with Bass's (1990) distinction between social and personal charisma, which is more of a value-judgment, productive charisma is the ability to put the narcissist's pull on others' emotions to her own purposes – that is, the effectiveness which with she is able to gain the emotional allegiance of followers to her vision, and to realize that vision in times of cataclysmic change and crisis. Narcissism, like charisma, is in itself neither honest nor crooked, wise nor foolish, healthy nor toxic, successful nor doomed to failure. The success of productive narcissism, as of productive charisma, is contingent on strategic factors and social/political/economic context, as well as the values orientation of the leader herself.

The charismatic relationship between leader and follower is a two-way street: the quality of charisma exists only so long as the extraordinariness of the leader is reaffirmed and validated by the follower (Bryman, 1992). This is strikingly resonant with the exaggerated need of narcissists for external affirmation of their extraordinariness.

Further overlaps between narcissism and charisma have been noted (Bass, 1990; Bryman, 1992; Tourish and Pinnington, 2002). The familiar characteristics we have seen used to describe narcissism also appear in the charisma literature: extreme self-confidence; high energy; drive for power and prestige; magnetic enthusiasm; vision; ruthlessness and Machiavellianism; tough decision-making, impression management and political skill. Each of these tendencies may be functional or dysfunctional, and its pros and cons have been amply discussed in the research and practitioner literature. Moving away from charisma as solely embodied within the persona of the leader, Burns (1978) and Bass (1990) incorporated charisma into a broader concept of transformational leadership, which Bass warned could be for the good but also the detriment of followers and society (Paul et al., 2002).

A brilliant comparison of transformational leadership and cults was contributed by Tourish and Pinnington (2002), which may well help us in our efforts to understand the two faces of narcissism and extraordinary leadership. The fundamental goal of transformational leadership is to create a single new culture, that is, for the transformational leader to incorporate followers into her overarching system of vision and values. The new culture may but need not be in the best interests of the followers. Bass (1990) underscores charisma as one of the main components in his concept of transformational leadership. The charismatic leader has extraordinary powers to energetically communicate the new vision, emotionally arouse and motivate followers to embrace that vision. Followers undergo a "collective rebirth" (Tourish and Pinnington, 2002, p. 151) into the leader's new dominant culture.

Maccoby (2000) expects the charismatic leader to be a narcissist, with an extremely well-developed self-image, self-confidence, strong convictions, and high need for power. Neither Maccoby (2000) nor Tourish and Pinnington (2002) downplay the dangers emanating from the charismatic leader's narcissism: perceptions of reality distorted by his or her own vision; lack of empathy or willingness to listen to followers; hyper-sensitivity to criticism, intense competitiveness and intolerance of dissent. "In such circumstances, corporate paranoia, frenetic activity and cultic norms that penalize open discussion may rapidly take root" (Tourish and Pinnington, 2002, p. 154), resulting in a dis-empowered followership, groupthink, and an insulation of the leadership against the possibility of corrective feedback, potentially leading to disastrous outcomes for the affected individuals, organization or society.

Conclusions and Applications

This chapter was developed around the notion of narcissism as a complex, multi-dimensional personality trait. Narcissism is not inherently functional or dysfunctional, and can be viewed as a powerful antecedent of both positive and negative leadership and organizational behavior. Narcissism as a construct is experiencing growing popularity among organizational scholars – is it because we relate to so many of its (what we hope are) admirable, success-related qualities? Clearly we are not suggesting that we should embrace pathological narcissists in our midst – but neither should our selection processes reject individuals on the basis of personality profiles toward which we feel so much ambivalence.

As our understanding of the narcissistic personality becomes more nuanced, one approach would be to distinguish between those sub-traits that tend to correspond to dysfunction or toxicity, versus those that correspond to creativity, vision, and engagement. I would go further, and argue that if we wish to accrue the tremendous contributions narcissists can bring to our organizations, we must explicitly recognize both the risks and payoffs these individuals offer, and manage the risks at a behavioral level. Our organizational cultures and human resource systems, including staffing, socialization, training, performance management, communication systems and policies, should explicitly address the toxic behaviors we wish to eliminate, without stifling the enthusiastic nonconformist in our midst. Effective anti-bullying policies, for example, would target abusive behaviors rather than stigmatize personality styles.

At the leadership level, we should look at those cases in which the leader's narcissism translates into bullying or destructive behavior. In some of these cases, the narcissism is blatant and ruthless, the bully proud of his abusive way of "getting things done." In these cases, there is probably little hope of reform, and the force of law, unions, or responsible corporate boards are needed to protect organization members and society from the narcissist.

However, in many cases, the "oblivious" narcissist is unaware either of her behaviors or of her toxic effect on the organization and its members. She may be interpreting all incoming data through her narcissistically distorted self-schemas and have little clue as to the cause of the poor outcomes she is experiencing. Freeman and Fox (2012) suggest that this narcissist might well profit from a form of executive coaching, a cognitive behavioral therapy (CBT)-based intervention that would address the cognitive and normative assumptions underlying her dysfunctional leadership. Narcissistic persons are more likely to inaccurately interpret situations when their self-worth is on the line, which is very much the case when the leader's efforts just don't seem to be working. The focus of CBT is on helping the individual identify and respond to his or her misattributions, impaired or limited problem solving, cognitive distortions, negative automatic thoughts, maladaptive schemas, and misperceptions (Freeman et al., 2004), and ultimately change to behaviors that derive from more realistic, healthier schemas. Coaching must be presented to the narcissist as the means to attain what she wants, that is, to help her demonstrate her superior leadership abilities and attain desired outcomes.

Conclusion

The purpose of this chapter has been to turn away from a unidimensional, reified judgment of narcissism in leadership and organizational behavior. Rather than rejecting narcissistic leaders and de-selecting narcissistic employees, or pretending that their narcissistic characteristics do not exist, we can deploy a more nuanced understanding to maximize the contributions and minimize the detriments of narcissism. Through individual, cultural, performance management and policy interventions, we can help our organizations profit from the talents and contributions of their most extraordinary members. We can channel their excitement, passion, and charisma from toxic self-serving narcissism to the highest levels of citizenship.

References

Ackerman, R.A., Witt, E.A., Donnellan, M.B., Trzesniewski, K.H., Robins, R.W. and Kashy, D.A. (2011) What does the Narcissistic Personality Inventory really measure? *Assessment*, 18, 67–87.

APA (2000) *Diagnostic and Statistical Manual of Mental Disorders*, Text Rev., 4th edn. Washington, DC: American Psychiatric Association.

Bass, B.M. (1990) *Bass and Stogdill's Handbook of Leadership: Theory, Research, and Managerial Applications*. New York: Free Press.

Brunell, A.B., Gentry, W.A., Campbell, W.K., Hoffman, B.J., Kuhnert, K.W. and DeMarree, K.G. (2008) Leader emergence: The case of the narcissistic leader. *Personality and Social Psychology Bulletin*, 34, 1663–76.

Bryman, A. (1992) *Charisma and Leadership in Organizations*. London: Sage.

Burns, J.M. (1978) *Leadership*. New York: Harper and Row.

Campbell, W.K. (2001) Is narcissism really so bad? *Psychological Inquiry*, 12, 214–16.

Chatterjee, A. and Hambrick, D.C. (2007) It's all about me: Narcissistic chief executive officers and their effects on company strategy and performance. *Administrative Science Quarterly*, 52, 351–86.

DuBrin, A.J. (2012) *Narcissism in the Workplace: Research, Opinion and Practice*. Cheltenham: Edward Elgar.

Einarsen, S., Aasland, M.S.U. and Skogstad, A. (2007) Destructive leadership behavior: A definition and conceptual model. *Leadership Quarterly*, 18, 207–16.

Emmons, R. (1984) Factor analysis and construct validity of the Narcissistic Personality Inventory. *Journal of Personality Assessment*, 48, 291–300.

Federn, P. (1952) *Ego Psychology and the Psychoses*. New York: Basic Books.

Fox, S. and Freeman, A.M. (2011) Narcissism and the deviant citizen: A common thread in CWB and OCB. *Research in Occupational Stress and Well-being*, 9, 151–96.

Fox, S., Spector, P.E., Goh, A., Bruursema, K. and Kessler, S.R. (2012) The deviant citizen: Measuring potential positive relations between counterproductive work behavior and organizational citizenship behavior. *Journal of Occupational and Organizational Psychology*, 8, 199–220.

Freeman, A.M. (2009) The narcissistic personality: Diagnosis and treatment in need of empirical support. Workshop presented at the Texas Behavioral Health Institute, July.

Freeman, A.M. and Fox, S. (2012) Cognitive behavioral perspectives on the theory and treatment of the narcissistic character. In J. Orgrodniczuk (ed.) *Treating Pathological Narcissism*. Washington, DC: American Psychological Association.

Freeman, A., Pretzer, J., Fleming, B. and Simon, K. (2004) *Clinical Applications of Cognitive Therapy*, 2nd edn. New York: Kluwer.

Hill, R.W. and Yousey, G.P. (1999) Adaptive and maladaptive narcissism among university faculty, clergy, politicians, and librarians. In N.J. Pallone (ed.) *Altruism Narcissism Comity*. New Brunswick, NJ: Transaction Publishers, 87–95.

John, O.P. and Robins, R.W. (1994) Accuracy and bias in self-perception: Individual differences in self-enhancement and the role of narcissism. *Journal of Personality and Social Psychology*, 66, 206–19.

Judge, T.A., LePine, J.A. and Rich, B.L. (2006) Loving yourself abundantly: Relationship of the narcissistic personality to self- and other perceptions of workplace deviance, leadership, and task and contextual performance. *Journal of Applied Psychology*, 91, 762–76.

Kernberg, O. (1975) *Borderline Conditions and Pathological Narcissism*. New York: Jason Aronson.

Kets de Vries, M.F.R. and Miller, D. (1985) Narcissism and leadership: An object relations perspective. *Human Relations*, 38, 583–601.

Kohut, H. (1971) *The Analysis of the Self: A Systematic Approach to the Psychoanalytic Treatment of Narcissistic Personality Disorders*. New York: International Universities Press.

Lord, R.G., De Vader, C.L. and Alliger, G.M. (1986) A meta-analysis of the relation between personality traits and leadership perceptions: An application of validity generalization procedures. *Journal of Applied Psychology*, 71, 402–10.

Lubit, R. (2002) The long-term organizational impact of destructively narcissistic managers. *Academy of Management Executive*, 16, 127–37.

Maccoby, M. (2000) Narcissistic leaders: The incredible pros, the inevitable cons. *Harvard Business Review*, 78, 69–77.

—— (2007) *Narcissistic Leaders: Who Succeeds and Who Fails*. Boston, MA: Harvard Business Review Press.

Matthews, B. and Norris, F.H. (2002) When is believing "seeing"? Hostile attribution bias as a function of self-reported aggression. *Journal of Applied Social Psychology*, 32, 1–32.

Morf, C.C. and Rhodewalt, F. (2001) Unraveling the paradoxes of narcissism: A dynamic self-regulatory processing model. *Psychological Inquiry*, 12, 177–96.

Morrison, E.W. and Milliken, F.J. (2000) Organizational silence: A barrier to change and development in a pluralistic world. *Academy of Management Review*, 25, 706–25.

O'Boyle, E.H., Forsyth, D.R., Banks, G.C. and McDaniel, M.A. (2012) A meta-analysis of the dark triad and work behavior: A social exchange perspective. *Journal of Applied Psychology*, 97, 557–79.

Paul, J., Costley, D.L., Howell, J.P. and Dorfman, P.W. (2002) The mutability of charisma in leadership research. *Management Decision*, 40, 192–200.

Penney, L.M. and Spector, P.E. (2002) Narcissism and counterproductive work behavior: Do bigger egos mean bigger problems? *International Journal of Selection and Assessment*, 10, 126–34.

Raskin, R. and Hall, C.S. (1979) A narcissistic personality inventory. *Psychological Reports*, 45, 159–62.

Raskin, R. and Terry, H. (1988) A principal-components analysis of the Narcissistic Personality Inventory and further evidence of its construct validity. *Journal of Personality and Social Psychology*, 54, 890–902.

Rose, P. (2002) The happy and unhappy faces of narcissism. *Personality and Individual Differences*, 33, 379–91.

Rose, P. and Campbell, W.K. (2004) Greatness feels good: A telic model of narcissism and subjective well-being. *Advances in Psychology Research*, 31, 3–27.

Rosenthal, S.A. and Pittinsky, T.L. (2006) Narcissistic leadership. *Leadership Quarterly*, 17, 617–33.

Samier, E.A. and Atkins, T. (2010) Preventing and combating administrative narcissism: Implications for professional programmes. *Journal of Educational Administration*, 48, 579–94.

Spector, P.E. and Fox, S. (2010) Counterproductive work behavior and organizational citizenship behavior: Are they opposite forms of active behavior? *Applied Psychology: An International Review*, 59, 21–39.

Tourish, D. and Pinnington, A. (2002) Transformational leadership, corporate cultism and the spirituality paradigm: An unholy trinity in the workplace? *Human Relations*, 55, 147–72.

Wallace, H.M. and Baumeister, R.F. (2002) The performance of narcissists' rise and falls with perceived opportunity for glory. *Journal of Personality and Social Psychology*, 82, 819–34.

Wu, J. and Lebreton, J.M. (2011) Reconsidering the dispositional basis of counterproductive work behavior: The role of aberrant personality. *Personnel Psychology*, 64, 593–626.

CHAPTER 6 Emotional Intelligence and Human Frailty at Work: Can We Be Too Emotionally Intelligent?

PETER J. JORDAN, ASHLEA C. TROTH
AND NEAL M. ASHKANASY

Introduction

Our aim in this chapter is to consider the nexus of emotional intelligence and human frailty at work. Burke (2010) recently equated frailty with personal shortcomings and moral weakness. He argues this is manifested in immoral or unacceptable behaviors such as lying, cheating, excessive gambling, and substance abuse. This interpretation has been used by a number of authors in relation to smoking (Higgs, 1993), making risky decisions (Mérö, 1998), lying and cheating (Mazar and Ariely, 2006), criminal acts (Hocking, 1999), and visceral over-indulgence (Ozdenoren, Salant and Silverman, 2012). Burke (2010) also argued that these fragile behaviors can be linked to extreme emotions such as passion or revenge. In this regard, social psychologist Roy Baumeister and his colleagues have made a strong case for a link between emotion and behavior (see Baumeister and Tierney, 2011; Baumeister et al., 2007).

Underlining our arguments in this chapter is the idea that emotion can act as both a precursor and a response to workplace behaviors; for example, verbal abuse (i.e., expressed anger) can come about in response to felt anger triggered by injustice perceptions (Weiss, Suckow and Cropanzano, 1999). We note the word "emotion" comes from the Latin verb *emovere*, which translates "to move out," and is intended to portray emotion as an underlying motivator of human action (Calne, 1999). In the case of human frailty, we argue in line with Weiss and his colleagues that it can also be generated in response to behaviors. In this respect, we note with interest that Burke's (2010) focus was on emotion *intensity* as a cause of human frailty with either positive (passion) or negative (revenge) emotion contributing to frailty.

While psychology literature has traditionally focused on negative emotions, more recently we have seen the emergence of positive psychology (Seligman, 2002), which promotes potential, human growth and emphasizes flow, meaningfulness, self-efficacy, human flourishing, and happiness (Seligman and Csikszentmihalyi, 2000).

From a positive psychology perspective, it is broadly assumed that positive emotions promote positive behaviors and outcomes, and that negative emotions tend to promote negative behaviors and outcomes (i.e., that include human frailty). Although we accept these relationships as generally valid, we also note that some emotions researchers have challenged the naive association of positive emotions and positive outcomes (and negative emotions and negative outcomes). In this respect, Lindebaum and Jordan (2012) recently called for researchers to focus on more interesting problems and to consider the utility of emotions for both positive and negative outcomes. These authors commented in particular, that positive emotions sometimes can give rise to negative outcomes (e.g., the use of inappropriate humor, see Smeltzer and Leap, 1988) and negative emotions can sometimes lead to positive outcomes (e.g., complaining leading to problem resolution, see Kowalski, 2002).

One construct in particular that has been offered as a set of abilities to improve human behavior (and therefore to minimize frailty) is emotional intelligence (Mayer and Salovey, 1997). In this respect, Mayer and Salovey defined emotional intelligence as "the abilities to accurately perceive emotions, to access and generate emotions so as to assist thought, to understand emotions and emotional knowledge, and to reflectively regulate emotions so as to *promote emotional and intellectual growth*" (p. 10, italics added). More recently, Mayer, Roberts and Barsade (2008) refined this definition to, "the ability to carry out accurate reasoning about emotions and the ability to use emotions and emotional knowledge *to enhance thought*" (p. 511, italics added). Brackett and Mayer (2003) argue, in particular, for a nexus of emotional intelligence and personal and subjective well-being. Similarly, Mayer and his associates (2008) commented that emotional intelligence researchers have traditionally associated emotional intelligence with positive traits including achievement motivation, flexibility, positive affectivity, and high self-esteem. The key issue here is that, based on Baumeister's Ego Depletion Theory (Baumeister et al., 1998; Baumeister, Muraven and Tice, 2000), researchers have come to understand that there is a link between emotional regulation (one of the abilities of emotional intelligence), and the types of behaviors and traits that may be seen to ameliorate human frailty (e.g., see Gino et al., 2011).

But is this necessarily so? Can individual emotional abilities serve to exacerbate (rather than to ameliorate) human frailty? In other words, as Baumeister and Alquist (2009) ask, "Is there a downside to good self-control?" (p. 115). And, if there is, under what circumstances? These are the specific questions we address in this chapter

Human Frailty

As we noted earlier, Burke (2010) equated human frailty with personal moral shortcomings. In other words, frailty is a weakness or susceptibility or fallibility of humans that is then likely to provide them with negative experiences down the track (e.g., a drug addict who suffers illness as a result of her addiction). If we accept that humans have aspirations to lead better lives and to improve themselves (i.e., as a path to happiness, see Seligman, 2002), then it follows that humans also have a need to ameliorate or to address any personal shortcomings. But to understand how we address these weaknesses and fallibilities and their relationship to emotions, we need a better picture of what behaviors constitute frailty.

The *Oxford Shorter Dictionary* refers to frailty as a "weakness in morals or character," while the *Merriam-Webster Dictionary* refers to frailty as a "fault due to weakness of moral character." It seems the concept of human frailty is generally defined a being linked to some form of character weakness. But this also begs the question: What is character? Shand (1896, p. 210) argues that "character ... includes ... thoughts and experiences as well as ... emotions and will." This view seems to have been sustained, despite the once popular view that intellect and character are separate (fine intellect/weak character, see Damasio, 1994).

In line with Shand (1896), Burke (2010) notes that frailty both affects us internally (through our thoughts) and is manifested externally (though our behaviors). Internally, frailty emerges in our thoughts in terms of doubts and a lack of resilience and self-pitying thoughts, while externally, it is manifested in our treatment of ourselves (e.g., low self-esteem and self-loathing); and particularly in our treatment of others and the relationships we form (e.g., parasitic/abusive relationships). If frailty emerges as thoughts and behaviors (driven by emotion and cognition), then the likelihood of a link between emotional intelligence (as a nexus between cognition and emotion), and frailty (specific behaviors) is possible. Still, the question remains as to the particular behaviors that reflect human frailty.

Hogan and Hogan (1989) offer an insight to the outcomes of what they term poor reliability of employees, and go on to develop a personality measure of organizational delinquency that includes a range of behaviors including "substance abuse, insubordination, absenteeism, excessive grievances, bogus worker compensation claims, temper tantrums, and various forms of passive aggression" (p. 273). Hogan and Hogan link this measure to counterproductive work behaviors and lower organizational performance. Clearly, within the scope of Burke's (2010) definition of frailty, these work behaviors certainly seem to fit the category of poor behaviors (identified by others, e.g., Higgs, 1993; Hocking, 1999; Mérö, 1998). We accept this view, and so we *define human frailty at work as a form of character weakness associated with undesirable behaviors and poor decision-making.*

HUMAN FRAILTY AND EMOTIONS

This then brings us to consider the specific relationship between emotions and human frailty. We distinguish in particular between emotions (short duration, usually intense, and associated with specific stimuli) and mood (long duration, chronic rather than acute, and usually not associated with a specific stimulus), and focus on emotions as a reaction to workplace stimuli. As we have already identified, emotions can be both precursors and responses to specific workplace behaviors (Elfenbein, 2007).

From the perspective of positive psychology, Peterson and Seligman (2004) identify 24 positive character strengths, including courage, bravery, persistence, kindness, and love. These types of behaviors represent the antithesis of human frailty, so the link between positive emotions and these character strengths is clear. On the other hand, when examining the links between negative emotion and human frailty, we find that emotions can be considered to be outcomes of human frailty (e.g., in the form of guilt and shame and remorse, Taylor, 1996) or precursors to human frailty (e.g., the effects of anger, see Hocking, 1999; or fear, see Clough, 2010).

As we noted above, we seek in this chapter to challenge the oft-stated assumption that there is necessarily an association between negative emotion and frailty, or the idea that negative emotions always induce frailty, or indeed are *always* a manifestation of frailty (noted by Keifer, 2002). We proffer that the experience of negative emotion is not analogous to the experience of frailty. We argue further that the experience of specific negative emotions is also not necessarily linked to the expression of specific types of frailty. For example, we reject the view, often stated in the positive psychology and emotional intelligence literature, that expressions of anger are indicative of personal weakness (Thomas, 1989).

On the contrary, anger is a natural human reaction (a response to perceived injustice, Weiss, Suckow and Cropanzano, 1999) and the expression of anger can generate a range of behaviors from inappropriate aggression to finding the strength to fight an injustice. Anger can also serve to promote passion (that in itself can be positive or negative); it can strengthen commitment to completing a course of action (particularly in relation to perceived injustice). Finally, we note that anger can also be generated when protecting specific personal values that are not related to human frailty (e.g., environmental protection or social justice).

So the experience of the emotion of anger per se is not always a source of human frailty. Instead, it may be the way emotion is expressed (and the behaviors that ensue) that determine if anger is, or is not, a precursor to human frailty (Geddes and Callister, 2007). Thus, on the one hand, an individual who chooses to use her or his anger arising from a social injustice to correct the situation would not normally be seen to be exhibiting human frailty. On the other hand, however, if the individual chooses to berate a fellow worker for no apparent reason in an angry outburst, then s/he will most likely be seen to be demonstrating human frailty.

Having established an association between emotions and human frailty and having questioned some of the assumptions regarding the link between negative emotions and frailty, it is appropriate now for us to move to the central aim of this chapter: to examine the links between emotional intelligence abilities and human frailty at work.

Emotional Intelligence

Emotional intelligence was proposed by Salovey and Mayer (1990) as a means to link thinking and feeling.[1] Over the years since 1990, emotional intelligence has undergone the sort of refinement that is typical of emerging constructs (Wieck, 1989), with a general consensus now emerging (see Ashkanasy and Daus, 2002) that emotional intelligence comprises four abilities: emotional awareness (perception and expression), emotional facilitation, emotional understanding, and emotional regulation/management (Mayer and Salovey, 1997; Mayer, Salovey and Caruso, 2000). Mayer, Caruso and Salovey (1999) present this "four-branch ability model" of emotional intelligence in a hierarchically and sequentially organized form, referred to by Joseph and Newman (2010) as the "cascading model" of emotional intelligence. In this model, the complexity of emotional abilities increases from simple emotional awareness though the facilitation and understanding to emotional management.

1 Although the term first appeared in a doctoral dissertation by Payne (1986), the concept was not developed fully, and the dissertation never published. Consequently, the Salovey and Mayer (1990) article is generally regarded as the initial introduction of emotional intelligence in the published literature.

In terms of understanding how emotional intelligence may be related to human frailty at work, it is useful to consider a concrete example outlined by Ashkanasy and Daus (2002) in terms of the cascading model. Ashkanasy and Daus describe the reactions of Ruth, an angry shop assistant, who eventually channels her feelings of anger at work into an act of sabotage (jamming a cash register). Ashkanasy and Daus reason that, in order to avoid this spontaneous act of sabotage and exercise her emotional intelligence, Ruth must first become aware that she is experiencing the emotion of anger. We consider, however, that this rationale may be overly simplistic. In this respect, it is instructive to consider the neurological processes underlying Ruth's emotional awareness.

To do this, we examine Ruth's actions in terms of her cognitive processing (LeDoux, 2003). In this instance, LeDoux, Farb and Romanski (1991) identified the pathways linking aural stimuli to behavior, which are first activated by initial recognition of the stimulus in the hypothalamus. This information is initially relayed to the amygdala, which stimulates hormonal and behavioral responses to the stimulus, and only then to the cerebral cortex (where it is subsequently cognitively processed). This primitive short-cut process via the amygdala is hardwired as a means to enable fast response to threat. Thus, it is possible that Ruth's initial processing of anger leads to a conditioned short-cut route between the hypothalamus and the amygdala (i.e., jamming the cash register without processing the consequences of her actions via the cortex). Weiss and Cropanzano (1996) refer to this as "affect-driven" behavior.

Ashkanasy and Daus (2002) then go on to discuss how Ruth might utilize her emotional intelligence to seek to understand the nature of her anger, and to reason with and about her anger to determine how this emotion might change over time. There is considerable evidence to show that anger often arises in response to perceptions of injustice (Solomon, 2000). In Ruth's case, it might be better understanding her feelings of anger are in response to perceived injustice (the organizational display rules that were at odds with her real feelings, Diefendorff and Greguras, 2009). Greater emotional understanding would also be shown by Ruth if she also recognized that her co-workers are subject to the same rules and that it is important for the organization that customers have a positive experience while shopping. Finally, Ashkanasy and Daus (2002) argue that Ruth needed to manage her anger in such a way that it would not impinge negatively, either on herself or her organization. In terms of addressing human frailties in the workplace, this may mean that Ruth has to channel her anger towards resolving the issues that she sees as being unfair in her work environment, rather than reacting so impulsively.

Essentially, Ruth's behavior comes down to an issue of self-control, also known as emotional regulation. According to Ego Depletion Theory (Baumeister et al., 1998; Baumeister, Muraven and Tice, 2000), when people engage in emotion regulation over a period of time, their "ego resources" become depleted, and they are less able to control their impulses – in Ruth's case to sabotage her cash register. Baumeister and Alquist (2009) note in particular that such lack of control can often be a downside of engaging in good self-control for an extended period, especially when the individual is in a negative mood state.

On the basis that self (emotional) control is the ultimate purpose of emotional intelligence (recall that emotional management is the last branch identified by Mayer and Salovey, 1997), we see this as supportive of our position that emotional intelligence is a key consideration in Ruth's behavior. In this respect, despite early concerns over the incremental predictive validity of some models of emotional intelligence

(Cherniss, 2010), there is now evidence that emotional intelligence predicts positive outcomes in organizations. Thus, in recent meta-analyses, Joseph and Newman (2010) and O'Boyle et al. (2011) reported that, across a wider range of situations, studies, and models, emotional intelligence predicted job performance. These authors therefore concluded that the construct is valid and provides incremental predictive validity for positive organizational outcomes over and above general intelligence and personality.

Looking now at the specific research evidence, we find that emotional intelligence and emotional regulation in particular have been shown to be associated with a range of positive outcomes in organizations such as better team performance (Troth et al., 2012), improved leader performance (Ashkanasy and Tse, 2000; DeWall et al., 2011), reduced turnover and higher job satisfaction (Jordan and Troth, 2011), higher levels of organizational citizenship behaviors (Côté and Miners, 2006; Ramachandran et al., 2011), more constructive conflict resolution outcomes (Jordan and Troth, 2004), and reduced job insecurity (Jordan, Ashkanasy and Härtel, 2002). Researchers have also investigated how emotional intelligence contributes to improved social relationships (Lopes et al., 2004) and higher levels of well-being (Mayer, Roberts and Barsade, 2008).

In summary, and as Cherniss (2010) noted, "most of the major theorists seem to accept (the Mayer and Salovey definition) as a common definition" (p. 115) of emotional intelligence. Moreover, a consensus seems to be emerging that emotional intelligence is in general associated with positive behaviors and outcomes in organizations.

But there is also a downside to this. Jordan, Ashton-James and Ashkanasy (2006), for example, note that popular writers have offered emotional intelligence as a universal panacea for a range of individual problems and organizational issues, in effect taking the concept to the brink of fad status. Avid promoters of emotional intelligence (e.g., Goleman, 1995) argue that the connection between emotional intelligence and better interpersonal outcomes (less personal shortcomings) is clear without further examination. Ignoring the hyperbole over emotional intelligence, we take the opportunity in this chapter to undertake a more objective view of the contribution of emotional intelligence to behavior and, in particular, its association with human frailty.

To this end, it is appropriate to step back from the multidimensional construct of emotional intelligence and to assess specific emotional intelligence abilities to determine if they serve either to reduce or to enhance human frailty in workplace settings. Building on a request to consider context in assessing emotional intelligence by Jordan et al. (2010) and heeding the calls of Lindebaum and Jordan (2012), we specifically examine the link between specific emotional abilities and human frailty and ask the question: Are there circumstances under which particular individual emotional abilities might serve to exacerbate human frailty in workplace settings?

This question emerges from two basic premises. The first is that occasionally people can be *too smart*, finding complicated causes for simple phenomena (Fine and Nevo, 2008). For example, a "smart" employee who devises a complicated accounting framework that other employees cannot understand, and therefore are reluctant to use, is not really contributing to the workplace. The idea may be brilliant in theory, but fails to take into account the practicality of day-to-day work practices that demand a simpler, more practical approach.

The second premise is exemplified in research by Foo et al. (2004), who suggested that high emotional intelligence is not always a good thing. In their research, Foo and his colleagues found that individuals who have high emotional intelligence actually do *worse* in negotiation outcomes than their low emotional intelligence counterparts. These authors reported that individuals with high emotional intelligence spent too much time ensuring that the relationship with their partners was good and as a result suffered in the fiscal outcomes of the negotiation. As a result of this type of research some researchers have begun to question whether the outcomes of high emotional intelligence are always positive (e.g., "the curse of emotions," Antonakis, Ashkanasy and Dasborough, 2009, p. 250). Overall, and in line with Sternberg (1985), we argue that the hallmark of an intelligence ability is that it should be purposive – directed towards goals and useful in resolving problems. In the next section of this chapter, we examine in particular the two EI abilities – emotional awareness (or perception) and emotional management (or regulation) – to determine the usefulness of these abilities in solving real-world problems and addressing human frailty.

Emotional Intelligence and Human Frailty

While we earlier referred to all four branches of emotional intelligence, in examining the relationship between individual emotional abilities and human frailty, we focus on the two pivotal abilities identified by Joseph and Newman (2010) in their cascading model. These are the start and end points of emotional intelligence: emotional awareness (or perception) and emotional management (or regulation). We focus in particular on the broader research relating to these abilities and examine the impact of extreme levels of emotional awareness and extreme levels of emotional management on human frailty.

EMOTIONAL AWARENESS/PERCEPTION

Joseph and Newman (2010) argue the link between improved human behavior and higher levels of emotional intelligence (and specifically emotional awareness) and suggest that:

> *individuals who are more aware of the verbal and nonverbal cues in their environments, as well as their own emotional states, subsequently have a larger base of emotional information. The accrual of a larger and more accurate base of emotional information then enables more accurate appraisal ... and more appropriate response formation. (p. 57)*

The clear inference here is that higher levels of awareness produce better outcomes (and by extension can address human frailties).

In fact, research into emotional awareness has been ongoing across a range of disciplines and beyond the emotional intelligence sphere. Lane et al., (1990) define emotional awareness in terms of how individuals cognitively process their emotional experiences. Lane and his colleagues go on to identify five types of awareness: (1) how we feel (sensations); (2) what we want to do (action); (3) experience of single emotions; (4) blends of emotions; and (5) combinations of blends of emotion.

Concomitantly, we argue that an individual's level of emotional awareness can be assessed on a continuum from high to low awareness. At the extreme low end, an individual's behavior is represented by the condition known as alexithymia (inability to experience emotions). Parker, Taylor and Bagby (2001) note in this respect that alexithymic individuals have difficulty monitoring and reading the feelings of others and in describing their own feelings; in other words, they have low (or even no) emotional awareness. Research identifies alexithymia as being problematic (the inability to experience emotions) and linked to the human frailties of alcohol abuse (Thorberg et al., 2009), poor nutrition and a sedentary lifestyle (Helmers and Mente, 1999), and self-injurious behaviors (Zlotnick et al., 1996). Clearly, raising emotional awareness abilities would be positive in this case, assisting to ameliorate human frailty.

At the other (high) end of the emotional awareness spectrum we find extreme emotional sensitivity (susceptibility to feeling emotions). In this case, Guarino, Roger and Olason (2007) note the strong relationship between the personality trait of neuroticism and extreme emotional sensitivity. Emotional sensitivity has also been noted in anxiety disorders (Novick-Kline et al., 2005). In this extreme state, individuals become so sensitized to emotions in themselves and others that this awareness becomes debilitating for them. In this respect, Davis (1983) found that individuals can become so sensitive to the emotions of others that they then begin to experience the same emotions and become incapacitated.

Researchers have found in particular high levels of emotional sensitivity to be associated with lessened self-control (Flett et al., 1989) and increased susceptibility to emotional contagion (Hsee et al., 1990). Again, high levels of emotional awareness are linked to behaviors associated with decreased human effectiveness, which (according to our definition) constitute human frailty. Thus, and in line with Jordan et al. (2010), it seems the relationship between emotional awareness and behavior may be curvilinear; both extremely low and extremely high levels of emotional awareness can contribute to human frailty.

While the discussion above is framed in general terms, it is clear that our conclusions can be applied in work settings. An employee who has either no emotional awareness or is over-sensitive emotionally is likely to exhibit human frailties in terms of counterproductive work behavior (rather than pro-social citizenship behavior (see Spector and Fox, 2010). Thus, the inability to perceive emotions can lead to aggression (Fox and Spector, 1999), while super-sensitivity to emotion can lead to loss of self-control (Flett et al., 1989) or susceptibility to emotional contagion (Hsee et al., 1990), both of which are sources of workplace ineffectiveness.

EMOTIONAL MANAGEMENT/REGULATION

The second branch of emotional intelligence we discuss is emotional management/regulation, defined by Mayer, Caruso and Salovey (1999, p. 270) as "the management and regulation of emotion, such as knowing how to calm down after being angry or being able to alleviate the anxiety of another person." In this respect, Gross defines emotional regulation as "the process by which individuals influence which emotions they have, when they have them, and how they experience and express these emotions" (1998, p. 275). Lawrence and her colleagues (2011) develop a model explaining emotional regulation at work and identify a common thread in which emotional regulation is not exclusively a trait or an ability, but better considered as a process. Drawing on Gross's extensive work on emotional regulation (Gross, 1998, 1999; Gross and Thompson, 2007), Lawrence et al. (2011) describe emotional regulation to include "behavioral strategies aimed at *increasing, maintaining, or decreasing* one or more components of emotion [*experiential, behavioral (expressions), physiological*], depending on an individual's goals" (p. 203, italics added). The significance of the Lawrence et al. (2011) model is that emotional regulation is a complex process that can occur at many stages of an interaction. It is not just about simply increasing control of emotion. In relation to human frailty, the question we need to address is whether extremes of emotional regulation exist and their impact on behavior.

In terms of Ego Depletion Theory, Baumeister and his colleagues (Baumeister et al., 1998; Baumeister Muraven and Tice, 2000) argue that individuals engaging in emotion regulation eventually become "tired" (Mead, Baumeister, Gino, Schweitzer and Ariely, 2009, p. 594), and their ability to regulate their emotions decreases and individuals (like Ruth in Ashkanasy and Daus's [2002] vignette) show signs of faulty decision-making and counter-productive behavior.

Given that a lack of emotional control (or regulation) is likely to be counterproductive in workplace settings (e.g., throwing tantrums at work, see Hogan and Hogan, 1989), it is instructive to ask if, at the other extreme, the opposite might be true. What of individuals who are able to regulate their emotions completely; or who are totally unemotional? In the popular literature, this is what "Mr Spock," a fictional character in the TV/movie series *Star Trek*, represents. Spock makes decisions in a completely rational and emotionless fashion and is presented in the show as a sort of human computer whose decision-making is uncolored by human frailties, and is therefore invariably impeccable. As such, he is regularly cited in the literature (e.g., see Baumeister and Lobbestael, 2011; Brotheridge and Lee, 2008; Tice, 2009) as the epitome of emotion regulation.

But is this real? Can someone devoid of emotions make perfect decisions? Evidence from the behavioral finance literature might seem to be supportive of this idea. Shiv et al. (2005) found that investors suffering from neurological deficiencies in emotion processing made better investment decisions than investors without such deficits. But, in fact, the deficiencies reported in this research were relatively mild. The results essentially tell us that *mild* levels of emotional deficiencies help in financial decision-making; not that high levels of deficiency (or indeed a total lack of emotional processing skill) improves decision-making. In fact, the evidence suggests that this is not at all facilitative of decision-making accuracy. For instance, Damasio (1994) describes the case of "Patient Elliot" who suffers from a brain lesion that prevents him from accessing his emotional feelings. Despite a high level of intellectual intelligence (as measured using standard IQ tests), Patient Elliot was incapable of making even simple decisions. Thus, and despite the perceived infallibility of Mr. Spock, the fact is that total rationality is a myth. As Damasio emphasizes, effective decision-making is made with reference to (what he calls) "somatic markers," or body states that provide essential references for human decision-making. As a consequence, elimiation of emotional information does not lead to improved decision-making; on the contrary, it leads to deficiencies in decision-mailing, resulting in increased human frailty.

Research into the effects of low levels of emotional control focus on emotional outbursts and include outcomes such as aggression and emotional abuse (Keashley, 2001). In terms of specific emotional outbursts in the form of extreme anger, the literature shows that this type of extreme emotional expression has an impact on the development of dysfunctional working relationships (Deffenbacher, Oetting and DiGiuseppe, 2002) and antisocial behavior such as theft, sabotage, and vandalism (Fox and Spector, 1999; Robinson and O'Leary-Kelly, 1998). Clearly, in this case, raising the level of emotional regulation will address human frailty and produce more positive outcomes.

As was the case in our analysis of emotional awareness/perception, we conclude that too much emotional management can be counterproductive and so increase human frailty, especially in workplace settings. At the high end of emotional management we have an inability to make decisions and a lack of appreciation of context in decision-making (Damasio, 1994). At the extreme low end of emotional management, we find more human frailty caused by extreme emotional outbursts. As such, and consistent with the conclusions reached by Jordan et al. (2010), we conclude that moderate levels of emotional management may be necessary to reduce human frailty, while high or low levels can actually serve to increase frailty.

Conclusion

In this chapter, we introduce the notion of human frailty at work, which we define as "a form of character weakness associated with undesirable behaviors and poor decision-making." We note that human frailty is related to emotions, and make the case that emotional intelligence, as defined in the Mayer and Salovey (1997) "four branch" model, is likely to play an important role. We present evidence that, while emotional intelligence abilities are important factors underlying human effectiveness and decision-making, and hence in ameliorating human frailty, too much emotional intelligence can sometimes have an opposite effect. In this respect, we questioned in particular the naïve assumption that more emotional intelligence is the answer to solving human frailty. Indeed, our arguments lead to the conclusion that, although emotional awareness and emotional regulation abilities are useful in reducing human frailty, that more is not always better. In this regard we note that excessive emotional abilities may result in more, rather than less, human frailty in workplace settings.

References

Antonakis, J., Ashkanasy, N.M. and Dasborough, M.T. (2009) Does leadership need emotional intelligence? *The Leadership Quarterly*, 20, 247–61.

Ashkanasy, N.M. and Daus, C.S. (2002) Emotion in the workplace: The new challenge for managers. *Academy of Management Executive*, 16(1), 76–86.

Ashkanasy, N.M. and Tse, B. (2000) Transformational leadership as management of emotions: A conceptual review. In N.M. Ashkanasy, C.E.J. Härtel and W.J. Zerbe (eds) *Emotions in the Workplace: Research, Theory, and Practice*. Westport, CT: Quorum Books, pp. 221–35.

Baumeister, R.F. and Alquist, J.L. (2009) Is there a downside to good self-control? *Self and Identity*, 8, 115–30.

Baumeister, R.F., Bratslavsky, E., Muraven, M. and Tice, D.M. (1998) Ego depletion: Is the active self a limited resource? *Journal of Personality and Social Psychology*, 74, 1252–65.

Baumeister, R.F. and Lobbestael, J. (2011) Emotions and antisocial behavior. *Journal of Forensic Psychiatry and Psychology*, 22(5), 635–49.

Baumeister, R.F., Muraven, M. and Tice, D.M. (2000) Ego depletion: A resource model of volition, self-regulation, and controlled processing. *Social Cognition*, 18, 130–50.

Baumeister, R.F. and Tierney, J. (2011) *Willpower: Rediscovering the Greatest Human Strength*. New York: Penguin Press.

Baumeister, R.F., Vohs, K.D., DeWall, C.N. and Zhang, L. (2007) How emotion shapes behavior: Feedback, anticipation, and reflection, rather than direct causation. *Personality and Social Psychology Review*, 11(2), 167–203.

Brackett, M. and Mayer, J.D. (2003) Convergent, discriminant, and incremental validity of competing measures of emotional intelligence. *Personality and Social Psychology Bulletin*, 29, 1147–58.

Brotheridge, C.M. and Lee, R.T. (2008) The emotions of managing: an introduction to the special issue. *Journal of Managerial Psychology*, 23(2), 108–17.

Burke, R.J. (2010) Risky business: Psychological, physical and financial costs of high risk behavior in organizations. In R.J. Burke and C.L. Cooper (eds) *Human Frailties and Toxic Organizations*. Farnham: Gower, pp. 3–63.

Calne, D.B. (1999) *Within Reason: Rationality and Human Behavior*. New York: Pantheon Books.

Cherniss, C. (2010) Emotional intelligence: Towards clarification of a concept. *Industrial and Organizational Psychology: Perspectives on Science and Practice*, 3, 110–26.

Clough, A. (2010) Loss of self-control as a defence: The key to replacing provocation. *Journal of Criminal Law*, 74(2), 118–26.

Côté, S. and Miners, C.T.H. (2006) Emotional intelligence, cognitive intelligence, and job performance. *Administrative Science Quarterly*, 51, 1–28.

Damasio, A.R. (1994) *Descartes' Error: Emotion, Reason and the Human Brain*. New York: Putnam.

Davis, M.H. (1983) Measuring individual differences in empathy: Evidence for a multidimensional approach. *Journal of Personality and Social Psychology*, 44, 113–26.

Deffenbacher, J.L., Oetting, E.R. and DiGiuseppe, R.A. (2002) Principles of empirically supported interventions applied to anger management. *The Counseling Psychologist*, 30(2), 262–80.

DeWall, C.N., Baumeister, R.F., Mead, N.L. and Vohs, K.D. (2011) How leaders self-regulate their task performance: Evidence that power promotes diligence, depletion, and disdain. *Journal of Personality and Social Psychology*, 100, 47–65.

Diefendorff, J.M. and Greguras, G.J. (2009) Contextualizing emotional display rules: Examining the roles of targets and discrete emotions in shaping display rule perceptions. *Journal of Management*, 35, 880–98.

Elfenbein, H.A. (2007) Emotion in organizations. *The Academy of Management Annals*, 1, 315–86.

Fine, S. and Nevo, B. (2008) Too smart for their own good? A study of perceived cognitive overqualification in the workforce. *International Journal of Human Resource Management*, 19, 346–55.

Flett, G.L., Blankstein, K.R., Bator, C. and Pliner, P. (1989) Affect intensity and self-control of emotional behaviour. *Personality and Individual Differences*, 10(1), 1–5.

Foo, M., Elfenbein, H.A., Tan, H. and Aik, V. (2004) Emotional intelligence and negotiation: The tension between creating and claiming value. *International Journal of Conflict Management*, 15, 411–29.

Fox, S. and Spector, P. (1999) A model of work frustration-aggression. *Journal of Organizational Behavior*, 20, 915–31.

Geddes, D. and Callister, R.R. (2007) Crossing the line(s): A dual threshold model of anger in organizations. *Academy of Management Review*, 32, 721–46.

Gino, F., Schweitzer, M.E., Mead, N.L. and Ariely, D. (2011) Unable to resist temptation: How self-control depletion promotes unethical behavior. *Organizational Behavior and Human Decision Processes*, 115, 191–203.

Goleman, D. (1995) *Emotional Intelligence: Why It Can Matter More Than IQ*. New York: Bantam Books.

Gross, J.J. (1998) The emerging field of emotion regulation: An integrative review. *Review of General Psychology*, 2, 271–99.

—— (1999) Emotion and emotion regulation. In L.A. Pervin and O.P. John (eds) *Handbook of Personality: Theory and Research*. New York: Guilford Press, pp. 525–52.

Gross, J.J. and Thompson, R.A. (2007) Emotion regulation: Conceptual foundations. In J.J. Gross (ed.) *Handbook of Emotion Regulation*. New York, NY: Guilford Press, pp. 3–24.

Guarino, L., Roger, D. and Olason, D. (2007) Reconstructing N: A new approach to measuring emotional sensitivity. *Current Psychology*, 26, 37–45.

Helmers, K.F. and Mente, A. (1999) Alexithymia and health behaviors in healthy male volunteers. *Journal of Psychosomatic Research*, 47, 635–45.

Higgs, R. (1993) Should smokers be offered coronary bypass surgery? Human frailty should not be penalized. *British Medical Journal*, 306(6884), 1049–50.

Hocking, B.A. (1999) Limited (and gendered?) concessions to human frailty: Frightened women, angry men and the law of provocation. *Psychiatry, Psychology and Law*, 6, 57–66.

Hogan, J. and Hogan, R. (1989) How to measure employee reliability. *Journal of Applied Psychology*, 74, 273–9.

Hsee, C.K., Hatfield, E., Carlson, J.G. and Chemtob, C. (1990) The effect of power on susceptibility to emotional contagion. *Cognition and Emotion*, 4, 327–40.

Jordan, P.J., Ashkanasy, N.M. and Härtel, C.E.J. (2002) Emotional intelligence as a moderator of emotional and behavioural reactions to job insecurity. *Academy of Management Review*, 27, 361–72.

Jordan, P.J., Ashton-James, C.E. and Ashkanasy, N.M. (2006) Evaluating the claims. In K.R. Murphy (ed.) *A Critique of Emotional Intelligence: What Are the Problems and How Can They Be Fixed?* Mahwah, NJ: Lawrence Erlbaum Associates, pp. 198–210.

Jordan, P.J., Dasborough, M.T., Daus, C.S. and Ashkanasy, N.M. (2010) A call to context. *Industrial and Organizational Psychology*, 3, 145–8.

Jordan, P.J. and Troth, A.C. (2004) Managing emotions during team problem solving: Emotional intelligence and conflict resolution. *Human Performance*, 17, 195–218.

—— (2011) Emotional intelligence and leader member exchange: The relationship with employee turnover intentions and job satisfaction. *Leadership and Organizational Development Journal*, 38, 260–80.

Joseph, D.L. and Newman, D.A. (2010) Emotional intelligence: An integrative meta-analysis and cascading model. *Journal of Applied Psychology*, 95, 54–78.

Keashly, L. (2001) Interpersonal and systemic aspects of emotional abuse at work: The target's perspective. *Violence and Victims*, 16, 233–68.

Kiefer, T. (2002) Understanding the emotional experience of organizational change: Evidence from a merger. *Advances in Developing Human Resources*, 4, 39–61.

Kowalski, R.M. (2002) Whining, griping, and complaining: Positivity in the negativity. *Journal of Clinical Psychology*, 58, 1023–35.

Lane, R.D., Quinlan, D.M., Schwartz, G.E., Walker, P.A. and Zeitlin, S.B. (1990) The Levels of Emotional Awareness Scale: A cognitive-developmental measure of emotion. *Journal of Personality Assessment*, 55, 124–34.

Lawrence, S.A., Jordan, P.J., Troth, A.C. and Collins, A.L. (2011) A review of emotion regulation and development of a framework for emotion regulation in the workplace. In P. Perrewe and D. Ganster (eds) *Research in Occupational Stress and Wellbeing*. Greenwich, CT: JAI Press, pp. 197–263.

LeDoux, J. (2003) The emotional brain, fear, and the amygdala. *Cellular and Molecular Neurobiology*, 23, 727–38.

LeDoux, J.E., Farb, C.R. and Romanski, L.M. (1991) Overlapping projections to the amygdala and striatum from auditory processing areas of the thalamus and cortex. *Neuroscience letters*, 134, 139–44.

Lindebaum, D. and Jordan, P.J. (2012) Positive emotions or negative emotions or the utility of emotions. *Journal of Organizational Behavior*, 33, 1027–30.

Lopes, P.N., Brackett, M.A., Nezlek, J.B., Schutz, A., Sellin, I. and Salovey, P. (2004) Emotional intelligence and social interaction. *Personality and Social Psychology Bulletin*, 30, 1018–34.

Mayer, J.D., Caruso, D.R. and Salovey, P. (1999) Emotional intelligence meets traditional standards for an intelligence. *Intelligence*, 27, 267–98.

Mayer, J.D., Roberts, R.D. and Barsade, S.G. (2008) Human abilities: Emotional intelligence. *Annual Review of Psychology*, 59, 507–36.

Mayer, J. and Salovey, P. (1997) What is emotional intelligence? In P. Salovey and D. Sluyter (eds) *Emotional Development and Emotional Intelligence: Implications for Educators*. New York: Basic Books, pp. 3–31.

Mayer, J.D., Salovey, P. and Caruso, D.R. (2000) Models of emotional intelligence. In R.J. Sternberg (ed.) *Handbook of Intelligence*, 2nd edn. New York: Cambridge University Press, pp. 396–420.

Mazar, N. and Ariely, D. (2006) Dishonesty in everyday life and its policy implications. *Journal of Public Policy and Marketing*, 25, 117–26.

Mead, N.L., Baumeister, R.F., Gino, F., Schweitzer, M.E. and Ariely, D. (2009) Too tired to tell the truth: Self-control resource depletion and dishonesty. *Journal of Experimental Social Psychology*, 45, 594–7.

Mérö, L. (1998) *Moral Calculations: Game Theory, Logic, and Human Frailty*. Amsterdam: Springer.

Novick-Kline, P., Turk, C.L., Mennin, D.S., Hoyt, E.A. and Gallagher, C.L. (2005) Level of emotional awareness as a differentiating variable between individuals with and without generalized anxiety disorder. *Journal of Anxiety Disorders*, 19, 557–72.

O'Boyle, E.H., Humphrey, R.H., Pollack, J.M., Hawver, T.H. and Story, P.A. (2011) The relation between emotional intelligence and job performance: A meta-analysis. *Journal of Organizational Behavior*, 32, 788–818.

Ozdenoren, E., Salant, S.W. and Silverman, D. (2012) Willpower and the optimal control of visceral urges. *Journal of the European Economic Association*, 10, 342–68.

Parker, J.D.A., Taylor, G.J. and Bagby, R.M. (2001) The relationship between alexithymia and emotional intelligence. *Personality and Individual Differences*, 30, 107–15.

Payne, W.L. (1986) A study of emotion. Developing emotional intelligence: Self-integration; relating to fear, pain, and desire. *Dissertation Abstracts International*, 47, 203A.

Peterson, C. and Seligman, M.E.P. (2004) *Character Strengths and Virtues: A Handbook and Classification*. Washington, DC: American Psychological Association.

Ramachandran, Y., Jordan, P.J., Troth, A.C. and Lawrence, S.A. (2011) Emotional intelligence, emotional labor and organisational citizenship behaviour in service environments, *International Journal of Work Organisation and Emotion*, 4, 136–57.

Robinson, S.L. and O'Leary-Kelly, A.M. (1998) Monkey see, monkey do: The influence of work groups on the antisocial behavior of employees. *Academy of Management Journal*, 41, 658–72.

Salovey, P. and Mayer, J. (1990) Emotional intelligence. *Imagination, Cognition and Personality*, 9, 185–211.

Seligman, M.E.P. (2002) *Authentic Happiness*. New York: Free Press.

Seligman, M.E.P. and Csikszentmihalyi, M. (2000) Positive psychology: An introduction. *American Psychologist*, 55, 5–14.

Shand, A.F. (1896) Character and the Emotions. *Mind*, 5, 203–26.

Shiv, B., Loewenstein, G., Bechara, A., Damasio, H. and Damasio, A.R. (2005) Investment behavior and the negative side of emotion. *Psychological Science*, 16, 435–9.

Smeltzer, L.R. and Leap, T.L. (1988) An analysis of individual reactions to potentially offensive jokes in work settings. *Human Relations*, 41(4), 295–304.

Solomon, R.C. (2000) The philosophy of emotions. In M. Lewis and J.M. Haviland-Jones (eds) *Handbook of Emotions*, 2nd edn. New York: Guilford, pp. 17–29.

Spector, P.E. and Fox, S. (2010) Counterproductive work behavior and organisational citizenship behavior: Are they opposite forms of active behavior? *Applied Psychology: An International Review*, 59(1), 21–39.

Sternberg, R.J. (1985) *Beyond IQ: A Triarchic Theory of Human Intelligence*. New York: Cambridge University Press.

Taylor, G. (1996) Guilt and remorse. In R. Harré and W.G. Parrott (eds) *The Emotions: Social, Cultural and Biological Dimensions*. London: Sage, pp. 57–73.

Thomas, S.P. (1989) Gender differences in anger expression: Health implications. *Research in Nursing and Health*, 12, 389–98.

Thorberg, F.A., Young, R.M., Sullivan, K.A. and Lyvers, M. (2009) Alexithymia and alcohol use disorders: A critical review. *Addictive Behaviors*, 34, 237–45.

Tice, D.M. (2009) How emotions affect self-regulation. In J.P. Forgas, R.F. Baumeister and D.M. Tice (eds) *Psychology of Self-regulation: Cognitive, Affective, and Motivational Processes*. New York: Psychology Press, pp. 201–15.

Troth, A.C., Jordan, P.J., Lawrence, S.A. and Tse, H.M. (2012) A multilevel model of emotional skills, communication performance, and task performance in teams. *Journal of Organisational Behavior*, 33, 700–722.

Weick, K. (1989) Theory construction as disciplined imagination. *Academy of Management Review*, 14, 516–31.

Weiss, H.M. and Cropanzano, R. (1996) Affective events theory: A theoretical discussion of the structure, causes, and consequences of affective experiences at work. In B.M. Staw and L.L. *Cummings* (eds) *Research in Organizational Behavior*, vol. 18. Greenwich, CT: JAI Press, pp. 1–74.

Weiss, H.M., Suckow, K. and Cropanzano, R. (1999) Effects of justice conditions on discrete emotions. *Journal of Applied Psychology*, 84, 786–94.

Zlotnick, C., Shea, M.T., Pearlstein, T., Simpson, E., Costello, E. and Begin, A. (1996) The relationship between dissociative symptoms, alexithymia, impulsivity, sexual abuse, and self-mutilation. *Comprehensive Psychiatry*, 37, 12–16.

CHAPTER 7

The Challenge of Heavy Work Investment (HWI)

RAPHAEL SNIR AND ITZHAK HARPAZ

Introduction

By the term workaholics, Oates (1971) refers to people whose need to work has become so exaggerated that it may constitute a danger to their health, personal happiness, interpersonal relations, and social functioning. Since 1995, the number of publications on the topic of workaholism appears to be increasing exponentially (Sussman, 2012). There is also considerable interest in related concepts, such as work engagement (e.g., Bakken and Torp, 2012), working long hours (e.g., Nakata, 2011), and overwork (e.g., Golden, 2009). In total, an estimated 22 percent of the global workforce (approximately 614 million workers) work more than 48 hours per week (Lee, McCann and Messenger, 2007). In this chapter, we address the concept of Heavy Work Investment (HWI), which constitutes a conceptual integration and extension of the present literature (Snir and Harpaz, 2012), and deal with its outcomes, as well as the challenge it poses for individuals, their families, work organizations, and society alike.

The Concept of Heavy Work Investment (HWI)

Snir and Harpaz (2012), who introduced the concept of Heavy Work Investment (HWI), maintain that *both* long hours and heavy effort are its core dimensions. Effort means the amount of either physical or mental energy allocated to work (Becker, 1985). There are some indications that time and effort investments in work are positively correlated. For instance, according to an Experience-Sampling study, in which respondents provided randomly sampled self-reports over a one-week period, daily work hours were found to be strongly correlated with performing work-related activity and thinking about work-related issues (Snir and Zohar, 2008).

Negative HWI Outcomes

There is growing evidence of the negative effects of long work hours and overtime work on health and health-related behavior (Caruso, 2006; Dembe et al., 2005; Hebrig and Palumbo, 1994; Iwasaki, Takahashi and Nakata, 2006; Raediker et al., 2006; Sparks et al., 1997;

van der Hulst, 2003; Wagstaff and Sigstad Lie, 2011). For example, Raediker et al. (2006) found a relation between the number of working hours per week and the frequencies of health complaints. This applies to both musculo-skeletal disorders and to psycho-vegetative complaints. In her review article, Caruso (2006) reports that working long hours is related to sleep deprivation, poor recovery from work, decrements in neuro-cognitive and physiological functioning, illnesses, adverse reproductive outcomes, and injuries. According to a recent literature review, work periods of more than eight hours carry an increased risk of accidents that cumulates, so that the increased risk of workplace accidents at around twelve hours is twice the risk at eight hours (Wagstaff and Sigstad Lie, 2011).

Risks of long work hours to families include delayed marriages and child bearing, and obesity in children. Mistakes by fatigued workers have broad-reaching impacts on the community: medical errors, automobile crashes with other drivers on the road, and industrial disasters that damage the environment (Caruso, 2006). Indeed, based on studies indicating the danger of working long hours for both residents' and patients' safety (e.g., Baldwin et al., 2003), since 2003 most residents in the United States have been limited to 80 working hours per week (which is still twice the hours of a "regular" workweek). The data as regards the utility of limiting residents' work hours are conflicting (e.g., Lockley et al., 2004; Howard, Silber and Jobes, 2004; Goldman and Fiebach, 2007).

In case of no or insufficient recovery from work, the effort process determines the costs in terms of decrement in work capacities, and in the long run in health (Meijman and Mulder, 1998). High work effort is one of several factors associated with the well-being of workers. The association between effort and two well-being measures (enthusiasm-depression and contentment-anxiety) is negative throughout the range of jobs (Green, 2008).

However, there are moderators in the relationship between HWI and its outcomes. For example, Sparks et al. (1997) describe a variety of moderators in the long work hours–health relationship, such as job type (e.g., the adverse effect of long work hours may be greater for jobs demanding excessive physical activity or repetitive work), the work environment (ill-effects of the work environment due to poor ergonomic design of the workstation, high level of noise, inadequate lighting, etc., may be exacerbated by working long hours), and age (employees aged over 40 may see themselves as more likely targets for redundancy, so they work longer hours under high stress). Tucker and Rutherford (2005) found that train drivers who lacked both schedule autonomy and social support showed a positive relation between hours worked per week and frequency of physical health symptoms. Conversely, a negative relation was observed among train drivers reporting low schedule autonomy together with high social support. Snir and Harpaz (2012) claim that, in addition to the possible moderators in the HWI-outcomes relationship, HWI predictors also play an important role in shaping its outcomes, as they determine its different subtypes.

Differentiating HWI Subtypes

Snir and Harpaz (2012) distinguish between two major types of heavy work investment. The first is situational, stemming from external and uncontrollable predictors. At least in the short range, external predictors such as basic financial needs (e.g., to support one's family, pay debts), and demanding supervisor or organizational culture (e.g., the overtime culture in high-tech organizations, and among hospital physicians) are uncontrollable. For example, Drago, Wooden and Black (2006) found that high levels of household debt are mainly associated with conscript status (i.e., working long hours but prefer not to). Although workers in the high-tech industry are theoretically free to work at their own pace, they tend to extend their work hours, putting in 50 to 70 hours per week (Sharone, 2004). Sharone (2004) shows how a culture of excellence and a structure of comparative performance generate the individual's "choice" to work long hours.

The second major type of heavy work investment is dispositional, stemming from personal characteristics. Snir and Harpaz (2012) further distinguish between two subtypes of dispositional heavy work investment. For instance, workaholism, which is based on an addiction to work (an internal, negative, uncontrollable, and stable predictor), and work devotion as an expression of a passion to work (an internal, positive, controllable, and stable predictor). According to Snir and Harpaz (2012), the difference between addiction and passion to work is similar to the distinction of Vallerand et al. (2003) between Obsessive Passion and Harmonious Passion. Obsessive Passion occurs when individuals feel compelled to engage in an activity because of internal contingencies that control them; whereas Harmonious Passion occurs when individuals have freely accepted an activity as important to them without any contingencies attached to it. Below we describe and compare outcomes of the different HWI subtypes.

WORKAHOLISM

Workaholism, has been found to be positively correlated with stress and health complaints (e.g., Spence and Robbins, 1992; Andreassen, Ursin and Eriksen, 2007), burnout (Burke and Matthiesen, 2004; Schaufeli, Taris and van Rhenen, 2008); and negatively related to life satisfaction (e.g., Aziz and Zickar, 2006; Bonebright, Clay and Ankenmann, 2000). According to a recent literature review (Sussman, 2012), workaholics experience relatively high work–family conflict and negative life outcomes including high perceived stress, low self-esteem, low life satisfaction, sleeping difficulties, career dissatisfaction and poor performance, delay of planned retirement, work burnout, and ill-health. Ill-health effects of workaholism include: exhaustion, weight gain, slightly worse social function, taking sick-leave, high blood pressure, anxiety and depression, and physical pain.

WORK DEVOTION

Work devotion is similar to Spence and Robbins's (1992) concept of work enthusiasm, as well as to the concept of work engagement, which refers to a positive, fulfilling, work-related state of mind characterized by vigor, dedication, and absorption (Schaufeli, Shimazu and Taris, 2009; Schaufeli, Taris and Bakker, 2006). Due to their positive attitude and activity level, engaged employees create their own positive feedback, in terms of appreciation, recognition, and success. Although engaged employees do feel tired after a long day of hard work, they describe their tiredness as a rather pleasant state because it is associated with positive accomplishments. Engaged employees also enjoy other things outside work. Virtually all studies on work engagement offer evidence for the benefits of the experience. Engaged employees have psychological capital, seem to create their own resources, perform better, and have happier clients (Bakker, Albrecht and Leiter, 2011).

SITUATIONAL HEAVY WORK INVESTMENT

Snir and Harpaz (2012) claim that the study of situational investors (i.e., the needy and the employer-directed), regardless of the specific terminology used to name them (e.g., reluctant hard workers: Buelens and Poelmans, 2004; the conscripts: Drago, Wooden and Black, 2006; unhappy workaholics: Friedman and Lobel, 2003; and the over-employed: Golden, 2006), is relatively scarce. For example, Buelens and Poelmans (2004) found that reluctant hard workers have a strong perception of external pressure and a low perception of growth culture. These workers were also dissatisfied with their salary and their superior. Future research is needed to advance our knowledge as to the outcomes of situational heavy work investment.

Comparing Outcomes of the Different HWI Subtypes

Workaholics were found to have lower levels of satisfaction with aspects of work (e.g., job, career), non-work (e.g., family, friends), and psychological well-being, in contrast to work enthusiasts across countries and occupations (e.g., Bonebright, Clay and Ankenmann, 2000; Burke and Fiksenbaum, 2009a, 2009b). In three recent studies comparing work engagement and workaholism, the former was associated with one's own better psychological and physical health, job and family satisfaction, and job performance. In addition, work engagement was associated with one's partner's better engagement among dual-earner couples. In contrast, workaholism was associated with one's own poor psychological and physical health, job and family satisfaction, work–family balance and job performance. In addition, workaholism was associated with one's partner's poor work–family balance (Shimazu, 2012).

According to the HWI model (Snir and Harpaz, 2012), a possible explanation for the above pattern is that workaholics, unlike work-devoted investors, are *not* in control of their HWI. The adverse effects of individuals' lack of control over long work hours on their well-being are documented (e.g., Golden and Wiens-Tuers, 2005; Sparks et al., 1997; van der Hulst and Geurts, 2001). Arguably, the needy heavy work investors, who resemble workaholics in the lack of control of their HWI, will also exhibit lower levels of satisfaction and well-being than work-devoted investors. We consider the employer-directed heavy work investors (e.g., high-tech workers, hospital physicians) a unique case. On the one hand they resemble workaholics in the lack of control of their work investment. On the other hand high-status employees reap greater remuneration as well as social rewards from their jobs than low-status employees (Hodson, 2004), which may compensate for the lack of control (of their HWI) and buffer its adverse effects.

Hence, Snir and Harpaz (2012) maintain that the different subtypes of dispositional and situational heavy work investors may experience different personal outcomes: negative personal work/non-work outcomes (e.g., burnout and stress) will be highest in workaholics and needy heavy work investors, lowest in work-devoted investors, and in between among employer-directed heavy work investors. However, positive personal work/non-work outcomes (e.g., work and life satisfaction) will be highest in work-devoted investors, lowest in workaholics and needy heavy work investors, and in between among employer-directed heavy work investors.

Major Dilemmas Concerning HWI

The phenomenon of HWI poses a challenge for individuals, their families, workplaces, and society alike. Namely: (1) which dimension of work investment should we value more – time or effort? (2) Should employers focus on HWI, or its outcomes? (3) In case of mixed HWI outcomes for the parties concerned, how should we weigh these outcomes? (4) Should employers encourage workers to strive for a one-size-fits-all simplistic notion of work-life balance or an individually-suited balance? (5) Should employers prefer heavy work investors over ordinary full-time workers or certain subtypes of heavy work investors over other subtypes? (6) How should organizations address the possible mismatches between actual and preferred work investment of their employees? Finally, (7) how should global organizations deal with cross-cultural differences in HWI?

WHICH DIMENSION OF HWI SHOULD WE VALUE MORE – TIME OR EFFORT?

Sometimes working long hours is a necessity – for instance, when having a high workload with tight deadlines, or in the need to communicate with colleagues and customers overseas. However, there are also jobs in which investing greater effort during a shorter time period could also lead to the desired work goal. The question – which dimension of HWI should we value more – time or effort – is strongly related to the issue of gender differences in time allocation to paid work. Of men's total (paid and unpaid) work time in 13 industrialized countries, roughly two-thirds were allocated to paid (market) activities and one-third to unpaid (non-market) activities (e.g., childcare, household chores). These proportions were reversed for women (United Nations, 1995). Wharton and Blair-Loy (2002) state that employed women in the industrialized world continue to bear more responsibility for family and children than do their male counterparts. Thus, they are more often considered candidates for part-time work. Indeed, based on a cross-national study of industrialized countries, for wives, being a parent was associated with a reduction in hours of paid work in all ten countries (Jacobs and Gornick, 2002). Furthermore, Rothbard and Edwards (2003) found that for women, increased time investment in either work or family reduced time invested in the other role. However, for men, increased time invested in work reduced time invested in family, but increased time investment in family did not affect time invested in work. Time invested in family was positively related to the number of children at home. Drago, Wooden, and Black (2006) found that women are relatively rare among long hours workers, and especially long hours volunteers (i.e., those who prefer to work long hours). In a relatively recent study, Snir, Harpaz and Ben-Baruch (2009) found that a contrasting parenthood effect on men and women prevails even in the demanding high-tech sector, where women are expected to work long hours and play down their care-giving activities. Fathers invested more weekly hours in work than childless men, whereas mothers invested fewer weekly hours in work than childless women. In the parents' sub-sample, mothers invested more hours per week in childcare than fathers did. The biosocial theory, which focuses on the interactive relations between physical attributes and related behaviors of men and women and the social contexts in which they live (Wood and Eagly, 2002), provides a possible explanation for these gender differences.

However, women may not necessarily be deterred from investment of heavy *effort* in work. According to Hewlett and Buck Luce (2006), extreme jobs demand a high number of responsibilities (five or more out of ten specific challenges, such as tight deadlines and responsibility for profit and loss), as well as a high number of work hours (60 or more a week). In a survey conducted in global companies they found that 39 percent of respondents holding jobs with reasonable hours but high number of responsibilities were women. By contrast, of those shouldering high number of responsibilities and putting in long hours, only 30 percent were women. Female respondents seemed particularly tuned into – and distressed by – the fallout of long work hours on their children.

To keep their jobs, mothers can compensate for their limited time investment in work through other inputs such as work effort. Research on this important issue is scarce, though there are some indications supporting the above notion. For instance, Bielby and Bielby (1988) found that women put substantially more effort into their jobs than men with similar household responsibilities and human capital and who worked in similar contexts. According to Gorman and Kmec (2007), even when women and men are matched on extensive measures of job characteristics, family and household responsibilities, and individual qualifications, women report that their jobs require more effort than men do.

In sum, the effort dimension of HWI is not less important than the time dimension. Work-effort-based rewards and promotion should be considered, at least concerning mothers having a career.

SHOULD EMPLOYERS FOCUS ON HWI, OR ITS OUTCOMES?

Employers tend to overvalue the tendency to work long hours, particularly when objective measures of productivity are hard to come by. Many employers may create a few shorter-hour jobs, as a way to screen out potentially less productive workers (Rebitzer and Taylor, 1995). Based on a study in a large high-tech corporation, managers also use bureaucratic means to control the hours that employees work, among them penalizing those who resist managerial control, even when they devise creative ways to schedule and complete their work (Perlow, 1998). Over time, there may be more jobs that valorize long hours, where requesting shorter hours is feared by employees to be a negative signal (Golden, 2009).

However, by definition, productivity is the degree of achieving ends at a low cost (of time, inter alia). Sometimes workers stay late in the office (while in fact hardly working) just to impress the boss (Snir and Harpaz, 2012), or simply due to bad time management. Indeed, work hours are not necessarily positively related to productivity (e.g., Baird and Beccia, 1980; Ben-David, 2003; Hanna, Taylor and Sullivan, 2005). For example, Hanna, Taylor and Sullivan (2005) reported a decrease in construction labor productivity as the number of hours worked beyond the typical 40 hours scheduled per week increased. One of the ways in which employees' long working hours and heavy work effort might impair productivity is by creating fatigue. According to Circadian (2000), production shutdowns and productivity losses caused by worker fatigue costs the US economy approximately $55 billion annually. Accordingly, it seems that if objective measures of productivity are available, it is better to reward employees mainly for work outputs rather than inputs. When productivity cannot be measured objectively, 360-degree performance appraisals concerning the employee (made by his/her supervisor, co-workers, subordinates, and so on) can be used.

IN CASE OF MIXED HWI OUTCOMES FOR THE PARTIES CONCERNED, HOW SHOULD WE WEIGH THESE OUTCOMES?

HWI may have different outcomes for the parties concerned (i.e., the individual, his/her family and workplace, and society). Moreover, the outcomes for a specific party are not necessarily uniform. For example, one's HWI may interfere with family, which on the other hand may enjoy a high material standard of living. One may exhibit organizational citizenship behavior, but also harm the morale of one's work group, by setting unrealistic standards of face time at the office (Snir and Harpaz, 2012). Besides, not all HWI outcomes are immediate, and their nature may change over time. For instance, Ng, Sorensen and Feldman (2007) expect workaholism to have more negative consequences in the long term than in the short term. Finally, a positive HWI subtype may have negative outcomes, and vice versa. For example, Bakker, Albrecht and Leiter (2011) claim that if engaged workers get overly involved in work activities, they may experience work–family conflict and other negative consequences. On the other hand, Shamai, Harpaz and Snir (2012) found that *all* four major subtypes of heavy work investors, *including* the workaholics, exhibit significantly higher levels of life satisfaction than common workers.

In the weighing of mixed HWI outcomes, we have to remember that extreme and continuous investment of time and effort in work might have grave repercussions, *regardless* of its predictors (external and uncontrollable ones, an addiction to work, or a passion to work). For example, "Karoshi" is a Japanese term, referring to death from overwork (Kanai, 2009). Most of its victims typically work 3,000–3,500 hours a year, commonly putting in 14-hour days and seven-day weeks. Most of the deaths occur due to subarachnoid hemorrhage or myocardial infarction (Hebrig and Palumbo, 1994). Relying on Morgan's (2006) insight as regard to creating learning organizations, we have to be aware of the importance of understanding the *limits* to be placed on action. In our context, organizations should avoid putting their employees at irreversible and serious health risk due to HWI, obligatory or voluntary alike.

Indeed, in the short term there may be a conflict of interests between one (or one's family) and one's workplace. For instance, to face a tight deadline, one invests heavily in one's work at the expense of spending time in leisure and familial activities. However, in the long term, if one's workplace continues to be overly demanding on one's time and energy, one may become fatigued and burned out, lose his/her vigor and creativity, develop health problems, and consequently exhibit poor performance at work, or even quit the job. Hence, one's workplace may lose a productive worker with valuable knowledge and skills, and face the costs of hiring and training a new employee with a potential similar occupational fate, due to organizational greediness. Namely, in the long term, all the concerned parties may benefit from one's work investment being not *too* heavy. Beyond that, there is a large subjective component in the weighing of mixed HWI outcomes.

SHOULD EMPLOYERS ENCOURAGE WORKERS TO STRIVE FOR A ONE-SIZE-FITS-ALL SIMPLISTIC NOTION OF WORK–LIFE BALANCE OR AN INDIVIDUALLY-SUITED BALANCE?

Along with the view of supportive (i.e., family-friendly) organizations, a one-size-fits-all simplistic notion of work–life balance has emerged (Friedman and Lobel, 2003). Dispositional heavy work investors, or at least workaholics, are less likely to approve of counseling/programs based on this notion. For them, the so-called "objective" imbalance may be in fact a subjective balance (Snir and Harpaz, 2012). Indeed, using the three-scale Workaholism Battery (Spence and Robbins, 1992), Russo and Waters (2006) found that workaholics, in contrast to their enthusiastic workaholic (those who score high in work involvement, enjoyment, and drive) counterparts, did not experience declining work–family conflict with increased access to flexible scheduling.

Furthermore, Snir, Harpaz and Ben-Baruch (2009) stress that a meaningful understanding of paid work hours and work–family conflict alike calls for analysis on the couple/household level (e.g., Clarkberg and Moen, 2001; Jacobs and Gerson, 2001; Medalia and Jacobs, 2008). One can invest one's time and energy in the family domain if one's spouse assumes the breadwinner role. By the same token, one's willingness to take care of the children and perform housework activities enables one's spouse to invest long hours in work. Hall and Hall (1979) identified four categories of couples based on the involvement of each party in work and family: accommodators (one party is highly involved in work and the other in family), allies (both parties are involved in the same sphere, with little identity tied to the other sphere), adversaries (each highly is involved in work but wants the other to do home tasks), and acrobats (each is highly involved in both home and work).

Hence, a couple of accommodators, in which one partner is highly invested in work and the other willingly takes on the caregiver role, may get along quite well. Such a couple represents a familial agreed-upon work–life balance, even though the heavy work investor among the two might be superficially perceived as suffering from imbalance at the individual level. On the other hand, a couple of adversaries (e.g., a dual-career couple) might face housework and care deficit, which could be resolved by paid help. Indeed, as a result of gender and family transformations, some upper-class and middle-class households in Western countries hire migrant domestics to outsource housework and care work. Hochschild (2000, p. 131) coined the term "global care chains," which describes "a series of personal links between people across the globe based on the paid or unpaid work of caring." Note though that the international transfer of caretaking facilitates the care deficit in the receiving countries at the expense of creating a worst deficit in the sending countries.

All in all, we maintain that employers should encourage workers to strive for an individually-suited work–life balance *within* reasonable limits.

SHOULD EMPLOYERS PREFER HEAVY WORK INVESTORS OVER ORDINARY FULL-TIME WORKERS OR CERTAIN SUBTYPES OF HEAVY WORK INVESTORS OVER OTHER SUBTYPES?

We have chosen to present this question, due to its prevalence. Note though that this is a misleading question, since it focuses on work inputs rather than outputs. That is to say, employers should prefer productive over non-productive workers. However, if in certain jobs HWI is an organizational necessity, and valid productivity measures are hard to come by, employers should prefer the work-devoted over the workaholics – present research indicates that they exhibit better work-related and non-work-related outcomes than the workaholics (e.g., Burke and Fiksenbaum, 2009a, 2009b; Shimazu, 2012).

HOW SHOULD ORGANIZATIONS ADDRESS POSSIBLE MISMATCHES BETWEEN ACTUAL AND PREFERRED WORK INVESTMENT OF THEIR EMPLOYEES?

Data from the 1997 International Social Survey Programme show that a majority of US employees prefer to work a different number of hours than they actually work. Many want to spend less time at work, but there are also many who want to increase their hours (Reynolds, 2003). Findings of the Australian Work and Life Index (AWALI) 2010 survey also indicate that many workers do not work the hours they would prefer: just over half of all workers worked more than half a day (4+ hours) more or less than they would prefer, taking account of the effect on their income. Most would like to work less (Pocock, Skinner and Pisaniello, 2010). Moreover, findings of the AWALI 2012 survey indicate that long hours and a poor fit between actual and preferred working hours are both associated with worse work–life outcome, and that most of those who work long hours would prefer not to (Skinner, Hutchinson and Pocock, 2012). Bell, Otterbach and Sousa-Poza (2011) examined the impact of the mismatch between actual and desired work hours on self-perceived health outcomes in Germany and the United Kingdom. They found that it has negative effects on workers' health. In particular, "overemployment" – working more hours than desired – has negative effects on different measures of self-perceived health.

Since organizations often require a variety of individuals in multiple roles, from ordinary full-time jobs to demanding ones, it may be important to search right from the start for the proper mix of employees to avoid mismatches between their actual and preferred work hours. In certain occupations, changing the reward system may also help. For example, according to Blair-Loy and Jacobs (2003), commission-based brokers have a personal clientele they have painstakingly built up over the years, whereas discount brokers provide a service for any of the firm's clients who may walk into a branch office or telephone a call center. Since discount brokers are paid a salary, they do not have to put in extremely long hours to generate the maximum commissions possible. In other occupations, changing work procedures may decrease the need for overemployment and its possible adverse outcomes. For instance, the 24-hour physician coverage of an emergency department usually requires long work hours, heavy effort, and shift work. A division of the 24-hour physician coverage into three ten-hour shifts (i.e., with a congruent two-hour interval between consecutive shifts to insure care continuity), which will also be adapted as far as possible for early-birds and night owls, may have the potential to reduce medical errors and better both residents' and patients' safety.

HOW SHOULD GLOBAL ORGANIZATIONS DEAL WITH CROSS-CULTURAL DIFFERENCES IN HWI?

With the new millennium witnessing an increase in economic activity on a global scale, individuals are increasingly encountering people of different nations across real and virtual borders (Aycan and Kanungo, 2001). Hence, an understanding of cross-cultural differences is becoming more critical than ever. However, relatively few studies have been published on possible cross-cultural differences concerning workaholism or HWI in general (e.g., Medalia and Jacobs, 2008; Snir and Harpaz, 2006, 2009; Wharton and Blair-Loy, 2006). For example, Snir and Harpaz (2009) have found that work investment is heavier in societies where survival values are important, as compared to societies where self-expression values are important. Situational heavy work investors are more common in societies where survival values are important, as compared to societies where self-expression values are important. On the other hand, work-devoted persons are more common in societies where self-expression values are important, as compared to societies where survival values are important.

According to the social identity theory, individuals are motivated to achieve a positive social identity. This desire will prompt them to make social comparisons between the in-group and the out-groups, with the ultimate aim of achieving a positive and distinct position for the in-group (Tajfel, 1978). Based on this reasoning, a person from a culture which values HWI may regard others from a culture which stresses a balance between work and leisure (e.g., the Western European culture) as lazy, whereas an individual from the latter culture may see heavy work investors as work addicts.

Therefore, global organizations should encourage awareness of and respect for cultural variations concerning HWI – namely, polycentric or at least geocentric HRM policies should be adopted, in spite of the temptation to utilize an ethnocentric policy. For example, in a selection process for relocation, the similarity between the candidate's homeland culture and the culture of the country of destination concerning work investment should be taken into account.

Hofstede (1994, p. 51) defines the individualism/collectivism dimension as follows:

> *individualism pertains to societies in which the ties between individuals are loose: everyone is expected to look after himself or herself and his or her immediate family. Collectivism as its opposite pertains to societies in which people from birth onwards are integrated into strong, cohesive in-groups, which throughout people's lifetime continue to protect them in exchange for unquestioning loyalty.*

Accordingly, we expect that in individualistic societies, HWI is more likely to be directed by self-related motivators, such as a high need for achievement, careerism, or a need for self-fulfillment. It is interesting to note in that respect that social loafing, the tendency of individuals to expend less effort when working collectively than when working individually, occurs in individualistic but not in collectivistic societies (Earley, 1989). On the other hand, in collectivistic societies HWI is more likely to be directed by group-related motivators – high commitment to the success of one's work-team or work-organization, or strong identification with a national enterprise. A recent example is the mobilization of the Chinese people for the success of the 2008 Beijing Olympic Games. The above means that building reward systems for multi-cultural (in respect of the individualism/collectivism dimension) work-teams can be quite tricky. As long as it does not compromise the achievement of the work-team goal, the reward system has to include *both* individual and team-based performance criteria.

Conclusion

In the present chapter we described the possible negative outcomes of HWI, presented HWI major subtypes, and dealt with the challenge it poses for individuals, their families, workplaces, and society alike. Based on our discussion we propose the following conclusions:

1. *Which dimension of HWI should we value more – time or effort?*
   The effort dimension of HWI is not less important than the time dimension. Work-effort-based rewards and promotion should be considered, at least as regard to mothers having a career.
2. *Should employers focus on HWI, or its outcomes?*
   If objective measures of productivity are available, it is better to reward employees mainly for work outputs rather than inputs. When productivity cannot be measured objectively, performance appraisals concerning the employee can be used.
3. *In case of mixed HWI outcomes for the parties concerned, how should we weigh these outcomes?*
   Extreme and continuous investment of time and effort in work might have grave repercussions, *regardless* of its predictors. In the long term, all the concerned parties may benefit from one's work investment being not *too* heavy. Beyond that, there is a large subjective component in the weighing of mixed HWI outcomes.
4. *Should employers encourage workers to strive for a one-size-fits-all simplistic notion of work–life balance or an individually-suited balance?*
   Employers should encourage workers to strive for an individually-suited work–life balance *within* reasonable limits.
5. *Should employers prefer heavy work investors over ordinary full-time workers or certain subtypes of heavy work investors over other subtypes?*
   Employers should prefer productive over non-productive workers. However, if in certain jobs HWI is an organizational necessity, and valid productivity measures are hard to come by, employers should prefer the work-devoted over the workaholics.
6. *How should organizations address the possible mismatches between actual and preferred work investment of their employees?*
   Organizations should search right from the start for the proper mix of employees to avoid mismatches between their actual and preferred work hours. In certain occupations, changing the reward system may also help. In other occupations, changing work procedures may decrease the need for overemployment and its possible adverse outcomes.
7. *How should global organizations deal with cross-cultural differences in HWI?*
   Global organizations should encourage awareness of and respect for cultural variations concerning HWI – namely, polycentric or at least geocentric HRM policies should be adopted, in spite of the temptation to utilize an ethnocentric policy. Building reward systems for multi-cultural (in respect of the individualism/collectivism dimension) work-teams can be quite tricky. As long as it does not compromise the achievement of the work-team goal, the reward system has to include both individual and team-based performance criteria.

References

Andreassen, C.S., Ursin, H. and Eriksen, H.R. (2007) The relationship between strong motivation to work, "workaholism," and health. *Psychology and Health*, 22(5), 615–29.

Aycan, Z. and Kanungo, R.N. (2001) Cross-cultural industrial and organizational psychology: A critical appraisal of the field and future directions. In N. Anderson, D.S. Ones, H.K. Sinangil and C. Viswesvaran (eds) *Handbook of Industrial, Work and Organizational Psychology*, vol. 1. London: Sage, pp. 385–408.

Aziz, S. and Zickar, M.J. (2006) A cluster analysis investigation of workaholism as a syndrome. *Journal of Occupational Health Psychology*, 11(1), 52–62.

Baird, L.S. and Beccia, P.J. (1980) The potential misuse of overtime. *Personnel Psychology*, 33, 557–65.

Bakken, B. and Torp, S. (2012) Work engagement and health among industrial workers. *Scandinavian Journal of Organizational Psychology*, 4(1), 4–20.

Bakker, A.B., Albrecht, S.L. and Leiter, M.P. (2011) Key questions regarding work engagement. *European Journal of Work and Organizational Psychology*, 20(1), 4–28.

Baldwin, D.C. Jr., Daugherty, S.R., Tsai, R. and Scotti, M.J. Jr. (2003) A national survey of residents' self-reported work hours: Thinking beyond specialty. *Academic Medicine*, 78, 1154–63.

Becker, G.S. (1985) Human capital, effort, and the sexual division of labor. *Journal of Labor Economics*, 3 (Supplement), S33–S58.

Bell, D., Otterbach, S. and Sousa-Poza, A. (2011) *Work Hours Constraints and Health*, IZA Discussion Paper No. 6126. Bonn: Institute for the Study of Labor (IZA).

Ben-David, D. (2003) The labor force in Israel from the international aspect. *Riv'on Le-Kalkala*, 50, 73–90 [Hebrew].

Bielby, D.D. and Bielby, W.T. (1988) She works hard for the money: Household responsibilities and the allocation of work effort. *The American Journal of Sociology*, 93(5), 1031–59.

Blair-Loy, M. and Jacobs, J.A. (2003) Globalization, work hours, and the care deficit among stockbrokers. *Gender and Society*, 17, 230–49.

Bonebright, C.A., Clay, D.L. and Ankenmann, R.D. (2000) The relationship of workaholism with work-life conflict, life satisfaction, and purpose in life. *Journal of Counseling Psychology*, 47(4), 469–77.

Buelens, M. and Poelmans, S. (2004) Enriching the Spence and Robbins' typology of workaholism: Demographic, motivational and organizational correlates. *Journal of Organizational Change Management*, 17(5), 440–58.

Burke, R.J. and Fiksenbaum, L. (2009a) Work motivations, work outcomes, and health: Passion versus addiction. *Journal of Business Ethics*, 84 (Supplement 2), 257–63.

—— (2009b) Work motivations, satisfactions, and health among managers: Passion versus addiction. *Cross-Cultural Research*, 43(4), 349–65.

Burke, R.J. and Matthiesen, S. (2004) Short communication: Workaholism among Norwegian journalists: Antecedents and consequences. *Stress and Health*, 20, 301–8.

Caruso, C. (2006) Possible broad impacts of long work hours. *Industrial Health*, 44, 531–6.

Circadian Technologies, Inc. (2000) *24x7 Operations: Optimizing Human Performance*. Cambridge, MA: Circadian Technologies, Inc.

Clarkberg, M. and Moen, P. (2001) Understanding the time-squeeze: Married couples' preferred and actual work-hour strategies. *American Behavioral Scientist*, 44, 1115–36.

Dembe, A.E., Erickson, J.B., Delbos, R.G. and Banks, S.M. (2005) The impact of overtime and long work hours on occupational injuries and illnesses: New evidence from the United States. *Occupational and Environmental Medicine*, 62, 588–97.

Drago, R., Wooden, M. and Black, D. (2006) *Long Work Hours: Volunteers and Conscripts*, Melbourne Institute Working Paper, No. 27/06. Victoria: Melbourne Institute of Applied Economic and Social Research, the University of Melbourne.

Earley, P.C. (1989) Social loafing and collectivism: A comparison of the United States and the People's Republic of China. *Administrative Science Quarterly*, 34(4), 565–81.

Friedman, S.D. and Lobel, S. (2003) The happy workaholic: A role model for employees. *Academy of Management Executive*, 17(3), 87–98.

Golden, L. (2006) How long? The historical, economic and cultural factors behind working hours and overwork. In R.J. Burke (ed.) *Research Companion to Working Time and Work Addiction*. Northampton, MA: Edward Elgar, pp. 36–57.

—— (2009) A brief history of long work time and the contemporary sources of overwork. *Journal of Business Ethics*, 84, 217–27.

Golden, L. and Wiens-Tuers, B. (2005) Mandatory overtime work: Who, what, and where? *Labor Studies Journal*, 30(1), 1–23.

Goldman, L. and Fiebach, N.H. (2007) Editorial. Hippocrates affirmed? Limiting residents' work hours does no harm to patients. *Annals of Internal Medicine*, 147(2), 143–4.

Gorman, E.H. and Kmec, J.A. (2007) We (have to) try harder: Gender and required work effort in Britain and the United States. *Gender and Society*, 21(6), 828–56.

Green, F. (2008) Work effort and worker well-being in the age of affluence. In R.J. Burke and C.L. Cooper (eds) *The Long Work Hours Culture: Causes, Consequences and Choices*. Bingley: Emerald Group Publishing, pp. 115–35.

Hall, F.S. and Hall, D.T. (1979) *The Two-Career Couple*. Reading, MA: Addison-Wesley.

Hanna, M.ASCE, A.S. Taylor, C.S. and Sullivan, K.T. (2005) Impact of extended overtime on construction labor productivity. *Journal of Construction Engineering and Management*, 131(6), 734–9.

Hebrig, P.A. and Palumbo, F.A. (1994) Karoshi: Salaryman sudden death syndrome. *Journal of Managerial Psychology*, 9(7), 11–16.

Hewlett, S.A. and Buck Luce, C. (2006) Extreme jobs and the dangerous allure of the 70-hour workweek. *Harvard Business Review*, 84(12), 49–59.

Hochschild, A.R. (2000) Global care chains and emotional surplus value. In W. Hutton and A. Giddens (eds) *Global Capitalism*. London: Jonathan Cape, pp. 130–46.

Hodson, R. (2004) Work life and social fulfillment: Does social affiliation at work reflect a carrot or a stick? *Social Science Quarterly*, 85(2), 221–39.

Hofstede, G. (1994) *Cultures and Organizations: Software of the Mind: Intercultural Cooperation and Its Importance for Survival*. London: HarperCollins.

Howard, D.L., Silber, J.H. and Jobes, D.R. (2004) Do regulations limiting residents' work hours affect patient mortality? *Journal of General Internal Medicine*, 19, 1–7.

Iwasaki, K., Takahashi, M. and Nakata, A. (2006) Health problems due to long working hours in Japan: Working hours, workers' compensation (Karoshi), and preventive measures. *Industrial Health*, 44, 537–40.

Jacobs, J.A. and Gerson, K. (2001) Overworked individuals or overworked families? *Work and Occupations*, 28, 40–63.

Jacobs, J.A. and Gornick, J.C. (2002) Hours of paid work in dual-earner couples: The United States in cross-national perspective. *Sociological Focus*, 35(2), 169–87.

Kanai, A. (2009) "Karoshi (work to death)" in Japan. *Journal of Business Ethics*, 84, 209–16.

Lee, S., McCann, D. and Messenger, J.C. (2007) *Working Time around the World: Trends in Working Hours, Laws, and Policies in a Global Comparative Perspective*. London: Routledge.

Lockley, S.W., Cronin, J.W., Evans, E.E., Cade, B.E. et al. (2004) Effect of reducing interns' weekly work hours on sleep and attentional failures. *New England Journal of Medicine*, 351, 1829–37.

Medalia, C. and Jacobs, J.A. (2008) Working time for married couples in 28 countries. In R.J. Burke and C.L. Cooper (eds) *The Long Work Hours Culture: Causes, Consequences and Choices*. Bingley: Emerald Group Publishing, pp. 137–57.

Meijman, T.F. and Mulder, G. (1998) Psychological aspects of workload. In P.J.D. Drenth, H. Thierry, and C.J. de Wolff (eds) *Handbook of Work and Organizational Psychology*, vol. 2, 2nd edn. Hove: Psychology Press, pp. 5–33.

Morgan, G. (2006) *Images of Organization*. Thousand Oaks, CA: Sage.

Nakata, A. (2011) Effects of long work hours and poor sleep characteristics on workplace injury among full-time male employees of small- and medium-scale businesses. *Journal of Sleep Research*, 20(4), 576–84.

Ng, T.W.H., Sorensen, K.L. and Feldman, D.C. (2007) Dimensions, antecedents, and consequences of workaholism: A conceptual integration and extension. *Journal of Organizational Behavior*, 28, 111–36.

Oates, W. (1971) *Confessions of a Workaholic: The Facts about Work Addiction*. New York: World Publishing.

Perlow, L.A. (1998) Boundary control: The social ordering of work and family time in a high-tech corporation. *Administrative Science Quarterly*, 43(2), 328–57.

Pocock, B., Skinner, N. and Pisaniello, S. (2010) *How Much Should We Work? Working Hours, Holidays and Working Life: The Participation Challenge. The Australian Work and Life Index 2010*. Adelaide, SA: The Centre for Work + Life, University of South Australia.

Raediker, B., Janssen, D., Schomann, C. and Nachreiner, F. (2006) Extended working hours and health. *Chronobiology International*, 23(6), 1305–16.

Rebitzer, J. and Taylor, L. (1995) Do labor markets provide enough short-hours jobs? An analysis of work hours and work incentives. *Economic Inquiry*, 33, 257–73.

Reynolds, J. (2003) You can't always get the hours you want: Mismatches between actual and preferred work hours in the US *Social Forces*, 81(4), 1171–99.

Rothbard, N.P. and Edwards, J.R. (2003) Investment in work and family roles: A test of identity and utilitarian motives. *Personnel Psychology*, 56, 699–730.

Russo, J.A. and Waters, L.E. (2006) Workaholic worker type differences in work-family conflict: The moderating role of supervisor support and flexible work scheduling. *Career Development International*, 11, 418–39.

Schaufeli, W.B., Shimazu, A. and Taris, T.W. (2009) Being driven to work excessively hard: The evaluation of a two-factor measure of workaholism in the Netherlands and Japan. *Cross-Cultural Research*, 43(4), 320–48.

Schaufeli, W.B, Taris, T.W. and Bakker, A.B. (2006) Dr Jekyll or Mr Hyde? On the differences between work engagement and workaholism. In R.J. Burke (ed.) *Research Companion to Working Time and Work Addiction*. Northampton, MA: Edward Elgar, pp. 193–217.

Schaufeli, W.B., Taris, T.W. and van Rhenen, W. (2008) Workaholism, burnout, and work engagement: Three of a kind or three different kinds of employee well-being? *Applied Psychology: An International Review*, 57(2), 173–203.

Shamai, O., Harpaz, I. and Snir, R. (2012) *Would You Be Happier if You Worked Harder? A Comparison of Life Satisfaction in Workers' Types*. The 2012 Academy of Management Annual Meeting, Boston, August 3–7.

Sharone, O. (2004) Engineering overwork: Bell-curve management at a high-tech firm. In C. Fuchs Epstein, and A.L. Kalleberg (eds) *Fighting for Time: Shifting Boundaries of Work and Social Life*. New York: Russell Sage Foundation, pp. 191–218.

Shimazu, A. (2012) *Is Working Hard Good or Bad for Employee Well-being? The Distinctiveness of Work Engagement and Workaholism*. The 30th International Congress on Occupational Health, Cancun, March 20.

Skinner, N., Hutchinson, C. and Pocock, B. (2012) *The Big Squeeze: Work, Home and Care in 2012 – The Australian Work and Life Index*. Adelaide, SA: The Centre for Work + Life, University of South Australia.

Snir, R. and Harpaz, I. (2006) The workaholism phenomenon: A cross-national perspective. *Career Development International*, 11(5), 374–93.

—— (2009) Cross-cultural differences concerning heavy work investment. *Cross-Cultural Research*, 43(4), 309–19.

—— (2012) Beyond workaholism: Towards a general model of heavy work investment. *Human Resource Management Review*, 22(3), 232–43.

Snir, R., Harpaz, I. and Ben-Baruch, D. (2009) Centrality of and investment in work and family among Israeli high-tech workers: A bicultural perspective. *Cross-Cultural Research*, 43(4), 366–85.

Snir, R. and Zohar, D. (2008) Workaholism as discretionary time investment at work: An experience-sampling study. *Applied Psychology: An International Review*, 57(1), 109–27.

Sparks, K., Cooper, C., Fried, Y. and Shirom, A. (1997) The effects of hours of work on health: A meta-analytic review. *Journal of Occupational and Organizational Psychology*, 70, 391–408.

Spence, J.T. and Robbins, A.S. (1992) Workaholism: Definition, measurement, and preliminary results. *Journal of Personality Assessment*, 58, 160–78.

Sussman, S. (2012) Workaholism: A review. *Journal of Addiction Research and Therapy*, S6, 1–10.

Tajfel, H. (1978) Social categorization, social identity, and social comparison. In H. Tajfel (ed.) *Differentiation between Social Groups*. London and New York: Academic Press, pp. 61–76.

Tucker, P. and Rutherford, C. (2005) Moderators of the relationship between long work hours and health. *Journal of Occupational Health Psychology*, 10(4), 465–76.

United Nations (1995) *Gender and Human Development* (Human Development Report 1995). New York: United Nations.

Vallerand, R.J., Blanchard, C., Mageau, G.A., Koestner, R., Ratelle, C., Leonard, M. and Gagne, M. (2003) Les passions de l'ame: On obsessive and harmonious passion. *Journal of Personality and Social Psychology*, 85(4), 756–67.

van der Hulst, M. (2003) Long workhours and health. *Scandinavian Journal of Work, Environment, and Health*, 29, 171–88.

van der Hulst, M. and Geurts, S. (2001) Associations between overtime and psychological health in high and low reward jobs. *Work and Stress*, 15(3), 227–40.

Wagstaff, A.S. and Sigstad Lie, J-A. (2011) Shift and night work and long working hours: A systematic review of safety implications. *Scandinavian Journal of Work, Environment, and Health*, 37(3), 173–85.

Wharton, A.S. and Blair-Loy, M. (2002) The "overtime culture" in a global corporation: A cross-national study of finance professionals' interest in working part-time. *Work and Occupations*, 29, 32–63.

—— (2006) Long work hours and family life: A cross-national study of employees' concerns. *Journal of Family Issues*, 27(3), 415–36.

Wood, W. and Eagly, A.H. (2002) A cross-cultural analysis of the behavior of women and men: Implications for the origins of sex differences. *Psychological Bulletin*, 128(5), 699–727.

CHAPTER 8

Bullying, Stress and Health in School Principals and Medical Professionals: Experiences at the "Front-Line"

PHILIP RILEY AND JANICE LANGAN-FOX

Introduction

A growing body of literature supports an association between occupational practices, psychological state, physical health and reactions to stress (for a review see Langan-Fox and Cooper, 2011). Psychosocial work conditions have a significant impact on health outcomes (Head et al., 2007; Kuper and Marmot, 2003; Marmot, 2006), while physical and psychological well-being have a significant effect on job performance (Cartwright and Cooper, 1997; Colligan and Higgins, 2005; Lyubomirsky, King and Diener, 2005). Income was not regarded as important when professionals judged job satisfaction (Lepnurm et al., 2006).

Bullying and Stress in the "Helping" Professions

In many helping professions, contact with colleagues is one of the major job rewards (Prossor et al., 1996, 1997, 1999; Reid et al., 1999). So, when this contact is *harmful*, the costs are likely to be higher than in other professions that are not so focused on people. The harmful contact ranges between disruptive behaviours, inappropriate conduct such as criticizing or shaming, confrontation or conflict, mobbing, verbal or physical abuse and sexual harassment (Felblinger, 2011). At low levels, harmful contact such as persistent bullying creates a "norm of incivility" which "leads to defensive posturing by workers. Trust is lacking and people use their emotional energy to address individual self-esteem issues and develop self-protective mechanisms" (Felblinger, 2011, p. 6).

School principals in remote locations experience many of the same difficulties. Moreover, like health workers, they can experience high levels of stress responding to externally set performance measures that may not take account of the context in which they work. This can have serious implications for workplace stress, tension and interpersonal professional relationships. Individuals who are overwhelmed by their level of responsibility can experience a crisis in both control and workload. This mismatch is reflected in the degree to which one's levels of responsibility exceed one's authority. "In fact, it is distressing for people when they feel responsible for producing results to which they are deeply committed while lacking the resources to deliver on that mandate" (Lasalvia, 2011, p. 57).

Opie, Lenthall and Dollard (2011) found that rural nurses experienced unrealistic demands from: community and employers; emotional demands; high workload; isolation; cross cultural issues and culture shock; staffing issues such as hard-to-fill vacancies and increased temporary staff who have been poorly oriented; poor management practices including lack of support compounded by distance; difficulties with equipment and infrastructure; and, were more likely to experience workplace violence than their urban counterparts.

A highly protective workgroup can offset some workplace stressors. However, these groups do not represent the norm (Lasalvia et al., 2009). In stressful workplaces, without a protective work group duration of tenure is associated with burnout (Lasalvia, 2011).

Bullying in the Health Services

In the health services, the impact of bullying on staff can be catastrophic – especially when perpetrated by other health staff. Staff-on-staff bullying is probably worse than patient-on-staff bullying because the latter is easily identified, is easily reported by health practitioners, and offensive behaviour can be terminated – through rejection of services to the offending patient, attendance by security services, or by the police. Furthermore, medical staff experiencing patient-on-staff bullying or violence can easily receive workplace counselling set up for this purpose, and receive sympathetic and moral support from other staff.

However, more often than not, research suggests that it is amongst the more senior and higher status staff in health systems who are the perpetrators of bullying, making reporting by victims more complicated, and more stressful, with serious ramifications for the victim's career and health. Trainees and interns are especially prone to experiencing bullying and harassment (for a complete review, see Langan-Fox and Vranic, 2011). Nurses frequently report bullying from other nursing professionals; the problem is at chronic proportions (e.g. Hutchinson et al., 2006; Johnson, 2009; Lewis, 2006).

There appears to be a "conspiracy of silence" (Adams, 1997) when it comes to staff-on-staff bullying. Unfortunately, even though highly-educated professional medical staff are engaged in vital patient care which requires fast, accurate, competent and "errorless" performance, hospitals and medical settings are just as likely as any other workplace to have bullying overlooked, ignored and not reported. There is no doubt that staff-on-staff bullying in these high-intense work situations, interferes with the optimal care of patients (Abe and Henly, 2010). Numerous studies across various countries reveal that harassment, abuse, bullying and victimization are commonly experienced by medical students, doctors, nurses, clinicians and paramedical staff in hospitals and healthcare systems (Ahmer et al., 2009; Askew et al., 2012; Cheema et al., 2005; Daugherty, Baldwin and Rowley, 1998). The abuse is frequently "top-down," and leads to medical staff absenteeism, stress, illness and staff turnover. The impact on patients can be direct or indirect, and lead to adverse events (i.e. complication of care). The consequences for hospitals and medical institutions and clinics have very serious cost implications and effect bottom line budgets.

For a system under stress, and one which is expected to experience higher demands in the future in both developed and developing countries, it is essential that health services staff are provided with workplace bullying management programmes with specific policies developed to cope with the problem (see e.g. Stagg et al., 2011 for a description).

The Changing Context of School Principals' Work

The background levels of stress that health workers and school principals have to cope with is growing rapidly under "scrutiny stress," which involves increased accountability, administrative reporting and persistent rumours (Lasalvia, 2011).

For school principals increasing scrutiny stress has been continuous and relentless over the last 10–15 years. The "first world" educational milieu has been changing rapidly and shows no sign of abatement (Matthews, Moorman and Nusche, 2007, p. 8). While no one disputes any governments' right to know how taxpayers' money is spent on education, the demands for simplistic accountability measures in the form of national literacy and numeracy tests and public comparison of schools on these simplistic measures seems insatiable, despite evidence that high-stakes testing is counterproductive (Campbell, 1976; Nichols, Berliner and Noddings, 2007). This has led to an ever-increasing emphasis on uniform curriculum and instruction reducing teachers' and principals' professional decision-making latitude. Prescription and instruction is in vogue with bureaucrats, and blaming teachers for poor results has reached epidemic proportions (Berliner, 2012; Darling-Hammond, 2010; Darling-Hammond, Newton and Wei, 2010). Sadly, learning, the real aim of education, has all but disappeared from the discourse, replaced with student outcomes, teacher performance, including performance pay for the "best and brightest" and culling of the bottom 5 percent (Berliner, 2012; Garrison, 2011; Podgursky and Springer, 2007), undermining professional collegiality and contributing to worsening workplace stress.

A notable exception to this trend is Finland, which has arguably the lowest scrutiny stress in the Western world. No national tests are conducted, teachers and principals are held in high esteem, and given the autonomy that goes with professional trust. Finish students routinely top the international comparisons such as PISA (Thomson et al., 2011) and TIMMS (Williams et al., 2007). In the UK, where schools have been increasingly held accountable for results via the publication of league tables, Phillips and Sen (2011, pp. 177–8) reported that "work related stress was higher in education than across all other industries ... with work-related mental ill-health ... almost double the rate for all industry."

Adding to workplace stress for principals is the decision by education ministries to devolve many administrative tasks. For example, many non-educational tasks such as payroll, budgeting and teacher employment have been partially devolved to schools. The work practices demanded by these changes have increased principals' work volume and accountability, while decreasing the amount of time they are able to spend on appropriate curriculum choice and implementation for their student population. The outcome is a substantial reduction in professional autonomy.

Extensive longitudinal, epidemiological research has been conducted on similar professional populations experiencing low autonomy and high accountability at work: middle-ranking UK public servants. The results have been reported in the Whitehall I and II studies dating back to the late 1960s (see Ferrie, 2004 for a review of the Whitehall II project). They have repeatedly found adverse health outcomes including decreased life expectancy resulting from high role demand and concurrent low decision latitude. The Whitehall studies indicate that if principals are experiencing the same levels of accountability and autonomy,

> *concurrent low decision latitude and high [role] demands cannot moderate the stress caused by the high demands through time management or learning new skills, and so become subject to high stress at work and are at increased risk of disease. (Kuper and Marmot, 2003, p. 147)*

More disturbing is that under these conditions younger people appear to be at greater risk of coronary heart disease than their older colleagues (Kuper and Marmot, 2003). Given the changes in school principals' work practices over the last 10–15 years, this finding is a real cause for concern. Therefore we examined the current occupational health, safety and well-being of Australian school principals.

Method

The reported data is drawn from the first wave of a larger longitudinal study examining trends in school principals' occupational health, safety and well-being. The detailed (raw) results are available from the project website: www.principalhealth.org/reports.php.

PARTICIPANTS

Every school principal in Australia was eligible to take part in the survey.

INSTRUMENT

The survey comprised 495 items designed to comprehensively capture three types of information drawn from existing robust and widely used instruments. Firstly, school demographic items drawn from the *Trends in International Mathematics and Science Study (TIMSS)* (Williams et al., 2007), *Program for International Student Assessment (PISA)* (Thomson et al., 2011), *My School* (ACARA, 2011) and *International Confederation of Principals* surveys were used to capture differences in occupational health and safety associated with the diversity of school settings and types. Secondly, personal demographic and historical information was collected. Thirdly, principals' quality of life and psychosocial coping was collected using the *Australian Quality of Life Questionnaire (AQoL-8D)* (Richardson et al., 2009) and the second iteration of the *Copenhagen Psychosocial Coping Questionnaire (COPSOQ-II)* (Pejtersen et al., 2010). Alcohol consumption was measured by the World Health Organization's, *Alcohol Use Disorders Identification Test (AUDIT)* (Babor et al., 2001). The combination of items from these instruments allowed opportunities for comprehensive analysis of variation in both OHS (occupational health and safety) and well-being as a function of school type, state and sector differences and the personal attributes of the principals themselves.

PROCEDURE

The survey was conducted between the end of August and end of October 2011. All principal professional organizations were consulted prior to the survey being undertaken and each agreed to invite their members on behalf of the researchers. Each organization independently sent invitations and reminder emails to participate to all member principals throughout the country. There is no way of accurately determining how many of the ~10,000 principals received an invitation, as there are 64 professional organizations, and many principals belong to more than one professional body. We were unable to determine how many principals do not belong to any organization and were therefore not invited to participate. With such a comprehensive survey, completion time and fatigue were concerns. The principals who took part in the research were allocated secure access to the survey website, allowing them to complete it over as many sessions as they needed during the two months the survey was open. Mean completion time for the survey was one hour. All data was analysed using SPSS 20.

Results

Responses from 2,050 principals are reported, representing a response rate of ~20 percent nationally. Males made up 56 percent and females 44 percent. Age ranged between 24 and 75 years (M = 51.35 SD = 7.49). Most were government employees (64.9 per cent) with Catholic schools making up a further 20.7 percent. The remainder were employed in the independent (private, fee paying) sector. Most had been in their current role for five years and leadership roles for 12, following 12 more years in teaching. Approximately 80 percent work upwards of 46 hours a week during term with just over one quarter working upwards of 61 hours per week. During school holidays, more than half work >25 hours per week. Annual salaries range from <\$50,000 to >\$160,00 per annum.

DEMOGRAPHICS AND WORK ENVIRONMENT ON SELF-REPORTED MENTAL HEALTH

As stress is correlated with mental health, multiple regression analysis was used to assess 13 demographic and work environment variables on the reported mental health subscale scores, from the AQoL-8D (Richardson et al., 2009), in a six-step hierarchy. Preliminary analyses were conducted to ensure assumptions of normality, linearity, multicollinearity and homoscedasticity were not violated. Inspection of the Mahalanobis distance revealed 29 outliers above the critical value (34.528, p <.001). Outliers were excluded from the analysis. The model summary appears in Table 8.1.

Table 8.1 Hierarchical multiple regression for demographic and work environment variables on the mental health subscale of the AQoL-8D

Step	R	R^2	Adjusted R^2	S.E.	Change Statistics				
					R^2 Change	F Change	df1	df2	p F Change
1	.091[a]	0.008	0.007	0.514	0.008	4.956	3	1787	0.002
2	.114[b]	0.013	0.010	0.513	0.005	4.388	2	1785	0.013
3	.152[c]	0.023	0.019	0.511	0.010	9.012	2	1783	<.001
4	.438[d]	0.192	0.188	0.465	0.169	186.271	2	1781	<.001
5	.465[e]	0.217	0.211	0.458	0.025	18.652	3	1778	<.001
6	.490[f]	0.241	0.235	0.451	0.024	56.022	1	1777	<.001

Predictors:

[a] = PrimSec–Other; Gender; Age

[b] = a + School sector; School Location

[c] = a + b + Mean hours worked per week during school terms; Mean hours worked per week during official school holiday periods

[d] = a + b + c + COPSOQ Demands at work – Hiding Emotions subscale; COPSOQ Demands at work – Emotional Demands subscale

[e] = a + b + c + d + Bullied by a colleague or superior; Experience of Physical Violence during last 12 months; Experience of Threats of Violence during last 12 months

[f] = a + b + c + d + e + AUDIT Alcohol use score

The total variance in Mental Health subscale scores explained by the model was 23.7 percent, F (1, 1987) = 53.437, p <.001. Each step of the model contributed statistically significant unique contributions to the total, however Step 4, Emotional Demands and Hiding Emotions, contributed 19.2 percent unique variance (Emotional Demands β = -.378, p <.001; Hiding Emotions (β = -.094, p = .001) R^2 change = .173, F change (2, 1991) = 214.419, p <.001. Inspection of mean scores revealed a number of differences in Mental Health that appear more related to work practices and situations than demographic differences. Mean scores and standard deviations for each of the subgroups appear in Table 8.3.

Table 8.2 Six-step multiple hierarchical regression showing mental health subscale scores for the AQoL-8D by participant subgrouping

Step	Independent Variables	Coefficients					Correlations			Collinearity	
		B	S.E.	β	*t*	*p*	Zero-order	Partial	Part	Tol	VIF
1	(Constant)	63.795	2.296		27.786	<.001					
	Gender	0.882	0.570	0.035	1.547	0.122	0.029	0.035	0.035	0.994	1.006
	Age	0.134	0.039	0.076	3.396	**0.001**	0.073	0.076	0.076	0.987	1.013
	School Type (Elem/Sec/Other)	-0.132	0.382	-0.008	-0.345	0.730	-0.001	-0.008	-0.008	0.993	1.007
2	(Constant)	64.207	2.538		25.299	<.001					
	Gender	0.850	0.571	0.033	1.489	0.137	0.029	0.033	0.033	0.986	1.014
	Age	0.127	0.040	0.072	3.196	**0.001**	0.073	0.071	0.071	0.963	1.039
	School Type	-0.101	0.382	-0.006	-0.265	0.791	-0.001	-0.006	-0.006	0.988	1.012
	Sector (Govt, Catholic, Ind)	1.021	0.393	0.059	2.600	**0.009**	0.062	0.058	0.058	0.975	1.026
	Location	-0.589	0.245	-0.055	-2.407	**0.016**	-0.069	-0.054	-0.054	0.960	1.042
3	(Constant)	67.625	2.711		24.944	<.001					
	Gender	0.649	0.573	0.025	1.133	0.257	0.029	0.025	0.025	0.971	1.030
	Age	0.128	0.040	0.073	3.243	**0.001**	0.073	0.072	0.072	0.960	1.041
	School Type	0.138	0.384	0.008	0.360	0.719	-0.001	0.008	0.008	0.967	1.034
	Sector	1.185	0.395	0.068	2.996	**0.003**	0.062	0.067	0.066	0.954	1.049
	Location	-0.583	0.244	-0.054	-2.390	**0.017**	-0.069	-0.053	-0.053	0.960	1.042
	Mean hours worked (school terms)	-0.361	0.159	-0.054	-2.273	**0.023**	-0.071	-0.051	-0.050	0.868	1.153
	Mean hours worked (holidays)	-0.522	0.196	-0.064	-2.656	**0.008**	-0.076	-0.059	-0.059	0.843	1.186
4	(Constant)	93.981	2.930		32.080	<.001					
	Gender	0.430	0.520	0.017	0.826	0.409	0.029	0.019	0.017	0.969	1.032
	Age	0.102	0.036	0.058	2.826	**0.005**	0.073	0.063	0.057	0.959	1.043
	School Type	-0.116	0.349	-0.007	-0.332	0.740	-0.001	-0.007	-0.007	0.965	1.036
	Sector	0.404	0.362	0.023	1.116	0.264	0.062	0.025	0.022	0.940	1.064
	Location	-0.678	0.221	-0.063	-3.064	0.002	-0.069	-0.069	-0.062	0.959	1.043

Step	Independent Variables	Coefficients					Correlations			Collinearity	
		B	S.E.	β	*t*	*p*	Zero-order	Partial	Part	Tol	VIF
	Mean hours worked (school terms)	0.042	0.145	0.006	0.288	0.773	-0.071	0.006	0.006	0.852	1.174
	Mean hours worked (holidays)	-0.091	0.179	-0.011	-0.507	0.612	-0.076	-0.011	-0.010	0.831	1.203
	COPSOQ Emotional Demands	-0.298	0.018	-0.378	-16.510	**<.001**	-0.423	-0.347	-0.332	0.771	1.297
	COPSOQ Hiding Emotions	-0.080	0.019	-0.094	-4.171	**<.001**	-0.268	-0.093	-0.084	0.793	1.261
5	(Constant)	93.288	2.891		32.264	<.001					
	Gender	0.075	0.515	0.003	0.146	0.884	0.029	0.003	0.003	0.961	1.041
	Age	0.096	0.035	0.055	2.705	**0.007**	0.073	0.061	0.054	0.957	1.045
	School Type	0.062	0.345	0.004	0.180	0.857	-0.001	0.004	0.004	0.956	1.047
	Sector	0.135	0.369	0.008	0.365	0.715	0.062	0.008	0.007	0.876	1.142
	Location	-0.612	0.218	-0.057	-2.802	**0.005**	-0.069	-0.063	-0.055	0.957	1.045
	Mean hours worked (school terms)	0.111	0.143	0.017	0.772	0.440	-0.071	0.017	0.015	0.848	1.179
	Mean hours worked (holidays)	-0.096	0.177	-0.012	-0.545	0.586	-0.076	-0.012	-0.011	0.831	1.203
	COPSOQ Emotional Demands	-0.271	0.018	-0.344	-14.896	**<.001**	-0.423	-0.317	-0.295	0.735	1.361
	COPSOQ Hiding Emotions	-0.071	0.019	-0.083	-3.724	**<.001**	-0.268	-0.083	-0.074	0.790	1.266
	Threats of Violence	-1.012	0.666	-0.039	-1.520	0.129	-0.147	-0.034	-0.030	0.601	1.663
	Physical Violence	0.602	0.710	0.021	0.847	0.397	-0.094	0.019	0.017	0.627	1.595
	Bullying	-4.308	0.559	-0.161	-7.700	**<.001**	-0.260	-0.170	-0.152	0.898	1.113
6	(Constant)	93.922	2.855		32.893	<.001					
	Gender	1.101	0.527	0.043	2.089	**0.037**	0.029	0.047	0.041	0.893	1.120
	Age	0.091	0.035	0.052	2.606	**0.009**	0.073	0.058	0.051	0.956	1.046
	School Type	0.166	0.341	0.010	0.486	0.627	-0.001	0.011	0.009	0.954	1.048
	Sector	-0.087	0.365	-0.005	-0.238	0.812	0.062	-0.005	-0.005	0.870	1.149
	Location	-0.656	0.216	-0.061	-3.042	**0.002**	-0.069	-0.068	-0.059	0.956	1.046
	Mean hours worked (school terms)	0.078	0.142	0.012	0.554	0.580	-0.071	0.012	0.011	0.847	1.181
	Mean hours worked (holidays)	-0.121	0.174	-0.015	-0.692	0.489	-0.076	-0.016	-0.014	0.831	1.203

Step	Independent Variables	Coefficients					Correlations			Collinearity	
		B	S.E.	β	*t*	*p*	Zero-order	Partial	Part	Tol	VIF
	COPSOQ Emotional Demands	-0.263	0.018	-0.334	-14.607	**<.001**	-0.423	-0.311	-0.285	0.732	1.366
	COPSOQ Hiding Emotions	-0.066	0.019	-0.078	-3.538	**<.001**	-0.268	-0.079	-0.069	0.789	1.267
	Threats of Violence	-0.952	0.657	-0.036	-1.449	0.148	-0.147	-0.032	-0.028	0.601	1.663
	Physical Violence	0.578	0.701	0.020	0.824	0.410	-0.094	0.018	0.016	0.627	1.596
	Bullying	-4.270	0.552	-0.159	-7.732	**<.001**	-0.260	-0.171	-0.151	0.898	1.113
	AUDIT alcohol score	-0.481	0.066	-0.150	-7.310	**<.001**	-0.172	-0.162	-0.143	0.912	1.097

Step 1: Age (6 levels) was significant F (3, 1994) = 4.392, p = .004. The trend was for younger principals to report lower levels of mental health than their more senior colleagues. Gender and School Type (Primary, Secondary, P-10, Early Childhood, Other) were not significant.

Step 2: School Location (Urban, Suburban, Regional, Rural, Remote) was significant after controlling for Gender, Age, School Type and School Sector (Government, Catholic, Independent). As distance from capital cities increased, reported mental health scores decreased, F (5, 1995) = 5.528, p <.001.

Step 3: The number of hours spent at work (10 levels: range <25 h/w – >70 h/w) significantly negatively impacted mental health scores after controlling all previous factors, F (7, 1993) = 6.627, p <.001. The greatest impact was the amount of work conducted during official holiday periods.

Step 4: After controlling all demographic variables, the COPSOQ II (Pejtersen et al., 2010) subscales Emotional Demands (15 levels: F (15, 1989) = 29.905, p <.001) and Hiding Emotions at work, F (9, 1991) = 53.907, p <.001, both significantly negatively impacted reported mental health scores.

Step 5: Threats of Violence, Physical Violence and Bullying by a colleague or superior in the workplace (2 levels: Experienced or Not Experienced in the previous 12 months) contributed to a statistically significant decline in reported mental health scores for principals F (12, 1998) = 47.099, p <.001. Inspection of the components revealed that only bullying contributed statistically significant unique variance (β = -.161, p <.001) R^2 change = .025, F change (3, 1998) = 21.645, p <.001.

Step 6: AUDIT (Babor et al., 2001). Alcohol use was examined after controlling for all other IVs (Range 0 (Teetotal) – 31). Scores of 8 or more indicate possible harmful/hazardous use and/or dependence). Increased alcohol intake was associated with decreased mental health, F (13, 1987) = 48.733, p <.001. At this step Gender became significant (t = 2.089, p = .037). Gender differences in AUDIT scores appear in Table 8.4 and Figure 8.1. Two thirds of the principals who reported drinking at potentially harmful levels are male.

Table 8.3 Mean mental health scores derived from the AQoL-8D disaggregated by demographic and workplace IVs

Subgroup (IV)s		Mental Health Subscale Score			
		M	SD	N	%
Gender	Female	3.95	0.49	1114	55.60
	Male	3.98	0.56	891	44.40
Age Group	25–34	3.89	0.65	54	2.70
	35–44	3.87	0.53	285	14.20
	45–54	3.94	0.51	890	44.40
	55–64	4.01	0.52	740	36.90
	>65	4.11	0.58	35	1.70
School Type	Elementary	3.96	0.52	1265	63.60
	Secondary	3.94	0.54	436	21.90
	P-10	3.85	0.58	43	2.20
	E C'hood	4.02	0.39	12	0.60
	Other	3.99	0.50	234	11.80
School Sector	Government	3.94	0.54	1439	71.80
	Catholic	3.98	0.51	281	14.00
	Independent	4.03	0.47	285	14.20
School Location	Urban	3.99	0.51	367	18.30
	Suburban	3.99	0.51	791	39.50
	Large Town	3.97	0.54	244	12.20
	Rural	3.91	0.54	516	25.70
	Remote	3.89	0.60	87	4.30
Hours Worked: Term	<25	4.14	0.66	22	1.10
	25–30	3.85	0.61	25	1.20
	31–35	3.92	0.62	21	1.00
	36–40	4.09	0.49	36	1.80
	41–45	3.98	0.51	91	4.50
	46–50	3.99	0.49	322	16.10
	51–55	4.02	0.49	411	20.50
	56–60	3.95	0.51	530	26.40
	61–65	3.89	0.58	259	12.90
	66–70	3.90	0.55	157	7.80
	>70	3.88	0.58	130	6.50
Threats of Violence	No	4.02	0.51	1248	62.20
	Yes	3.87	0.54	757	37.80

Subgroup (IV)s		Mental Health Subscale Score			
		M	SD	N	%
Physical Violence	No	3.99	0.52	1464	73.00
	Yes	3.88	0.53	541	27.00
Bullying	No	4.06	0.48	1320	65.80
	Yes	3.77	0.56	685	34.20
Hours Worked: Holidays	<25	4.02	0.51	904	45.10
	25–30	3.94	0.53	629	31.40
	31–35	3.91	0.51	153	7.60
	36–40	3.81	0.58	156	7.80
	41–45	4.02	0.43	58	2.90
	46–50	3.87	0.51	37	1.80
	51–55	3.88	0.50	17	0.80
	56–60	3.80	0.46	19	0.90
	61–65	4.10	0.68	5	0.20
	66–70	4.04	0.56	9	0.40
	>70	3.75	0.63	17	0.80

Table 8.4 Mean alcohol use (AUDIT) scores reported by gender and potential harmful/hazardous use

		Mean	SD	N	%	*F*	*df*	*p*
Teetotal	Female			94	60.30			
	Male			62	39.70			
AUDIT Score	Female	3.79	3.321	1114	55.60	143.950	1, 2003	<.001
	Male	5.93	4.636	891	44.40			
AUDIT Score >7	Female	11.05	3.493	127	33.80	4.115	1, 374	0.043
	Male	11.90	4.050	249	66.20			

CLUSTER ANALYSIS

Three clusters of principals were statistically and theoretically supported based on the participants' scores for: Confidence in "Managing myself and my time" and "Dealing with stress and pressure"; AQoL-8D subscales (Happiness, Mental Health, Coping, Relationships and Self Worth); and, COPSOQ subscales (Interpersonal Relations and Leadership; Social Support from Colleagues; Job Insecurity; Job Satisfaction; Work–Family Conflict; General Health, Burnout, Stress, Sleeping Problems, Depressive Symptoms, Somatic Stress Symptoms, Cognitive Stress Symptoms, and Self-Efficacy). There were significant main effects of cluster on each variable included in the clustering algorithm. Cluster 1 contained 487 participants who gave the highest ratings for all positive factors and the lowest scores for all the negative factors, and so were named *Supported Copers*. They appeared to be reasonably well suited to their working conditions, manage their time well and enjoyed strong, supportive relationships at home and from colleagues in the workplace. Cluster 2 contained 651 participants whose responses were opposite to Cluster 1. This group was named the *Unsupported Outsiders*, due to their high scores on Work–Family Conflict, Stress, Burnout, Somatic and Depressive Symptoms, Emotional Demands and Hiding Emotions, and low scores on Mental Health, Support from Colleagues, Job Rewards, and Commitment to the Workplace. They did not appear well suited to, or well supported in their work or home environments. Cluster 3 contained 896 participants, who were positioned roughly equidistant from the two other groups, but with interesting variations on the stress subscales (see Figures 8.2–8.5). This group reported the same perceived ability to deal with stress as the Supported Copers, and significantly higher Social Support from Colleagues ($M = 57.25$) than the Unsupported Outsiders ($M = 43.80$), but not as high as the Supported Copers ($M = 64.41$). They were named the *Emotional Rollercoasters* as they showed similar aspects of functioning to each of the other two groups. They also reported high levels of Emotional Demands and having to Hide Emotions at work, less Support from Colleagues, and high levels of Family–Work Conflict.

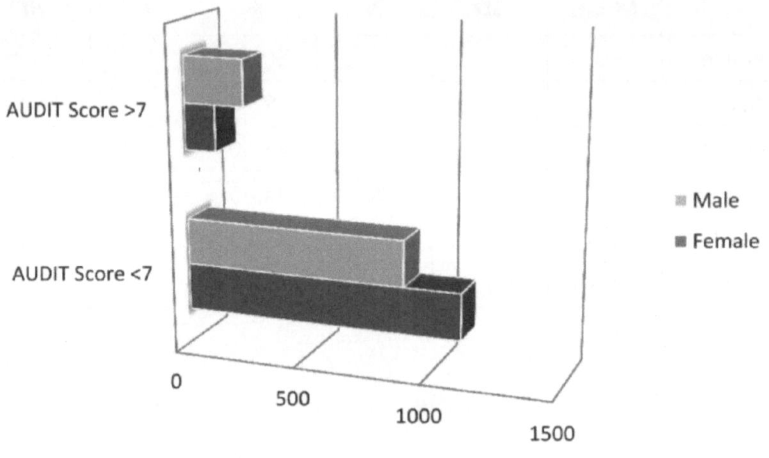

Figure 8.1 Self-reported AUDIT scores above and below the cut-off for potential harm/dangerous use

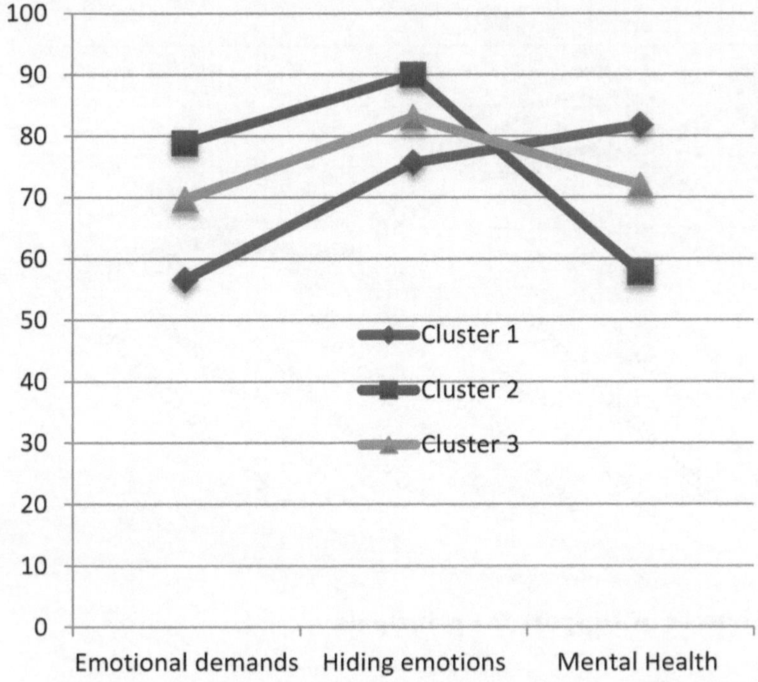

Figure 8.2 Principals' mean scores on emotional demands, emotional labour and mental health by cluster grouping

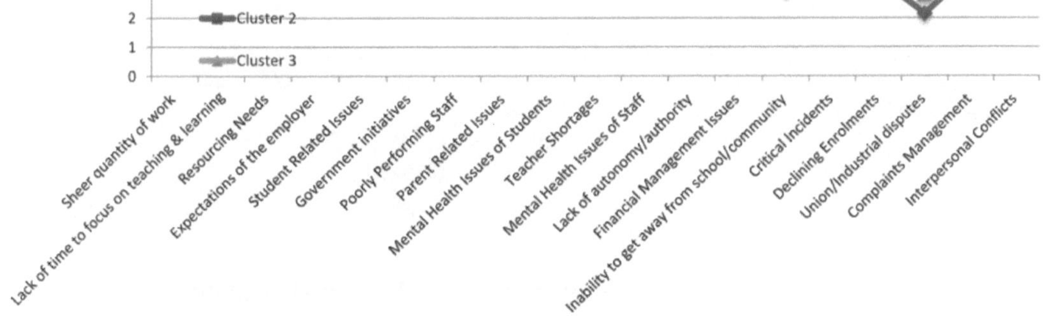

Figure 8.3 Self-reported workplace stressors rated on a 10-point scale disaggregated by cluster group

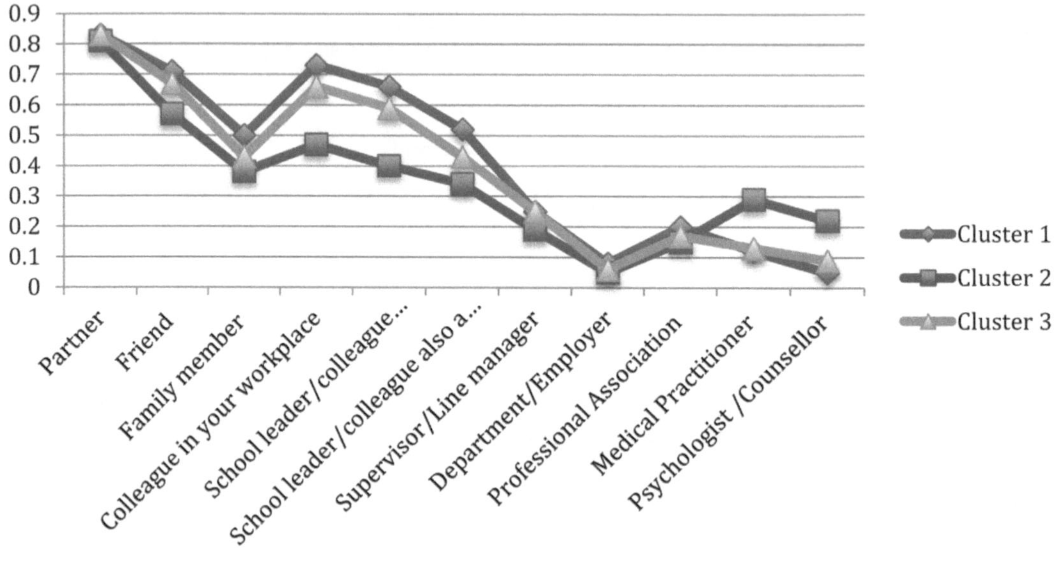

Figure 8.4 Sources of support for principals

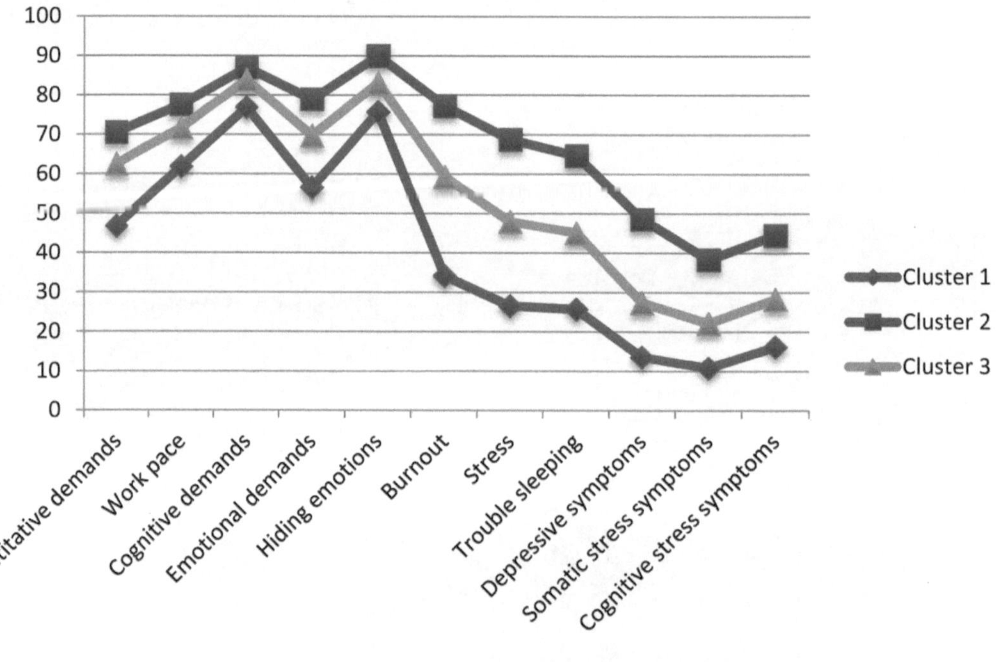

Figure 8.5 COPSOQ subscale scores disaggregated by cluster group

Implications

The results reported in this chapter show that the occupational health, safety and well-being of Australia's principals is quite varied. Three distinct clusters of principals were deduced from the data: *Supported Copers*, who show many signs of thriving in the role; *Unsupported Outsiders*, who struggle with the emotional demands of the job and see the need to keep their emotions hidden; and *Emotional Rollercoasters*, who show some of the positive and negative characteristics of the other two cluster groups. The three groups appear to operate distinctly differently from each other in terms of how they manage workplace stress and the level of support they perceive from others, both inside and outside of the workplace. While gender and school type do not appear to impact well-being levels significantly, the sector in which the principal works and the geographical location of the school does. As with other helping professionals those in remote locations experience bigger threats to their well-being, particularly mental health, partly as a result of the isolation, but also because of the nature of the communities in which they work: like remote area nurses they are often seen as outsiders (Opie, Lenthall and Dollard, 2011).

Being perceived as a leader in the community but not of the community can preclude principals in rural and remote locations from accessing local support networks. High autonomy was less likely in remote locations, and more likely in the independent sector. Principals with the highest levels of autonomy report higher levels of well-being and lower levels of occupational stress. Autonomy and accountability are inexorably linked. This places independent school principals at an advantage over their government and Catholic school colleagues. Independent school principals are generally accountable only to a school board that is small enough to allow regular personal contact and more likely to be philosophically aligned with the principal or they would not have appointed him or her in the first place. Principals from the large government and Catholic systems have a significantly larger hierarchy above them, who exercise significant direct and indirect control over schools. This is probably reflected in the higher levels of bullying experienced by government and Catholic school principals. Principals from these sectors may not know their superiors well and are more likely to meet with them irregularly and in groups. They are also likely to differ in their ontological commitments and epistemologies from at least some of those in the hierarchy that control their work practices. In the worst cases reported here this is perceived as bullying by a significant proportion of principals.

An interesting finding from the cluster analysis is that the largest group, Cluster 3 ($N = 896$), seems to be wavering between coping well and just surviving in the job. This is a positive finding because it suggests that if some work practice changes can be introduced to help this group the school sector generally may receive a significant boost through the sheer weight of the numbers of this group. The factors that appear to distinguish this cluster group relate to the emotional labour of the role, with high scores on Emotional Demands and Hiding Emotions at Work strongly influencing the regression coefficients determining principals' mental health outcomes after controlling for eight demographic and work practice variables. Relationships with colleagues and family also appear to be very powerful predictors of success in the role. When work practices produce work–family conflicts the mental health costs paid by principals is large. Building stronger relationships at work is not reliant on a large injection of funds, and always leads to school improvement (Fullan, 2008). Stronger relationships are likely to provide the conditions for the protective workgroup found by Lasalvia and colleagues (2009) to reduce stress. Strong professional relationships were correlated with increased mental health of the principal. An interesting follow-up study would be to measure the teachers' self-reported mental health in the same schools as the principals. Logic suggests when the principals' mental health improves so does the teachers'. Data from this project indicates that relationship strength may be the catalyst.

School principals' stress levels have long been known to be high. So the stress levels reported in this study are consistent with the literature. Given that this study replicates previous findings, these results give pause for thought. The findings are challenging to those charged with responsibility for looking after the occupational health, safety and well-being of principals. More research is needed to determine if the sample in this study is representative of the whole country. The worst-case scenario is that the respondents to this survey are the most functional group: able to give an hour of their time to complete the survey. Those who could not see their way to doing this could be the majority. Alternatively, this sample may comprise those who are most in need, and may be using the survey to highlight this. If so, responsible authorities would do well to take heed and design better support systems based on human-to-human communication rather than economic incentives. Performance-based pay, for example, appears unlikely to change the amount of hours principals devote to the job. They already work very long hours both during term time and in the holidays, with holiday hours contributing to lower levels of mental health. Help with time management and administrative tasks that would allow principals to concentrate more effort on teaching and learning may significantly reduce the amount of stress they report and increase the amount of time spent on facilitating teaching and learning. Schools need to be managed, but the question of how much of the principals' time should be devoted to tasks for which no specific pedagogical skill is needed remains open.

Workplace interventions that will be useful to principals need to be developed with a full understanding of occupational health and safety theory, and based on evidence from other industries, particularly other helping professions. This study forms part of a comprehensive risk assessment for principals, by capturing baseline data for principals from a wide range of circumstances. Further analysis is beginning to identify risk and protective factors for those motivated to join the profession of education and become leaders within it. The motivation itself may be a sensible place to begin to identify groups of potential principals likely to find the going difficult and target pre-leadership programmes to address the issues causing them the most difficulty. Any interventions developed need to be tailored to suit the diversity of principals' workplaces, such as sector, size and location, but also remain flexible and adaptable for implementation in specific situations with individual principals and/or aspirants. Interventions which facilitate self-understanding, competency building in managing complex, highly-charged emotional situations and related skill development are important as, at the organizational level, they build leadership and management capability across the system, while developing people to become fully self-actualized.

Conclusion

School leaders and medical professionals work in highly demanding professions. Efforts to understand the health and workforce needs of these professionals are urgently needed. So too are specific training and counselling programmes to enable such professionals to adequately cope with their job, to provide leadership, and to help others endure and prosper in contexts that are often experienced as a "battle zone." At stake, is not only the health of those who work in these professions, but also, those in the community, and the future educational and occupational prospects of our younger generations. They need to be able to recognize a positive career which is wholeheartedly supported by those in authority and leadership.

References

Abe, K. and S.J. Henly (2010) Bullying (ijime) among Japanese hospital nurses: Modeling responses to the revised Negative Acts Questionnaire. *Nursing Research*, 59(2), 110–18.

Adams, A. (1997) Bullying at work. *Journal of Community and Applied Social Psychology*, 7(3), 177–80.

Ahmer, S., Yousafzai, A.W., Siddiqi, M., Faruqui, R., Khan, R. and Zuberi, S. (2009) Bullying of trainee psychiatrists in Pakistan: A cross-sectional questionnaire survey. *Academic Psychiatry*, 33(4), 335–9.

Askew, D.A., Schluter, P.J., Dick, M.L., Régo, P.M., Turner, C. and Wilkinson, D. (2012) Bullying in the Australian medical workforce: Cross-sectional data from an Australian e-Cohort study. *Australian Health Review*, 36(2), 197–204.

Australian Curriculum and Assessment Reporting Authority (ACARA) (2011) *My School*. Available at: http://www.myschool.edu.au/ [accessed: May 12, 2011].

Babor, T.F., Higgins-Biddle, J.C., Saunders, J.B. and Monteiro, M.G. (2001) *AUDIT: The Alcohol Use Disorders Identification Test. Guidelines for Use in Primary Care*, 2nd edn. Geneva: World Health Organization.

Berliner, D. (2012) Confusing assessment with testing and quantification: The overzealous promotion of value-added assessment of teachers. Paper presented at the Joint Australian Association for Research in Education and Asia-Pacific Education Research Association Conference World Education Research Association Focal Meeting: Regional and Global Cooperation in Educational Research, University of Sydney, December 2–6.

Campbell, D.T. (1976) *Assessing the Impact of Planned Social Change*. Hanover, NH: The Public Affairs Center, Dartmouth College.

Cartwright, S. and Cooper, C.L. (1997) *Managing Workplace Stress*. Thousand Oaks, CA: Sage.

Cheema, S., Ahmad, K., Giri, S.K., Kaliaperumal, V.K. and Naqvi, S.A. (2005) Bullying of junior doctors prevails in Irish health system: A bitter reality. *Irish Medical Journal*, 98(9), 274–5.

Colligan, T.W. and Higgins, E.M. (2005) Workplace stress: Etiology and consequences. *Journal of Workplace Behavioral Health*, 21(2), 89–97.

Darling-Hammond, L. (2010) Teacher education and the American future. *Journal of Teacher Education*, 61(1–2), 35–47.

Darling-Hammond, L., Newton, X. and Wei, R.C. (2010) Evaluating teacher education outcomes: A study of the Stanford Teacher Education Programme. *Journal of Education for Teaching: International Research and Pedagogy*, 36(4), 369–88.

Daugherty, S.R., Baldwin, J.D.C. Jr. and Rowley, B.D. (1998) Learning, satisfaction, and mistreatment during medical internship: a national survey of working conditions. *JAMA: The Journal of the American Medical Association*, 279(15), 1194–9.

Felblinger, D.M. (2011) Incivility and bullying in the nursing workplace. In J. Langan-Fox and C.L. Cooper (eds), *Handbook of Stress in the Occupations*. Cheltenham: Edward Elgar, pp. 5–15.

Ferrie, J.E. (ed.) (2004) *Work, Stress and Health: The Whitehall II Study*. London: Public and Commercial Services Union on behalf of Council of Civil Service Unions/Cabinet Office.

Fullan, M. (2008) *The Six Secrets of Change: What the Best Leaders Do to Help Their Organizations Survive and Thrive*. San Francisco, CA: Jossey-Bass.

Garrison, M. (2011) The political economy of educational restructuring: On the origin of performance pay and Obama's "blueprint" for education. In P.R. Carr and B.J. Porfilio (eds) *The Phenomenon of Obama and the Agenda for Education: Can Hope Audaciously Trump Neoliberalism*. Charlotte, NC: IAP Information Age Publishing, pp. 211–24.

Head, J., Kivimaki, M., Siegrist, J., Ferrie, J.E., Vahtera, J., Shipley, M.J. and Marmot, M.G. (2007) Effort-reward imbalance and relational injustice at work predict sickness absence: The Whitehall II study. *Journal of Psychosomatic Research*, 63(4), 433–40.

Hutchinson, M., Vickers, M., Jackson, D. and Wilkes, L. (2006) Workplace bullying in nursing: Towards a more critical organisational perspective. *Nursing Inquiry*, 13(2), 118–26.

Johnson, S. (2009) International perspectives on workplace bullying among nurses: A review. *International Nursing Review*, 56(1), 34–40.

Kuper, H. and Marmot, M. (2003) Job strain, job demands, decision latitude, and risk of coronary heart disease within the Whitehall II study. *Journal of Epidemiology and Community Health*, 57(2), 147–53.

Langan-Fox, J. and Cooper, C.L. (eds) (2011) *Handbook of Stress in the Occupations*. Cheltenham: Edward Elgar.

Langan-Fox J. and Vranic, V. (2011) Intern coping and stress: The price of developing medical expertise. In J. Langan-Fox and C.L. Cooper (eds) *Handbook of Stress in the Occupations*. Cheltenham: Edward Elgar, pp. 91–108.

Lasalvia, A. (2011) Occupational stress, professional burnout and job satisfaction among psychiatrists. In J. Langan-Fox and C.L. Cooper (eds), *Handbook of Stress in the Occupations*. Cheltenham: Edward Elgar, pp. 49–68.

Lasalvia, A., Bonetto, C., Bertani, M., Bissoli, S., Cristofalo, D., Marrella, G., Ceccato, E., Cremonese, C., De Rossi, M., Lazzarotto, L., Marangon, V., Morandin, I., Zucchetto, M., Tansella, M. and Ruggeri, M. (2009) Influence of perceived organisational factors on job burnout: Survey of community mental health staff. *British Journal of Psychiatry*, 195(6), 537–44.

Lepnurm, R., Dobson, R., Backman, A. and Keegan, D. (2006) Factors explaining career satisfaction among psychiatrists and surgeons in Canada. *Canadian Journal of Psychiatry*, 51(4), 243–55.

Lewis, M.A. (2006) Nurse bullying: Organizational considerations in the maintenance and perpetration of health care bullying cultures. *Journal of Nursing Management*, 14(1), 52–8.

Lyubomirsky, S., King, L. and Diener, E. (2005) The benefits of frequent positive affect: Does happiness lead to success? *Psychological Bulletin*, 131(6), 803–55.

Marmot, M.G. (2006) Status syndrome: A challenge to medicine. [Editorial]. *JAMA: Journal of the American Medical Association*, 295(11), 1304–7.

Matthews, P., Moorman, H. and Nusche, D. (2007) *School Leadership Development Strategies: Building Leadership Capacity in Victoria, Australia: A Case Study Report for the OECD Activity Improving School Leadership*. Paris: OECD.

Nichols, S.L., Berliner, D.C. and Noddings, N. (2007) *Collateral Damage: How High-Stakes Testing Corrupts America's Schools*. Cambridge, MA: Harvard Education Press.

Opie, T., Lenthall, S. and Dollard, M.F. (2011) Occupational stress in the remote area nursing profession. In J. Langan-Fox and C.L. Cooper (eds), *Handbook of Stress in the Occupations*. Cheltenham: Edward Elgar, pp. 16–32.

Pejtersen, J.H., Kristensen, T.S., Borg, V. and Bjorner, J.B. (2010) The second version of the Copenhagen Psychosocial Questionnaire. *Scandinavian Journal of Public Health*, 38(Suppl 3), 8–24.

Phillips, S. and Sen, D. (2011) Stress in head teachers. In J. Langan-Fox and C.L. Cooper (eds), *Handbook of Stress in the Occupations*. Cheltenham: Edward Elgar, pp. 177–201.

Podgursky, M. and Springer, M.G. (2007) Credentials versus performance: Review of the teacher performance pay research. *Peabody Journal of Education*, 82(4), 551–73.

Prosser, D., Johnson, S., Kuipers, E., Szmukler, G., Bebbington, P. and Thornicroft, G. (1996) Mental health, "burnout" and job satisfaction among hospital and community-based mental health staff. *The British Journal of Psychiatry*, 169(3), 334–7.

—— (1997) Perceived sources of work stress and satisfaction among hospital and community mental health staff, and their relation to mental health, burnout and job satisfaction. *Journal of Psychosomatic Research*, 43(1), 51–9.

Prosser, D., Johnson, S., Kuipers, E., Dunn, G., Szmukler, G., Reid, Y., Bebbington, P. and Thornicroft, G. (1999) Mental health, "burnout" and job satisfaction in a longitudinal study of mental health staff. *Social Psychiatry and Psychiatric Epidemiology*, 34(6), 295–300.

Reid, Y., Johnson, S., Morant, N., Kuipers, E., Szmukler, G., Thornicroft, G., Bebbington, P. and Prosser, D. (1999) Explanations for stress and satisfaction in mental health professionals: A qualitative study. *Social Psychiatry and Psychiatric Epidemiology*, 34(6), 301–8.

Richardson, J., Khan, M., Iezzi, A., Sinha, K., Mihalopoulos, C., Herrman, H., Hawthorne, G. and Schweitzer, I. (2009) *The AQoL-8D (PsyQoL) MAU Instrument: Overview September 2009*. Melbourne: Centre for Health Economics, Monash University.

Stagg, S.J., Sheridan, D., Jones, R.A. and Speroni, K.G. (2011) Evaluation of a workplace bullying cognitive rehearsal program in a hospital setting. *The Journal of Continuing Education in Nursing*, 42(9), 395–403.

Thomson, S., Bortoli, L.D., Nicholas, M., Hillman, K. and Buckley, S. (2011) *Challenges for Australian Education: Results from PISA 2009*. Camberwell: Australian Council for Educational Research.

Williams, T., Ferraro, D., Roey, S., Brenwald, S., Kastberg, D., Jocelyn, L., Smith, C. and Stearns, P. (2007) *TIMSS 2007 US Technical Report and User Guide*. Washington DC: National Center for Education Statistics, Institute of Education Sciences, US Department of Education.

CHAPTER 9

Counterproductive Work Behavior: Where We Have Been and Where We Are Going

LISA M. PENNEY AND STACEY R. KESSLER

Introduction

Counterproductive work behavior or CWB refers to employee actions that have the potential to harm an organization and/or the people connected to it (e.g., employees, customers, shareholders; Berry, Carpenter and Barratt, 2011; Sackett and DeVore, 2002; Spector and Fox, 2005). Organizations and managers view CWB as contrary to their legitimate business interests largely because CWB is a prevalent and costly problem. For example, employee theft alone has been estimated to cost US businesses between \$40 and \$600 billion every year (Govoni, 1992; Greenberg, 1997). Despite the negative financial impact of these behaviors, employees may not always engage in CWB to harm the organization's interests (although some certainly do). In fact, recent research suggests that employees may engage in CWB for a number of reasons, only some of which include deliberately harming an organization.

In this chapter, we review the theoretical and empirical literature on CWB to date with the primary goal of understanding what motivates employees to engage in CWB. We begin by providing an overview of CWB and what we refer to as "classic" (i.e., affect-based) models of CWB; that is, we focus on theories that frame CWB as a response to negative work conditions and the negative emotions that accompany them. Then, we present alternative perspectives that investigate CWB as behavior that is instrumentally driven (i.e., performed in pursuit of a goal) and discuss future research needs in this area. We close with a discussion of how these varied perspectives can be leveraged to develop solutions for individuals and organizations.

CWB

CWB is employee behavior that has the potential to harm an organization and/or the people associated with an organization (i.e., employees, customers) and is but one label given to this class of behavior. For example, researchers have studied similar behaviors under various construct labels depending on their theoretical lens. These labels include workplace aggression (Baron and Neuman, 1996), employee deviance, (Robinson and Bennett, 1995), retaliation (Skarlicki and Folger, 1997), revenge (Bies and Tripp, 1998), organization-motivated aggression (O'Leary-Kelly, Griffin and Glew, 1996), organizational delinquency (Hogan and Hogan, 1989), and antisocial behavior (Giacalone and Greenberg, 1997). Despite the diversity of terms used to describe this class of behavior, measures of these constructs generally assess an overlapping set of behavior that includes arguing with, ignoring, bullying, or threatening others at work; deliberately withholding information and/or effort; wasting, stealing, or destroying company or employee property; wasting time; and withdrawal (e.g., taking longer breaks or leaving earlier than allowed, calling in "sick").

Neuman and Baron (2005) argued that the term workplace aggression should be used in lieu of CWB because it provides a more direct path to using aggression theory as an organizing framework. Indeed, some of the earliest research on CWB drew heavily from the aggression literature. Whereas we acknowledge the value in using an established framework to capitalize on the commonalities shared within this class of behavior, Neuman and Baron's definition of workplace aggression as "any form of behavior directed by one or more others in a workplace toward the goal of harming one or more others in that workplace (or the entire organization) in ways the intended targets are motivated to avoid" (2005, p. 18) limits our examination of CWB to behavior that is motivated by harmful intent. As we discuss later in the chapter, researchers acknowledge that some CWB may be performed for reasons that do not necessarily involve malicious or harmful intent. For example, actors may not be aware of the potential for harm when performing CWB (Tunstall et al., 2006), and some CWB may be performed for prosocial motives (e.g., deontic response, Folger, 2001). Thus, following other scholars in this area (e.g., Gruys and Sackett, 2003; Sackett, 2002) we use the term CWB to refer to this broad class of behavior.

FORMS OF CWB

CWB is described as a multi-dimensional construct, and several strategies for parsing the dimensional structure of CWB have been offered (Bennett and Robinson, 2000; Sackett and DeVore, 2002; Spector et al., 2006). Robinson and Bennett (1995) created an influential categorization that classifies CWB along two continua: Serious/Minor and Interpersonal/Organizational. The Serious/Minor dimension refers to the severity of CWB, whereas Interpersonal/Organizational refers to the target of CWB – the organization itself or other individuals working in the organization. This categorization scheme allows CWB to be classified within four quadrants: minor acts directed towards the organization (e.g., leaving early, wasting resources), serious acts directed towards the organization (e.g., sabotage, theft), minor acts directed towards individuals (e.g., gossiping, blaming others) and serious acts directed towards individuals (e.g., verbal abuse, endangering others). However, most researchers focus solely on the Interpersonal/Organizational distinction (e.g., Berry, Ones and Sackett, 2007).

Others suggest a finer categorization of CWB. For example, Spector et al. (2006) distinguished five CWB dimensions: abuse (harmful behaviors directed towards others that injure the person either physically or psychologically), production deviance (intentional failure to complete aspects of the job properly), sabotage (destruction of organizational property), theft, and withdrawal. Sackett and colleagues (e.g., Gruys and Sackett, 2003; Sackett, 2002) identified eleven different dimensions of CWB: (1) theft and related behavior, (2) destruction of property, (3) misuse of information, (4) misuse of time and resources, (5) unsafe behavior, (6) poor attendance, (7) poor work quality, (8) alcohol use, (9) drug use, (10) inappropriate verbal actions, and (11) inappropriate physical actions. As we discuss later, distinguishing among various types of CWB is important because research suggests that different CWBs have different antecedents which may underlie the motivation behind various forms of CWB. However, we begin our exploration of the underlying motivations by reviewing classical models of CWB.

Classical Theoretical Models of CWB

Over the years, a number of organizational researchers have sought to better understand and control these behaviors and mitigate their negative impact on others and organizations. Some of the earliest research in this area was done by Spector (1975, 1978). In one of the first studies to examine aggression outside of a laboratory setting, Spector (1975) surveyed a field sample of employees from a mental health facility. He found that frustrated employees were more likely to engage in a variety of aggressive acts in the workplace including aggression against others (e.g., pranks, being nasty to others), wasting time and materials (e.g., daydreaming), interpersonal hostility (e.g., arguing), complaining, sabotage (e.g., damaging or defacing organizational property), and apathy (e.g., deliberately performing work incorrectly, drug use on the job). Building on the frustration-aggression hypothesis (Dollard et al., 1939), Spector (1978) outlined a model of organizational frustration in which he described how conditions at work can interfere with individual goal attainment resulting in frustration. In turn, Spector argued that the physiological arousal associated with feelings of frustration and anger would manifest in aggressive action directed toward the organization or other people and inhibit effective task performance.

Over the years, the theoretical framework developed by Spector and Fox (Fox and Spector, 1999; Fox and Spector, 2006; Spector, 1998; Spector and Fox, 2002; Spector and Fox, 2005) has evolved to include a broader range of conditions and negative emotions that may drive CWB. In particular, the stressor-emotion model of CWB (Spector and Fox, 2005) positions CWB as a response to stressful conditions (i.e., stressors) in the work environment. The core of the stressor-emotion model (see Figure 9.1) emphasizes the cognitive and emotional processes that mediate the stressor-CWB relationship. Similar to transactional stress models (Lazarus and Folkman, 1984), the stressor-emotion model of CWB emphasizes individuals' perception or interpretation of events, as opposed to the event itself, as being the primary driver of negative emotions and subsequent CWB. For example, an objective stressor would be an organization announcing impending layoffs. An employee who perceives the pending layoffs as an opportunity to trade a dissatisfying job for one that is more fulfilling is unlikely to experience frustration or other negative emotions or to respond with CWB. However, an employee who perceives the layoffs as the result of mismanagement at the highest levels of the organization is likely to become frustrated or angry. Those angry feelings may be expressed or released through complaining and yelling at others, damaging company property, taking long breaks, and/or leaving work early.

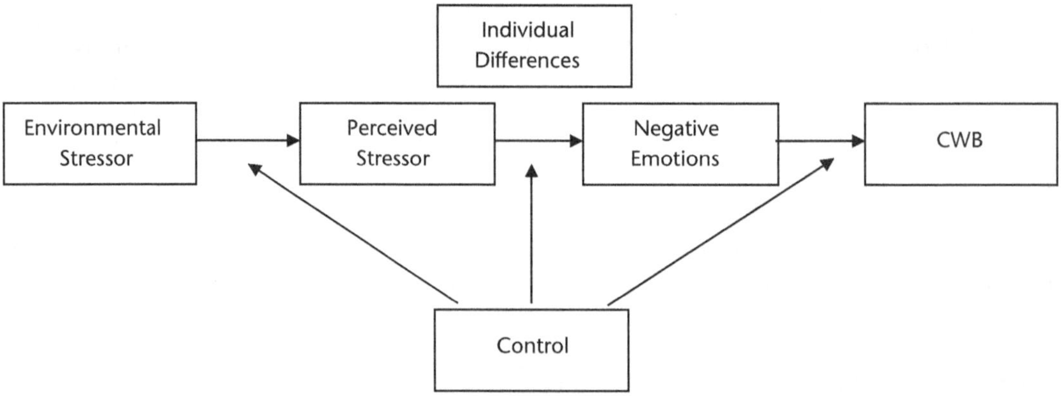

Figure 9.1 Stressor-emotion model (CITE)

Control is positioned as an important moderator that can affect different potions of the stressor-emotion model. High levels of control (e.g., employee perceptions of the controllability of a stressor, perceived or actual control over the work environment) generally reduce the experience of negative emotions and the tendency to take counterproductive action. Personality may influence nearly every step in the model as individual differences may affect: a) the extent to which people perceive stressors or experience negative emotions; b) how people respond to those stressors or emotions; and c) the tendency to engage in CWB.

A number of other theories have also been offered to describe CWB, including the causal reasoning model of CWB (Martinko, Gundlach and Douglas, 2002), the elaboration likelihood model for workplace aggression (Douglas et al., 2008), and the affective events theory (Weiss and Cropanzano, 1996). Despite the diversity in theoretical perspectives and elaborations offered by each, these models share a common emphasis on the central roles of cognition and emotion in driving CWB.

EVIDENCE FROM RESEARCH

The relationships proposed by classic theoretical models of CWB have been supported in dozens of empirical studies. For example, research supports the positive association between CWB and specific negative emotions such as anger, frustration (Chen and Spector, 1992; Douglas and Martinko, 2001; Storms and Spector, 1987), and hostility (Judge, Scott and Ilies, 2006; Lee and Allen, 2002), as well as the experience of negative emotions more broadly (Aquino, Lewis and Bradfield, 1999; Bruk-Lee and Spector, 2006; Fox and Spector, 1999; Fox, Spector and Miles, 2001; Lee and Allen, 2002). Dalal et al. (2009) used two experience sampling studies to examine the relationship between negative affect and CWB. In their studies, participants reported on their experience of negative emotions and performance of CWB twice a day for three weeks. Dalal et al. (2009) found that within person variance in the performance of CWB was related to the experience of state negative affect. That is, the performance of CWB throughout a workday is related to momentary changes in the experience of negative emotions throughout the day.

A number of stressors have also been linked to CWB both directly and indirectly through negative emotions. Some stressors primarily reflect characteristics of jobs or the work itself. For example, organizational constraints refer to conditions at work that interfere with task performance. These include insufficient time, budgetary support, equipment, or other resources. Constraints have been negatively related to CWB in a number of studies (Bowling and Eschleman, 2010; Fox and Spector, 1999; Fox et al., 2012; Keenan and Newton, 1984). Further, Fox, Spector and Miles (2001) showed that the relationship between constraints and CWB is mediated by negative emotions. Hindrance stressors are similar to constraints in that they reflect "work circumstances that ... interfere with or hinder an individual's ability to achieve valued goals" (Cavanaugh et al., 2000, p. 67); these include organizational politics, red tape, and concerns about job security. Like constraints, hindrance stressors have also been found to predict CWB (Ilie et al., 2012; Rodell and Judge, 2009). Other work conditions including conflicting role demands, role ambiguity, and having too much to do (i.e., quantitative workload) have also been related to CWB (Chen and Spector, 1992; Miles et al., 2002; Tucker et al., 2009).

Other stressors reflect characteristics of the social environment including negative social exchanges or poor interpersonal relations. For example, employees who feel they are treated unfairly or unjustly by their organization or supervisors are more likely to experience negative emotions (e.g., Fox, Spector and Miles, 2001) and to engage in CWB (Greenberg, 1990, 1993; Ilie et al., 2012; Jones, 2009; Skarlicki and Folger, 1997). Interpersonal conflict, one of the most common sources of stress at work, is also related to CWB (Bruk-Lee and Spector, 2006; Fox and Spector, 1999; Fox, Spector and Miles, 2001; Fox et al., 2012; Spector et al., 2006). Even relatively mild forms of interpersonal mistreatment, such as workplace incivility, have been related to CWB (Cortina et al., 2001; Penney and Spector, 2005; Sakurai and Jex, 2012). Taken together, these results support the contention that CWB may be performed as a reaction to stressful work conditions and the negative emotional arousal they provoke.

Studies also suggest that different forms of CWB may have different antecedents. In their meta-analysis, Herschovis et al. (2007) reported that interpersonal CWB was more strongly predicted by interpersonal conflict, whereas organizational CWB was more strongly related to situational constraints and job dissatisfaction. Spector et al. (2006) found different patterns of antecedents for finer categories of CWB which they suggest may indicate different underlying motivations for each. For example, they found that theft was unrelated to stressors or emotions indicating that it may be driven by instrumental motives. In contrast, withdrawal, production deviance, and abuse against others were related to stressors and negative emotions. Abuse was most strongly associated with interpersonal conflict and feelings of anger suggesting hostile motives and retaliation.

Research also suggests that control is an important factor in employee CWB. For example, Storms and Spector (1987) found that locus of control (LOC, i.e., individuals' beliefs about whether rewards in life are largely due to one's own actions or external forces) moderates the relationship between perceived frustration and CWB such that the relationship between frustration and CWB was more strongly positive for those with an external as opposed to internal LOC. Similar results were reported by Fox and Spector (1999).

However, research on other forms of control and CWB has been somewhat contradictory. For example, Vardi and Weitz (2003) reported a positive relationship between overall CWB and autonomy – i.e., the degree of control employees have in determining where, when, and how they work. However, Bruursema and Spector (2005) and Fox, Spector and Miles (2001) found that autonomy was positively related to organizational CWB, but not interpersonal CWB. Further, Fox, Spector and Miles (2001) reported weak evidence for autonomy moderating the relationship between organizational justice and CWB that was also in an unexpected direction; the relationship was stronger for those with high autonomy. Also, Tucker et al. (2009) found that perceived job control moderated the relationship between workload and soldier indiscipline in both a concurrent and six-month lagged model. However, in the concurrent model, high control was associated with less indiscipline, but in the lagged model, high control was associated with more indiscipline. These findings suggest that the role of control may be more complex than indicated by the stressor-emotion model.

CWB AND PERSONALITY

In addition to environmental factors, most models of CWB including the stressor-emotion model acknowledge that individual differences may affect CWB as well. Because these models feature negative emotions as a key variable, many researchers have focused on how affective traits can affect CWB by increasing the likelihood that employees perceive stressors and experience negative emotions. For example, trait negative affectivity (NA) refers to the dispositional tendency to experience a variety of negative emotional states, such as anxiety, distress, guilt, anger, rejection, and sadness (Watson and Clark, 1984). According to Watson and Clark (1984), individuals high in NA are "in any given situation, more likely to experience a significant level of distress ... (and are) particularly sensitive to minor failures, frustrations and irritations in daily life as evidenced by the likelihood, magnitude and duration of their reactions" (p. 466). The tendency of high NA individuals to experience negative emotions suggests they are more likely to engage in CWB. Indeed, Aquino et al. (1999) found that NA accounted for significant unique variance in both interpersonal and organizational CWB beyond perceived injustice. The dispositional tendencies to experience anger and anxiety more specifically (i.e., trait anger and trait anxiety) have also been found to predict CWB (Fox and Spector; 1999; Fox, Spector and Miles, 2001). Moreover, individuals who are predisposed to experience negative emotions also appear to respond to stressors with less equanimity than others. Skarlicki, Folger and Tesluck (1999) and Penney and Spector (2005) found that the relationships between both justice and incivility, respectively, and CWB were stronger for individuals high as opposed to low in NA. Similar findings regarding the moderating effect of trait anger were reported by Fox, Spector and Miles (2001) and Ilie et al. (2012). That is, when environmental stressors are high, individuals high in trait anger reported higher levels of CWB compared to those low in trait anger.

Other personality traits, including those from the Big Five, have also been examined in relation to CWB. In their meta-analysis, Berry et al. (2007) found that among the Big Five traits, conscientiousness, agreeableness, and emotional stability were the strongest predictors of CWB, although they demonstrated different patterns. Conscientiousness was more strongly related to organizational than interpersonal CWB, whereas agreeableness was more strongly related to interpersonal than organizational CWB. Emotional stability was equally related to both. Two traits from the "dark triad" (Paulhus and Williams, 2002), namely narcissism (Judge, LePine and Rich, 2006; Penney and Spector, 2002) and Machiavellianism (Kessler et al., 2010), have also been linked to the performance of CWB.

As with affective traits, studies have shown that one's standing on these personality traits also moderates the relationship between perceptions of the work environment and CWB (e.g., Bowling and Eschleman, 2010; Colbert et al., 2004; Marcus and Schuler, 2004; Marcus and Wagner, 2007; Penney and Spector, 2002). That is, whether or not individuals respond to stressful working conditions in a counterproductive manner depends in part on their personality.

As evinced by the volume of research on personality and CWB, researchers deem individual differences to be an important factor in understanding CWB. However as Spector (2011a) noted, the research on personality has not been well integrated into the theoretical frameworks of CWB. The lack of integration can be partially attributed to personality research that is geared primarily toward employee selection, although the tendency of classical CWB theories to focus primarily on environmental as opposed to individual antecedents of CWB is also a likely contributing factor.

Limitations of Classical Approach

The stressor-emotion model and other classical CWB theories that emphasize negative emotion as the mediating mechanism between negative environmental conditions and CWB have clearly contributed much to our understanding of these costly behaviors. However, the classical approach is not without limitations. First and foremost, these models present CWB as a reaction employees have as a result of exposure to stressful conditions and the subsequent negative emotions they experience. In other words, employees are positioned as reacting to their work environment and concomitant negative emotions as opposed to actively shaping their experiences. However, as we discuss later, employees may use some CWB as a means to proactively shape their environment and their emotional experiences. Along those same lines, classical CWB theories emphasize the role of negative emotion as the primary mediating mechanism in precipitating CWB. However, to the extent that individual behavior, including CWB, is goal-directed, there may be other reasons why employees engage in CWB that preclude the experience of negative emotions.

Another limitation with the classical models of CWB is that they do not consider how outcomes or anticipated outcomes for CWB affect employees' willingness to engage in these behaviors. Indeed, employees generally persist in CWB (i.e., most do not simply perform CWB once), and thus must expect some reward or at least lack of punishment that does not discourage future CWB (Fox and Spector, 2010). Human behavior is not random but is at least partially determined by individuals' expectations of reinforcements or punishments. CWB is no exception, but these factors which may contribute to the performance of CWB have not received significant attention in the literature.

Instrumental CWB

As noted earlier, CWB research has its origins in the broader aggression literature. Aggression researchers distinguish between aggression that is performed in reaction to a provocative event (i.e., hostile aggression) and aggression that is performed to obtain some desired end (i.e., instrumental aggression; Neuman and Baron, 2005). The classical models of CWB discussed so far largely position CWB as a reaction to negative work conditions and emphasize the mediating role of emotion; thus, they are consistent with hostile motives (i.e., emotion serves as a catalyst for behavior). However, CWB may be performed to achieve ends that are unrelated to expressing negative emotions or reacting to work stressors. That is, some CWB may be instrumentally driven. As noted by Diefendorff and Mehta (2007) and Fox and Spector (2010), instrumental motives for CWB have been largely unexplored. In the following sections, we discuss the literature pertaining to instrumentally-driven CWB. We begin by explaining how existing literature on CWB and related constructs (e.g., revenge, retaliation, coping) can be framed as instrumental CWB and discuss burgeoning perspectives on instrumental CWB that integrate CWB with theories of cognition, decision-making, and social information processing.

REVENGE AND RETALIATION

Perhaps some of the most widely examined instrumental motives of CWB are those that pertain to revenge and retaliation. Aquino, Tripp, and Bies (2001) defined revenge as "action in response to some perceived harm or wrongdoing by another party that is intended to inflict damage, injury, discomfort, or punishment on the party judged responsible" (p. 53). Similarly, the term retaliation is generally used in lieu of CWB in order to convey the idea that these behaviors are used as a means to balance the justice/equity equation (Adams, 1965). Thus, both revenge and retaliation are generally positioned as responses to perceived injustice (Bies and Tripp, 1998, 2005; Greenberg, 1990, 1993; Skarlicki and Folger, 1998). That is, they are motivated by a desire to restore justice or redress a perceived wrong.

Research by Aquino, Tripp and Bies (2001, 2006) indicates that employees often desire revenge over reconciliation or forgiveness in response to a perceived personal offense. Further, they found that the desire for revenge is exacerbated when the procedural justice climate is low or when the target is of lower status than the offender. That is, when formal organizational mechanisms/procedures to preserve justice are lacking or when employees have legitimate power over an offender, they are more likely to desire revenge. Jones (2009) went a step further and found that the desire for revenge partially mediated the relationships between interpersonal justice and CWB directed toward supervisors, and between procedural justice and CWB directed toward the organization. In other words, employees direct CWB toward their supervisors or organizations at least in part because of their desire to avenge perceived injustice. Similarly, Hung, Chi and Lu (2009) found that the desire for revenge against the organization and co-workers mediated the relationships between co-worker loafing and organization-directed CWB and person-directed CWB, respectively. Together, these studies indicate that the desire for revenge is an important mediating mechanism that links workplace injustice to CWB.

In describing retaliatory behavior, Folger and Skarlicki (2005) describe a process very similar to the cognitive-emotion models of CWB. Applying fairness theory (Folger and Cropanzano, 1998, 2001), they suggest that the perception of injustice, which is accompanied by an assignment of blame, gives rise to moralistic anger and a deontic response. They suggest that moralistic or deontic anger evolved to restrict abuses of power that could otherwise jeopardize the well-being and survival of social groups. From this perspective, taking action to correct a wrong (i.e., a deontic response) and thereby protect the larger social order borders on a moralistic imperative. In this respect, retaliation can be seen as having a prosocial motive. Furthermore, Kelloway et al. (2010) suggest that retaliation and deontic response can also be a group-level response. Specifically, they suggest that CWB can function as group protest or collective action by employees to express dissatisfaction with or to correct undesirable circumstances and injustice at work.

Framing CWB as retaliation and deontic response provides an interesting contrast to examining CWB in an aggression framework which presumes that harm is the intent of the actor (Neuman and Baron, 2005). Although these frameworks include emotional response (deontic anger) as antecedent to retaliation/revenge, these CWBs are framed as primarily instrumental in that they are driven by a desire to right a perceived wrong rather than performed as a behavioral manifestation of angry feelings.

EMOTION REGULATION AND COPING

Another instrumental motive of CWB that is related to emotion is the desire to regulate emotions or cope with environmental stressors. Applying Gross's (1998) framework on emotional regulation, Penney and Spector (2008) suggested that some CWBs may reflect instrumentally motivated behavior driven by a desire to manage the emotions one experiences at work. Gross (1998) defined emotion regulation as "the processes by which individuals influence which emotions they have, when they have them and how they experience and express these emotions" (p. 275). Because people are hedonically driven, they tend to engage in behavior that will result in positive emotions and take action to avoid or reduce negative emotions (Dalal et al., 2009). For instance, CWB such as withdrawal may occur because employees want to avoid unpleasant work conditions and the anxiety or frustration that arises by being in them. Boredom, a low arousal, negative emotion associated with insufficient stimulation (Mikulas and Vodonavich, 1993), often occurs in jobs that are tedious, dull, or otherwise uninteresting. To overcome boredom, employees may spend time online communicating with friends or play practical jokes on others simply because it is fun (Fisher, 1993; Penney and Spector, 2008). Indeed, Bruurseema, Kessler and Spector (2011) reported that both job boredom and dispositional boredom were positively related to various forms of CWB, including horseplay (i.e., playful and time- or resource-wasting behavior).

Coping is related to emotion regulation and represents individuals' attempts to reduce negative emotions or the conditions that give rise to them (Lazarus and Folkman, 1984). As Spector (1998) noted, employee coping can be productive or counterproductive from an organization's perspective. For instance, when frustrated by a co-worker who fails to provide necessary job-relevant resources, an employee who attempts to obtain the resource by gently explaining the importance of the resource to the co-worker may obtain the information and reduce frustration while also building a positive relationship with him/her. In contrast, an employee who yells at or gossips about the negligent co-worker to alleviate frustration is unlikely to gain the necessary resources or foster trust among colleagues.

Although many have described CWB as a form of coping (e.g., Spector and Fox, 2002), few empirical studies have investigated whether or not CWB may be used to successfully cope with stressors. A recent exception is the study by Krischer, Penney and Hunter (2010) who investigated whether production deviance and withdrawal mitigate the emotional exhaustion associated with unjust treatment. They found that among employees experiencing low levels of distributive justice, those who reported engaging in high levels of withdrawal and production deviance reported lower levels of emotional exhaustion compared to employees who refrained from these CWBs. They reported similar findings for low procedural justice and withdrawal. Krischer, Penney and Hunter's (2010) findings suggest that some forms of CWB may help employees reduce emotional exhaustion.

A "COLD COGNITIVE" APPROACH

Whereas the emotion regulation/coping and revenge/retaliation perspectives on CWB identify a specific motive, both do so within frameworks that retain affective processes as a key mediating mechanism and most proximal antecedent to CWB. Neither considers motives for CWB that may preclude the experience of negative emotions. However, as Fox and Spector (2010) argue, some CWBs may be unrelated to negative emotions or stressful work events, but instead driven by planful, cognitive processes associated with goal achievement.

Fox and Spector (2010) applied Ajzen's (2002) theory of planned behavior to explain purely instrumental CWB. According to the theory of planned behavior, the best predictor of a behavior is one's intentions to perform the behavior. Behavioral intentions are described as being influenced by a number of social-cognitive processes including one's *attitude toward the behavior* (i.e., individual beliefs about whether the behavior will benefit the actor), *social norms* regarding the behavior (i.e., beliefs about whether or not relevant others implicitly or explicitly approve of the behavior), and *perceptions of control* (e.g., actual ability to control outcomes or beliefs about one's ability to control outcomes). Using the example of theft of organizational equipment to use for work performed at home, Fox and Spector suggest that if an employee feels entitled to the equipment and believes taking the equipment home will facilitate job performance during off-hours (attitude), believes that supervisors value performance and co-workers resent paying for needed supplies out of their own pockets (social norms), and have the opportunity and ability to take the cable (control), then theft is likely.

Although at this writing, no empirical studies have examined CWB within the framework of the theory of planned behavior, research in the behavioral ethics literature provides some insight into how unethical behavior, including some CWB, may be instrumentally driven. For example, Treviño, Weaver and Reynolds (2006) define behavioral ethics as, "individual behavior that is subject to or judged according to generally accepted moral norms of behavior" (p. 952). They note that research on unethical behavior has generally focused on lying, cheating, and stealing – behaviors that are also considered CWB. Research on unethical behavior is generally studied within frameworks of ethical decision-making (e.g., Kohlberg, 1969; Lewicki, 1983; Rest, 1986) which, like the theory of planned behavior, focuses on various cognitive processes, including behavioral intention, that influence behavior. Thus, we consider them relevant to our discussion.

At least two studies on unethical behavior provide insight into how CWB may be instrumentally driven. Schweitzer, Ordóñez and Douma (2004) conducted a laboratory study to examine how performance goals affect participants' unethical behavior; the specific behavior they investigated was overstating one's level of task performance (i.e., cheating/lying). Participants were randomly assigned to receive one of three goal conditions: (1) general, do-your-best goals, (2) mere performance goals, and

(3) performance goals accompanied by financial rewards for goal completion (reward goal). They found that participants given the reward goal engaged in more unethical behavior compared to participants who had do-your-best goals or mere performance goals.

Gino and Margolis (2011) conducted a series of laboratory studies to examine how differences in regulatory focus affect unethical behavior. Specifically, they examined two strategies for goal achievement: promotion focus and prevention focus (Higgins, 1996). They found that individuals induced to have a promotion focus (i.e., emphasis on attaining desirable states) engaged in more unethical behavior than those induced to have a prevention regulatory focus (i.e., emphasis on avoiding negative outcomes). Further, they found that the effects of regulatory focus on unethical behavior were amplified when individuals' induced regulatory focus (promotion or prevention) were consistent with their perceived organization's regulatory focus.

Together these studies suggest that unethical behavior, including some CWB, may be leveraged to achieve performance-related goals or at least to maintain the appearance of achieving performance-related goals. These studies also provide indirect support for the utility of the theory of planned behavior as a framework for understanding instrumental CWB as both goals or regulatory focus (i.e., attitude toward behavior) and subjective norms about the behavior (i.e., what the organization values) predicted unethical or counterproductive behavior.

SOCIAL INFLUENCES AND NORMS

The theory of planned behavior and theories of ethical decision making are cognitive theories that emphasize individual attitudes and objectives while also incorporating aspects of social information processing (e.g., norms) to predict behavior. However, the influence of the social environment can also play a more central role in driving individual CWB.

Research suggests that conformity to group norms is important to maintaining one's position within a group as a member in good standing as many groups strongly enforce norms (Spector, 2011b). For example, Robinson and O'Leary-Kelly (1998) leveraged several theories, including the attraction-selection-attrition model (ASA, Schneider, 1975), social information processing theory (Salancik and Pfeffer, 1978), and social learning theory (Bandura, 1977) to explain how CWB (they used the term antisocial behavior) of work group members affects individual-level CWB. They argued that individuals are likely to be attracted to, self-select into, and remain in organizations where co-workers have similar attitudes and behavior, including CWB, thereby leading to greater homogeneity in the level of CWB within work groups. Further, they suggested that because work group members share a work environment, they should be exposed to similar social cues regarding the appropriateness of CWB, as well as ample opportunities to observe and model others' CWB. Indeed, Robinson and O'Leary-Kelly (1998) found that employees were more likely to engage in high levels of antisocial behavior if members of their work group also engaged in high levels of antisocial behavior. This effect was amplified for employees who had longer tenure with their work group and greater task interdependence among group members. Similarly, Glomb and Liao (2003) found that the aggregate interpersonal aggression performed within a work group explained significant incremental variance in individual interpersonal aggression beyond individual differences (trait anger, negative affectivity, self-monitoring), workplace stressors, and being the target of others' aggression.

A related line of research concerns violence climate, that is employee perceptions of an organization's policies, procedures, and practices around the prevention and control of physical violence and verbal aggression (Kessler et al., 2008; Spector et al., 2007). According to Levinson (1965) and organizational support theory (Eisenberger et al., 1986), employees tend to anthropomorphize their organizations by attributing the intentions and behavior of organizational representatives to the organization. Because of this tendency to think of organizations in a manner similar to the way they think of people, employees may model the actions of their organization concerning interpersonal relations by observing how their organization, through both formal and informal policies, treats its people. Thus, a positive violence climate signals to employees that their organization and supervisor are aware of and deem important the prevention of violence and aggression at work. To the extent that employees model these values, violence and aggression, including some forms of CWB, should be reduced. Indeed, Kessler et al. (2008) found that employees who perceived a positive violence climate reported less exposure to physical violence and verbal aggression. Further, Chang et al. (2012) found that a positive violence climate was related to higher levels of employee violence prevention behavior.

Together, these studies emphasize the importance of the social environment in predicting CWB. Specifically, they suggest that some CWB may be motivated by desire to conform to social norms. They also emphasize the role that supervisors and organizations play in reducing severe CWB by establishing expectations through policies, procedures, and practices.

Solutions for Individuals and Organizations

There are numerous solutions that both employees and organizations can implement to reduce CWB. On the individual side, it is necessary for employees to implement their own coping strategies to reduce their level of CWB. Coping skills are particularly applicable to boring jobs and to customer-service related jobs. Regarding job boredom, employees should learn to recognize when they are engaging in particularly boring tasks and take frequent breaks from these tedious tasks or ask supervisors to rotate these types of tasks among team members.

The second scenario, that of customer service, is a little more complex given the unique stressors employees experience while working directly with customers. Dormann and Zapf (2004) cite four distinct types of stressors that customer service employees routinely encounter. These include disproportionate customer expectations, customer verbal aggression, customers disliked by employees, and ambiguous customer expectations. Disproportionate customer expectations include customers making exorbitant demands on employees or expecting special treatment. Customer verbal aggression refers to customers shouting or attacking an employee verbally. The disliked customer factor refers to when employees are required to engage with customers who are hostile, unpleasant, or even lacking a sense of humor. Finally, the ambiguous customer expectations factor consists of customers expressing contradictory or unclear wishes/requests. Many of these behaviors are inherent to customer service and employees need to learn coping skills to handle these issues. For example, employees should ask customers for clarification in the case of ambiguous requests. Employees should also learn to diffuse situations with angry customers and seek the guidance of managers if the anger escalates. Organizations may also consider offering training to help employees acquire more productive strategies to cope with unpleasant customers. For example, training programs could teach employees to engage in deep acting to cognitively reframe an unpleasant situation in a more positive light (Grandey, 2003).

At the same time that employees engage in coping skills, there are solutions that organizations can implement. Some evidence suggests that it is possible to use selection techniques to "weed out" employees who are likely to commit CWB (Ones, Viswesvaran and Schmidt, 1993; Van Iddekinge et al., 2012). Specifically, integrity tests can be used to assess employee honesty so as to reduce on the job theft.

However, it should be noted that using integrity testing as part of a comprehensive selection system will only help incrementally for a number of reasons. First, despite measures to prevent "faking," it is still possible for employees to "beat" the test. Moreover, it is often environmental factors that lead employees to engage in CWB (Robinson and O'Leary-Kelly, 1998; Spector and Fox, 2002). As Spector and Fox (2002) first proposed, job stressors are among the greatest predictors of CWB because of the negative emotions they provoke and because employees may use CWB to reduce or eliminate them. Job stressors include work overload, various organizational constraints, interpersonal conflict, and injustice. The remainder of this section will be devoted to discussing ways for organizational leaders to reduce each of these job stressors.

WORK OVERLOAD (INCLUDING COMPETING DEMANDS)

Given external organizational threats including economic conditions and the globalization of the workforce, employees have to handle an overload of work and disparate demands. With the economic downturn, work overload has become the norm since positions have been eliminated and multiple jobs have become unified under one position. Ideally, organizational leaders would be sensitive to this trend and avoid enlarging jobs. However, this might not be a realistic option. Rather, organizational leaders could be helpful in assisting employees in handling multiple, competing demands. One way of doing this is for leaders to prioritize each of the demands and communicate these priorities to employees. This way, employees can set clear plans for tackling their work.

ORGANIZATIONAL CONSTRAINTS

Spector and Jex (1998) list a number of organizational constraints that restrict employees' abilities to do their work effectively. Examples of these include having poor (or even lacking) needed equipment and supplies, inadequate training, lacking necessary information related to work, frequent interruptions, and receiving incorrect instructions. Because some employees may leverage CWB to obtain the resources they need or to draw attention to problems, organizational leaders should actively seek to reduce these stressors by constantly seeking feedback from employees about the constraints they encounter each day and by ensuring that necessary equipment is available and working properly. In many cases, this means ensuring that the budget for equipment (and repairing equipment) is adequate. Additionally, when hiring new employees, leaders should carefully evaluate the skills the employee might lack and arrange for appropriate training. Leaders should also ensure that newly hired employees have been properly trained to navigate the organization. Finally, leaders should be sensitive to the interruptions employees face throughout the day and help the employee to minimize these disruptions, especially when the employee is working on a project with an impending deadline. Organizational leaders can be flexible by allowing employees to work from home and/or work at off hours if this helps the employee to minimize disruptions.

INTERPERSONAL CONFLICT

Interpersonal conflict is one of the widest and most disastrous organizational stressors; it can fuel the desire for revenge and create norms that encourage interpersonal aggression and abuse. However, its effects are often underestimated by organizational leaders. Therefore, it is important for leaders to manage interpersonal conflict in a constructive way. One of the first steps leaders can take is to separate interpersonal conflict from task and process conflict. These latter types of conflicts are actually productive and involve disagreement over the tasks themselves or how to accomplish these tasks. To some extent leaders should encourage these types of disagreements among employees in order to combat groupthink and stimulate creativity. Leaders should also remind employees that they should strive to keep disagreements over the tasks and how to accomplish the tasks. This way, leaders can prevent conflicts from becoming personal as many interpersonal conflicts at work are likely to have their roots in task and/or process conflicts. In the event that interpersonal conflicts emerge, leaders should be careful to contain the conflict to the employees involved and prevent additional parties from joining the conflict and/or taking sides. Leaders should attempt to mediate the conflict between the two parties by carefully listening to the issues and then proposing solutions.

INJUSTICE

Organizational injustice has profound effects on organizations and organizational members. Specifically, employees who suffer unfair treatment are likely to retaliate against the organization through CWB. While leaders should be careful to be fair to all employees, it should be noted that actually *being* fair is not enough. Rather, employees need to *perceive* that fairness within the organization. Therefore, leaders should clearly explain all policies and be sure to apply them consistently. Leaders should also explain the reasons for rewards given to employees. Additionally, organizational leaders should create an open environment where employees feel comfortable asking leaders about decisions and voicing their feelings/perceptions of injustice.

Future Directions

Whereas hostile motives for CWB have been widely examined in research, instrumental motives have received comparatively less attention. Thus, there are a number of opportunities for future research to broaden our understanding of why employees engage in actions that organizations deem counterproductive. For example, research on revenge/retaliation indicates that the desire for revenge is the mediating process explaining the relationship between injustice and CWB (Hung, Chi and Lu, 2009; Jones, 2009); that is, these findings suggest that revenge motivates CWB. However, no studies to date have directly examined whether the desire to regulate emotions to increase positive feelings or reduce negative feelings mediates the stressor-CWB relationship.

Furthermore, researchers suggest that employees engage in CWB to correct an injustice, regulate emotions, cope with stressful work conditions or achieve other work-related goals. However, little is known about whether or not CWB is an effective means for achieving these outcomes. Do revenge/retaliation and deontic responses result in more just conditions, or do actors simply believe that they do? Likewise, are counterproductive coping strategies associated with outcomes associated with effective coping strategies such as the reduction of emotional distress (Folkman and Lazarus, 1980), protection of self-esteem (Lazarus, 1991), increasing personal control (Allen and Greenberger, 1980), solving problems (Brown, Westbrook and Challagalla, 2005; Laux and Weber, 1991), or achieving work-related goals (e.g., improving performance, eliminating obstacles)? To answer these questions, researchers may consider the use of longitudinal and diary studies to determine if the performance of CWB is associated with positive outcomes. Such research would help organizational scientists understand whether employees experience rewards as a result of their CWB that may outweigh managerial or organizational attempts to discourage CWB through formal or informal sanctions.

The notion that CWB may be the result of "cold" cognitive processes as opposed to an expression of "hot" emotional processes (Fox and Spector, 2010) is another area requiring empirical investigation. Specifically, research is needed to examine how the cognitive process described in the theory of planned behavior relates to the performance of CWB. Do employees believe that CWB can be an effective strategy for achieving desired goals? Which forms of CWB do employees believe are most effective for different goals? For example, employees may believe that production deviance (i.e., deliberately performing work slowly or incorrectly) and withdrawal are effective tactics to protest and eventually change unreasonable performance goals, whereas verbal abuse is not. Also, how do employee perceptions of control or actual control influence CWB? To date, the research on how control impacts CWB has been mixed. Perhaps examining employee control within the framework of the theory of planned behavior will shed more light on the complex role that control plays in employee CWB. Moreover, what kind of social norms influence CWB? Highly political climates (Ferris, Russ and Fandt, 1989) may indicate organizational norms that encourage self-interested and aggressive tactics, including CWB, whereas high levels of organizational support (Eisenberger et al., 1986) may reflect norms that discourage CWB.

Along those same lines, much is left to be explored regarding how other social factors influence employee CWB. Research indicates that employees are more likely to engage in CWB if their co-workers also engage in CWB, but are all forms of CWB equally subject to social influences? Are employees more likely to model behavior targeting the organization rather than other people? Does the severity of others' CWB affect whether or not the behavior will be modeled? How does the attractiveness of a potential behavioral role model affect an observer's likelihood of imitating CWB? Observing others receiving rewards or punishment for CWB should also affect employee attitudes about the effectiveness of CWB to achieve different goals (Bandura, 1977). We expect that investigations into how social factors influence CWB may lead to insights that could inform management practices to control CWB.

Conclusion

Finally, as Spector (2011a) noted, the research on personality and CWB has not been well integrated into theoretical frameworks of CWB. However, recent theorizing and research by Barrick and his colleagues (e.g., Barrick, Mitchell and Stewart, 2003; Barrick, Stewart and Piotrowski, 2002) among others (Hogan, 1996; Hogan and Holland, 2003; Kanfer and Ackerman, 2000) describes the motivational processes that mediate the personality-performance relationship. Briefly stated, they suggest that personality traits are associated with broad intentions to pursue certain types of goals. When those goals are congruent with organizational goals or job requirements, traits are likely to enhance performance (e.g., conscientiousness and achievement orientation). Extending this theoretical approach, focusing on motivation may be one avenue via which the relationship between personality and CWB may be placed in a more solid theoretical framing.

For example, Penney, Hunter and Perry (2011) applied the conservation of resources theory (Hobfoll, 1989) to explain how conscientiousness and emotional stability are associated with resource management strategies (i.e., motivational tendencies) relevant to CWB. They suggested that because conscientiousness is associated with achievement orientation, highly conscientious employees are likely to be motivated to invest their time, energy, attention, and other resources toward behavior that will facilitate task performance and away from actions that detract from performance (i.e., CWB). However, when highly conscientious employees are also low in emotional stability, they may leverage CWB a) as a strategy to conserve resources that have been depleted by their need to manage their frequent and high levels of anxiety and other negative emotions (e.g., by taking frequent and long breaks), and/or b) in a desperate attempt to obtain resources to avoid failure (e.g., harassing co-workers for help or needed resources). They found that the relationship between conscientiousness and CWB was negative for individuals high in emotional stability, but positive for those low in emotional stability. However, although they offered goals and motivation as explanations for the relationship between these traits and CWB, they did not examine these motivational mechanisms directly. Thus, more research is needed to determine if the motivational mechanisms that have shown to mediate the personality-performance relationship (e.g., Barrick, Stewart and Piotrowski, 2002) are also relevant for the personality-CWB relationship.

References

Adams, J.S. (1965) Inequity in social exchange. In L. Berkowitz (ed.) *Advances in Experimental Social Psychology*, Vol. 2. New York: Academic Press, pp. 267–99.

Ajzen, I. (2002) Perceived behavioral control, self-efficacy, locus of control, and the theory of planned behavior. *Journal of Applied Social Psychology*, 32, 665–83.

Allen, V.L. and Greenberger, D.B. (1980) Destruction and perceived control. In A. Baum and J.E. Singer (eds) *Applications of Personal Control*. Hillsdale, NJ: Erlbaum, pp. 85–109.

Aquino, K., Lewis, M.U. and Bradfield, M. (1999) Justice constructs, negative affectivity, and employee deviance: A proposed model and empirical test. *Journal of Organizational Behavior*, 20, 1073–91.

Aquino, K., Tripp, T.M. and Bies, R.J. (2001) How employees respond to personal offense: The effects of blame attribution, victim status, and offender status on revenge and reconciliation in the workplace. *Journal of Applied Psychology*, 861, 52–9.

—— (2006) Getting even or moving on? Power, procedural justice, and types of offense as predictors of revenge, forgiveness, reconciliation, and avoidance in organizations. *Journal of Applied Psychology*, 913, 653–68.

Bandura, A. (1977) *Social Learning Theory*. Oxford: Prentice-Hall.

Baron, R.A. and Neuman, J.H. (1996) Workplace violence and workplace aggression: Evidence on their relative frequency and potential causes. *Aggressive Behavior*, 22, 161–73.

Barrick, M.R., Mitchell, T.R. and Stewart, G.L. (2003) Situational and motivational influences on trait-behavior relationships. In M.R. Barrick and A.M. Ryan (eds) *Personality and Work: Reconsidering the Role of Personality in Organizations*. San Francisco, CA: Jossey-Bass, pp. 60–82.

Barrick, M.R., Stewart, G.L. and Piotrowski, M. (2002) Personality and job performance: Test of the mediating effects of motivation among sales representatives. *Journal of Applied Psychology*, 87, 43–51.

Bennett, R.J. and Robinson, S.L. (2000) The development of a measure of workplace deviance. *Journal of Applied Psychology*, 85, 349–60.

Berry, C.M., Carpenter, N.C. and Barratt, C.L. (2012) Do other-reports of counterproductive work behavior provide an incremental contribution over self-reports? A meta-analytic comparison. *Journal of Applied Psychology*, 973, 613–36.

Berry, C.M., Ones, D.S. and Sackett, P.R. (2007) Interpersonal deviance, organizational deviance, and their common correlates: A review and meta-analysis. *Journal of Applied Psychology*, 92, 410–24.

Bies, R.J. and Tripp, T.M. (1998) Revenge in organizations: The good, the bad, and the ugly. In R.W. Griffin, A. O'Leary-Kelly, and J.M. Collins (eds) *Dysfunctional Behavior in Organizations: Violent and Deviant Behavior. Monographs in Organizational Behavior and Industrial Relations*, vol. 23, parts A and B. Stamford, CT: JAI Press, pp. 49–67.

—— (2005) The study of revenge in the workplace: Conceptual, ideological, and empirical issues. In S. Fox and P.E. Spector (eds) *Counterproductive Work Behavior: Investigations of Actors and Targets*. Washington, DC: American Psychological Association, pp. 65–81.

Bowling, N.A. and Eschleman, K.J. (2010) Employee personality as a moderator of the relationships between work stressors and counterproductive work behavior. *Journal of Occupational Health Psychology*, 151, 91–102.

Brown, S.P., Westbrook, R.A. and Challagalla, G. (2005) Good cope, bad cope: Adaptive and maladaptive coping strategies following a critical negative work event. *Journal of Applied Psychology*, 90, 792–8.

Bruk-Lee, V. and Spector, P.E. (2006) The social stressors-counterproductive work behaviors link: Are conflicts with supervisors and coworkers the same? *Journal of Occupational Health Psychology*, 11, 145–56.

Bruursema, K., Kessler, S.R. and Spector, P.E. (2011) Bored employees misbehaving: The relationship between boredom and counterproductive work behaviour. *Work and Stress*, 252, 93–107.

Bruursema, K. and Spector, P.E. (2005) Leadership style and the link with counterproductive work behavior CWB. Paper presented at the meeting of the Society for Industrial and Organizational Psychology, Los Angeles, April 15–17.

Cavanaugh, M., Boswell, W., Roehling, M. and Boudreau, J. (2000) An empirical examination of self-reported work stress among US managers. *Journal of Applied Psychology*, 851, 65–74.

Chang, C., Eatough, E.M., Spector, P.E. and Kessler, S.R. (2012) Violence-prevention climate, exposure to violence and aggression, and prevention behavior: A mediation model. *Journal of Organizational Behavior*, 335, 657–77.

Chen, P.Y. and Spector, P.E. (1992) Relationships of work stressors with aggression, withdrawal, theft and substance use: An exploratory study. *Journal of Occupational and Organizational Psychology*, 65, 177–84.

Colbert, A.E., Mount, M.K., Harter, J.K., Witt, L.A. and Barrick, M.R. (2004) Interactive effects of personality and perceptions of work situation on workplace deviance. *Journal of Applied Psychology*, 89, 599–609.

Cortina, L.M., Magley, V.J., Williams, J.H. and Langhout, R.D. (2001) Incivility in the workplace: Incidence and impact. *Journal of Occupational Health Psychology*, 61, 64–80.

Dalal, R.S., Lam, H., Weiss, H.M., Welch, E.R. and Hulin, C.L. (2009) A within-person approach to work behavior and performance: Concurrent and lagged citizenship-counterproductivity associations, and dynamic relationships with affect and overall job performance. *Academy of Management Journal*, 525, 1051–66.

Diefendorff, J.M. and Mehta, K. (2007) The relations of motivational traits with workplace deviance. *Journal of Applied Psychology*, 924, 967–77.

Dollard, J., Doob, L.W., Miller, N.E., Mowrer, O.H. and Sears, R.R. (1939) *Frustration and Aggression*. New Haven, CT: Yale University Press.

Dormann, C. and Zapf, D. (2004) Customer-related social stressors and burnout. *Journal of Occupational Health Psychology*, 9(1), 61–82.

Douglas, S.C., Kiewitz, C., Martinko, M.J., Harvey, P., Kim, Y. and Chun, J. (2008) Cognitions, emotions, and evaluations: An elaboration likelihood model for workplace aggression. *The Academy of Management Review*, 332, 425–51.

Douglas, S.C. and Martinko, M.J. (2001) Exploring the role of individual differences in the prediction of workplace aggression. *Journal of Applied Psychology*, 864, 547–59.

Eisenberger, R., Huntington, R., Hutchison, S. and Sowa, D. (1986) Perceived organizational support. *Journal of Applied Psychology*, 71, 500–507.

Ferris, G.R., Russ, G.S. and Fandt, P.M. (1989) Politics in organizations. In R.A. Giacalone and P. Rosenfeld (eds) *Impression Management in the Organization*. Hillsdale, NJ: Lawrence Erlbaum, pp. 143–70.

Fisher, C.D. (1993) Boredom at work: A neglected concept. *Human Relations*, 46, 395–418.

Folger, R. (2001) Fairness as deonance. In S.W. Gilliland, D.D. Steiner and D.P. Skarlicki (eds) *Research in Social Issues in Management*. Greenwich, CT: Information Age, pp. 3–31.

Folger, R. and Cropanzano, R. (1998) *Organizational Justice and Human Resource Management*. Thousand Oaks, CA: Sage.

—— (2001) Fairness theory: Justice as accountability. In J. Greenberg and R. Cropanzano (eds) *Advances in Organizational Justice*. Stanford, CA: Stanford University Press, pp. 1–55.

Folger, R. and Skarlicki, D.P. (2005) Beyond counterproductive work behavior: Moral emotions and deontic retaliation versus reconciliation. In S. Fox and P.E. Spector (eds) *Counterproductive Work Behavior: Investigations of Actors and Targets*. Washington, DC: American Psychological Association, pp. 83–105.

Folkman, S. and Lazarus, R.S. (1980) An analysis of coping in a middle-aged community sample. *Journal of Health and Social Behavior*, 21, 219–39.

Fox, S. and Spector, P.E. (1999) A model of work frustration-aggression. *Journal of Organizational Behavior*, 206, 915–31.

—— (2006) The many roles of control in a stressor-emotion theory of counterproductive work behavior. In P.L. Perrewé and D.C. Ganster (eds) *Employee Health, Coping and Methodologies*. Amsterdam and Boston, MA: Elsevier Science/JAI Press, pp. 171–201.

—— (2010) Instrumental counterproductive work behavior and the theory of planned behavior: A "cold cognitive" approach to complement "hot affective" theories of CWB. In L.L. Neider and C.A. Schriesheim (eds) *The "Dark" Side of Management*. Charlotte, NC: Information Age Publishing, pp. 93–114.

Fox, S., Spector, P.E., Goh, A., Bruursema, K. and Kessler, S.R. (2012) The deviant citizen: Measuring potential positive relations between counterproductive work behaviour and organizational citizenship behaviour. *Journal of Occupational and Organizational Psychology*, 851, 199–220.

Fox, S., Spector, P.E. and Miles, D. (2001) Counterproductive work behavior CWB in response to job stressors and organizational justice: Some mediator and moderator tests for autonomy and emotions. *Journal of Vocational Behavior*, 59, 291–309.

Giacalone, R.A. and Greenberg, J. (1997) *Antisocial Behavior in Organizations*. Thousand Oaks, CA: Sage.

Gino, F. and Margolis, J.D. (2011) Bringing ethics into focus: How regulatory focus and risk preferences influence unethical behavior. *Organizational Behavior and Human Decision Processes*, 1152, 145–56.

Glomb, T.M. and Liao, H. (2003) Interpersonal aggression in work groups: Social influence, reciprocal, and individual effects. *Academy of Management Journal*, 464, 486–96.

Govoni, S.J. (1992) To catch a thief. *CFO*, February, 24–32.

Grandey, A.A. (2003) When "the show must go on": Surface acting and deep acting as determinants of emotional exhaustion and peer-rated service delivery. *Academy of Management Journal*, 46(1), 86–96.

Greenberg, J. (1990) Employee theft as a reaction to underpayment inequity: The hidden cost of pay cuts. *Journal of Applied Psychology*, 75, 561–8.

—— (1993) Stealing in the name of justice: Informational and interpersonal moderators of theft reactions to underpayment inequity. *Organizational Behavior and Human Decision Processes*, 54, 81–103.

—— (1997) *Occupational Crime*, 2nd edn. Chicago, IL: Nelson-Hall.

Gross, J.J. (1998) The emerging field of emotion regulation: An integrative review. *Review of General Psychology*, 2, 271–99.

Gruys, M.L. and Sackett, P.R. (2003) Investigating the dimensionality of counterproductive work behavior. *International Journal of Selection and Assessment*, 111, 30–42.

Hershcovis, M.S., Turner, N., Barling, J., Arnold, K.A., Dupre, K.E., Inness, M., LeBlanc, M.M. and Sivanathan, N. (2007) Predicting workplace aggression: A meta-analysis. *Journal of Applied Psychology*, 92, 228–38.

Higgins, E.T. (1996) The "self digest": Self-knowledge serving self-regulatory functions. *Journal of Personality and Social Psychology*, 71, 1062–83.

Hobfoll, S.E. (1989) Conservation of resources: A new attempt at conceptualizing stress. *American Psychologist*, 44, 513–24.

Hogan, R. (1996) A socioanalytic perspective on the Five-Factor Model. In J.S. Wiggens (ed.) *The Five Factor Model of Personality*. New York: Guilford Press, pp. 163–79.

Hogan, J. and Hogan, R. (1989) How to measure employee reliability. *Journal of Applied Psychology*, 742, 273–9.

Hogan, J. and Holland, B. (2003) Using theory to evaluate personality and job performance relations. *Journal of Applied Psychology*, 88, 100–112.

Hung, T., Chi, N. and Lu, W. (2009) Exploring the relationships between perceived coworker loafing and counterproductive work behaviors: The mediating role of a revenge motive. *Journal of Business and Psychology*, 243, 257–70.

Hunter, E.M. and Penney, L.M. (2007) *The Waiter Spit in My Soup! Counterproductive Behavior toward Customers*. Poster presented at the annual meeting of the Society of Industrial and Organizational Psychology, New York, April.

Ilie, A., Penney, L.M., Ispas, D. and Iliescu, D. (2012) The role of trait anger in the relationship between stressors and counterproductive work behaviors: Convergent findings from multiple studies and methodologies. *Applied Psychology: An International Review*, 613, 415–36.

Jones, D.A. (2009) Getting even with one's supervisor and one's organization: Relationships among types of injustice, desires for revenge, and counterproductive work behaviors. *Journal of Organizational Behavior*, 304, 525–42.

Judge, T.A., LePine, J.A. and Rich, B.L. (2006) Loving yourself abundantly: Relationship of the narcissistic personality to self and other perceptions of workplace deviance, leadership, and task and contextual performance. *Journal of Applied Psychology*, 94, 762–76.

Judge, T.A., Scott, B.A. and Ilies, R. (2006) Hostility, job attitudes, and workplace deviance: Test of a multilevel model. *Journal of Applied Psychology*, 911, 126–38.

Kanfer, R. and Ackerman, P.L. (2000) Individual differences in work motivation: Further explorations of a trait framework. *Applied Psychology: An International Review*, 49, 470–82.

Keenan, A. and Newton, T.J. (1984) Frustration in organizations: Relationships to role stress, climate, and psychological strain. *Journal of Occupational Psychology*, 57, 57–65.

Kelloway, E., Francis, L., Prosser, M. and Cameron, J.E. (2010) Counterproductive work behavior as protest. *Human Resource Management Review*, 201, 18–25.

Kessler, S.R., Bandelli, A.C., Spector, P.E., Borman, W.C., Nelson, C.E. and Penney, L.M. (2010) Re-examining Machiavelli: A three-dimensional model of Machiavellianism in the workplace. *Journal of Applied Social Psychology*, 408, 1868–96.

Kessler, S.R., Spector, P.E., Chang, C. and Parr, A.D. (2008) Organizational violence and aggression: Development of the three-factor Violence Climate Survey. *Work and Stress*, 222, 108–24.

Kohlberg, L. (1969) Stage and sequence: The cognitive–developmental approach to socialization. In D.A. Goslin (ed.) *Handbook of Socialization Theory and Research*. Chicago, IL: Rand McNally, pp. 347–480.

Krischer, M.M., Penney, L.M. and Hunter, E.M. (2010) Can counterproductive work behaviors be productive? CWB as emotion-focused coping. *Journal of Occupational Health Psychology*, 15, 154–66.

Laux, L. and Weber, H. (1991) Presentation of self in coping with anger and anxiety: An intentional approach. *Anxiety Research*, 3, 233 55.

Lazarus, R.S. (1991) Progress on a cognitive-motivational-relational theory of emotion. *American Psychologist*, 46, 819–34.

Lazarus, R.S. and Folkman, S. (1984) *Stress, Appraisal and Coping*. New York: Springer.

Lee, K. and Allen, N.J. (2002) Organizational citizenship behavior and workplace deviance: The role of affect and cognitions. *Journal of Applied Psychology*, 871, 131–42.

Levinson, H.H. (1965) Reciprocation: The relationship between man and organization. *Administrative Science Quarterly*, 9(4), 370–90.

Lewicki, R.J. (1983) Lying and deception: A behavioral model. In M.H. Bazerman and R.J. Lewicki (eds) *Negotiating in Organizations*. Beverly Hills, CA: Sage, pp. 68–90.

Marcus, B. and Schuler, H. (2004) Antecedents of counterproductive behavior at work: A general perspective. *Journal of Applied Psychology*, 89, 647–80.

Marcus, B. and Wagner, U. (2007) Combining dispositions and evaluations of vocation and job to account for counterproductive work behavior in adolescent job apprentices. *Journal of Occupational Health Psychology*, 12, 161–76.

Martinko, M.J., Gundlach, M.J. and Douglas, S.C. (2002) Toward an integrative theory of counterproductive workplace behavior: A causal reasoning perspective. *International Journal of Selection and Assessment*, 10, 36–50.

Mikulas, W.L. and Voadanovich, S.J. (1993) The essence of boredom. *The Psychological Record*, 43, 3–12.

Miles, D.E., Borman, W.E., Spector, P.E. and Fox, S. (2002) Building an integrative model of extra role work behaviors: A comparison of counterproductive work behavior with organizational citizenship behavior. *International Journal of Selection and Assessment*, 101–2, 51–7.

Neuman, J.H. and Baron, R.A. (2005) Aggression in the workplace: A social-psychological perspective. In S. Fox and P.E. Spector (eds) *Counterproductive Work Behavior: Investigations of Actors and Targets*. Washington, DC: American Psychological Association, 13–40.

O'Leary-Kelly, A.M., Griffin, R.W. and Glew, D.J. (1996) Organization-motivated aggression: A research framework. *Academy of Management Review*, 21, 225–53.

Ones, D.S., Viswesvaran, C. and Schmidt, F.L. (1993) Comprehensive meta-analysis of integrity test validities: Findings and implications for personnel selection and theories of job performance. *Journal of Applied Psychology*, 78, 679–703.

Paulhus, D.L. and Williams, K.M. (2002) The dark triad of personality: Narcissism, Machiavellianism, and psychopathy. *Journal of Research in Personality*, 36, 556–63.

Penney, L.M., Hunter, E.M. and Perry, S.J. (2011) Personality and counterproductive work behaviour: Using conservation of resources theory to narrow the profile of deviant employees. *Journal of Occupational and Organizational Psychology*, 841, 58–77.

Penney, L.M. and Spector, P.E. (2002) Narcissism and counterproductive work behavior: Do bigger egos mean bigger problems? *International Journal of Selection and Assessment*, 10, 59–67.

—— (2005) Job stress, incivility, and counterproductive workplace behavior CWB: The moderating role of negative affectivity. *Journal of Organizational Behavior*, 26, 777–96.

—— (2008) Emotions and counterproductive work behavior. In N.M. Ashkanasy and C.L. Cooper (eds) *Research Companion to Emotion in Organizations*. Cheltenham: Edward Elgar, pp. 183–96.

Rest, J. (1986) *Development in Judging Moral Issues*. Minneapolis, MN: University of Minnesota Press.

Robinson, S.L. and Bennett, R.J. (1995) A typology of deviant workplace behaviors: A multidimensional scaling study. *Academy of Management Journal*, 38, 555–65.

Robinson, S.L. and O'Leary-Kelly, A.M. (1998) Monkey see, monkey do: The influence of work groups on the antisocial behavior of employees. *Academy of Management Journal*, 41, 658–72.

Rodell, J.B. and Judge, T.A. (2009) Can "good" stressors spark "bad" behaviors? The mediating role of emotions in links of challenge and hindrance stressors with citizenship and counterproductive behaviors. *Journal of Applied Psychology*, 946, 1438–51.

Sackett, P.R. (2002) The structure of counterproductive work behaviors: Dimensionality and relationships with facets of job performance. *International Journal of Selection and Assessment*, 10, 5–11.

Sackett, P.R. and DeVore, C.J. (2002) Counterproductive behaviors at work. In N. Anderson, D.S. Ones, H. Sinangil and C. Viswesvaran (eds) *Handbook of Industrial, Work and Organizational Psychology*. Vol. 1, *Personnel Psychology*. Thousand Oaks, CA: Sage, 145–64.

Sakurai, K. and Jex, S.M. (2012) Coworker incivility and incivility targets' work effort and counterproductive work behaviors: The moderating role of supervisor social support. *Journal of Occupational Health Psychology*, 172, 150–61.

Salancik, G.J. and Pfeffer, J. (1978) A social information processing approach to job attitudes and task design. *Administrative Science Quarterly*, 23, 224–53.

Schneider, B. (1975) Organizational climates: An essay. *Personnel Psychology*, 28, 447–80.

Schweitzer, M.E., Ordóñez, L. and Douma, B. (2004) Goal setting as a motivator of unethical behavior. *Academy of Management Journal*, 473, 422–32.

Skarlicki, D.P. and Folger, R. (1997) Retaliation in the workplace: The roles of distributive, procedural, and interactional justice. *Journal of Applied Psychology*, 82, 434–43.

—— (1998) A popcorn metaphor for employee aggression. In R.W. Griffin, A. O'Leary-Kelly and J.M. Collins (eds) *Dysfunctional Behavior in Organizations: Violent and Deviant Behavior*. Amsterdam and Boston, MA: Elsevier Science/JAI Press, 43–81.

Skarlicki, D.P., Folger, R. and Tesluk, P. (1999) Personality as a moderator in the relationship between fairness and retaliation. *Academy of Management Journal*, 42, 100–108.

Spector, P.E. (1975) Relationships of organizational frustration with reported behavioral reactions of employees. *Journal of Applied Psychology*, 60, 635–7.

—— (1978) Organizational frustration: A model and review of the literature. *Personnel Psychology*, 31, 815–29.

—— (1998) A control theory of the job stress process. In C.L. Cooper (ed.) *Theories of Organizational Stress*. Oxford: Oxford University Press, 153–69.

—— (2011a) *Industrial and Organizational Behavior*, 6th edn. New York: John Wiley and Sons.

—— (2011b) The relationship of personality to counterproductive work behavior CWB: An integration of perspectives. *Human Resource Management Review*, 214, 342–52.

Spector, P.E., Coulter, M.L., Stockwell, H.G. and Matz, M.W. (2007) Perceived violence climate: A new construct and its relationship to workplace physical violence and verbal aggression, and their potential consequences. *Work and Stress*, 212, 117–30.

Spector, P.E. and Fox, S. (2002) An emotion-centered model of voluntary work behavior: Some parallels between counterproductive work behavior CWB and organizational citizenship behavior OCB. *Human Resources Management Review*, 12, 269–92.

—— (2005) The stressor-emotion model of counterproductive work behavior. In S. Fox and P. Spector (eds) *Counterproductive Work Behavior: Investigations of Actors and Targets*. Washington, DC: American Psychological Association, 151–74.

Spector, P.E., Fox, S., Penney, L.M., Bruursema, K., Goh, A. and Kessler, S. (2006) The dimensionality of counterproductivity: Are all counterproductive behaviors created equal? *Journal of Vocational Behavior*, 68, 446–60.

Spector, P.E. and Jex, S.M. (1998) Development of four self-report measures of job stressors and strain: Interpersonal conflict at work scale, organizational constraints scale, quantitative workload inventory, and physical symptoms inventory. *Journal of Occupational Health Psychology*, 3, 356–67.

Storms, P.L. and Spector, P.E. (1987) Relationships of organizational frustration with reported behavioral reactions: The moderating effect of perceived control. *Journal of Occupational Psychology*, 60, 227–34.

Treviño, L.K., Weaver, G.R. and Reynolds, S.J. (2006) Behavioral ethics in organizations: A review. *Journal of Management*, 326, 951–90.

Tucker, J.S., Sinclair, R.R., Mohr, C.D., Adler, A.B., Thomas, J.L. and Salvi, A.D. (2009) Stress and counterproductive work behavior: Multiple relationships between demands, control and solider indiscipline over time. *Journal of Occupational Health Psychology*, 143, 257–71.

Tunstall, M.M., Penney, L.M., Hunter, E.M. and Weinberger, E. (2006) A closer look at CWB: Emotions, targets, and outcomes. Poster presented at the annual meeting of the Society of Industrial and Organizational Psychology, Dallas, TX, May.

Van Iddekinge C.H., Roth P.L., Raymark P.H. and Odle-Dusseau, H.N. (2012). The criterion-related validity of integrity tests: An updated meta-analysis. *Journal of Applied Psychology*, 97, 499–530.

Vardi, Y. and Weitz, E. (2003) Personal and positional antecedents of organizational misbehaviour. In A. Sagie, S. Stashevsky and M. Koslowsky (eds) *Misbehaviour and Dysfunctional Attitudes in Organizations*. New York: Palgrave Macmillan, 173–93.

Watson, D. and Clark, L.A. (1984) Negative affectivity: The disposition to experience aversive emotional states. *Psychological Bulletin*, 963, 465–90.

Weiss, H.M. and Cropanzano, R. (1996) Affective Events Theory: A theoretical discussion of the structure, causes and consequences of affective experiences at work. In B.M. Staw and L.L. Cummings (eds) *Research in Organizational Behavior: An Annual Series of Analytical Essays and Critical Reviews*, vol. 18. Amsterdam and Boston, MA: Elsevier Science/JAI Press, 1–74.

PART III

Addressing Human Frailties in the Workplace

CHAPTER 10

Recovery from Work Stress as an Opportunity to Foster Well-being and Performance

ANNA ROSA KOCH, VERENA C. HAHN AND CARMEN BINNEWIES

Introduction

For today's workforce experiencing stress at work and at home seems to be an everyday experience as most workers have access to technology such as laptops, smartphones and constant internet access and therefore can work 24/7 wherever they are (Park, Fritz and Jex, 2011). As boundaries between work and private life become more and more blurred, in many jobs employees may find it more and more difficult to unwind from daily work stress and find time to recharge their batteries. However, this process of unwinding – namely recovery – is the process which reverses negative consequences of stress (Meijman and Mulder, 1998) and thus plays a crucial role in preventing the development of strain and diseases as a reaction to stress at work (Geurts and Sonnentag, 2006). Accordingly, both employees and organizations should be interested in promoting employees' recovery as a way to foster health and performance complementary to stress-reducing interventions.

This chapter provides an overview of research on recovery from work stress and sums up how this research can help employees to stay healthy and fit. We first describe the concept of recovery and briefly summarize the most important theoretical frameworks explaining the recovery process. In the following, we point out the different options employees have to recover before we explain how recovery during vacations, during daily leisure time and during work breaks contribute to employees' well-being and health. We further discuss workplace factors and factors outside work that facilitate or impede recovery during leisure time and discuss research examining performance-related outcomes of recovery. Finally, we point out implications for individuals and organizations that can be drawn from recovery research.

Recovery from Work Stress

Throughout the work day employees have to expend effort to fulfill their work requirements and to deal with job demands (Meijman and Mulder, 1998). As a result, employees' physical and mental resources are depleted and employees feel exhausted and in need of recovery after the work day (Sluiter, van der Beek and Frings-Dresen, 1999). During leisure time, employees normally have time to rest, unwind from work stress, and recharge their batteries for the next work day. The functional systems that have been taxed during the work day can return to their baseline levels and the resources that have been drained can be replenished (Meijman and Mulder, 1998). This process of unwinding and resource replenishment is called recovery. The recovery process can be seen as a process opposite to the strain process as the negative effects of dealing with job demands are reversed and employees' impaired well-being is restored (Sonnentag and Fritz, 2007).

Accordingly, successful recovery is indicated by a reduction of the negative effects of job demands. As dealing with daily job demands can impair employees' psychological (e.g., fatigue, affect), physiological (e.g., cardiovascular and neuroendocrine), and behavioral outcomes (e.g., performance), successful recovery can become apparent in changes in these three types of outcomes (Sonnentag and Geurts, 2009). For example, recovery after work is indicated by decreases in negative affect and increases in positive affect (e.g., Fritz, Sonnentag, Spector and McInroe, 2010; Hahn, Binnewies and Haun, 2012; Sonnentag, Binnewies and Mojza, 2008), by a decreasing heart rate or adrenaline excretion (e.g., Saxbe, Repetti and Nishina, 2008), or by improved task and contextual performance at work (e.g., Binnewies, Sonnentag and Mojza, 2009a; Sonnentag, 2003; Trougakos et al., 2008). Moreover, recovery is directly indicated by an employees' subjective feeling of being recovered after a rest period (e.g., Binnewies, Sonnentag and Mojza, 2009a, 2010).

Research on recovery from work stress has usually been based on the notion that employees have to expend personal resources to fulfill their work tasks and that their personal resources are limited (Trougakos and Hideg, 2009). As engaging in effortful work activities depletes an employees' limited personal resources, recovery is needed to replenish an employees' exhausted resources. Two theories utilizing the concept of limited personal resources have been predominantly used in the recovery literature: the effort-recovery model (Meijman and Mulder, 1998) and the conservation of resources theory (Hobfoll, 1989).

According to the effort-recovery model (Meijman and Mulder, 1998), the expenditure of effort throughout the work day leads to load reactions such as fatigue or physiological activation which deplete an employee's energy resources. These load reactions are reversible: when job demands are absent during recovery periods, the psychophysiological systems that were activated during work return to a baseline level. However, if time for recovery is not sufficient, an employee's psychophysiological systems cannot return to their baseline level. Consequently, when the employee starts to work, he or she is still in a suboptimal state and has to mobilize compensatory effort in order to perform adequately at work. When recovery is insufficient over longer periods of time, load reactions can accumulate and result in irreversible consequences such as severe health complaints.

According to the conservation of resources theory (Hobfoll, 1989), people strive to possess and protect personal resources. These personal resources include objects, personal characteristics, conditions, and energies that are either valued in themselves or serve as means for obtaining other valued resources. When employees experience an actual or potential loss of resources or when they cannot regain resources after having invested them, they are assumed to experience stress. To recover from work stress, employees have to engage in activities that help them to gain new resources and restore threatened or lost resources. Engaging in certain leisure time activities can require the investment of a certain amount of resources such as energy or self-regulation to gain further resources. For example, engaging in sport activities or voluntary work involves investing a certain amount of energy and self-regulatory resources, but is beneficial for employees' recovery (Mojza, Sonnentag and Bornemann, 2011; Sonnentag and Jelden, 2009). Taken together, the effort-recovery model and the conservation of resources theory suggest that recovery from work stress can occur when employees are no longer exposed to job demands that tax their resources and when they can replenish their drained resources or build new resources.

Recently, Trougakos and Hideg (2009) proposed Muraven and Baumeister's (2000) ego-depletion theory as a complementary limited resource perspective that is particularly useful for studying momentary recovery from work stress. This theory suggests that regulating one's own behavior requires the expenditure of a central limited personal resource. Each time individuals engage in some form of self-regulatory behavior (e.g., completing an assigned work task), this central resource is depleted. As a result, after engaging in self-regulatory behavior, subsequent regulatory efforts become increasingly difficult. Individuals can replenish their self-regulatory strength under favorable conditions. Specifically, Trougakos and Hideg (2009) proposed that employees can replenish their self-regulatory resources in two possible ways: either by stopping a task that depletes their regulatory resources, or by engaging in a preferred behavior that does not require self-regulation.

Recovery can occur over different time periods: during vacations providing a recovery period of several days or even weeks, during daily leisure time, and during the weekend as well as during the workday when taking work breaks. In the following, we will summarize and discuss recovery research addressing these different time periods.

Going on Holiday: Vacations' Contribution to Recovery

Probably most people first think of vacation when thinking about recovery from work stress and most people can hardly wait for the holiday season to come. Vacation is defined as a longer period absent from work which is usually not interrupted by work tasks and should therefore allow employees to recover from work stress (de Bloom et al., 2010). Recovery research has confirmed vacations' recovering effect (de Bloom et al., 2009); most people know from their own experience.

Two mechanisms through which vacations contribute to recovery have been postulated. First, a passive mechanism can be assumed (de Bloom et al., 2010). During vacations, job demands such as time pressure or work-related problems are usually removed from employees. Employees do not have to participate in job-related activities as reading business emails or preparing a presentation for the next working day. Instead, individuals have the time to recharge their batteries and restore energy, for example while being on a holiday trip or enjoying a relaxing time at home. Therefore, unwinding from work stress is enabled and recovery can occur (Meijman and Mulder, 1998). Second, vacations contribute to recovery through active engagement in recovering activities (de Bloom et al., 2010). As individuals have the chance to participate in preferred leisure activities such as doing sports or visiting their family, they can restore resources such as feelings of competence and self-esteem.

A recent meta-analysis revealed that vacations also have a positive effect on employees' well-being and self-rated mental health (de Bloom et al., 2009). Immediately after a vacation, employees report fewer burnout symptoms, fewer health complaints, and higher psychological well-being than before the vacation (de Bloom et al., 2009). Effects on performance are inconsistent. Still, it has been shown that vacations decrease effort expenditure at work: after vacations employees need less effort and energy to fulfill their daily work tasks (Fritz and Sonnentag, 2006). Furthermore, vacations contribute to employees' work engagement. In the long run, a number of vacations was found to decrease mortality, especially mortality due to coronal heart diseases (Gump and Matthews, 2000).

What individuals can do to benefit the most from their vacation was the aim of Fritz and Sonnentag's (2006) longitudinal study. Fritz and Sonnentag (2006) distinguished between resource-providing and resource-consuming vacation experiences. Vacation activities during which employees experienced challenges (referred to as mastery experiences) or relaxation were found to be resource-providing vacation experiences. Reflecting positively about their own job during vacations, for example about achieved goals and supportive colleagues, was also found to be an effective way to rebuilt resources during vacation (Fritz and Sonnentag, 2006). Negative work-related thoughts were found to be a resource-consuming vacation experience. Also Davidson and colleagues (2010) showed that well-being does not improve during a sabbatical leave if the one on sabbatical is not able to detach mentally from work problems. Negative work-related thoughts, for example about unsolved problems or conflicts at work kept work stress present during vacation time. Additionally, non-work hassles such as conflicts with spouse and children during family trips drained resources such as mental energy and were found to be detrimental for employees' recovery (Fritz and Sonnentag, 2006). Strauss-Blasche, Ekmekcioglu and Marktl (2000) found that employees who took control over their vacation and were able to arrange their vacation in a pleasant way benefitted most from vacation. Therefore, both recovering days spent at home and others spent away on a holiday trip contribute to employees' recovery from work stress (Strauss-Blasche, Ekmekcioglu and Marktl, 2000). Concerning the length of vacation, surprisingly longer vacations do not increase employees' well-being to a larger extent than shorter vacations (de Bloom et al., 2009). Taken together, it can be suggested that individuals participating in resource-providing activities during vacation (Fritz and Sonnentag, 2006) and who feel satisfied with their vacation time (Westman and Eden, 1997) benefit mostly from their vacation in terms of their own well-being, health, and performance.

Vacation effects on well-being and performance are substantive and one might think that vacation could be sufficient to prevent negative consequences of daily work stress. However, this is not the case as vacation effects quickly fade away (Fritz and Sonnentag, 2006; Kühnel and Sonnentag, 2011; Westman and Eden, 1997). De Bloom and colleagues' meta-analysis (2009) showed that vacation's beneficial effects on well-being and performance faded out after two to four weeks. At least four weeks after their vacation, employees felt as exhausted and stressed as before. If employees were confronted with high job demands such as time pressure immediately after their vacation, fade-out was even sped up (Kühnel and Sonnentag, 2011). However, Kühnel and Sonnentag (2011) also showed that vacation fade-out was delayed for employees who experienced more relaxation during daily leisure time after vacation.

Recovery Activities and Experiences during Leisure Time

During leisure time individuals participate in various leisure activities. Besides enjoying hobbies, personal duties and household activities (e.g., banking activities, washing the dishes) have to be performed during leisure time. As one can imagine, not all of these activities contribute to recovery. Several studies have focused on distinguishing between different classes of leisure activities and examining the effect of leisure activities on an individual's health and well-being.

Sonnentag (2001) distinguished between high-duty-leisure activities and activities with recovery potential. High-duty leisure activities comprise work-related activities such as checking one's business mail, task-related activities such as paying bills, and domestic activities such as doing one's chores. As activities with high-duty profile further deplete resources which have already been drained during work or put additional demands on individuals, they impede recovery. Activities with recovery potential comprise low-effort activities such as reading a book, social and physical activities. Sonnentag (2001) suggested that activities with recovery potential allow individuals to leave job demands behind and recovery to occur.

Unexpectedly, not all high-duty-leisure activities were negatively related to recovery and well-being. While work-related activities decreased employees' well-being (Sonnentag, 2001; Sonnentag and Zijlstra, 2006), no detrimental effect was found for domestic (e.g., household and child-care activities) and private task-related activities (e.g., banking activities). Taking care of children or family members seems to be not only demanding but also restorative. In line with these findings, Steptoe, Lundwall and Cropley (2000) compared employees living with a family including children, employees living with a partner, and employees living alone. In their study, recovery was assessed with physiological measures. The authors showed that a decrease in blood pressure, i.e. cardiovascular recovery during the evening, was largest for individuals living with a family, intermediate for individuals living with a partner, and smallest for individuals living alone.

Concerning activities with recovery potential, Sonnentag (2001) found that low-effort, social and physical activities pursued after work positively contribute to an individual's well-being before going to sleep. The beneficial effect of physical activities during leisure time has also been confirmed by several other studies (e.g., Sonnentag and Bayer, 2005; van Hooff et al., 2011). Next to physical activities, low-effort activities were found to increase individuals' well-being. If employees participate in low-effort leisure activities, they feel better recovered the next day, report a better sleep and lower fatigue (Tucker et al., 2008). Concerning the effect of social activities on well-being, results are mixed. Sonnentag and Zijlstra (2006) confirmed the beneficial effect of Sonnentag's (2001) study, whereas another study (Sonnentag and Natter, 2004) showed that flight attendants who participate in social activities during leisure time feel more depressed at night time. On first view, the finding is surprising as meeting with friends or chatting with family members on the phone seem to be enjoyable activities for most people. On the other hand, Sonnentag and Natter (2004) argued that in jobs with high social demands, such as flight attendants, social activities during leisure time further drain the resources that have already been used up at work. For employees working in socially demanding jobs it could be better for recovery to relieve social resources by withdrawing and spending some time alone (Sonnentag and Natter, 2004). Besides physical, low-effort, and social activities, the role of volunteer work has been studied as a potential recovery activity. Volunteer work during leisure time was found to be positively related with different work outcomes, for example affect at work. Employees who participate in volunteer work activities in the evening can satisfy their needs for competence, autonomy, and relatedness and therefore feel better recovered when returning to work the next day (Mojza, Sonnentag and Bornemann, 2011).

As engaging in activities is to a great extent an idiosyncratic experience that can largely differ between persons, Sonnentag and Fritz (2007) suggested that it is not the nature of leisure activities per se but the individual experience that is important in the promotion of recovery and well-being. Sonnentag and Fritz (2007) identified four recovery experiences that account for differences in individual recovery and well-being: psychological detachment, relaxation, mastery experiences, and control during leisure time.

Psychological detachment refers to mentally refraining from job demands during leisure time. Psychological detachment goes beyond physical absence from the work place and implies mentally "switching off" from work. It implies that individuals do not participate in work-related activities (e.g., answering business mails) or work-related thoughts when away from work. The impact of detachment for recovery can be explained using the effort-recovery model (Meijman and Mulder, 1998). As psychological detachment allows refraining from job demands, it contributes to recovery and increases well-being. Several studies have confirmed the beneficial effect of psychological detachment for recovery and well-being. Psychological detachment was found to be positively related to mood and feelings of recovery, and negatively related to health complaints, emotional exhaustion, depressive symptoms, need for recovery, and sleep problems (Sonnentag and Fritz, 2007). If employees cannot detach they are confronted with job demands during leisure time (Fritz and Sonnentag, 2006) and may experience prolonged activation (Brosschot, Pieper and Thayer, 2005). In sum, there is much empirical evidence that psychological detachment increases well-being, whereas insufficient detachment has a contrary effect. But does that mean that all work-related thoughts during leisure time are detrimental to ones' health? This question was addressed by Fritz and Sonnentag's (2005) study. They examined how different weekend experiences contribute to employees' well-being and performance after the weekend. The authors found that individuals who reflected positively about their work, for example about supportive colleagues or achieved goals, during the weekend benefitted in terms of well-being and performance. Employees reported increased pursuit of learning and decreased feelings of burnout after the weekend. Binnewies, Sonnentag and Mojza' (2009b) study confirmed also the positive effect of positive work-related thoughts during leisure time on employees' job performance. It can be concluded, therefore, that it is not necessary to refrain from all work-related thoughts during leisure time. Positive work-related thoughts can even contribute to one's recovery, while only negative, ruminative thoughts about work seem to be detrimental to one's recovery (Fritz and Sonnentag, 2006).

Relaxation during leisure time comprises activities characterized by low activation and positive affect. Relaxation may result from diverse activities, such as listening to music or reading a book. Relaxing activities put no social, physical, and intellectual demands on resources normally required (Tinsley and Eldredge, 1995). Therefore no expenditure of effort is needed, stress reactions are reversed, and well-being increased (Sonnentag, Binnewies and Mojza, 2008). Research confirms the assumed positive effect of relaxation. Hartig et al. (2003) showed that taking an easy walk in a natural environment reduces blood pressure and feelings of anger and increases affect and performance when returning back to work. Furthermore, relaxation predicts affect (Fritz, Sonnentag et al., 2010), feelings of recovery (Binnewies, Sonnentag and Mojza, 2010), health complaints, feelings of burnout, sleep problems, and life satisfaction (Sonnentag and Fritz, 2007). In addition, Siltaloppi, Kinnunen and Feld (2009) reported that relaxation buffers detrimental effects of work stressors. Under high time pressure, relaxation protects against exhaustion.

Mastery experiences refer to leisure activities that foster recovery by providing challenges and learning opportunities (Sonnentag and Fritz, 2007). Typical activities that allow experiencing mastery are rock climbing, taking adult education classes and learning new hobbies (Fritz and Sonnentag, 2006). Volunteering was also identified as a leisure activity evoking mastery experiences (Mojza, Sonnentag and Bornemann, 2011). Although these activities put extra demand (e.g., social engagement, self-regulation) on individuals, they are beneficial in terms of recovery, relying on the conservation of resources theory (Hobfoll, 1989). Mastery experiences contribute to recovery by offering opportunities to experience competence and increase confidence and self-efficacy. Empirical evidence supports the beneficial effect of mastery experiences for recovery. For example, Sonnentag and Fritz (2007) showed that mastery experiences are negatively associated with emotional exhaustion, depressive symptoms, and the need for recovery. Binnewies, Sonnentag and Mojza (2010) reported that individuals who experience mastery during the weekend feel more recovered at the beginning of the working week.

Control during leisure time is an external resource that describes an individual's ability to choose from two or more options (Sonnentag and Fritz, 2007). Having control during leisure time implies that an individual can freely decide which leisure activity to pursue as well as when and how to pursue the activity. Control during leisure time may increase feelings of self-efficacy in relation to recovery during leisure time and should therefore contribute to recovery, in line with the conservation of resources theory (Hobfoll, 1989). Empirical evidence supports this assumption. Griffin et al. (2002) showed in a longitudinal study that low control at home is associated with depression and anxiety symptoms in the long run. Furthermore, control was found to be associated with more favorable affective states (Fritz, Sonnentag et al., 2010), higher life satisfaction and fewer health complaints, burnout depression symptoms, and sleep problems (Sonnentag and Fritz, 2007).

Recovery during Breaks

While vacations, free weekends, and free evenings allow employees to recover from job demands outside work, work breaks offer employees the opportunity to restore their energies within the work day. Even though employees may start their work day feeling completely recovered and refreshed, throughout the day their ability to concentrate and to sustain their effort on work tasks may diminish and they may feel the need to make a break before they can continue to work efficiently (Trougakos and Hideg, 2009). In a literature review, Tucker (2003) showed that work breaks indeed seem to be an effective means of maintaining performance and managing fatigue over prolonged task performance.

Traditionally, the role of work breaks was mainly investigated in the ergonomics literature. Researchers in this domain mostly examined the frequency and timing as well as the length of work breaks as they were interested in the role of work breaks as means to alleviate musculoskeletal discomfort and strain (cf. Tucker, 2003). Only recently, recovery researchers began to focus on the role of rest periods during the work day in the recovery process. As work breaks represent short periods of time during which work-relevant tasks are not required or expected (Trougakos et al., 2008), they can help people to replenish drained self-regulatory and affective resources that are needed for maintaining one's energies at work and completing one's work tasks. A daily diary study by Sanz-Vergel et al. (2010) showed that recovery resulting from work breaks helped employees to maintain their energy throughout the day. Specifically, the authors showed that an employee's feeling of being refreshed and revitalized after work breaks was associated with high levels of vigor in the evening after work.

Employees may use their work breaks for a wide range of activities from running errands, having a snack, or taking a nap. Fritz, Lam and Spreitzer (2011) surveyed a sample of knowledge workers about behaviors they use to maintain their energy at work. The five most common break-related strategies include drinking some water, having a snack, going to the bathroom, drinking a caffeinated beverage, and doing some form of physical activity including walks or stretching. Not all break activities may be equally effective in restoring employees' resources. Trougakos and Hideg (2009) proposed that the nature of work breaks and the activities employees engage in during the work breaks influence the levels of psychological resources, which in turn influence various workplace outcomes. They distinguished two kinds of break activities, namely respites and chores. Respites refer to low-effort or preferred choice activities and thus help to stop resource drain. Chores refer to break activities that continue to draw on the resources utilized during work and thus do not allow employees to recover from the negative effect of work.

In a diary study with cheerleading instructors, Trougakos et al. (2008) examined the effects of respites and chores on emotional states and positive affective displays in customer interactions as one aspect of performance after the breaks. They found that engaging in chore activities during breaks (e.g., practicing material, continuing to work with customers, preparing for upcoming work, running errands) predicted an increase in negative emotional states after the break. Engaging in respite activities (e.g., napping, relaxing, socializing) was positively related to positive emotional states and negatively related to negative emotional states after the breaks. Moreover, engaging in respite activities predicted the cheerleading instructors' positive affective displays in interactions with their students in the after-break sessions.

A study by Krajewski, Sauerland and Wieland (2011) further suggests that not all respite activities may be equally effective. They compared a group of call center agents who practiced progressive muscle relaxation in a silent room cabin during their lunch break to a group of call center agents who spend their lunch break with small talk in the company's social room. Only the progressive muscle relaxation break reduced post-lunchtime and afternoon strain.

A diary study on the effects of several lunch-break activities in a sample of university employees points in the same direction (Trougakos, Hideg and Cheng, 2011). Trougakos, Hideg and Cheng (2011) found that engaging in relaxing lunch-time activities reduced employees' workday fatigue as rated by their co-workers, whereas engaging in social activities and work-related activities increased fatigue. Additionally, they showed that employees' control over how to utilize their lunch break moderated the relations between lunch-break activities and fatigue. Employees high in control were less fatigued by working during the lunch break than employees low in control who worked during the break. People high in control experienced less fatigue when engaging in social lunch-break activities than people low in control. These results suggest that employees' control over their lunch-break activities (i.e., their personal choice) is crucial for the extent to which these activities facilitate or hinder recovery.

Moreover, the study by Trougakos, Hideg and Cheng (2011) further suggests that it is important to investigate boundary conditions of the recovery processes during within-day breaks. Accordingly, Trougakos and Hideg (2009) suggested studying employees' individual characteristics (e.g., extraversion) and work characteristics (e.g., job demands) as potential moderators of the recovery effect of work-break activities.

Individual differences may influence how break activities are appraised and that appraisal may lead to different resource levels. For example, employees high in extraversion may appraise spending the lunch break socializing with colleagues as a preferred choice activity while introverts may not be able to recover their resources during a group lunch. Regarding employees' work characteristics, employees facing high job demands may be more likely to engage in more chore activities during the work break such as working over lunchtime or running errands because they will have to work long. Moreover, quick respites may not be sufficient for employees with high job demands to recover. However, a study by Demerouti et al. (2012) suggested that enjoyment at work as one aspect of work-related flow may compensate for insufficient recovery from work breaks.

Predictors of Recovery during Leisure Time

So far, we have discussed which recovery activities and experiences benefit employees' psychological and physical well-being which in turn benefits well-being and performance at work. Over the last years, research has accumulated showing that the workplace also partly affects employees in the way they engage in and enjoy different activities and experiences during leisure time. Accordingly, Kinnunen et al. (2011) argued that recovery experiences play an important role in how job characteristics are related to employee well-being. Extending the Job Demands–Job Resources model of Demerouti et al. (2001) they proposed that recovery experiences play a mediating role between job demands and job resources on the one hand and employee well-being on the other. According to their reasoning, job demands do not only affect employees at work, they also impair employees' recovery at home by draining employees' resources during the working day, resulting into decreased well-being. Similarly, they assume that job resources benefit employees' recovery at home as job resources are motivating and increase employees' resources, which enables employees to better recover from work stress during leisure time. In their cross-sectional study, Kinnunen et al. (2011) found partial support for their model: higher job demands were associated with decreased psychological detachment and relaxation during leisure time, while higher job resources were related to increased mastery experiences and control during leisure time. Several other studies found support for the assumption that job demands are related to impaired recovery during leisure time (e.g., Cropley, Dijk and Stanley, 2006; Rau and Triemer, 2004; Sonnentag and Bayer, 2005; Sonnentag and Fritz, 2007).

Recently, empirical studies also suggest that employees' segmentation of work and private life foster their psychological detachment (Sonnentag, Kuttler and Fritz, 2010; Park, Fritz and Jex, 2011; Hahn and Dormann, 2013). Additionally, Park and colleagues (2011) also found that work group norms of segmentation of work and private life influence employees' ability to detach from work.

However, until today our knowledge on work-related predictors of recovery is very limited. Knowing which factors at work impair and promote employees' recovery during leisure time is extremely important for organizations as it is the basis for work place design and interventions to foster employees' recovery and work–life balance.

Besides, work-related predictors of recovery, recent research examined the role of employees' spouses or partners as facilitators or inhibitors of recovery. In a study on recovery during the weekend, Hahn, Binnewies and Haun (2012) found that being absorbed in joint activities with the partner fostered employees' recovery experiences. In another study, Hahn and Dormann (2013) found that partners' work–home segmentation preference as well as partners' psychological detachment were associated with employees' psychological detachment.

Consequences of Recovery for Employees' Performance-related Outcomes

Over the last years, recovery research also addressed the question if recovery also benefits performance-related outcomes, which is of utmost important to organizations. Several diary studies showed that when employees are better recovered in the morning they experience more work engagement during the day, they report their work to be less effortful, and display better task performance at work and particularly higher levels of extra-role behaviors such as being proactive, engaging in learning activities, and helping co-workers (Binnewies, Sonnentag and Mojza, 2009a; Kühnel, Sonnentag and Bledow, 2012; Sonnentag, 2003; Sonnentag et al., 2012). Similarly, Binnewies, Sonnentag and Mojza (2010) provided evidence that employees showed higher task performance, more proactive behavior, and more helping behavior in weeks when they felt better recovered after the weekend. Fritz and Sonnentag (2005) also examined recovery during the weekend and found evidence that specific recovery processes, namely social activities (meeting friends, performing activities with others) and positive work reflection (thinking about the positive aspects of one's job) were related to improved job performance after the weekend. Specifically, social activities predicted improved task performance and positive work reflection predicted improved pursuit of learning. In a longitudinal study, Binnewies, Sonnentag and Mojza (2009b) found that feeling recovered was related to an increase in task performance over time mediated by an increase in occupational self-efficacy. Additionally, the authors showed that positive work reflection during leisure time was related to an increase in extra-role behaviors, specifically in proactivity, helping behavior, and creativity. All studies summarized so far relied on self-reports of performance leaving the question if recovery is related to more objective ratings of performance. Fritz, Yankelevich, Zarubin and Barger (2010) examined the role of psychological detachment for employees' task performance and proactive performance using co-worker ratings of performance. Results showed a curvilinear relationship between psychological detachment and both performance dimensions: a medium level of detachment was most beneficial while low and high levels of detachment were associated with lower job performance.

Taken together, several studies showed positive relationships between employees' recovery and different dimensions of job performance. Although not explicitly tested in the studies, relationships were strongest for different extra-role behaviors, specifically proactive behavior, creativity, and helping behavior. It seems that recovery particularly contributes to the flourishing of individuals (Gable and Haidt, 2005) promoting experiences and behaviors (e.g., work engagement, proactive behavior) characterizing employees' active mental health (Warr, 1994). Consequently, promoting employees' recovery and thus fostering their flourishing may be a more effective way to foster desired organizational outcomes such as proactivity and creativity compared to organizational health management interventions which aim at reducing job demands and associated impairments in well-being.

Conclusion: Practical Implications

So far we have outlined that recovery from work stress plays an important role for employees' health and well-being as it is the process reversing the negative consequences of work stress. In addition, recovery positively contributes to work engagement and different performance-related outcomes (e.g., Binnewies, Sonnentag and Mojza, 2010; Fritz, Yankelevich, Zarubin and Barger, 2010; Sonnentag, 2003). Consequently, both employees and organizations should be interested in fostering and maintaining successful recovery. In the following, we discuss potential implications for employees and organizations.

Concerning the implications regarding employees' vacations, it is definitely important for employees to take vacations even if effects are short-lived. Vacations constitute a time period during which individuals feel happy and healthy and which are enjoyed for their own sake (de Bloom et al., 2010). As detaching from work problems is important for vacation's recovering effect, employees should try to minimize contact with their company during vacation (Davidson et al., 2010). Also supervisors and colleagues can contribute to employees' well-being by establishing norms and rules that employees on vacation must not be contacted by phone or email. Additionally, as vacation length does not matter for employees' well-being (de Bloom et al., 2009) it seems to be advisable to take several short vacations over the year instead of taking one long vacation once a year.

Regarding daily recovery and recovery during the weekends, employees and organizations can take different actions. First, research showed that recovery experiences can be fostered by training (Hahn et al., 2011), enabling employees themselves to improve their recovery behavior and enabling organizations to offer recovery training in addition to other personnel development interventions. Second, work design interventions reducing job demands and increasing job resources should both directly and indirectly benefit employees' health as such interventions foster employees' energy resources and other personal resources which are also needed for initiating and engaging in different recovery activities. In addition, organizations can support their employees by providing a recovery-friendly environment. Such a recovery-friendly environment may include providing recreation opportunities (e.g., sports facilities), norms valuing employees' recovery as an important part of employees' life to stay healthy and fit for work (e.g., communicating recovery-promoting initiatives and interventions), or work-time arrangements that allow employees to organize their work and leisure time in a way that supports their recovery.

In sum, employees and organizations alike should become aware that recovery is an important mechanism in preventing the development of strain and diseases in reaction to work stress. Therefore, interventions promoting and enabling recovery should become an integral part of organizations' personnel and organizational development programs to foster employees' health and performance in the short and in the long run.

References

Binnewies, C., Sonnentag, S. and Mojza, E.J. (2009a) Daily performance at work: Feeling recovered in the morning as a predictor of day-level job performance. *Journal of Organizational Behavior*, 30, 67–93.

—— (2009b) Feeling recovered and thinking about the good sides of one's work. A longitudinal study on the benefits of non-work experiences for job performance. *Journal of Occupational Health Psychology*, 14, 243–56.

—— (2010) Recovery during the weekend and fluctuations in weekly job performance: A week-level study examining intra-individual relationships. *Journal of Occupational and Organizational Psychology*, 83, 419–41.

Brosschot, J., Pieper, S. and Thayer, J. (2005) Expanding stress theory: Prolonged activation and perseverative cognition. *Psychoneuroendocrinology*, 30, 1043–9.

Cropley, M., Dijk, D.-J. and Stanley, N. (2006) Job strain, work rumination, and sleep in school teachers. *European Journal of Work and Organizational Psychology*, 15, 181–96.

Davidson, O.B., Eden, D., Westman, M., Cohen-Charash, Y., Hammer, L.B., Kluger, A.N., Krausz, M., Maslach, C., O'Driscoll, M., Perrewe, P.L., Quick, J.C., Rosenblatt, Z. and Spector, P.E. (2010) Sabbatical leave: Who gains and how much? *Journal of Applied Psychology*, 95, 953–64.

de Bloom, J., Geurts, S.A.E., Taris, T.W., Sonnentag, S., de Weerth, C. and Kompier, M.A.J. (2010) Effects of vacation from work on health and well-being: Lots of fun, quickly gone. *Work and Stress*, 24, 196–216.

de Bloom, J., Kompier, M., Geurts, S., de Weerth, Taris, T. and Sonnentag, S. (2009) Do we recover from vacation? Meta-analysis of vacation effects on health and well-being. *Journal of Occupational Health Psychology*, 51, 13–25.

Demerouti, E., Bakker, A.B., Nachreiner, F. and Schaufeli, W.B. (2001) The job demands-resources model of burnout. *Journal of Applied Psychology*, 86, 499–512.

Demerouti, E., Bakker, A.B., Sonnentag, S. and Fullagar, C.J. (2012) Work-related flow and energy at work and at home: A study on the role of daily recovery. *Journal of Organizational Behavior*, 33, 276–95.

Fritz, C., Lam, C.F. and Spreitzer, G.M. (2011) It's the little things that matter: An examination of knowledge workers' energy management. *The Academy of Management Perspectives*, 25, 28–39.

Fritz, C. and Sonnentag, S. (2005) Recovery, health and job performance: Effects of weekend experiences. *Journal of Occupational Health Psychology*, 10, 187–99.

—— (2006) Recovery, well-being and performance-related outcomes: The role of work load and vacation experiences. *Journal of Applied Psychology*, 91, 936–45.

Fritz, C., Sonnentag, S., Spector, P.E. and McInroe, J.A. (2010) The weekend matters: Relationships between stress recovery and affective experiences. *Journal of Organizational Behavior*, 31, 1137–62.

Fritz, C., Yankelevich, M., Zarubin, A. and Barger, P. (2010) Happy, healthy and productive? The role of detachment from work during leisure time. *Journal of Applied Psychology*, 95, 977–83.

Gable, S.L. and Haidt, J. (2005) What (and why) is positive psychology? *Review of General Psychology*, 9, 103–10.

Geurts, S.A.E. and Sonnentag, S. (2006) Recovery as an explanatory mechanism in the relation between acute stress reactions and chronic health impairment. *Scandinavian Journal of Work, Environment and Health*, 32, 482–92.

Griffin, J.M., Fuhrer, R., Stansfeld, S.A. and Marmot, M. (2002) The importance of low control at work and home on depression and anxiety: Do these effects vary by gender and social class? *Social Science and Medicine*, 54, 783–98.

Gump, B.B. and Matthews, K.A. (2000) Are vacations good for your health? The 9-year mortality experience after the multiple risk factor intervention trial. *Psychosomatic Medicine*, 62, 608–12.

Hahn, V.C., Binnewies, C. and Haun, S. (2012) The role of partners for employees' recovery during the weekend. *Journal of Vocational Behavior*, 80, 288–98.

Hahn, V.C., Binnewies, C., Sonnentag, S. and Mojza, E.J. (2011) Learning how to recover from job stress: Effects of a recovery training program on recovery, recovery-related self-efficacy, and well-being. *Journal of Occupational Health Psychology*, 16, 202–16.

Hahn, V.C. and Dormann, C. (2013) The role of partners and children for employees' psychological detachment from work and well-being. *Journal of Applied Psychology*, 98(1), 26–36.

Hartig, T., Evans, G.W., Jamner, L.D., Davis, D.S. and Gärling, T. (2003) Tracking restoration in natural and urban field settings. *Journal of Environmental Psychology*, 23, 109–23.

Hobfoll, S.E. (1989) Conservation of resources: A new attempt at conceptualizing stress. *American Psychologist*, 44, 513–24.

Kinnunen, U., Feldt, T., Siltaloppi, M. and Sonnentag, S. (2011) Job demands-resources model in the context of recovery: Testing recovery experiences as mediators. *European Journal of Work and Organizational Psychology*, 20, 805–32.

Krajewski, J., Sauerland, M. and Wieland, R. (2011) Relaxation-induced cortisol changes within lunch breaks: An experimental longitudinal worksite field study. *Journal of Occupational and Organizational Psychology*, 84(2), 382–94.

Kühnel, J. and Sonnentag, S. (2011) How long do you benefit from vacation? A closer look at the fade-out of vacation effects. *Journal of Organizational Behavior*, 32, 125–43.

Kühnel, J., Sonnentag, S. and Bledow, R. (2012) Resources and time pressure as day-level antecedents of work engagement. *Journal of Occupational and Organizational Psychology*, 85, 181–98.

Meijman, T.F. and Mulder, G. (1998) Psychological aspects of workload. In P.J.D. Drenth and H. Thierry (eds) *Handbook of Work and Organizational Psychology*. Vol. 2, *Work Psychology*, 2nd edn. Hove: Psychology Press/Erlbaum Taylor and Francis, pp. 5–33.

Mojza, E.J., Sonnentag, S. and Bornemann, C. (2011) Volunteer work as a valuable leisure-time activity: A day-level study on volunteer work, non-work experiences, and well-being at work. *Journal of Occupational and Organizational Psychology*, 84, 123–52.

Muraven, M. and Baumeister, R.F. (2000) Self-regulation and depletion of limited resources: Does self-control resemble a muscle? *Psychological Bulletin*, 126, 247–59.

Park, Y., Fritz, C. and Jex, S.M. (2011) Relationships between work-home segmentation and psychological detachment from work: The role of communication technology use at home. *Journal of Occupational Health Psychology*, 16, 457–67.

Rau, R. and Triemer, A. (2004) Overtime in relation to blood pressure and mood during work, leisure, and night time. *Social Indicators Research*, 67, 51–73.

Sanz-Vergel, A.I., Demerouti, E., Moreno-Jiménez, B. and Mayo, M. (2010) Work-family balance and energy: A day-level study on recovery conditions. *Journal of Vocational Behavior*, 76, 118–30.

Saxbe, D.E., Repetti, R.L. and Nishina, A. (2008) Marital satisfaction, recovery from work, and diurnal cortisol among men and women. *Health Psychology*, 27, 15–25.

Siltaloppi, M., Kinnunen, U. and Feldt, T. (2009) Recovery experiences as moderators between psychosocial work characteristics and occupational well-being. *Work and Stress*, 23, 330–48.

Sluiter, J.K., van der Beek, A.J. and Frings-Dresen, M.H.W. (1999) The influence of work characteristics on the need for recovery and experienced health: A study on coach drivers. *Ergonomics*, 42, 573–83.

Sonnentag, S. (2001) Work, recovery activities, and individual well-being: A diary study. *Journal of Occupational Health Psychology*, 6, 196–210.

—— (2003) Recovery, work engagement, and proactive behavior: A new look at the interface between nonwork and work. *Journal of Applied Psychology*, 88, 518–28.

Sonnentag, S. and Bayer, U.-V. (2005) Switching off mentally: predictors and consequences of psychological detachment from work during off-job time. *Journal of Occupational Health Psychology*, 10, 393–414.

Sonnentag, S., Binnewies, C. and Mojza, E.J. (2008) "Did you have a nice evening?" A day-level study on recovery experiences, sleep and affect. *Journal of Applied Psychology*, 93, 674–84.

Sonnentag, S. and Fritz, C. (2007) The Recovery Experience Questionnaire: Development and validation of a measure for assessing recuperation and unwinding from work. *Journal of Occupational Health Psychology*, 12, 204–21.

Sonnentag, S. and Geurts, S.A.E. (2009) Methodological issues in recovery research. In S. Sonnentag, P.L. Perrewé and D.C. Ganster (eds) *Current Perspectives on Job-Stress Recovery*, vol. 7. Bingley: JAI Press/Emerald Group Publishing, pp. 1–46.

Sonnentag, S. and Jelden, S. (2009) Job stressors and the pursuit of sport activities: A day-level perspective. *Journal of Occupational Health Psychology*, 14, 165–81.

Sonnentag, S., Kuttler, I. and Fritz, C. (2010) Job stressors, emotional exhaustion, and need for recovery: A multi-source study on the benefits of psychological detachment. *Journal of Vocational Behavior*, 76(3), 355–65.

Sonnentag, S., Mojza, E.J., Demerouti, E. and Bakker, A.B. (2012) Reciprocal relations between recovery and work engagement: The moderating role of job stressors. *Journal of Applied Psychology*, 97, 842–53.

Sonnentag, S. and Natter, E. (2004) Flight attendants' daily recovery from work: Is there no place like home? *International Journal of Stress Management*, 11, 366–91.

Sonnentag, S. and Zijlstra, F.R.H. (2006) Job characteristics and off-job activities as predictors of need for recovery and well-being. *Journal of Applied Psychology*, 91, 330–50.

Steptoe, A., Lundwall, K. and Cropley, M. (2000) Gender, family structure and cardiovascular activity during the working day and evening. *Social Science and Medicine*, 50, 531–9.

Strauss-Blasche, G., Ekmekcioglu, C. and Marktl, W. (2000) Does vacation enable recuperation? Changes in well-being associated with time away from work. *Occupational Medicine*, 50, 167–72.

Tinsley, H. and Eldredge, B.D. (1995) Psychological benefits of leisure participation: A taxonomy of leisure activities based on their need-gratifying properties. *Journal of Counseling Psychology*, 42, 123–32.

Trougakos, J.P., Beal, D.J., Green, S.G. and Weiss, H.M. (2008) Making the break count: An episodic examination of recovery activities, emotional experiences, and affective delivery. *Academy of Management Journal*, 51, 131–46.

Trougakos, J.P. and Hideg, I. (2009) Momentary work recovery: The role of within-day work breaks. In S. Sonnentag, P.L. Perrewé and D.C. Ganster (eds) *Current Perspectives in Job-Stress Recovery. Research in Organizational Stress and Well-Being*, vol. 7. Bingley: Emerald Group Publishing, pp. 37–84.

Trougakos, J.P., Hideg, I. and Cheng, B.H. (2011) Lunch breaks unpacked: Examining the effect of daily lunch break activities and control over break activities on fatigue. Paper presented at the Academy of Management annual conference San Antonio, TX, August.

Tucker, P. (2003) The impact of rest breaks upon accident risk, fatigue and performance: A review. *Work and Stress*, 17, 123–37.

Tucker, P., Dahlgren, A., Akerstedt, T. and Waterhouse, J. (2008) The impact of free-time activities on sleep, recovery and well-being. *Applied Ergonomics*, 39, 653–62.

van Hooff, M.L.M., Geurts, S.A.E., Beckers, D.G.J. and Kompier, M.A.J. (2011) Daily recovery from work: The role of activities, effort and pleasure. *Work and Stress*, 25, 55–74.

Warr, P. (1994) A conceptual framework for the study of work and mental health. *Work and Stress*, 8, 84–97.

Westman, M. and Eden, D. (1997) Effects of a respite from work on burnout: Vacation relief and fade-out. *Journal of Applied Psychology*, 82, 516–27.

CHAPTER 11 Respite Redux

DOV EDEN AND MINA WESTMAN

Introduction

A little more than a decade ago reviews of the respite research that had been conducted up to that time were published (Eden, 2001a, 2001b). The present chapter summarizes briefly what we knew then and reviews, but does not exhaust, what we have learned since. Spawned from methodological considerations, respite research had expanded into research on a variety of off-the-job respites including forced leave due to computer shutdowns, holidays, vacations, semester breaks, reserve military duty, and business trips. Since then research has waxed both in volume and in variety. Researchers have studied the effects of short respites such as evenings and weekends at home and of much longer respites, namely, a year-long sabbatical leave. Furthermore, researchers have expanded the methods beyond comparing individuals before and after respites from work to colleagues that remain at work using interrupted time-series survey designs to diary analysis. Using more articulated data collection methods, researchers have begun learning about the importance of what happens during the respite: how, where, and with whom off-the-job respite time is spent. Finally, respite research has been enriched by broader theoretical conceptualization leading to greater understanding and initial notions about practical applications to capitalize on respite's potential benefits. Suggestions for advancing future research into such issues as the respite–work–family interface and application of experimental design to issues such as respite length, timing, frequency, and content are provided.

Why Study Respites?

Prior to the advent of respite research (Eden, 1982, 1990), most job stress research was based on causally ambiguous correlations between stressors and strains. Such correlations can be attributed to the hypothesized causal effects of stress on strain and equally plausibly to the effects of strain on stress (for an object-lesson in the ambiguity of correlational data and reverse causality, see Lowen and Craig, 1968); individuals experiencing a great deal of strain may perceive greater stress. Experimentation is ruled out because ethical considerations preclude exposing participants to unnecessary stressors merely to study their ill-effects. Maximal internal validity in an ethically-acceptable design on the effects of stress can best be achieved using the on-again off-again nature of respite research. A pattern of rising and falling levels of measured subjective stress and strain that coincides with corresponding alternating periods of objectively stressful and relaxed or routine circumstances, confirms the stress hypothesis.

Beginnings

Caplan and Jones (1975) measured stress and strain among students just prior to an acutely stressful computer shutdown and several months later, after the summer semester break. Stress and strain were higher on the first occasion than on the second. Although Caplan and Jones focused on stress, they did show a respite effect without so dubbing it. Next, Eden (1982) studied the effects of two "critical job events" among student nurses by measuring stress and strain five times, before, during, and after each objectively stressful event. Stress and strain peaked on the stressful occasions and ebbed between them, evidencing what Eden dubbed "respite effects." Both of these studies involved comparison of objectively highly stressful and less stressful occasions; vacation itself was not the focus of the hypotheses.

Unrelated to these studies, Lounsbury and Hoopes (1986) studied vacation using a single-group pre-test/post-test design measuring well-being on two occasions, just before and just after vacation. They found that after vacation job involvement declined and life satisfaction and turnover intentions increased. They had no observation during the vacation, rendering causal attribution risky. Then Eden (1990) replicated and extended Caplan and Jones' computer shutdown study including more occasions, one of which was a holiday vacation, again with the intention of studying the effects of stress using the vacation respite as a control occasion. One of the measuring occasions was during the holiday while participants were at home. Again, subjective stress rose and fell as predicted, but contrary to prediction, strain remained constant. This unexpected pattern of findings sparked a discussion of what could explain why strain remained unabated during the vacation despite the reduction in subjective stress and the construct of "vacation stress" was introduced. From these beginnings, vacation emerged as a focus of research in its own right, not merely as a control condition to highlight the effects of job stress.

Vacation as Job Stress Relief Emerges as a Focus

Research integrating the study of job stress and vacation as a type of respite relief soon followed. Increasing the number of occasions studied, Westman and Eden (1997) measured stress and strain among clerks twice before, once during, and twice after a vacation. They detected a respite effect and also a fadeout effect, as strain returned half way to its pre-vacation level by three days after return to work and dissipated completely by three weeks later. They found also that women reported greater pre-vacation stress, greater respite relief, and greater post-vacation return to their pre-vacation level. Another moderator effect detected was for vacation satisfaction: individuals who enjoyed their vacations also enjoyed respite relief, whereas those who did not enjoy their vacations got no relief. Westman and Eden discussed burnout and its relief in terms of "burnout climate" at work and in terms of interpersonal stress crossover (see Westman, 2001). Finally, they invoked Hobfoll's conservation of resources (COR) theory (see below) to explain respite effects; previous respite research had been conspicuously atheoretical.

Etzion and Sapir (1997) measured stress and burnout among industrial workers before their vacations and twice after returning to work. They also had a comparison group of workers that remained on the job during this time. They found a respite effect. Their study appears to have been the first to put the focus on vacation as the topic of respite research, rather than as a "control" event useful for studying the ill-effects of job stress.

Moving beyond previous studies, Westman and Etzion (2001) added self-report measures of performance and retrieved data on absenteeism from personnel files in a food manufacturing company. They found substantial respite effects and fadeout. Furthermore, self-reported performance was significantly higher immediately after vacation than before vacation; however, it faded, returning to its pre-vacation level a month after returning to work. Health-related absenteeism immediately after vacation did not differ significantly from the rate before vacation but it dropped significantly four weeks after vacation. Absenteeism for other reasons was lower two weeks after vacation than before vacation. Four weeks after vacation absenteeism was significantly lower than prior to vacation but higher than immediately after the vacation; it was trending toward fadeout. Finally, moderator analysis did not replicate the previous findings of Westman and Eden; there were no differences between men and women or between those who enjoyed their vacations and those who did not. Replication using objective performance measures and absentee rates would establish respites as a potential source of renewed human energy to fuel organizational effectiveness.

Beyond Vacation: Other Types of Respites

Arguing that active reserve service in the Israel Defense Forces serves as a release mechanism for "letting off steam" among Israeli men, Etzion, Eden and Lapidot (1998) predicted that being away from job stressors would have an ameliorative impact on burnout. Previous respite research had lacked a comparison group of similar others not simultaneously experiencing a respite. Etzion et al. rectified this by comparing 81 men who were mobilized for active reserve service to 81 matched controls in the same company who were not mobilized during the same period. Each reservist and his control completed questionnaires shortly before the former left work for service and immediately upon his return. Job stress and burnout declined among those who were mobilized. There was no change among the control respondents. The quality of reserve service and the degree of psychological detachment from work moderated these respite effects; the greater the detachment, the stronger the effect that positive reserve service experience had in relieving reservists of stress and burnout. Those who failed to detach during reserve service respite failed to reap its respite benefits. Thus, reserve service is a special case of stress-relieving get-away from work that may relieve stress and strain as does vacation. The magnitude of the respite effect depends on the amount of psychological detachment from the job back home. As an aside, Etzion et al. suggested that psychological detachment may be as important on the job as during respites. Since this study, psychological detachment during vacation and other respites has emerged as a major moderator of respite effects.

Seeking evidence for crossover of strain between partners in two studies, Etzion and Westman (2001) analyzed the relationships between stress and burnout among dual-career couples on two occasions, one stressful and the other a less stressful respite. They found that crossover of burnout occurred on the stressful occasion but not during the respite. Of course, a simple explanation of Etzion and Westman's findings is that there was no stress crossover during the low-stress respite because there was little stress to cross over. An intriguing implication of these findings is that contact between spouses may or may not occasion contagion, depending on when the contact occurs. If Etzion and Westman's findings can be replicated, then salutogenic interventions geared toward facilitating cross-partner relief (e.g., reducing a wife's strain in order to facilitate a reduction in the husband's strain) may be worthwhile. However, this may occur only during stressful times when there is abundant strain to relieve, but not during a respite, when the partner's strain is already lower. At any rate, comparing stress-strain crossover relationships during high and low stress periods is an innovation that might spur further use of respite occasions in moderator analyses to help clarify the high-stress/low-stress conditions under which other variables relate to each other.

A special kind of respite from chronic job stress with unique characteristics is international business travel, defined as travelling for the organization for periods of a week or so while crossing international borders. A business trip seems to be a dual experience, consisting of hassles and uplifts, losses and gains, all impacting the well-being of the travelers. According to conservation of resources theory (COR; Hobfoll, 1989; see below), resource gain enables individuals to combat stress and any kind of respite is a time for launching a gain spiral and recharging batteries. In this respect, international business trips are similar to other kinds of respite. Resource gain during the trip may help in buffering and ameliorating the effect of resource loss in the pre-trip stage. Thus, COR theory lends a wide theoretical ground to the area of business travel. By leaving the routine working atmosphere and distancing oneself from chronic job demands, the travelers might not only cease the loss of resources resulting from job pressure and family demands, but also gain new ones such as new friends, increased sense of self-efficacy, new cultural experiences, rest, pleasant experiences, detachment, and the like. Thus, though business travelers are exposed to job demands while away, they are not exposed to the authentic organizational physical environment and direct contact with bosses and peers. Furthermore, according to COR theory, the pre- and post-stages of the trip are characterized by losses whereas the trip itself (being away) is a period that enables recharging batteries, accumulating resources and initiating a resource spiral.

Westman and Etzion (2002) were the first to study the impact of overseas business trips on job stress and burnout. They studied 57 employees who travel abroad on average four times per year for an absence of six days on average as part of their job. Substantial declines in stress and burnout were detected immediately after the trip. These respite effects were larger among those who were most satisfied with their trip. Westman and Etzion opined that an overseas business trip does not have the same impact as a vacation though the employee is absent from his or her routine work environment. They attributed the high level of burnout prior to the trip to excessive overload, ambiguity, and threatening job demands, and described the period abroad as also characterized by ambiguity and overload. Both the anticipation of the overseas trip and the work abroad itself may have had a negative impact on employees. Only when they return to their routine jobs does their burnout wane.

Westman and Etzion showed that a working respite is not the same as a vacation respite. Their participants reported less stress and strain after return, indicating a delayed, post-respite effect. This is different from a vacation respite effect, which is experienced *during* the respite. This points to the need for a typology of respites, each type with its distinguishing characteristics and degree of relief from stress and strain that it affords. We need research on other types of working respites, such as when absenting the routine workplace for training. Finally, it became apparent that sounder theoretical underpinnings were needed for respite research to advance.

Aiming to replicate Westman and Etzion's (2002) findings, Westman and her colleagues conducted two additional studies to explore fluctuations of work–family conflict and burnout. They focused on the work–family interface, as the potential for stresses arising from the work and family domains that exists in most occupations is even more apparent for people engaged in business travel, particularly at the interface of family and work demands. The work–family interface is affected by the structural characteristics of the two roles. Work-related travel renders the traveler temporarily unavailable to fulfill his/her family-related roles. This can increase work–family conflict (WFC) and strain such as burnout. On the other hand, a business trip can be perceived as a respite from the overt WFC, as the person is away from home.

Westman, Etzion and Gurtler (2004) examined fluctuations in the experience of conflict between work and family (WFC) and burnout in different phases of business travel among 58 business travelers (74 percent male) who completed questionnaires at three points in time: prior to going abroad, during the stay abroad, and after their return. They detected a different pattern of fluctuations in the levels of both WFC and burnout according to gender. Gender moderated the fluctuations of WFC, demonstrating that WFC remains constant for men before and during the trip but decreases significantly during the post-trip phase. Among women, WFC decreased from pre-trip to mid-trip and then increased significantly upon returning home. Thus, whereas for men the least WFC is experienced upon returning home, for women the lowest level is during the trip and the highest level of WFC is experienced upon returning home. No differences were detected for men in mean burnout during the various stages of the trip, whereas women's burnout was similar both before and during the trip but decreased significantly upon returning home. These findings lend support to Westman and Etzion's (2002) suggestion that business travel is a special kind of respite that affords detachment and gain of resources, thus reducing stress and strain.

In a follow-up study, Westman, Etzion and Gattenio (2008) similarly examined fluctuations in the levels of work–family conflict (WFC), family–work conflict (FWC), and burnout during three different stages of international business trips among 66 business travelers (70 percent male) who completed questionnaires prior to the trip, during the stay abroad, and after the trip. As between and within-individual sources of variation were analyzed, the design captured the dynamic nature of work and family roles. Analysis of variance detected differences in WFC, FWC, and burnout levels among the three stages of the trip, moderated by gender. WFC, FWC, and burnout fluctuated across trip stages; all three decreased during the trip and increased after the trip. Gender moderated these fluctuations for both WFC and FWC but not for burnout. Men experienced no significant change in WFC and FWC in the different stages of the trip. In contrast, women's WFC fluctuated: it was lowest during the trip and highest after the trip. Burnout decreased among women from the pre-trip stage to the trip itself. No significant differences were detected for men in mean burnout during the various stages of the trip, whereas women's burnout was highest during the pre-trip stage and decreased significantly during the trip. These results may be considered similar to past findings that burnout was at its lowest during different kinds of respite (e.g., Davidson et al., 2010; Westman and Eden, 1997).

The literature concerning the role of gender on respite is scant. Westman and Eden (1997) found that women had higher levels of burnout than men before and after vacation. They also found that women benefited more from vacation as they had lower levels of burnout than men during the vacation, perhaps because women have a greater need of respite due to their exposure to additional home–work conflict stressors. During vacation home–work conflict vanishes and burnout wanes. Future research on the role of gender in respite phenomena is likely to yield greater understanding of respite effects and dynamics.

Double-whammy Theoretical Underpinning for Respite Research Emerges

The earliest respite research was notably atheoretical (e.g., Eden, 1982, 1990). Westman (1999) and Westman and Eden (1997) enriched the theoretical basis of respite research by embedding it in Hobfoll's (1989, 1998, 2001) conservation of resources (COR) theory. In the current chapter we embed respite research also in the JD-R model. Together the JD-R model and COR theory offer complementary theoretical perspectives for respite research.

Conservation of resources (COR) theory's basic tenet is that individuals are seen as motivated to obtain, retain, foster, and protect those things they value (food, shelter, a positive sense of an effective self, and primary social ties). Further, secondary resources are needed to preserve these primary resources. These secondary resources include such things as work, family, insurance, time, credit, and other concrete and abstract structures and entities that are part and parcel of the cultural web that all cultures create to support primary resources. COR theory is both a stress theory and a motivational theory that outlines how individuals and organizations are likely to be impacted by stressful circumstances, and how individuals and organizations act in order to garner and protect their resources. According to COR theory, resource loss is the primary operating mechanism driving stress reactions. COR theory suggests that, in the face of adversity, people mobilize their remaining resources to offset the ongoing challenges that confront them. To the extent that they succeed in limiting resource loss, they manifest fewer negative outcomes. This is because these resources are integral to the individuals' ability to offset stress, improve their conditions, and deter future stressful experiences. COR theory also posits that resource gain has less impact than does resource loss. However, gain in some resources becomes especially important during periods of loss in other resources. Research must examine not only resource loss but also resource gain processes.

The JD-R model supplements COR theory. Bakker and Demerouti (e.g., Bakker and Demerouti, 2007; Demerouti et al., 2001) developed the JD-R model as a resource-based approach that focuses on the dynamics of resources and their outcomes. This model is a heuristic model that specifies how two specific sets of working conditions, namely job demands and job resources, contribute to employee well-being. According to the JD-R model, job demands are physical, psychological, social, or organizational aspects of the job that require sustained effort (e.g., workload, emotional demands) and are therefore associated with physiological and psychological costs. Job resources are those physical, psychological, social, or organizational aspects of the job that (a) reduce job demands and their associated physiological and psychological costs, (b) are functional in achieving work goals, or (c) stimulate personal growth, learning, and development.

According to Bakker and Demerouti (2007), the JD-R model postulates the coexistence of two underlying psychological processes. The *strain* process occurs when chronic job demands exhaust employee energy. This process is in line with COR theory's (Hobfoll, 2001) loss cycles whereby initial loss begets further loss, creating loss spirals that lead to resource depletion and strain. The *motivational* process implies that job resources have an arousing, energizing potential because they foster employee growth, learning, and development. Job resources may fulfill basic human needs such as autonomy, relatedness, and competence. We hypothesize that respites facilitate this need fulfillment. This aspect of resources leading to positive outcomes such as engagement and performance are not apparent in COR theory. The role of the recourses in COR theory is to prevent loss and to create a "resource caravan" that will be used in case of loss or threat of loss. The addition of the positive outcomes in the JD-R, becoming engaged during vacation, may enhance the advantage of respite and may slow post-vacation fadeout.

Hobfoll (1998) developed COR theory as a general approach to understanding stress and coping in life whereas Bakker and Demerouti (2007) intended JD-R theory specifically to explain stress and strain at work. JD-R constructs are clearer and easier to measure. Furthermore, the JD-R model suggests that when studying a specific profession researchers may focus on demands and resources specific to this profession or occupation.

A further addition of the JD-R model is the buffering hypothesis. The model proposes that job resources may buffer the impact of job demands on negative job-related outcomes. The buffering hypothesis explains interactions between job demands and job resources by proposing that the relationship between job demands and strain is weaker for those enjoying a large amount of job resources. This buffering notion supports predictions regarding the level of strain or motivation as a function of levels of demands and resources. Thus, resources serve not only to prevent stress but also to moderate, or buffer the relationship between stress and strain.

Thus, both COR and JD-R theories emphasize the importance of resources. This theoretical integration is directed toward a more elaborate comprehension of the dynamics underlying human experiences and behavior in work and non-work environments. COR theory and the JD-R model provide grounds for conceptualizing vacation as an opportunity for a beneficial process of reducing stress and decreasing strain (burnout) while JD-R also emphasizes that enhancing resources leads to job engagement and other positive outcomes.

The practical upshot is that, based on COR theory and the JD-R model, managers can improve employee well-being by enriching employee resources. Understanding the results of the various combinations of demands and resources can help organizations plan respites in such a way that they will generate important benefits for employee well-being. For example, they could provide opportunities to gain resources and train employees how to gain resources whether from active or passive experiences and try to find a fit between needs and experiences during respite.

Greater Articulation and Elaboration of the Respite Relief Process

Subsequent research has been more theory-based and has shed light on four important issues that the research reviewed above raised but did not specifically address. These include (a) the length of the respite, (b) fadeout, (c) the nature of the activities respitees (individuals on respite) engage in and with whom, and (d) how respitees subjectively experience these activities. Below we review some of the research that sheds light on these issues; space limitation does not allow for a comprehensive review of all the relevant research. These studies expanded the data collection methods (e.g., diaries) and the types of respites studied (evenings at home, weekends, ski vacations, etc.). The division into subsections is arbitrary and could be done in various ways because all four of these issues are interconnected and some studies have addressed more than one issue.

BRIEF AND LONGER RESPITES: EVENINGS AT HOME, WEEKENDS, AND SHORT AND LONG VACATIONS

De Bloom et al.'s (2009) meta-analysis of vacation research showed that vacation has small, positive effects on health and well-being and that these positive effects fade fast. However, most of the earlier studies lacked observation during vacation and some studies even neglected to report the duration of the vacation. In other studies (e.g. Strauss-Blasche, Ekmekcioglu and Marktl, 2000; Westman and Eden, 1997; Westman and Etzion, 2001), the length of the vacation was rather long, ranging between nine and 14 days. Accordingly, most of the effects found till now are relevant mainly to vacations of this length. Nevertheless, the relationship between length of vacation and the strength and duration of vacation relief effects is still unclear. Further disentangling of this relationship could imply practical guidance in vacation planning to conserve long-term health and well-being. For example, consider five three-day weekends off work, which would include five days off beyond the standard five-day work-week and two-day weekend. This would accumulate the equivalence of a whole work-week off. Spreading out the respite days in this manner may or may not bring overall greater relief and rejuvenation than would a whole week off. Management could try to maximize individual respite relief by letting individual employees choose how to spread out their vacation days over the year. Allowing individuals to bunch them up or spread them out – or to take some vacation days bunched and some spread out – according to their own personal predilection may result in greater overall personal benefit. Letting individuals choose for themselves is an important value in itself; it may increase subjective well-being. However, the benefits – or lack thereof – of such spreading has yet to be tested. We need research that contrasts the amount and duration of the relief provided by short, intermediate, and long respites.

De Bloom, Geurts and Kompier (2012) investigated whether employee health and well-being improved during vacations of only four or five days. They also determined how long any improvement lasts after returning home and resuming work and to what extent vacation activities and experiences during such short vacations explain health improvements during and after the vacations. They measured five times (two weeks before vacation, once during vacation, on the day of returning home, and on the third and tenth day after returning). Employees reported higher health and well-being during these short vacations. However, fadeout came quickly; on the third day after returning home all participants had resumed work, and positive vacation effects had faded out entirely. These and other fadeout findings suggest that work resumption and the associated increased strain due to renewed exposure to job stressors cause the dissipation of positive vacation effects very soon after returning to work.

Despite the fact that positive respite effects wash out so rapidly after work resumption, regular vacations seem to be of truly vital importance. Gump and Matthews (2000) followed 12,338 men at risk for coronary heart disease and found that not taking annual vacations is associated with an increased risk of morbidity and even mortality nine years later. A question that remains unanswered still is how long vacations must be to generate such healthy and life-giving benefits.

SABBATICAL: THE LONGEST RESPITE

The sabbatical study was in the proposal stage when the Eden (2001a, 2001b) reviews were published. Davidson et al. (2010) conducted a rigorous, longitudinal, quasi-experiment to test the ameliorative effects of a sabbatical leave as a special case of respite from routine work among academics. Basing their research on COR theory and positive psychology, they hypothesized that respite increases resource level and well-being. The sample included 129 faculty members on sabbatical and 129 matched controls at ten universities in three countries. Sabbatees and their controls completed measures of resource gain, resource loss, and well-being before, during, and after the sabbatical. The results confirmed COR theory. Among the sabbatees (i.e., individuals on sabbatical leave), resource loss and negative well-being diminished whereas resource gain and positive well-being waxed during the sabbatical. The matched controls showed no change. Analyses revealed that resource gain and resource loss mediated the respite effects. Several individual differences and respite features moderated these respite effects; those who reported higher respite self-efficacy and greater control, were more detached, and had a more positive sabbatical experience, enjoyed more enhanced well-being than others. Finally, sabbatees that spent their sabbatical outside their home country gained less while away and lost more upon returning home. An unexpected finding was that life satisfaction showed a gradual, year-long decline among the control colleagues; the sabbatical respite offset and actually reversed this downward slide into increasing burnout. This finding fits well with Gump and Matthews' (2000) morbidity and mortality results.

Sabbatical is the longest respite studied so far. Previous evaluations of sabbatical leave were mostly anecdotal. Davidson et al. did the first internally valid research that confirmed the commonly held view that sabbaticals are not merely maxi-vacations that pamper privileged professors; rather, during the sabbatical respite important positive things happen to bolster well-being and, potentially, future productivity. However, inasmuch as psychological detachment was the most consistent moderator in the sabbatical study, the detachment that enables respite relief is threatened by the advent of communication devices that enable cheap back-home communication anytime, anywhere. It is predictable that, as future sabbatees remain in constant contact with the back-home department and colleagues, these electronic tethers will deny them some – if not all – of the salutogenic value of their sabbatical respite.

VACATION ACTIVITIES AND EXPERIENCES: WHAT ONE DOES DURING RESPITE RELATES TO ITS CONSEQUENCES

It is abundantly clear from the research reviewed above that vacation and other respites from work offer the chance to recover from work demands and to build new resources. Advancing beyond this dichotomous comparison of respite versus no respite, De Bloom et al.'s (2009) theoretical thinking led them to propose that vacation is a most powerful respite due to two underlying mechanisms. The "passive" mechanism produces the relief from daily job demands whereas the "active" mechanism involves engagement in potentially restorative activities. These mechanisms relate to resource gain and loss and are conceptually consistent with COR theory and JD-R theory, as proposed in this chapter. These theoretical propositions imply that what one does during a respite may be as important as respite's length and frequency. Thus, there may be specific experiences that have positive – or negative – impact on recovery processes and subsequent well-being. Without basing it on any particular theoretical grounds, Eden (2001a) proposed that vacations may not be uniformly positive experiences but, they may provide "relief or misery" depending on various individual factors as well as respite features and the fit between them. Eden (2001a) called for further research on how the type of activity individuals engage in during respites influences well-being (Eden, 2001b). Subsequent research has begun examining this issue.

Following Hobfoll (1998) and results of several vacation studies (Eden, 1990; Etzion, Eden and Lapidot, 1998; Fritz and Sonnentag, 2005), one should differentiate experiences that consume resources from experiences that generate resources. Vacation experiences that consume resources pose additional demands on the individual, which may increase perceived stress, decrease well-being, and impair job performance after vacation. That is, there is "vacation stress" and it has consequences. In contrast, vacation experiences that bolster an individual's resources result in enhanced well-being and job performance after vacation. These are the experiences that produce "vacation relief."

Further research has shown that the specific activity does not necessarily help people to recover from job stress. Rather, it is the underlying psychological experience associated with the activity that produces the effect. Studying flight attendants, Sonnentag and Natter (2004) found that, in addition to off-job time activities, how they experienced the off-job time also predicted well-being. They posited recovery experiences as respitees' perception that the activities they are pursuing help in restoring their resources. Sonnentag and Natter (2004) concluded, "Thus, it is not just the type of the activity per se and the time devoted to it that makes recovery happen: *experiencing* an activity as recovery seems to be important" (p. 373). We understand this to mean that it is not the passage of time away from the situs where the job stress and strain arise nor the particular activities a respitee engages in but, rather, an internal, psychological process in which the individual consciously interprets the activities and events that have or have not occurred while away during the respite.

Further articulating how respitees experience respite activities, Sonnentag and Fritz (2007) proposed and validated four types of recovery experiences: psychological detachment from work, relaxation, mastery, and control. Detachment refers to both being free of work-related duties and disengaging mentally from work (see Etzion, Eden and Lapidot, 1998). To illustrate, Sonnentag and Bayer (2005) found that people who detached from their work during off-job time reported greater well-being than people who thought about their work.

When respitees don't detach, they work. Further confirmation of the value of detachment comes from research on respitees who work during their respites. Sonnentag (2001) maintained that when employees are busy with work related-activities (e.g., conversations regarding work issues, task preparations) during vacation, their resources, previously threatened and diminished on the job, continue to be challenged and little or no recovery occurs. This also might accelerate the fadeout process as the individual may return to work with weaker resource pools. Sonnentag and Natter (2004) studied a sample of flight attendants who completed daily surveys on four evenings when they stayed at home or at a hotel. They found that time spent on work-related activities decreased their levels of well-being. Obviously, being detached from the workplace but continuing to work during the respite cannot be expected to bring much relief from job stress.

Relaxation implies low levels of activation, little physical or intellectual effort, few demands, and high levels of positive affect. Mastery experiences are challenging activities that build up such resources as skills, competency, and proficiency in non-work domains. Control characterizes the degree to which a person has the discretion to decide which activity to pursue, when, how, and with whom. Sonnentag and Fritz (2007) suggested that these four types of recovery experiences or any combination of them may decrease stress and strain and increase well-being. Implications for practical application of Sonnentag and her colleagues' conceptualization and validation seem numerous and achievable.

Fritz and Sonnentag (2005) examined the effect of experiences during a weekend on health and job performance. Eighty-seven employees of emergency medical services completed questionnaires at the end of the work week, on Sunday evening (end of weekend) and at the beginning of the new following work week. They found that positive reflection decreased feelings of burnout; however, it did not improve general well-being. Social activities during the weekend decreased burnout and fostered well-being after the weekend. Furthermore, social activities were positively related to work performance after the weekend. The authors suggested that future research should investigate the role of social activity and its relationship with social support.

Fritz and Sonnentag (2006) then conducted a longitudinal study (one week before, during, and two days and two weeks after a one-week vacation) to examine effects of a vacation on well-being and performance-related outcomes among 221 non-academic university employees. They focused on specific respite experiences (positive and negative work reflection, relaxation, mastery experience, and non-work hassles) during the vacation. They found that vacation experiences were related to exhaustion after vacation. Respondents high in negative work reflection felt more exhausted on their return to work two weeks later. Similarly, non-work hassles during vacation increased exhaustion after vacation. Positive vacation experiences contributed to all indicators of well-being immediately after vacation and two weeks later. The authors concluded that resource-consuming experiences during vacation hinder the recovery process whereas positive experiences seem to rebuild resources as reflected in the well-being after vacation. Psychological detachment from work doesn't help relieve job stress and strain if respitees encounter new non-work-related stressors and hassles during their respite.

Fritz and Sonnentag suggested that findings regarding specific vacation effects can provide information on how to create vacation experiences that result in improved well-being and job performance and on how to allocate work in organizations during and after an employee's vacation. For example, they suggested that employers should design jobs in ways that facilitate recovery from work demands during the weekend. Furthermore, employees should be trained in the use of positive reflection and other recovery experiences to enhance recuperation. Work-related activities and worrying about work should be avoided during vacation in order to achieve high levels of detachment. Relaxation could be promoted by engaging in pleasant activities with a high relaxation potential, such as reading a magazine, going for a walk, physical activities (sport), or taking a bath.

Etzion and Zvi (2004) measured stress and burnout among students a week before a two-week Passover holiday break and a week following the break. They found a decline in stress and burnout after the vacation. However, vacation activities such as "studying" and "working for a living" were positively related to post-vacation burnout and negatively related to vacation satisfaction; it was social activities during vacation that produced restorative respite effects. These included visiting friends and sightseeing, which were negatively related to post-vacation stress and burnout and positively related to vacation satisfaction.

Several researchers (e.g., Iso-Ahola and Park, 1996; Larson, Mannell and Zuzaneck, 1986; Rook, 1987; Rook and Zijlstra, 2006) have found that leisure-generated companionships buffer the adverse effects of life stress on physical and mental health. These researchers have suggested that while engaging in non-work social activities job demands are removed, less emotion regulation is needed and therefore individual resources may be replenished. Thus, resources gained by social interactions during vacation may buffer the effect of prospective job demands. Similarly, De Bloom, Geurts and Kompier (2012) found that respondents who conversed extensively and positively with their partner during their vacations benefitted more from their vacation, felt more detached from work, felt more relaxed, and derived more pleasure from their activities. Thus, a vacation may act as an interpersonal relationship booster by increasing the number of positive interactions with the partner. Social activities are potential recovery actions as they offer opportunities for social support. However, Sonnentag and Natter (2004) found that the time flight attendants spent on social activities increased depression during the evening and at bedtime. For flight attendants spending time on social activities draws on their resources. This may be specific to this and similar vocational groups that face a high degree of emotional labor that social activities impede their well-being. Thus, the fit between specific individual or sector needs and type of respite activities should be investigated further.

Another kind of fit was studies by Utecht and Aldag (1989). They focused on five vacation indices that tap discrepancies between ideal and actual vacation objective characteristics (e.g., duration, nature of vacation) and found that when vacation expectations are fulfilled (i.e., the discrepancy is low) in an area of importance to the individual, the outcome to the individual and the organization (e.g., absenteeism) is beneficial. Thus, it may be that the particular type of activity people engage in is less important than the personal preference for an activity and the satisfaction with this activity. Focusing on discrepancies is an important contribution to vacation research; it implies the need to tailor respite characteristics to the individual's preferences.

Sonnentag (2001) and Sonnentag and Natter (2004) found that time spent on physical activities during off-job time predicts low depression, high vigor, and high well-being at bed time. Physical activities include physical effort invested in exercise, sports, walking, cycling, and the like. Hassman, Koivula and Uutela (2000), Penedo and Dahn (2005), and Tatlor (2000) reported beneficial effects of physical leisure activities on psychological and physiological health. Coleman and Iso-Ahola (1995) suggested that physical activities involve valuable features of self-determination that are related to choice and enjoyment.

Nawijn (2010) found that vacation effects were similar for three types of vacation activity (i.e., sightseeing, shopping, and relaxing). Nawijn (2011) subsequently found no relationship between the type of activity and affect during vacation. However, Nawijn's studies were cross-sectional and compared different types of vacations and differences in activities between persons. Therefore, more research into the role of vacation activities and a greater diversity of experiences in different types and durations of vacations is needed.

The role of vacation activities and experiences in the vacation effects is a relatively neglected topic. The findings from the very few studies that have investigated the role of vacation activities and experiences are somewhat contradictory. Moreover, in most of these studies the data on vacation activities and experiences were collected retrospectively after resuming work. Future research should collect such data during vacation and look for mediators such as profession, sex, and personality.

Time in Respite Research

Sonnentag (2012) has discussed some implications of the neglect of time as an important variable in organizational theory and research in general. The role of time in respite research also requires theoretical development. Time is involved in two still unresolved issues in respite research. One is respite length. We still do not know how long a respite must be – or how short it can be – for it to have salutogenic effects. Researchers have found beneficial effects of respites ranging from a workday evening at home to a year-long sabbatical. That cannot mean that all respites have equal effects, regardless of their length. But we are currently far from being able to pinpoint the ideal length of various respites. A weekend can be two or three days off work but we don't know if three days bring more relief than two days. A vacation can be a few days, like an extended weekend, or up to, say, a month off work. We don't know whether the latter brings more relief than the former.

Time also plays into consideration of fadeout effects. One of the most consistent findings in respite research, second only to the decline of stress and strain during respites, is the quick return of stress and strain to pre-respite levels after return to work. We need research on ways of helping returnees to delay fadeout. We know of no research on this potentially fruitful issue. The only idea we have been able to come up with is to suggest that returnees use their photos from their enjoyable vacations as a screen saver; perhaps seeing over and over again the sites and scenes that they enjoyed so much while away will extend their savoring of the positive experiences that otherwise would naturally recede into the less accessible parts of their awareness and memory.

Future Respite Research

Virtually all respite research to date has been on off-the-job respites. Etzion, Eden and Lapidot's (1998) suggestion that research on on-the-job respites might be fruitful. This would tie in with research on coffee and lunch breaks and may lead to some useful ways to make respites more beneficial.

A glaring deficiency in respite research is the lack of a metric to assess the magnitude of respite effects. Perusing the graphs displaying respite effects in the many articles, a major shortcoming is apparent: they all look alike. They all show a dip in stress and strain during the respite, followed by a rise after the return to work. If you've seen one respite effect, you've seen them all. There must be an obvious distortion when a weekend and a sabbatical look alike. This is the result of our lack of measures that might be sensitive to such differences, somehow quantifying the qualitative differences that must characterize these drastically different – but similar-appearing – respites. Creating such measures would be a major boost for respite research.

Respite research originated as a more internally valid way to study job stress (Eden, 1982). Thirty years on, it has advanced job-stress research to a degree of internal validity far superior to the older, causally ambiguous, correlational studies. However, it may now be ripe to advance again to a higher level by subjecting some of the issues raised above to experimental testing. For example, we could randomly assign employees about to depart for weekends, vacations, or business trips to different experimental conditions. The experimenter could provide advice on how to maximize respite benefits to the experimental participants and withhold such advice from the control employees. One group could get vouchers for a physically active weekend or vacation while the control group gets treated to some kind of sedentary respite. One group could get five three-day weekends while another group gets an uninterrupted five-day break. To test detachment experimentally, one group could have their work cell phones and notebooks deposited at work during their vacation while another group takes their devices with them. Such experimentation will render causal interpretation more convincing and bring our growing knowledge about respite moderators closer to practical application.

One domain that can be integrated into respite research is crossover (Westman, 2001). Crossover has been defined traditionally as the process through which psychological stress or strain experienced by one individual affects the stress or strain of another individual in the same social environment. Recently, crossover research has been expanded to include positive experiences (Westman, Etzion and Chen, 2009) and also to focus on teams and not only on dyads (Westman, Bakker, Roziner and Sonnentag, 2011). Thus, when a person gains resources during respite and experiences positive feelings, these feelings and experiences can also cross over to the partner and also to team members. Thus, crossover can create a kind of spiraling relief effect from one person to another and from a person to a team. Future research should focus on dyads and teams when the focal person has benefited from respite.

The connectivity revolution is upon us and it is fueling integration of respite research and work-family research. As the nature of work changes, so changes the nature of respites and so must the ways in which we study respites. Eden (2001a) spoke of the need to overcome "high-tech tethers." He warned that the evolution of communication devices that enable employees to be connected to their back-home workplace from anywhere and at any time would put an end to psychological detachment and reduce the restorative value of respites. By issuing employees smart phones, portable electronic notebooks, and other communication devices, organizations are not pampering them. Rather, they are chaining them to the organization 24/7 with high-tech devices that render detachment difficult if not impossible. In recent years, employees have eagerly adopted these devices, adapted to them, and relinquished their psychological detachment during their respites. With these devices, individuals can be away from the workplace geographically yet still be "there" electronically and psychologically. It remains to be seen whether the restorative powers of off-job respites can survive. We need research comparing individuals who take such devices with them on vacation to others who don't have such tethers or who leave them home.

Both of these last two issues have been addressed together in a single recent study. Richardson and Thompson (2012) studied the use of mobile communication devices among employees of a media company during evenings, weekends, and vacations. They found that the more these individuals used their devices, the greater the work–family conflict. Not surprisingly, the more these individuals used their devices during their various respites, the less detached they were from work. So early suspicions have been confirmed: telecommunication device use reduces detachment and diminishes the value of respites away from work. Tethered employees benefit less restorative effects from their respites. This must be weighed against any benefits to the company, and to the individual, that these tethers may provide.

Conclusion

So what have we learned? The casual reader may shrug, thinking that respite researchers studied and found the obvious: employees enjoy vacations more than working. This may have plagued the first generation of respite research. However, the developments of the past decade have deepened our understanding of the nature of respites, articulated different types of respites, illuminated some of the psychological processes at work in producing respite relief, and embellished respite findings with some notion of individual traits that may moderate who benefits more and who less, opening the way to consider tailoring respite type and timing to maximize its salutogenic value. Thus, we are learning new things about various aspects of respite, and the future bodes learning more how to turn respites into a more reliable salutogenic tool for maximizing individual well-being.

References

Bakker, A.B. and Demerouti, E. (2007) The job demands-resources model: State of the art. *Journal of Managerial Psychology*, 22(3), 309–28.

Caplan, R.D. and Jones, K.W. (1975) Effects of work load, role ambiguity, and Type-A personality on anxiety, depression and heart rate. *Journal of Applied Psychology*, 60, 713–19.

Coleman, D. and Iso-Ahola, S. (1995) Leisure and health: The role of social support and self determination. *Journal of Leisure Research*, 25, 111–28.

Davidson, O., Westman, M. and Eden, D., Cohen-Charash, Y., Hammer, L.B., Kluger, A.N., Krausz, M., Maslach, C., O'Driscoll, M., Perrewé, P.L., Quick, J.C., Rosenblatt, Z., Spector, P.E. (2010) Sabbatical leave relief from job stress: Who gains and how much? *Journal of Applied Psychology*, 95, 953–64.

De Bloom, J., Geurts, S. and Kompier, M. (2012) Effects of short vacations, vacation activities and experiences on employee health and well-being. *Stress and Health*, 28, 305–18.

De Bloom, J., Kompier, M., Geurts, S., De Weerth, C., Taris, T. and Sonnentag, S. (2009) Do we recover from vacation? Meta-analysis of vacation effects on health and well-being. *Journal of Occupational Health*, 51, 13–25.

Demerouti, E., Bakker, A.B., Nachreiner, F. and Schaufeli, W.B. (2001) The job demands-resources model of burnout. *Journal of Applied Social Psychology*, 86(3), 499–512.

Eden, D. (1982) Critical job events, acute stress, and strain: A multiple interrupted time series. *Organizational Behavior and Human Performance*, 30, 312–29.

—— (1990) Acute and chronic job stress, strain, and vacation relief. *Organizational Behavior and Human Decision Processes*, 45, 175–93.

—— (2001a) Job stress and respite relief: Overcoming high-tech tethers. In P.L. Perrewé and D.C. Ganster (eds) *Research in Occupational Stress and Well-being: Exploring Theoretical Mechanisms and Perspectives*, vol. 1. New York: JAI Press/Elsevier Science, pp. 143–94.

—— (2001b) Vacations and other respites: Studying stress on and off the job. *International Review of Industrial and Organizational Psychology*, 16, 121–46.

Etzion, D., Eden, D. and Lapidot, Y. (1998) Relief from job stressors and burnout: Reserve service as a respite. *Journal of Applied Psychology*, 83, 577–85.

Etzion, D. and Sapir, O. (1997) Annual vacation: Duration and relief from job stress and burnout. Paper presented at the 12th Annual Conference of the Society for Industrial and Organizational Psychology, St. Louis, April.

Etzion, D. and Westman, M. (2001) Vacation and the crossover of strain between spouses: Stopping the vicious cycle. *Man and Work*, 11, 106–18.

Etzion, D. and Zvi, E. (2004) *Stress and Burnout among Students before and after the Passover Break: Vacation Activities and Personality Variables as Moderators*. Working paper No. 11/04, The Henry Crown Institute of Business Research in Israel, Faculty of Management, The Leon Recanati Graduate School of Business Administration, Tel Aviv University.

Fritz, C. and Sonnentag, S. (2005) Recovery, health, and job performance: Effects of weekend experiences. *Journal of Occupational Health Psychology*, 10, 187–99.

—— (2006) Recovery, well-being, and performance-related outcomes: The role of workload and vacation experiences. *Journal of Applied Psychology*, 91, 936–45.

Gump, B.B. and Matthews, K.A. (2000) Are vacations good for your health? The 9-year mortality experience after the multiple risk factor intervention trial. *Psychosomatic Medicine*, 62, 608–12.

Hassman, P., Koivula, N. and Uutela, A. (2000) Physical exercise and psychological well-being: A population study in Finland. *Preventive Medicine*, 30, 17–25.

Hobfoll, S.E. (1989) Conservation of resources: A new attempt at conceptualizing stress. *American Psychologist*, 44, 513–24.

—— (1998) *Stress, Culture and Community: The Psychology and Philosophy of Stress*. New York: Plenum.

—— (2001) The influence of culture, community, and the nested self in the stress process: Advancing conservation of resources theory. *Applied Psychology: An International Review*, 50, 337–70.

Iso-Ahola, S.E. and Park, C.J. (1996) Leisure-related social support and self-determination as buffers of stress-illness relationship. *Journal of Leisure Research*, 28, 169–87.

Larson, R., Mannell, R. and Zuzaneck, J. (1986) Daily well-being of older adults with friends and family. *Journal of Psychology and Aging*, 1, 117–26.

Lounsbury, J.W. and Hoopes, L.L. (1986) A vacation from work: Changes in work and nonwork outcomes. *Journal of Applied Psychology*, 71, 392–401.

Lowen, A. and Craig, J.R. (1968) The influence of level of performance on managerial style: An experimental object-lesson in the ambiguity of correlational data. *Organizational Behavior and Human Performance*, 3, 440–58.

Nawijn, J. (2010) Happiness through vacationing: just a temporary boost or long term benefits? *Journal of Happiness Studies*, 12, 651–65.

—— (2011) The holiday happiness curve: A preliminary investigation into mood during a holiday abroad. *International Journal of Tourism Research*, 12, 281–90.

Penedo, F.J. and Dahn, J.R. (2005) Exercise and well-being: A review of mental and physical health benefits associated with physical activity. *Current Opinion in Psychiatry*, 18, 189–93.

Richardson, K. and Thompson, C. (2012) High tech tethers and work-family conflict: A conservation of resources approach. *Engineering Management Research*, 1, 29–43.

Rook, K.S. (1987) Social support versus companionship: Effects on life stress, loneliness and evaluations by others. *Journal of Personality and Social Psychology*, 52, 1132–47.

Rook, J.W. and Zijlstra, F.R.H. (2006) The contribution of various types of activities to recovery. *European Journal of Work and Organizational Psychology*, 15, 218–40.

Sonnentag, S. (2001) Work, recovery activities, and individual well-being: A diary study. *Journal of Occupational Health Psychology*, 6, 196–210.

—— (2012) Time in organizational research: Catching up on a long neglected topic in order to improve theory. *Organizational Psychology Review*, 2, 361–8.

Sonnentag, S. and Bayer, U. (2005) Switching off mentally: Predictors and consequences of psychological detachment from work during off-job time. *Journal of Occupational Health Psychology*, 10, 393–414.

Sonnentag, S. and Fritz, C. (2007) The recovery experience questionnaire: Development and validation of a measure for assessing recuperation and unwinding from work. *Journal of Occupational Health Psychology*, 12, 204–21.

Sonnentag, S. and Natter, E. (2004) Flight attendants' daily recovery from work: Is there no place like home? *International Journal of Stress Management*, 11, 366–91.

Strauss-Blasche, G., Ekmekcioglu, C. and Marktl, W. (2000) Does vacation enable recuperation? Changes in well-being associated with time away from work. *Occupational Medicine*, 50, 167–72.

Tatlor, A. (2000) Physical activity, anxiety and stress. In S.J.H. Biddle, K.R. Fox and S.H. Boutcher (eds) *Physical Activity and Psychological Well Being*. London: Routledge, pp. 10–46.

Utecht, K. and Aldag, R. (1989) Vacation discrepancy: Correlates of individual differences and outcomes. *Psychological reports*, 65, 867–82.

Westman, M. (1999) *Applying Hobfoll's conservation of resources (COR) theory to respite research*. Working Paper No. 29/99. The Israel Institute of Business Research, Tel Aviv University.

—— (2001) Stress and strain crossover. *Human Relations*, 54, 557–91.

Westman, M., Bakker, A.B., Roziner, I. and Sonnentag, S. (2011) Crossover of job demands and emotional exhaustion within teams: A longitudinal multilevel study. *Anxiety, Stress, and Coping*, 24, 561–77.

Westman, M. and Eden, D. (1997) Effects of vacation on job stress and burnout: Relief and fade-out. *Journal of Applied Psychology*, 82, 516–27.

Westman, M. and Etzion, D. (2001) The impact of vacation and job stress on burnout and absenteeism. *Psychology and Health*, 16, 595–606.

—— (2002) The impact of short overseas business trips on job stress and burnout. *Applied Psychology: An International Review*, 51, 582–92.

Westman, M., Etzion, D. and Chen, S. (2009) The crossover of exhaustion and vigor between international business travelers and their spouses. *Journal of Managerial Psychology*, 24, 269–84.

Westman, M., Etzion, D. and Gattenio, E. (2008) Business travels and the work-family interface: A longitudinal study. *Journal of Organizational and Occupational Psychology*, 81, 459–80.

Westman, M., Etzion, D. and Gurtler, E. (2004) The work-family interface and burnout. *International Journal of Stress Management*, 11, 413–28.

CHAPTER 12 Proposed Frailties of Courage and Related Interventions

CYNTHIA L.S. PURY

Introduction

How can people become more courageous? The quest for a basic science modeling courage is ongoing: there are no empirically-validated interventions to increase courage at the time this chapter is being written. However, we appear to have a good start on delineating the primary features of courageous behavior. This chapter will present a theoretical overview of courage research and its implications to date, including defining features, different types of courage, associated frailties, and implications for the design and validation of courage interventions.

Historical Views of the Psychology of Courage

Like many topics in positive psychology, the virtue of courage has been relatively neglected by researchers in favor of exploring aspects of related frailties (e.g., fear, avoidance, sensation seeking). A notable early exception is Lord (1918), who proposed that courage occurs when the base sentiment of fear is overruled by another, usually more noble, sentiment. In keeping with the times, Lord's treatise then goes on to assert a scaling for noble sentiments, including, in rough ascending order: self-assertion, protection of kin, honor, love of country, and, at the pinnacle, devotion to a sacred lost cause. This ordering is applied to the then-current World War I, and ends with the comforting proposition that the German soldiers are surely less courageous than the Allied soldiers.

These and similar subjective assumptions are thoroughly rejected in behaviorist conceptions of courage. In the third quarter of the 1900s, advances in behavior therapy drove and were driven by empirical theories of emotion. Rachman (1978) proposed that the tripartite model of emotion could be used to explain fear as a combination of subjective and cognitive changes, specific psychophysiological changes associated with dramatically increased arousal, and an action tendency of avoidance or flight. Under this model, courage occurs when the subjective and/or psychophysiological markers of fear are present but the action tendency elicited is approach rather than avoidance or flight (Rachman, 1990).

Using this approach to courage, paratrooper trainees can be classified as courageous (moderate optimism and moderate fear of jumping), fearless (high optimism, low fear of jumping), and overconfident (over-predicted confidence and under-predicted fear of jumping, McMillan and Rachman, 1988). The Courage Measure (CM) (Norton and Weiss, 2009) utilizes a similar approach: respondents are first given a definition of courage as acting despite fear, then asked 12 Likert-type questions about their willingness to act despite fear. The measure predicts behavioral approach scores to taxidermied spiders in high spider fear individuals (Norton and Weiss, 2009), children's self-reports of feeling more courageous when standing up to fear (Muris, 2009), and parent reports of their children's courage (Muris, Mayer and Schubert, 2010).

However, this behavioral approach also leads to paradoxical findings, most notably that more courageous people experience fear less intensely. Decorated bomb disposal operators have less subjective and psychophysiological signs of fear under laboratory stress (Cox et al., 1983; O'Connor, Hallam and Rachman, 1985). Similar responses were found in veterans of a decorated (non-bomb disposal) military combat unit (McMillan and Rachman, 1987). Children who score high on the CM report less anxiety symptoms and feeling less afraid during a past courageous action (Muris, 2009; Muris, Mayer and Schubert, 2010). Thus, the behavioral definition of courage as standing up to fear leads to a conundrum: to be courageous, a person needs to stand up to their fear, with more fear conquered equaling higher courage. However, people who have acted quite courageously actually experience fear less intensely than others. Rachman (e.g., 1990) raises the question if these individuals might instead be classified as fearless rather than courageous.

A more problematic implication of the behaviorist model leads to the moderately high correlation (.63) of children's CM scores with sensation-seeking (Muris, 2009). Without specifying any sort of reason for taking action despite fear, little separates this type of courage from the excess of rashness raised by Aristotle (1999) in ancient Greece. If we are judged as courageous for not giving into fear and for that alone, then we end up with some peculiar accolades. Imagine three burn patients, all equally injured, all experiencing identical levels of fear while confronting a raging fire. One went into the fire to save a child, one to save a unique and valuable piece of art, and one to experience how it feels to be surrounded by flames. According to the behaviorist definition, all three are equally courageous. This notion seems at odds with most popular conceptions of courage.

Volition, Risk, and a Worthwhile Goal

An alternate approach, distilling both lay and expert implicit theories of courage, yields a definition that, to date, appears to avoid these concerns. Using a multi-method empirical approach, Chris Rate and his colleagues (Rate, 2010; Rate et al., 2007) derived a multipart definition of a courageous action as a deliberate, intentional action; taken despite risk to the actor; and in pursuit of a noble or otherwise worthwhile goal. The subjective sense of risk might or might not lead to the emotion of fear. Regardless, the actor is aware of the risk to him or herself (Rate et al., 2007).

One of the appealing features about this definition is that it does a better job of differentiating different types of courageous behaviors. The philosophy literature has long distinguished between physical and moral courage (Lopez, O'Byrne and Petersen, 2003; Putman, 2010), and additional subtypes of courage including vital courage (thriving despite serious medical or psychological illness, Finfgeld, 1995, 1999) and psychological courage (risking psychological stability by, for example, reliving traumatic events during psychotherapy, Putman, 1997; Putman, 2004) have been proposed in recent years. These types, I propose, exist because certain types of goals and the required risks to reach them are commonly paired in nature. For example, the physical courage of saving someone from a physical danger frequently involves facing that danger yourself: the rough ocean that threatens the drowning person also threatens the rescue swimmer. The moral courage of standing up to a bully involves risking that same bully's wrath. However, not all courageous acts are as easy to classify: what about civil rights pioneers who risked their lives to stand up for what is right? Or someone who leads an intervention to save the life of a substance-dependent friend, while risking social rejection by that same friend? By considering risks and goals separately, these actions can be said to have the risks of one type of courage while having the goals of another.

Another, even more appealing feature of this definition is that it explains our gut instinct: that risky actions taken for a valuable goal matter more than the same actions taken for a goal of limited value. The three burn patients described above are very likely to be evaluated quite differently: the rescuer is a hero and the thrill-seeker a fool. But what of the art collector? It may depend on how much the person making the assessment of courage values art.

Charles Starkey and I (Pury and Starkey, 2010) propose that there is a fundamental distinction between viewing courage as a process – or an actor's internal experience of overcoming a sense of risk or fear to pursue a valuable goal; and courage as an accolade – or an observer's conclusion that an act was courageous. Worth or nobility of goal has the same relationship to both process and accolade courage. The greater the perceived worth or nobility of the goal the greater chance that the action is taken (process courage) and the greater the perceived courage (accolade courage). Risk, however, has an opposite relationship with process and accolade courage. For process courage, the greater the perceived risk of the action, the less likely it should be taken. On the other hand, for accolade courage, the greater the perceived risk, the more courageous the act should seem.

For both risk and worthiness, it is important to note that these are subjective judgments on the part of both the actor and the observer. For example, one common response to asking participants about a time they acted courageously is a time someone overcame a fear or obstacle that was specific to them (Pury and Kowalski, 2007; Pury, Kowalski and Spearman, 2007). These instances, high in personal courage (Pury, Kowalski and Spearman, 2007), commonly involve overcoming specific or social phobias that even the actor may acknowledge as irrational. Yet, the sense of risk and fear remains, with fear predicting how courageous the action was for that particular participant but not for how courageous the action would have been for anyone else (Pury, Kowalski and Spearman, 2007).

Specific Frailties of Courage

Considering the three key working parts of courage – volition, risk, and a worthwhile goal – can help us create a theoretical taxonomy of specific frailties of courage, such as: cowardice, rashness, indecision, ineffectiveness, indifference, and bad courage. Two of these proposed frailties, cowardice and rashness, were proposed by Aristotle in ancient times (Aristotle, 1999). In Aristotle's system, they were the vices at extreme ends of the same continuum; while courage represented their mean and was a virtue. In our theory, both are dependent on a faulty weighting of risk in process courage. Cowardice describes those occasions on which an actor may overvalue the risk of a particular action; thus, no matter what the goal, the person gives more weight to risk than they ought and thus does not take action even when they risks are small and should seem outweighed by the goals. While it might be that risk is given a greater weight due to a strong accompanying sense of fear, theoretically, this might not be true in all cases.

Rashness, on the other hand, might describe those situations in which an individual gives too little weight to risk in process courage. Thus, the individual may be more apt to engage in actions high in accolade courage, such as risking his or her own life to save another person, but the same process might also lead to risking one's life for a less worthy goal, such as to show off.

Other frailties of courage may involve a dysfunction of parts of the deliberate, volitional part of courageous action. This part of courage implies that the potentially courageous actor must form a plan to reach the goal. In some cases, the individual may be indecisive, or unable to form or commit to a plan. Such indecisiveness can lead to a frailty that prevents courageous action, and may be particularly problematic for goals that have a short window of opportunity for action, such as emergencies.

Another related hypothetical frailty of courage, ineffectiveness, may occur when the person develops a plan that is not likely to lead to reaching the goal, even if executed perfectly. Even when the actor is not to blame for success or failure, risky actions that fail to reach their goal are rated as less courageous than those that succeed (Pury and Hensel, 2010).

Finally, frailties of courage may involve problems with valuation of the goal. Indifference to the worth of a goal should make a courageous action less likely to happen, and, from an accolade standpoint, may make an observer think less of the actor for not pursuing it. As an extreme example, a parent who does not rescue a child from physical danger may be seen as morally deficient.

Perhaps more concerning for society at large, bad courage (Pury and Starkey, 2010) is theorized to occur when the actor values a goal that is seen as worthless, or even worse, evil by most observers. Suicide attempts, going into a dangerous situation to seek drugs, and even reckless stunts done for the thrill of it might be seen as the pursuit of goals of limited or negative value for the individual. Other bad goals involve actively harming others. Former terrorists describe planting bombs as something that was dangerous and frightening but in support of a worthwhile cause (at least, at the time; Silke, 2004).

These frailties of courage are, for the most part, largely theoretical at the moment and rest upon a modified version of Rate et al.'s (2007) definition of courage as a voluntary planned action in pursuit of a noble or worthwhile goal despite risk to the actor. To the extent that this theory is supported by future research, these frailties may likewise be of empirical interest.

Courage Interventions

While few if any empirically-validated interventions to increase courage exist, we can use the existing findings about courage to suggest targets of such an intervention. One place to begin is by looking to see what sort of self-regulatory thoughts or actions people take to increase their own courage. In prior research, we asked participants to describe a time they acted courageously, then asked them if they did or thought anything in particular to increase their courage. Twelve percent tried to increase their efficacy by practicing or mentally rehearsing their actions (Pury, 2008). Thirty percent of participants focused on reducing risk or the sense of felt risk: reminding themselves it will be alright or trying to relax, for example. Forty-two percent reported focusing on the goal they were trying to reach, including reminding themselves of how important the goal is to them or, in the case of moral courage, simply that it is the right thing to do (Pury, 2008). In addition to providing support for a view of courage very much in line with Rate et al.'s (Rate, 2010; Rate et al., 2007) consensus definition, these results suggest that the process of taking courageous action might be made easier by considering specific frailties of three main areas: risk, worthwhile goal, and efficacy.

Initially, we may be inclined to think of courage interventions as making up for the most obvious frailty of courage: cowardice. Reducing a sense of felt risk or fear is a common way people try to increase their own courage. A wide variety of cognitive-behavioral and other techniques are available to treat irrational or exaggerated fear, and those techniques might be profitably incorporated into courage interventions when excessive fear leads to cowardice.

Based on our preliminary data on self-regulation strategies (Pury, 2008), the most common self-regulation strategy to increase courage does not target cowardice but instead targets indifference. By focusing on the value of the goal, our participants may have been reminding themselves that any risk taken would be worth it. The commitment component of Acceptance and Commitment Therapy (e.g., Hayes et al., 2011; Hayes, Strosahl and Wilson, 1999) might be adapted for use in interventions to combat indifference-related frailties.

Ineffectiveness also has an associated self-regulation strategy: practice or rehearsal (Pury, 2008). Elements of guided practice and similar existing interventions might be incorporated into a hypothetical courage intervention to guard against ineffectiveness. Such interventions may also help to combat a sense of felt risk when failure is the largest risk of the potential courageous action, for example, before an important public performance.

Of the remaining three hypothetical frailties, indecisiveness may also be combat using similar techniques, depending upon the cause. Indecisiveness due to the distractions of fear, ultimately, should decline as fear declines. Indecisiveness due to uncertainty may be reduced by therapeutic techniques aimed at decision-making (e.g., Bell and D'Zurilla, 2009) or philosophical examinations of what is right (Pury et al., in press).

The two remaining frailties of courage may not appear to the person experiencing them as a problem with courage. Interventions for rashness may resemble treatments for extreme impulsivity such as borderline personality disorder. Again, therapies that support decision-making skills could be appropriated, but, in this case, the goal of treatment is to decrease risky decision-making rather than to decrease indecisiveness (e.g., Svaldi, Philipsen and Matthies, 2012).

All of the above frailties have involved a general support of client goals – helping the client to overcome fear or other barriers to reach a desired goal. But what about bad courage – when the goal itself is faulty? Traditional therapeutic techniques are designed to help clients reach existing goals, discover new goals, and even throw over some goals, like getting high, for others (e.g., motivational interviewing, Miller and Rose, 2009). However, these techniques do not address what to do if the goal the client desires is morally wrong. We (Pury et al., in press) suggest elsewhere that therapists and coaches consider including philosophical techniques of right and wrong.

The problem of bad courage, while likely to be infrequent, is serious enough to warrant a serious pause in developing courage interventions. It changes the original question posed in this chapter: "How can people become more courageous?" to a more fundamental question: "Should people become more courageous?" While I believe that in most cases the answer to this second question is yes, it is not universally yes.

A final consideration for courage interventions is making sure that whatever we develop, it works. One of the difficulties in courage research that is likely to carry over to intervention testing is selecting valid outcome measures. Are we interested in increasing courage in general, a specific type of courage (e.g., physical, moral, or psychological courage), or in increasing a particular desired behavior (e.g., increased incident of firing a weapon during battle, increased bystander intervention in bullying, or increased enrollment in difficult courses)? More specific outcome measures are likely to be easier to measure reliably and validly; however, they are also by definition less generalizable.

Conclusion

Psychologists have only recently begun to investigate courage. Models of courage are still being developed and validated. Based on the limited data available at the current time, we might start to think about interventions centered on six hypothetical frailties of courage and specific strategies to combat them. Further research and development, including rigorous empirical testing, are clearly needed before any courage intervention is ready for large-scale implementation.

References

Aristotle (1999) *Nicomachean Ethics*, trans. M. Ostwald. Upper Saddle River, NJ: Prentice Hall.

Bell, A.C. and D'Zurilla, T.J. (2009) Problem-solving therapy for depression: A meta-analysis. *Clinical Psychology Review*, 29(4), 348–53.

Cox, D., Hallam, R., O'Connor, K. and Rachman, S. (1983) An experimental analysis of fearlessness and courage. *British Journal of Psychology*, 74(1), 107–17.

Finfgeld, D.L. (1995) Becoming and being courageous in the chronically ill elderly. *Issues in Mental Health Nursing*, 16(1), 1–11.

—— (1999) Courage as a process of pushing beyond the struggle. *Qualitative Health Research*, 9(6), 803–14.

Hayes, S.C., Levin, M.E., Plumb-Vilardaga, J., Villatte, J.L. and Pistorello, J. (2011) Acceptance and commitment therapy and contextual behavioral science: Examining the progress of a distinctive model of behavioral and cognitive therapy. *Behavior Therapy*, 44(2), 180–98.

Hayes, S.C., Strosahl, K.D. and Wilson, K.G. (1999) *Acceptance and Commitment Therapy: An Experiential Approach to Behavior Change*. New York: Guilford Press.

Lopez, S.J., O'Byrne, K.K. and Petersen, S. (2003) Profiling courage. In S.J. Lopez and C.R. Snyder (eds) *Positive Psychological Assessment: A Handbook of Models and Measures*. Washington, DC: American Psychological Association, pp. 185–97.

Lord, H.G. (1918) *The Psychology of Courage*. Boston, MA: John W. Luce.

McMillan, T.M. and Rachman, S.J. (1987) Fearlessness and courage: A laboratory study of paratrooper veterans of the Falklands War. *British Journal of Psychology*, 78(3), 375–83.

—— (1988) Fearlessness and courage in paratroopers undergoing training. *Personality and Individual Differences*, 9(2), 373–8.

Miller, W.R. and Rose, G.S. (2009) Toward a theory of motivational interviewing. *American Psychologist*, 64(6), 527–37.

Muris, P. (2009) Fear and courage in children: Two sides of the same coin? *Journal of Child and Family Studies*, 18(4), 486–90.

Muris, P., Mayer, B. and Schubert, T. (2010) "You might belong in Gryffindor": Children's courage and its relationships to anxiety symptoms, Big Five personality traits, and sex roles. *Child Psychiatry and Human Development*, 41(2), 204–13.

Norton, P.J. and Weiss, B.J. (2009) The role of courage on behavioral approach in a fear-eliciting situation: A proof-of-concept pilot study. *Journal of Anxiety Disorders*, 23(2), 212–17.

O'Connor, K., Hallam, R.S. and Rachman, S. (1985) Fearlessness and courage: A replication experiment. *British Journal of Psychology*, 76(2), 187–97.

Pury, C.L.S. (2008) Can courage be learned? In S.J. Lopez (ed.) *Positive Psychology: Exploring the Best in People*. Vol 1, *Discovering Human Strengths*. Westport, CT: Praeger Publishers/Greenwood Publishing, pp. 109–30.

Pury, C.L.S. and Hensel, A.D. (2010) Are courageous actions successful actions? *The Journal of Positive Psychology*, 5(1), 62–72.

Pury, C.L.S. and Kowalski, R.M. (2007) Human strengths, courageous actions, and general and personal courage. *Journal of Positive Psychology*, 2(2), 120–28.

Pury, C.L.S., Kowalski, R.M. and Spearman, J. (2007) Distinctions between general and personal courage. *Journal of Positive Psychology*, 2(2), 99–114.

Pury, C.L.S. and Starkey, C.B. (2010) Is courage an accolade or a process? A fundamental question for courage research. In C.L.S. Pury and S.J. Lopez (eds) *The Psychology of Courage: Modern Research on an Ancient Virtue*. Washington, DC: American Psychological Association, pp. 67–87.

Pury, C.L.S., Starkey, C.B., Breeden, C., Kelley, C., Murphy, H. and Lowndes, A. (eds) (in press). *Courage Interventions: Future Directions and Cautions*. Oxford: Wiley-Blackwell.

Putman, D. (1997) Psychological courage. *Philosophy, Psychiatry and Psychology*, 4(1), 1–11.

—— (2004) *Psychological Courage*. Dallas, TX: University Press of America.

—— (2010) Philosophical roots of the concept of courage. In C.L.S. Pury and S.J. Lopez (eds) *The Psychology of Courage: Modern Research on an Ancient Virtue*. Washington, DC: American Psychological Association, pp. 9–22.

Rachman, S.J. (1978) Human fears: A three systems analysis. *Scandinavian Journal of Behaviour Therapy*, 7(4), 237–45.

—— (1990) *Fear and Courage*, 2nd edn. New York: W.H. Freeman/Times Books/Henry Holt and Co.

Rate, C.R. (2010) Defining the features of courage: A search for meaning. In C.L.S. Pury and S.J. Lopez (eds) *The Psychology of Courage: Modern Research on an Ancient Virtue*. Washington, DC: American Psychological Association, pp. 47–66.

Rate, C.R., Clarke, J.A., Lindsay, D.R. and Sternberg, R.J. (2007) Implicit theories of courage. *Journal of Positive Psychology*, 2(2), 80–98.

Silke, A. (2004) Courage in dark places: Reflections on terrorist psychology. *Social Research*, 71, 177–98.

Svaldi, J., Philipsen, A. and Matthies, S. (2012) Risky decision-making in borderline personality disorder. *Psychiatry Research*, 197(1–2), 112–18.

CHAPTER 13 Professional Moral Courage: Establishing Ethical Strength in Organizational Settings

LESLIE E. SEKERKA

Whatever we learn to do, we learn by actually doing it.

– Aristotle (384–322 BCE)

Introduction

What do Mark Hurd (former CEO of Hewlett-Packard), John Ensign (former Senator of Nevada), Lee Farkas (former Chairman of Taylor, Bean and Whitaker), and Scott Thompson (former CEO of Yahoo) all have in common? One cannot help but notice the fact that the word "former" is now a prominent feature associated with their names. Yet another, albeit presumed, commonality, is that these men did not wake up one morning and say to themselves, "Today I plan to submit false expense reports, create a monetary payoff scheme, engage in bank fraud, or cheat on my resume." These types of unethical acts rarely occur as one-time events; rather, they are choices depicted in a pattern of behavior that emerges over time. When leaders engage in unethical action it puts their reputations and organizations at risk, often costing them their jobs, relationships, and likely much more. One might ask, where was their corporate social responsibility? Where was their moral courage to do well and do good in business? Where was their foundation of character strength, an expected feature of leadership? Clearly, these people were grossly remiss in ethical strength and far from practicing the art of ethics in business.

As explained by George (2011), being a leader can cultivate distortions in one's view of the self. In a sustained effort to prove their worth, people may ultimately have difficulty in acknowledging anything less than perfection in their performance. Sadly, this strong drive to succeed can go awry, fueling the belief that failure is unacceptable. If failure does occur, it must be attributed elsewhere. With a mix of personal biases, inaccurate perceptions, fear of failure, and a little hubris, people can become very vulnerable to ethical risk. Typically, moral lapses start out small, are rationalized, and then increase in frequency and magnitude over time. Being unethical is rarely a one-time isolated occurrence. It is often the result of thought and behavioral patterns that accumulate over time, leading to habits that skim or dip below the moral minimum.

Such a lack of moral fortitude in management is not that hard to diagnose. People provide signals that can suggest cause for concern. Walking the edge of the moral line, this type of manager may take advantage of others and take credit for their accomplishments. They tend to skim the truth, exaggerate, or demonstrate hypocrisy – saying one thing and doing another. The behaviors they model may be different from the values they claim to uphold. Unethical managers tend to demonstrate a hard focus on short-term gains for themselves, with a soft focus on the long-term good of others. I argue that this lack of ethics, a distortion in business success, evolves over time but can be mitigated. While many leaders strive to meet regulatory requirements with the best of intentions, when compliance is considered the gold standard for ethics in the workplace, people are likely to fall short. This is not because compliance is ineffective; rather, it is because it serves to instill the bare minimum (Sekerka, in press). In other words, rules and regulations provide a framework for ethical action, not the means to produce ethical strength.

To help ensure the ethical health of an organization, more attention must be directed toward building moral fortitude in employees' everyday task actions. To address this concern this chapter begins with a consideration of how ethics is broached in the workplace today. It then draws upon prior research, arguing that professional moral courage (PMC) is needed to supplement baseline compliance-driven practices. Recommendations for adult moral development are provided, including a technique to exercise and build moral competencies in organizational settings.

Ethics Driven by Compliance

Given the parade of ethical mishaps associated with every realm of business, government, and nonprofit enterprise, a wave of ethical reforms have emerged. The Federal Sentencing Guidelines for Organizations (FSGO), Sarbanes Oxley Act (SOX), and Foreign Corruption Practices Act (FCPA) are a few examples of elevated requirements and restrictions imposed upon organizations in the United States, mandates designed to mitigate illegal enterprise and to promote ethics in business. These laws have imposed some success toward preventing ethical dysfunction, via the adoption of more comprehensive compliance/ethics programs and the creation of a new profession of ethics and compliance professionals to develop and implement them (Sekerka, in press). Additionally, legal requirements have been toughened by governing bodies, boards of directors and senior corporate management, and corporate leaders who have taken responsibility for promoting law-compliant organizations.

Regardless of well-intended regulatory controls, a firm's ethical character is still shaped by the people who work there. In metaphorical terms the organization is the "barrel," providing the context for ethics (Treviño and Youngblood, 1990). But it is also the character of the "apples" in that barrel, the employees, who have a compelling influence on the organization's ethical health. While improvements have been implemented, a study conducted by the Ethics Resource Center (ERC) reflects that a staggering number of employees still observe misconduct at work (45 percent) and a disconcerting number of employees report feeling pressure to compromise their ethical standards to achieve their performance goals (13 percent) (ERC, 2011). Still, more work is needed to fortify the ethical health of peoples' daily operations, according to a review team who examined the impact of the FSGO mandates since their inception 20 years ago (ERC, 2012). Their report outlines key areas where challenges to organizational ethics remain:

1. few ethical malfeasance cases involve large companies; criminal lawsuits against big corporate defendants are detoured within the judicial system;
2. inconsistency in policies across the various government agencies that play a role in corporate law enforcement and regulation;
3. compliance/ethics programs fall short, as portions of the FSGO remain unclear;
4. a less than effective "check the box" approach remains the norm; "going through the motions" does not create a culture of ethical strength.

Recommendations based on these observations entail directives imposed upon the Department of Justice and Congress (among other governmental agencies). The review team also advised the private sector to do more than attend to the requirements, directing leaders to impose greater diligence toward the spirit of the standards, not just a surface approach via box-checking activities. The report suggests this begins by "defining the mission of a company as comprising both strong financial performance and a strong commitment to integrity" (ERC, 2012, p. 13). The recommendations go on to state, "boards of directors and senior executives should demand compliance/ethics programs that are effective in preventing and detecting misconduct and help build ethical and law-abiding cultures" (p. 13). By implication, this means leaders need to invest in initiatives that raise the bar for business ethics best practices.

Slowly but surely, managers, practitioners, and scholars alike are realizing that compliance-driven approaches can help people become aware of the rules, but do not build the moral competencies necessary for ethical action. Furthermore, without an explicit and measured effort to achieve principled performance, demands to meet quarterly goals can impose pressures that contribute to ethical dysfunction. To understand how this happens over time, it is important to see how people fall short of the ethical baseline, when ethical health relies upon regulation alone. It will become clearer as to why organizations must couple compliance with professional moral courage (PMC). If leaders want to establish a more durable form of organizational ethics, they need to go beyond compliance. One way that some leaders have attempted to do this is by applying a Corporate Social Responsibility (CSR) framework to their business strategy.

Corporate Social Responsibility

Primary benefits of a capitalist system include its ability to generate economic growth, promote wealth accumulation, and protect liberty through its emphasis on protecting private property rights and individual choice. A strong argument for the benefits of capitalism rests upon Adam Smith's concept of the "invisible hand." Organizations, acting in their own self-interest, are driven to create products that serve society's best interest (Smith, 1976). But economist Milton Friedman (1970) argued that businesses' sole purpose is to generate shareholder profit. He explained that companies who adopt responsible attitudes face binding constraints – requirements that render them less competitive. By definition, business means upholding a fiduciary responsibility to the firm's investors

(Vogel, 2006). This shareholder approach is essentially self-centered enterprise, motivating management to protect the life of the firm through profit generation. In this light, ethics can be reduced to adherence to regulations imposed by law, unless monetary returns are generated by leveraging social responsibility as a marketable commodity.

Conversely, the stakeholder approach integrates considerations for people and the planet in conjunction with making a profit. This type of organization tends to undertake deeper forms of ethical responsibility, which is manifest in the firm's core values and reflected in the firm's purpose, mission, and strategy. Leaders holding a stakeholder approach understand it is their duty to generate investor returns, but they are moved to do so with responsibility and consideration toward others' needs. In other words, corporate performance is not just measured in dollars. Value creation is established with moral awareness, including respect for the future inhabitants of the earth in years to come. Firms striving to supersede ethical compliance are largely stakeholder-driven, because they inculcate CSR into their organizational identity, which fuels operational strategies and performance goals. The academic literature is rife with explanations about CSR and how it can be implemented (cf. Carroll, 1999; Jones, 1983, 1995; Porter and Kramer, 2006; Windsor, 2001). Yet, sustaining a commitment to aspirational goals in conjunction with profitable performance is challenging, especially during protracted recessionary periods (Sekerka and Stimel, 2011).

Global leaders have called for a new kind of capitalism, one that leverages the benefits of a free-market coupled with a foundation of sound ethics and a strong sense of morality (Guth, 2008). The notion of creative capitalism, coined by Bill Gates and Warren Buffett, supports this idea. John Mackey, CEO of Whole Foods, uses the term "conscious capitalism." He explains that social purpose and profit are balanced through voluntary cooperation (Sacks, 2009). Mackey claims self-interest and altruism can not only coexist, they can thrive simultaneously without government intrusion. Such a platform assumes leaders will adopt a shared sense of responsibility and commit to a balance – a weave between shareholder and stakeholder strategic perspectives (Sekerka and Stimel, 2011). This also entails a shift in how performance is measured, advancing CSR through triple bottom line (TBL) reporting. The TBL process requires firms account for the social, ecological, and economic value in how they measure business performance. This assumes everyone associated with the firm has a stake in its actions (customers, suppliers, members, the environment, etc.).

Firms typically exist on a continuum between the two perspectives (stake- and shareholder orientations), influenced by factors such as management goals, pressure from external stakeholders, governmental regulation, industry type, and geographic location. Shareholder-driven organizations dominate the market in the United States, yet management scholars continue to suggest that a stakeholder-driven operation is actually more productive for the long-term interests of the firm (Boatright, 2006). When considering their level of commitment to principled performance, management generates organizational goals based on assumptions rooted in the firm's identity (Sekerka and Stimel, 2011). Strategies emerge and reinforce existing beliefs about how to conduct business. When asked about how companies keep up their CSR efforts, one leader summed up the point:

> *If they see it as a "nice to have" but not a necessity for the sustainability of their business, then it will not be a priority. ... Often, the issue is the time frame within which returns are*

expected. Most sustainability initiatives are long-term commitments and, therefore, often do not fit within the quarterly profits model. (Marshall, 2009)

Whether or not CSR is a core part of a firm's strategy, it cannot be assumed that such a stance is incorporated into the bottom line (Marshall and Brown, 2003). For example, firms with favorable CSR reputations (e.g., General Electric (GE), Pacific Gas and Electric Company, and Procter and Gamble), are typically shareholder-driven (2012). GE Chairman and CEO Jeff Immult suggests, "There is a green lining among the current economic storm clouds and GE customers and investors are benefiting" (GE Press Release, 2008). GE's eco-focus does not stem from a deep sense of social responsibility; rather, it uses CSR as a strategic initiative to gain position in a range of high-growth and high-margin emerging markets. This represents the healthy drive of free market capitalism, a cornerstone of Western enterprise. But it also reflects the fact that companies may espouse an ethic of care, with an intention to do well and do good, yet it is an identity adopted because it is deemed profitable. Therefore, ethics are still likely viewed as requirements imposed by law or industry standards. When CSR is a revenue source, rather than a component of the firm's core identity, the organizations remain susceptible to ethical risk.

Because organizations are manmade, they reflect the will of human achievement as expressed by innovation and performance. Like people, even so-called "good" organizations are fallible. People and organizations can fail to live up to their own standards. To explore this concern, we now examine what causes people to fall short of their values. And, to address our human vulnerabilities, I argue that aiming higher, working to achieve ethical strength, is a necessary and recommended way forward.

Human Vulnerability

There are a host of reasons why so-called ethical people engage in unethical acts. Research reflects how susceptible people are to the influence of social norms (Shadnam and Lawrence, 2011). Looking at groups of people, it is easy to see how interpersonal and environmental forces can be deleterious to one's character. Stanley Milgram, noted for one of the most famous experiments in social psychology, showed how reasonably thoughtful citizens could be swayed, choosing to inflict harm on others so long as the responsibility for this action was assumed by an authority figure. As described by Milgram, it is not so much the kind of person one is, as much as the situation one is in, that helps determine people's actions (1974). Scholars continue to reflect on this disconcerting aspect of humanity, working to understand our inherent ethical malleability.

Drawing insight from his Stanford Prison Experiment, Philip Zimbardo continued to study this issue, as demonstrated in the Abu Ghraib prison scandal (2007). In testifying as an expert witness, he described how certain environments can corrupt even those who have vowed to uphold ethical standards as a part of their social identity (e.g., military service personnel). Zimbardo's work to determine how people can become grossly separated from their ethical or moral selves, led him to create a list of criteria that contribute to the corruption of people's identity in social settings. To illustrate just how susceptible people are to ethical dysfunction, Zimbardo set forth a list of circumstances that move good people to do bad things (2004). Examples include:

- organization's performance system justifies questionable actions, legitimated with rewards;
- management models engagement in this performance system, but also demonstrate adherence to compliance mandates;
- management appears to be just and, at times, even compassionate; yet, can also become dictatorial;
- rules are vague and changing;
- exiting the situation is difficult.

These points illustrate how people can work for managers who may deter the desire to engage in principled performance. When striving to achieve their goals, people do not always realize how behavior may deteriorate, forming patterns of moral weakness. A lack of ethical fortitude can also be exacerbated by personal short-comings such as selfishness, greed, arrogance, and laziness, along with real or perceived social pressure. Fear of job loss and lack of information can also contribute to ethical fallibility.

Everyone has weaknesses and strengths in their character and situational contexts can bring out the best or worst in us. We are all vulnerable to ethical lapses, as are the organizations we represent. Dennis Moberg, an expert in organizational ethics, explains that employees may not be aware they are losing clarity of thought around ethical discernment and prudential judgment (Moberg, 2006). This can foster an environment where moral myopia can cloud decision-making. Employees' ability to give voice to ethical concerns can become thwarted due to competing values coupled with misperceptions (Bird and Waters, 1989; Drumwright and Murphy, 2004). Scholars have taken care to ascertain how unethical acts form, spread, and establish influence on processes and even shape entire industries. I argue that if we expect to create organizations that are ethically healthy, we must aim higher than achieving a compliance-driven baseline. While adherence to rules and regulations is essential, leaders must also create an environment where moral competency is a part of the expected performance goals. And people need to become more aware of how certain contexts can deplete their ethical resources and to learn how to exercise moral courage in these situations through practice.

Table 13.1 depicts how firms relate ethics to performance (see Sekerka, 2011). The center section represents an ethical baseline, achieved through compliance. Legal adherence does not necessarily include any efforts to build ethical strength. The far left illustrates firms that fall below the baseline, deficient and morally weak. The far right exemplifies what it looks like to go beyond compliance, doing more than what is required and pursuing ethical development to instill practices that support principled performance. This stance helps to attain compliance via consideration of both the spirit and letter of the law. Moreover, this approach considers how the firm impacts others, with profits generated in a socially responsible manner.

Firms in the United States are required to attend to rules that stem from governmental regulatory agencies. The organization's ethical identity is often visible in their mission, code of conduct, and operating stance. But sometimes values are stated but not fully exercised. Compliance measures are intended to help firms avoid wrongdoing, but people who work to achieve compliance alone are unlikely to exceed it. It is important firms create practices and processes within their operations that meet and exceed this moral minimum. To accomplish this, leaders must aspire to achieve principled performance

Table 13.1 The ethical performance continuum

Ethical Weakness	Ethical Compliance	Ethical Strength
Does harm	Does no harm	Reduces harm
Non-adherence to regulation	Adherence to regulation	Supersedes regulation and advocates social responsibility in the firm's purpose
External punishment for noncompliance	Compliance-based training and compliance-driven performance goals	Compliance-based training and ethical development, ethics woven into the criteria for principled performance goals, rewards for professional moral courage

|--|--|

Moral Weakness	Moral Minimum	Moral Fortitude

as a part of the organization's mission. Cameron (2007) illustrates this point by framing performance driven by negative or positive deviance (a continuum representing harmful on the one end and virtuous on the other). To establish a workplace that possesses ethical strength, it is important to add granularity to the topic of ethical health; namely, making a distinction between illness and survival, and health and wellness.

DEFICITS AND STRENGTHS

When companies aim for the moral baseline by viewing compliance as the ethical target, they tend to maintain a problem-orientated approach. Management studies have described this as a deficit-based approach to organizational development (Sekerka et al., 2006). This helps explain why business ethics become especially relevant in organizations when malfeasance occurs. In short, when there is trouble, there is action. When issues emerge, management addresses them in a reactionary diagnostic fashion. This aligns with a medical health model, which is also typically how people navigate the world around them. When there is a dysfunction, the response is to identify its cause by examining unwanted symptoms. Business managers work to resolve problematic conditions via inquiry, case comparison, and analyses, then offer recommendations, corrective measures, or a plan to create remedy or change. This problem-orientated approach, according to systems theorist Peter Senge, helps to resolve immediate issues (1990). Such advances, however, never change the system (in this case the organization) that created the issue in the first place. Senge explains that diagnostic methods are inherently "band-aid" fixes – resolving current issues, but never altering the system that created the problem in the first place. Unless the organization challenges its own deeply-held assumptions and engages in learning, the same issues will occur again and again (Kanter, Stein and Jick, 1992; Senge et al., 2008).

This deficit-based approach has been a driving force in how scholars have framed research inquiry for decades. More than 99 percent of psychological research in the last 50 years has focused on problems, illnesses, or human malfunction, rather than ascertaining what contributes to human thriving, resilience, and well-being (Seligman, 2002). Similarly, most organizational and management research is structured in this manner. Business tends to pay far more heed to solving problems, surmounting obstacles, battling competitors, and closing deficit gaps than identifying the flourishing and life-giving aspects of organizational life – looking for ways to create strength from existing strength (Cooperrider and Sekerka, 2006). Pro-social behavior and a focus on abundance are often dismissed or they are mere transactional efforts cloaked as righteousness to achieve gain, rather than authentic motives to generate goodness (Cialdini et al., 1987).

With the advent of Positive Psychology, new areas of research have emerged in Positive Organizational Scholarship and Positive Organizational Ethics to address strength-based approaches to achieve business success. This platform has been edified, with theoretical and empirical evidence to support the idea that organizational dynamics can benefit from a more proactive approach to healthy performance (Sekerka, Godwin and Charnigo, 2012). Such research has brought fresh insight, with management scholars working to understand how ethical strength can become a sustained component of business strategy. A more balanced approach is essential if we expect a shift from the current reactionary stance to one that is more holistic and sustainable. This means management must provide the tools employees need to exercise ethical strength in their daily task actions. If an organization wants to establish a more durable form of ethics, leaders need to complement their fixation on problems with establishing environments of ethical health, that is, work to create organizations that support the development and maintenance of healthy ethical habits for employees (Nielsen, 1989; Sekerka, 2011). Rather than waiting for the unethical mishap to occur, why not also address ethics by focusing on building strength?

Professional Moral Courage

Assuming people have choices, when they see an opportunity to engage in malfeasance, moral courage is needed to withstand the pressure or temptation to engage. This is especially the case if the person feels wronged in some way and negative emotions such as anger, disgust, fear, hubris, or greed are present. But a variety of negative elements can influence people to redirect their intentions to protect or advance their own self-interest. Empirical research shows that bad often drives psychological reactions, whereas good often propels behavior (Wang, Galinsky and Murnighan, 2009, Baumeister et al., 2001). The challenge is that "bad" is often stronger than "good," suggesting that people tend to be motivated to avoid the negative, rather than to pursue the positive. Thus, when faced with an alternative decision, to stand tall (moral fortitude) or to take the easier, softer way (moral weakness), people must be prepared to muster courage and possess the personal resolve to step up to the plate and face the ethical challenge.

The idea of *professional moral courage* (PMC) and the internal processes that support it, have added depth to the notion of building organizational ethical strength (Sekerka, Bagozzi and Charnigo, 2009). If leaders want employees to maintain principled performance, they must support and model how to face everyday operations with moral competence. The image that individuals with PMC are somehow like superheroes, extraordinary people with particular moral fortitude, is just not realistic. In fact, those with ethical strength often experience worry or anger, and report losing sleep over the ethical issues they face (Sekerka, 2011). Despite these feelings, they learn to proceed, moving through and beyond this distress and toward moral action.

Motives for unethical activities may be driven by conscious and unconscious desires to enhance or protect the self or one's organization. Moreover, when personal and collective principles vie for placement in decision-making priorities, people experience tension and pressure to make choices among competing values. Sometimes, even without being aware of it, individuals select self-serving paths that can erode their integrity, which may ultimately lead to broader and more frequent engagement in less than ethical thoughts, decisions, and actions.

A person who possesses ethical strength has a moral identity that includes moral awareness and the desire to achieve principled right action. To deal effectively with ethical challenges people need internal processes – personal skills that help them navigate workplace issues with PMC. One's freedom to choose "right" action can be obfuscated by negative emotions (anticipated and experienced) (Sekerka and Bagozzi, 2007). Fears of potential loss can mitigate the desire to maintain a courageous stance. In some cases, a lack of willingness to go along with others may pose a perceived or real threat. Thus, the choice to follow laws, policies, and ethical principles set forth by the government, industry, and organizations, in conjunction with one's own moral identity, necessitates the use of internal efforts. In particular, efforts to support PMC in the moral decision-making path.

Definition of PMC

A variety of issues emerge when companies engage managers in ethics workshops. People respond to ethical challenges in different ways. Transcripts of critical incident interviews with hundreds of managers reveal a host of details related to their various workplace scenarios. One study with the United States Navy Supply Corps found that officers' core ethical issues were: (1) rule bending to accomplish tasks; (2) rule bending to accommodate senior management; and (3) inappropriate use of funds or missing funds and resources (Sekerka and Zolin, 2007). While it is feasible that other issues were embedded within these top three concerns, 42 percent of their challenges were situations framed as rule bending (Sekerka, 2011). This finding suggests that when organizations are laden with rules, policies, and procedures to guide task accomplishment, employees experience ethical challenges as they try to navigate compliance with performance expectations. With pressure to get the job done, meet target goals, and please superiors, ethics depicted as the rules end up competing against a desire to succeed. People then move to negotiate what they see as a dilemma, sometimes manufacturing justifications and rationalizations to support "workarounds" or "rule bending" activities (Sekerka and Zolin, 2005, 2007).

Through qualitative analysis of ethical scenarios presented by managers, researchers have determined what ethical strength looks like in everyday work life – referring to this effort as PMC. Those who possess PMC demonstrate it in their decision-making process and behavioral choices; they go beyond adherence to regulations, striving to achieve a morally principled response despite the perceived barriers. More specifically, PMC is marked by the presence of five key themes (Sekerka, Bagozzi and Charnigo, 2009):

1. *Moral Agency*: possesses a predisposition to be a moral agent;
2. *Multiple Values*: uses multiple value sets to determine moral action;
3. *Endures Threat*: faces danger or threat, yet pursues moral action;

4. *Supersedes Compliance*: applies rules but goes beyond compliance to consider what is right, just, and appropriate; and
5. *Moral Goal*: moves to complete tasks with the application of moral principles to achieve a moral outcome.

It is important to understand the skills that support PMC if we hope to establish ethical health in organizational life.

Moral Competencies

Professional moral courage has been associated with specific moral competencies, particular skills present when a person engages in addressing an ethical challenge with moral fortitude. They include: (1) emotional signaling; (2) reflective pause; (3) self-regulation; and (4) moral preparation (Sekerka, McCarthy and Bagozzi, 2010). Competencies that support PMC are essential in maintaining the desire to proceed with right action, as people work through the issue and determine if they will act and what they might do. Classic decision making models focus on awareness of the issue, forming the intent to proceed, making a judgment, and then engaging in an ethical action (Rest, 1986). A problem with these path models is they rely upon rational thought, often paying little heed to the affective elements that influence people's decisions and behavioral responses. Moreover, most people decide things – after the fact. In post-hoc analysis people justify or rationalize whatever behavior they demonstrated rather than actually having made a decision prior to action (Bazerman and Tenbrunsal, 2011). More attention is needed to help employees become aware of this tendency and to learn how to sustain the desire to proceed with moral action. People need to practice paying attention to what they are doing and why they are doing it, before they act. One way to prompt moral awareness and to sustain the desire to act ethically is to build personal moral competencies. If people have the skills needed to respond to their ethical challenges, and leaders encourage and model ethical strength, employees are more likely to use them. A description is now presented in greater detail.

A. EMOTIONAL SIGNALING

Emotions and cognition are intertwined, working together to help people make sense of the world. Emotions contain important signals that influence the cerebral process of ethical decision making. Haidt (2001) distilled four families of moral emotions referring to them as: other-condemning (contempt, anger, and disgust), self-conscious (shame, embarrassment, and guilt), other-suffering (compassion), and other-praising (gratitude and elevation). These sentiments play a critical role in motivating or hindering the choice to engage in PMC. But there are other affective sentiments that managers feel in the midst of moving to resolve an ethical challenge, including worry, loneliness, fear, shock, surprise, and feelings of hurt (often stemming from a sense of betrayal). A common theme among those who demonstrate PMC is an initial sense of confusion, agitation, or helplessness. In such a state, there is a concern for the potential of personal harm (e.g., being fired), which is accompanied by emotional discomfort and distress (Sekerka, McCarthy and Bagozzi, 2010).

Individuals with moral fortitude do not ignore, repress, or sublimate them. Those with PMC use this affective information as a cue. Individuals with ethical strength are enabled by their emotional awareness rather than being blocked or thwarted by it. Those with PMC proceed with a more informed decision-making process, honoring visceral reactions and addressing the seriousness of these cues as cautionary, but also managing and directing the energy toward right action. Use of emotional signaling is a prompt, helping to facilitate caution, care, and mindful decision-making. When attentions are directed toward one's affective cues, a reflective pause is needed to better understand their cause and how to proceed effectively.

B. REFLECTIVE PAUSE

The use of a reflective pause represents an ability, regardless of time constraints, to purposively self-impose a time-out. During this break, individuals examine possible avenues for right action. These individuals weigh the pros and cons of the situation by thinking about different periods of time and potential implications (i.e., past and present). This display of prudential judgment appears to be an important component of PMC that manifests during these reflection periods (Sekerka and Zolin, 2007). The time-out helps people discern options, and then build informed momentum toward moral action. Individuals also use this period to gather additional insight about the rules and other particulars regarding the situation. Taking time to reflect often alters, overrides, or postpones some initial reactions while also weighing alternative responses for appropriateness. When applied as a daily habit this kind of reflection may serve as a portal for the other moral competencies, but it is especially important for self-regulation.

C. SELF-REGULATION

The initial reaction to an ethical challenge requires the use of emotional signaling and reflection. But to habitually pursue right action, effectively managing tough ethical decisions, individuals must balance their reactions and know how to manage responsibilities alongside their own personal desires. Managers have a variety of goals; therefore, they must be adept at balancing the pursuit of task accomplishment while also incorporating ethical means. The ways people achieve principled performance means they effectively know when and how to tackle the ethical challenges that emerge. People must discern whether to postpone a response or engage in immediate action. This requires an ability to regulate one's reactions, an understanding of restraint coupled with an ability to move forward – despite perceptions that negative impacts to self or others may be present. This effort can be particularly difficult when peers or leaders are the ones engaged in questionable activities, or when asked to engage in actions that are deemed ethically unsound. Self-regulation employs personal governance, reflecting an ability to restrain the impulse to act (or not act), as well as to know when to proceed.

In working with managers reflecting on their ethical challenges, many express regret from not having acted sooner. They recant that respect, appreciation, or care for someone, moreover their sense of loyalty to senior management may inhibit self-regulation (at least initially) and ultimately curtail their decision to act. In addition, the fear of losing one's job, being ostracized, or being excluded from the group may also be present. Use of self-regulation serves as an inner prompt and compass that helps appropriately assign motivation and direction, often developed through personal struggle. Individuals must be willing to demonstrate ethical strength even when those around them, including leaders and peers, do not. This form of self-control has been regarded as the moral muscle – an inner directive to alter one's immediate responses and to redirect them toward the overall good of others. Psychologists have referred to self-regulation as the cornerstone of virtuous behavior (Baumeister and Exline, 1999). In rare cases some may apply this moral competency naturally, but there is enormous potential for further development of this competency in most people (Sekerka and Bagozzi, 2007). Learning to quiet one's impulse to react or ignore the problem, then reflecting upon and managing immediate thoughts and feelings, can begin a course of advanced moral development marked by habits of self-regulation.

D. MORAL PREPARATION

A commitment to right action is developed through a deep understanding of self. Such an understanding is fueled by a prefactual thought process concerning how one will and will not act when faced with an ethical challenge – in the future. There is widely held concurrence that moral action stems from a dynamic relationship between moral motivation, moral emotions, virtue and vice, identity, reasoning, choice, and action (Bergman, 2002; Hardy and Carlo, 2005). A manager with ethical strength appears to think through consequences, related to themselves and others, before real-time ethical challenges occur. This ongoing preparatory effort includes a consideration of the circumstances surrounding whether a person acts (or fails to act), and includes an evaluation of the emotions, appraisals, and thoughts that serve to influence their decisions and actions. People who continue to be aware of how their emotions and situational factors influence their reactions can then consciously tailor their reactions in appropriate ways, before or as scenarios emerge. This pre-planning appears to develop a heightened level of moral preparedness for ethical challenges to come. It is sometimes expressed by continued vigilance of the "moral line," working to remain above reproach before situational problems can occur.

Preparation is a core feature of sustained ethical strength. It involves the practice of thinking through the positive and negative consequences of acting and not acting. Individuals with PMC recognize and manage their emotions, develop a conscious awareness of where the ethical risk areas may be, but do so even before ethical events arise. This engrained rehearsal process helps prepare individuals for a thoughtful response-action when problems do occur. By working to make sure one's everyday actions are above the ethical line, compliance is achieved along with building moral strength. By working in this way, a misstep is unlikely to be a gross infraction.

Moral preparation relies upon the use of the other moral competencies. To build the gestalt capacity of personal governance, people learn to continually self-monitor and work to maintain an ongoing understanding of their own motives. This includes a preparation phase that requires sustained self-awareness and introspection. In aggregate, it is important to recognize that the practices outlined herein can never be perfected. Because each person and every situation is different, responses to an ethical challenge vary. Therefore, it is essential that people focus on their ongoing moral development, not simply relying upon their organization to uphold the moral line.

Ethical strength means being a moral agent before an ethical challenge emerges. Like a volunteer emergency responder, people and organizations need to determine their ethical identity before an ethical crisis occurs. A person knows he or she is a moral agent because he or she made a decision to be that type of person – prior to an ethical event. It is not an assumption; it is who that person is, as a part of their identity. When faced with ethical challenges, people with PMC have already made a decision to act ethically, before issues arise. Thus, when faced with an ethical issue the question is not, "Should I, or should I not engage in this activity?" Rather, the question is, "What is the next ethical thing to do now?"

Positive Organizational Ethics

In shaping their organization's ethical identity, leaders, managers, and employees will need to work together to go beyond a surface compliance-based approach. If the main thrust of the firm's ethics program is to convey rules, codes, regulations, and reporting channels, then the value placed on ethical performance is dubious. If management values moral action in the workplace, it needs to establish a broad developmental effort with ethics criteria directly linked to performance goals. To embrace such efforts, employees need to become part of the process – to engage in regular activities that exercise their personal governance practices.

Although the competencies have been set forth independently in this article, they are not meant to be taught in isolation, as sequential lectures, or as online training units. Psychologists explain that moral judgment is a function of our cognitive and intuitive-emotional systems – both rational and affective components play a role in ethical behavior (Haidt, 2001; Narvaez, 2010; Sekerka and Bagozzi, 2007). This underscores why employees need to learn how PMC comes from within, learning to balance internal competing values and external pressures. Personal governance must be driven from an inner desire to maintain personal and organizational integrity. This helps provide the initial motivation and direction to face corruption. But people must also simultaneously deal with their internal desires and fears that can derail an intended course toward moral action. Therefore, it is important to practice the use of personal governance in a social context with other members of the organization. It is recommended that this type of discourse occurs across functional groups (e.g., marketing and accounting) and among different levels (e.g., first line supervisors and senior executives).

If an organization is truly committed to positive organizational ethics, techniques that draw upon employees' experiences are particularly useful (Sekerka and Godwin, 2010). By embracing ethical development as a collective endeavor, personal governance can be adopted at both the individual and organizational levels. The idea of infusing ethics into ongoing organizational learning means employees continually work to develop the desire to do the "right" thing, weaving ethical strength into their daily task actions. Establishing a desire for PMC means to inculcate this expectation into the meaning of work itself. This necessitates shared understanding about what successful performance means and developing the skills to achieve it. Change management techniques are useful in fostering reflective dialogue, which can empower employees to build positive momentum and the capacity for discovery and learning. And, rather than limiting ethics to rules, facilitated guided inquiry can help employees co-create the conditions that help render skill development in support of ethical strength.

An examination of best practices in ethics education and training in the workplace shows that employees need to engage in face-to-face interaction to address collectively the ethical risks and strengths that exist in the current system (Sekerka, 2009). It is important for people to feel they are part of a learning community, working together to address the challenge of ethical corrosion with support from their peers, managers, and leaders. The issues that individuals perceive to be salient are an important focus for interactive experiential learning processes.

Balanced Experiential Inquiry

To achieve this type of open developmental effort in organizational settings, management should implement processes that support dialogue, reflection, and shared discovery. One process, balanced experiential inquiry (BEI), has been empirically shown to increase curiosity, decrease negative emotions, and bolster managers' desire to proceed with moral action, without the need for external affirmations or praise (Sekerka and Godwin, 2010). It is considered a hybrid approach to organizational learning because it weaves two very different core change management techniques together to form a useful management exercise (diagnostic- and appreciative-based inquiry). With BEI, employees share their ethical challenges, airing both successes and times of difficulty. This provides a platform that offers a way to learn how to conduct ongoing reflection and discovery in the organizational setting. Activities like BEI help people unearth and review how they overcame barriers to moral action or were blocked by them. Employees are asked to use their own stories to determine what strengths can be leveraged, as well as how to resolve their moral deficits. Unsettled conflicts are often related to internal inconsistencies that contribute to deception, setting the stage for ethical corrosion.

Techniques like BEI are used to enhance the knowledge and skills of industry leaders and their stakeholders including managers, regulators, consultants, and policy makers in support of sustainable business practices. As management works to plan and execute strategies that preserve the commercial, social, economic, and ecological well-being of companies and their constituents, working together is essential to stimulate collective interest and shared understanding. BEI activities are often included in management education. For example, recently leaders from the energy and extraction industries gathered to prompt collaborative discovery into CSR. Starting from the assumption that managers want to be ethical, seminar participants worked through a series of questions designed to strengthen their ability to (1) apply multiple value sets to determine the right decision; (2) identify and overcome dangers and threats in pursuing the right action; and (3) move beyond compliance to deliver decisions that are right and just for stakeholders.

Participants experience the process of sharing their ethical challenges in a public forum, practicing collective discourse on how to proceed with right action in difficult situations. Those engaged are strongly encouraged to take this technique in-house, incorporating ethical development into strategy discussions, planning meetings, and everyday conversations. Initially, a trainer or practitioner facilitates this process. It is essential, however, that such activities become inculcated into workplace routines. The goal is to help managers and supervisors conduct BEI as a part of group staff meetings, as well as integrating it into individual coaching and feedback sessions. Techniques like BEI help employees reach a deeper level of learning as they engage in critical thinking about their decision-making processes, and begin to understand how to practice new behaviors. Such activities are necessary elements of work life if ethical strength is to become a part of employees' expected performance capability. Information gleaned from BEI sessions help people identify where potential ethical risks reside and how employees can pursue moral action with personal governance. As organizational inconsistencies emerge, members in different roles, functions, and status practice working together to see where their assets reside and where improvements need to be exacted.

Because BEI is a balanced approach, employees can draw upon their greatest assets as they work to develop their shortcomings, in an environment that values transparency in concert with others. In so doing, employees become more aware of and sensitive to their emotional signals and can then self-regulate these feelings as they prepare for moral action. But the actions of management are what ultimately serve as the cornerstone of the organization's ethical health. While individual contributors need to practice and exercise personal governance, management is responsible for setting a consistent example and creating an environment that expects, supports, and nurtures ethical strength. This means a workplace where everyday habits move to achieve principled performance. It also means not waiting for issues to emerge, but looking for how and where practices and assumptions in operations may be vulnerable to ethical corrosion and where ethical risks reside.

It is essential that managers choose to model, endorse, and strengthen moral competencies as an ongoing part of their operations. Unfortunately, this is not always the case. High level personnel have been known to expect ethical performance without congruency in their own actions. This underscores the essential nature of ethical leadership and how it rests on the shoulders of every organizational member.

Conclusion

The competencies discussed in this chapter are the moral muscles that support and build a healthy ethical organizational culture. Toning these strengths necessitates assuming personal responsibility to self-monitor one's thoughts and feelings. In so doing, employees can continually work at being more honest with themselves – and each other. Ethical strength is about having a clear understanding of motives and recognizing the purpose of one's actions. By addressing ethical challenges in a more mindful way, people can learn to ascertain if their intentions are driven by self-interest and, if so, to consider how this shapes their performance.

Organizational members who demonstrate PMC maintain ethical vigilance, looking for the ethical aspects of every circumstance. By honing in on the potential for ethical concerns in advance, people can learn to address the potential for ethical problems – before they arise. By inculcating these practices in everyday workplace routines, organizations can become more nimble, looking for ways to improve and leverage existing ethical strengths while attending to potential ethical risks. Having a desire to engage in ongoing learning and continuous improvement can help people deal with similar or nuanced conditions that have the potential to emerge repeatedly. The goal, of course, is to create systemic change so that cycles of moral weakness are altered, and management does not have to continual broach organizational ethics from a reactionary stance. Moral preparation in support of PMC necessitates sustained self-awareness, personal introspection, and the willingness to consider multiple vantage points, attending to both short- and long-term potential outcomes.

One thing to remember is that transgressions can be a powerful resource to fuel a change. Ethical mishaps can certainly be a catalyst for building ethical strength, especially when they encourage transformational change and humility. Humility is central to principled performance, because it keeps egos in check, ushering in a kind of freedom to strive and achieve, but recognizing that self-interest must be reframed to incorporate a greater holistic self. Keeping hubris in check is essential for sustained ethical health. Humility helps stabilize and maintain the desire for moral action over sheer personal gain.

Because individuals, situations, and organizations are different, and the current state (physical and emotional) of a person is constantly changing, there is no guarantee people will respond with the same level of ethical commitment at all times. If employees are expected to rally against moral weakness, they must work to continually maintain their ethical health, which ultimately supports the ethical strength of the organization. Of course, management must reward employees who exercise moral competence and model the behaviors they wish to see. Finally, it is important to remember that we, as humans, are all fallible. The temptations of power and money, the desire to belong and be valued, and the fear of being short-changed, ostracized, can influence our ethical acuity. If management expects principled performance, ethical strength must be supported and exercised in everyday organizational life. As described by the early Greek philosophers, bringing out the best in humanity comes from learning, born from sustained commitment and ongoing practice.

References

Aristotle (1980) *The Nicomachean Ethics*, trans. Ross. Oxford: Oxford University Press.

Baumeister, R., Bratslavsky, E., Finkenauer, C. and Vohs, K. (2001) Bad is stronger than good. *Review of General Psychology*, 5, 323–70.

Baumeister, R.F. and Exline, J.J. (1999) Virtue, personality, and social relations: Self-control as the moral muscle. *Journal of Personality*, 33(1), 1165–94.

Bazerman, M.H. and Tenbrunsal, A.E. (2011) *Blind Spots: Why We Fail to Do What's Right and What to Do About It*. Princeton, NJ: Princeton University Press.

Bergman, R. (2002) Why be moral? A conceptual model from developmental psychology. *Human Development*, 45, 104–24.

Bird, F.B. and Waters, J.A. (1989) The moral muteness of managers. *California Management Review*, 32 (Fall), 73–88.

Boatright, J.R. (2006) What's wrong – and what's right – with stakeholder management. *Journal of Private Enterprise*, Spring, 106–30.

Cameron, K. (2007) Positive organizational scholarship. In S. Clegg and J. Bailey (eds) *International Encyclopedia of Organization Studies*. Beverly Hills, CA: Sage, pp. 1261–7.

Carroll, A.B. (1999) Corporate social responsibility: Evolution of a definitional construct. *Business and Society*, 38(3), 268–95.

Cialdini, R.B., Schaller, M., Houlihan, D., Arps, K., Fultz, J. and Beaman, A. (1987) Empathy based helping: Is it selflessly or selfishly motivated? *Journal of Personality and Social Psychology*, 52, 749–58.

Cooperrider, D. and Sekerka, L.E. (2006) Toward a theory of positive organizational change. In J.V. Gallos (ed.) *Organization Development: A Jossey-Bass Reader*. San Francisco, CA: Jossey-Bass, pp. 223–38.

Drumwright, M.E. and Murphy, P.E. (2004) How advertising practitioners view ethics: Moral muteness, moral myopia, and moral imagination. *Journal of Advertising*, 33 (Summer), 7–24.

Ethics Resource Center (2011) *National Business Ethics Survey: Workplace Ethics in Transition*. Arlington, VA: Ethics Resource Center.

—— (2012) *The Federal Sentencing Guidelines for Organizations at Twenty Years*. Arlington, VA: Ethics Resource Center.

Friedman, M. (1970) The social responsibility of business is to increase profits. *New York Times Magazine*, September 13, 122–6.

General Electric (GE) (2008) Press Release (October 21): GE's 2008 Ecomagination Revenues to Rise 21%, Cross $17 Billion. Available at: http://www.genewscenter.com/content/detail.aspx?releaseid=4266&newsareaid=2 [accessed May 1, 2012].

George, B. (2011) Why leaders lose their way. *Harvard Business School Working Knowledge*. Available at: http://hbswk.hbs.edu/item/6741.html [accessed May 26, 2012].

Guth, R.A. (2008) Bill Gates issues call for kinder capitalism: Famously competitive billionaire now urges business to aid the poor. *Wall Street Journal*, January 24. Available at: http://www.sidley.com/newsresources/newsandpress/detail.aspx?news=3701 [accessed May 1, 2012].

Haidt, J. (2001) The emotional dog and its rational tail: A social intuitionist approach to moral judgment. *Psychological Review*, 108(4), 814–34.

Hardy, S. and Carlo, H. (2005) Identity as a source of moral motivation. *Human Development*, 48, 232–56.

Jones, T. (1983) An integrating framework for research in business and society: A step toward the elusive paradigm? *Academy of Management*, 8(4), 559–64.

—— (1995) Instrumental stakeholder theory: A synthesis of ethics and economics. *Academy of Management*, 20(2), 404–37.

Kanter, R.M., Stein, B.A. and Jick, J.D. (1992) *The Challenge of Organizational Change: How Companies Experience It and Leaders Guide It*. New York: Free Press.

Marshall, J. (2009) Is corporate green getting a yellow light? *Financial Executives International*, 25(5). Available at: http://www.thefreelibrary.com/Is+corporate+green+getting+a+yellow+light%3F-a0202922850 [accessed May 28, 2012].

Marshall, R.S. and Brown, D. (2003) Corporate environmental reporting: What's in a metric? *Business Strategy and the Environment*, 12, 87–103.

Milgram, S. (1974) *Obedience to Authority: An Experimental View*. New York: Harper and Row.

Moberg, D. (2006) Ethics blind spots in organizations: How systematic errors in person perception undermine moral agency. *Organization Studies*, 27, 413–28.

Narvaez, D. (2010) Moral complexity: The fatal attraction of truthiness and the importance of mature moral functioning. *Perspectives on Psychological Science*, 5, 163–81.

Nielsen, R.P. (1989) Changing unethical organizational behavior. *Academy of Management Executive*, 3(2), 123–31.

Porter, M. and Kramer, M. (2006) Strategy and society: The link between competitive advantage and corporate social responsibility. *Harvard Business Review*, 84(12), 78–92.

Rest, J.R. (1986) The major component of morality. In W.M. Kurtines and J.L. Gerwitz (eds) *Morality, Moral Behavior, and Moral Development*. New York: Wiley, pp. 24–38.

Sacks, D. (2009) John Mackey's whole foods vision to reshape capitalism. *Fast Company*, December 1. Available at: http://www.fastcompany.com/magazine/141/the-miracle-worker.html?page=0%2C0 [accessed May 1, 2012].

Sekerka, L.E. (2009) Organizational ethics education and training: A review of best practices and their application. *International Journal of Training and Development*, 13(2), 77–95.

—— (2011) Preserving integrity in the face of corruption: Exercising moral muscle in the path to right action. *Journal of Organizational Moral Psychology*, 1(3), 1–14.

—— (in press) Compliance as a subtle precursor to ethical corrosion: A strength-based approach as a way forward. *Wyoming Law Review*.

Sekerka, L.E. and Bagozzi, R.P. (2007) Moral courage in the workplace: Moving to and from the desire and decision to act. *Business Ethics: A European Review*, 16(2), 132–42.

Sekerka, L.E., Bagozzi, R.P. and Charnigo, R. (2009) Facing ethical challenges in the workplace: Conceptualizing and measuring professional moral courage. *Journal of Business Ethics*, 89(4), 565–79.

Sekerka, L.E., Brumbaugh, A., Rosa, J. and Cooperrider, D. (2006) Comparing appreciative inquiry to a diagnostic technique in organizational change: The moderating effects of gender. *International Journal of Organization Theory and Behavior*, 9(4), 449–89.

Sekerka, L.E. and Godwin, L. (2010) Strengthening professional moral courage: A balanced approach to ethics training. *Training and Management Development Methods*, 24(5), 63–74.

Sekerka, L.E., Godwin, L. and Charnigo, R. (2012) Use of balanced experiential inquiry to build ethical strength in the workplace. Special Issue on Experiential Learning for the *Journal of Management Development*, 30(3), 275–86.

Sekerka, L.E., McCarthy, D. and Bagozzi, R. (2010) Developing the capacity for professional moral courage: Facing daily ethical challenges in today's military workplace. In D. Comer and G. Vega (eds) *Moral Courage in Organizations: Doing the Right Thing at Work*. Armonk, NY: M.E. Sharpe, pp. 130–41.

Sekerka, L.E. and Stimel, D. (2011) How durable is sustainable enterprise? Ecological sustainability meets the reality of tough economic times. *Business Horizons*, 54(2), 115–24.

Sekerka, L.E. and Zolin, R. (2005) Proactive versus reactive approaches to ethical dilemmas: Battling moral mediocrity with professional courage. *Business and Professional Ethics Journal*, 24(4), 27–50.

—— (2007) Rule bending: Can prudential judgment affect rule compliance and values in the workplace? *Public Integrity*, 9(3), 225–44.

Seligman, M.E.P. (2002) *Authentic Happiness*. New York: Free Press.

Senge, P.M. (1990) *The Fifth Discipline: The Art and Practice of the Learning Organization*. New York: Doubleday.

Senge, P., Smith, B., Schlev, S., Laur, J. and Kruschwitz, N. (2008) *The Necessary Revolution: How Individuals and Organizations Are Working Together to Create a Sustainable World*. New York: Doubleday.

Shadnam, M. and Lawrence, T.B. (2011) Understanding widespread misconduct in organizations: An institutional theory of moral collapse. *Business Ethics Quarterly*, 21(3), 379–407.

Smith, A. (1976 [1759]) *The Theory of Moral Sentiments*, D.D. Raphael and A.L. Macfie (eds). New York: Oxford University Press.

Treviño, L.K. and Youngblood, S.A. (1990) Bad apples in bad barrels: A causal analysis of ethical decision-making behavior. *Journal of Applied Psychology*, 75(4), 378–86.

Vogel, D. (2006) *The Market for Virtue: The Potential and Limits of Corporate Social Responsibility*. Washington, DC: The Brookings Institution Press.

Wang, C.S., Galinsky, A.D. and Murnighan, J.K. (2009) Bad drives psychological reactions, but good propels behavior: Responses to honesty and deception. *Psychological Science*, 20(5), 634–44.

Windsor, D. (2001) The future of corporate social responsibility. *International Journal of Organizational Analysis*, 9(3), 225–56.

World Health Organization (2003) *Definition of Health*. Available at: https://apps.who.int/aboutwho/en/definition.html [accessed May 28, 2012].

Zimbardo, P.G. (2004) A situationist perspective on the psychology of evil: Understanding how good people are transformed into perpetrators. In A. Miller (ed.) *The Social Psychology of Good and Evil*. New York: Gilford Press, 21–5.

—— (2007) *The Lucifer Effect: Understanding How Good People Turn Evil*. New York: Random House.

Index